CAMBRIDGE ASIA-PACIFIC STUDIES

Cambridge Asia-Pacific Studies aims to provide a focus and forum for scholarly work on the Asia-Pacific region as a whole, and its component sub-regions, namely Northeast Asia, Southeast Asia and the Pacific Islands. The series is produced in association with the Research School of Pacific and Asian Studies at the Australian National University and the Australian Institute of International Affairs.

Editor: John Ravenhill

Editorial Board: James Cotton, Donald Denoon, Mark Elvin, Hal Hill, Ron May, Anthony Milner, Tessa Morris-Suzuki, Anthony Low

Recent titles in the series:
Samuel S. Kim (ed.) *Korea's Globalization*
    0 521 77272 9 hardback 0 521 77559 0 paperback
Gregory W. Noble and John Ravenhill (eds) *The Asian Financial Crisis and the Architecture of Global Finance*
    0 521 79091 3 hardback 0 521 79422 6 paperback
Peter Dauvergne *Loggers and Degradation in the Asia-Pacific: Corporations and Environmental Management*
    0 521 80661 5 hardback 0 521 00134 X paperback
Anthony J. Langlois *The Politics of Justice and Human Rights: Southeast Asia and Universalist Theory*
    0 521 80785 9 hardback 0 521 00347 4 paperback
Alan Dupont *East Asia Imperilled: Transnational Challenges to Security*
    0 521 81153 8 hardback 0 521 01015 2 paperback
William T. Tow *Asia-Pacific Strategic Relations: Seeking Convergent Security*
    0 521 80790 5 hardback 0 521 00368 7 paperback
John Ravenhill *APEC and the Construction of Pacific Rim Regionalism*
    0 521 66094 7 hardback 0 521 66797 6 paperback
Graham Hassall and Cheryl Saunders *Asia-Pacific Constitutional Systems*
    0 521 59129 5 hardback

Economic Crisis and Corporate Restructuring in Korea
Reforming the *Chaebol*

Asian business conglomerates have clearly been successful agents of growth, mobilizing capital, borrowing technology from abroad, and spearheading Asia's exports. However, these firms have long had a number of organizational and financial weaknesses, including heavy reliance on debt, that make them vulnerable to shocks. Nowhere was this more true than in Korea, where the large corporate groups known as *chaebol* have dominated the economic landscape. This collection of essays by leading political scientists and economists provides a comprehensive examination of the *chaebol* problem in the wake of the Asian financial crisis. The authors consider the historical evolution of the *chaebol* and their contribution to the onset of economic turmoil in 1997. The book analyzes the government's short-run response to corporate and financial distress, and outlines an agenda for longer-term reform of the financial system, corporate governance and the politics of business–government relations.

Stephan Haggard is the Lawrence and Sallye Krause Professor at the Graduate School of International Relations and Pacific Studies, University of California, San Diego. His publications include *The Political Economy of the Asian Financial Crisis* (2000).

Wonhyuk Lim is a Research Fellow in the Law and Economics Division of the Korea Development Institute. His books include *The Origin and Evolution of the Korean Economic System* (2000).

Euysung Kim is Assistant Professor of Economics at Yonsei University, Korea. He has written *Trade Liberalization and Productivity Growth in Korean Manufacturing Industries* (2000).

Economic Crisis and Corporate Restructuring in Korea
Reforming the *Chaebol*

Edited by

Stephan Haggard
University of California, San Diego

Wonhyuk Lim
Korea Development Institute

Euysung Kim
Yonsei University

CAMBRIDGE
UNIVERSITY PRESS

CAMBRIDGE UNIVERSITY PRESS
Cambridge, New York, Melbourne, Madrid, Cape Town, Singapore,
São Paulo, Delhi, Dubai, Tokyo

Cambridge University Press
The Edinburgh Building, Cambridge CB2 8RU, UK

Published in the United States of America by Cambridge University Press, New York

www.cambridge.org
Information on this title: www.cambridge.org/9780521131711

First published 2003
This digitally printed version 2010

A catalogue record for this publication is available from the British Library

National Library of Australia Cataloguing in Publication data
Economic crisis and corporate restructuring in Korea:
reforming the chaebol
Bibliography.
Includes index.
ISBN 0 521 82363 3.
1. Korea–Economic conditions– 1945– . 2. Corporate
reorganizations–Korea. I. Haggard, Stephan. II. Kim,
Euysung. III. Lim, Wonhyuk. (Series: Cambridge
Asia-Pacific studies).
339.409519

ISBN 978-0-521-82363-0 Hardback
ISBN 978-0-521-13171-1 Paperback

Contents

Figures

Tables

Preface and Acknowledgements

The origins of this project go back to a grant that Lawrence Krause submitted to the Korea Foundation just as the economic crisis in East Asia was unfolding. At the time, Krause was the Director (and founder) of the Korea Pacific Program (KPP) at the Graduate School of International Relations and Pacific Studies (IR/PS) at the University of California, San Diego. With this generous grant in hand, Krause and Stephan Haggard, also at IR/PS, approached the Korea Development Institute (KDI) about the prospect of collaborating on a project on the crisis and its aftermath.

On coming to office, Kim Dae-jung had outlined an ambitious reform program in four areas: corporate restructuring; the financial sector; labor markets and social policy; and government institutions. All posed challenging inter-disciplinary issues, but after consultation with colleagues at KDI and the KDI School, including Hong-Tack Chun, Seong Min Yoo and Sang-woo Nam, Haggard and Krause narrowed their focus to the area of corporate restructuring. Reform of the *chaebol* has long been a privileged issue in Korea, and the economic crisis added a new sense of urgency to it. They presented their ideas to KDI president Jin-soon Lee and got a supportive response.

The Asian financial crisis and the issue of corporate restructuring had already captured the attention of both institutions. At IR/PS, Haggard and Krause had convened a faculty seminar on the crisis that included among others Peter Gourevitch, Takeo Hoshi, Miles Kahler, Euysung Kim, Andrew MacIntyre, John McMillan, Peter Timmer, and Christopher Woodruff. That seminar spurred a substantial and diverse body of research. Krause had been commissioned by the Council on Foreign Relations to write an early assessment of the crisis, which appeared as *The Economics and Politics of the Asian Financial Crisis of 1997-98*. Krause's analysis was the first to include serious consideration of political issues. Fred Bergsten at the Institute for International Economics encouraged Haggard to write a book on the politics of the crisis, which appeared in late 2000 (*The Political Economy of the Asian Financial Crisis*). Hoshi had been working on the Japanese financial system for some time, and published important work on the topic including *Crisis and Change in the Japanese Financial System* (co-edited with Hugh Patrick, 2000) and *Corporate Financing and Governance in Japan* (with Anil Kashyap, 2001). Haggard and MacIntyre collaborated on several articles on the crisis, and MacIntyre initiated a book that offered a comparative look at the Southeast Asian cases (*The Power of Institutions: Political Architecture and Governance*, 2002).

As a public research institute supported by taxpayers, KDI was intimately involved in the policymaking process in the wake of the crisis. Jun-Il Kim participated in Korea's debt rescheduling negotiations and provided policy advice to the Minister of Finance and Economy as his Senior Adviser. Bum Soo Choi and Seong Min Yoo held similar positions at the Financial Supervisory Commission and the Fair Trade Commission. At KDI itself, an institute-wide effort was organized to craft a master plan to clean up nonperforming loans and carry out structural reform. This effort culminated in the publication of *A Master Plan for Overcoming the Crisis and Restructuring the Economy* (in Korean) in April 1998. In the summer of the same year, Dong Chul Cho argued that the IMF's high interest rate policy had served its purpose and made a strong and ultimately successful case for reflationary policy.

As the tumultuous year of 1998 came to a close and the Korean economy began to show signs of recovery, KDI researchers finally found time to turn to more academic endeavors. Youngjae Kang and Il-Chong Nam organized a conference with OECD on corporate governance in Asia, later published as an OECD report. Dong Chul Cho, Joon-Ho Hahm, Chin Hee Hahn, Kiseok Hong, Sung Wook Joh, and Inseok Shin collaborated with American economists to publish *The Korean Crisis: Before and After*. In a joint project with the National Institute of Research Advancement of Tokyo, Ha Won Jang, Youngjae Lim, Wonhyuk Lim, and Jung-Dong Park worked with Japanese scholars to produce *An Institutional Perspective on the Korean Crisis and Implications for Japan*.

The definition and initial organization of this project were undertaken by Stephan Haggard and Seong Min Yoo, but Yoo left KDI in February 2000 and the management of the project there was taken over by Wonhyuk Lim. Euysung Kim (IR/PS and KDI School at the time) also joined the team. They quickly saw eye-to-eye on two critical issues. First, although the area of corporate restructuring involved a number of complex economic questions, it also engaged the domains of law, public policy and politics. Although most of the participants in the project were economists, it would be important to draw in political scientists and to urge economists to consider political economy and legal issues. Chung-in Moon, Byung-Kook Kim and Jongryn Mo all agreed to participate early in the project adding their strong reputations to the project. Second, the co-editors agreed that the breadth of the project required that it draw talent from as wide a pool as possible. Connections to a variety of institutions, including Korea and Yonsei Universities, the Korea Institute for International Economic Policy (KIEP) and the Korea Institute of Finance (KIF), allowed us to identify a diverse and high-quality team of participants.

The first project meeting was held in Seoul in March 2000. In addition to the paper presenters, the workshop had the benefit of high-quality commentary from Sriram Aiyer, Peter Beck, Sea-Jin Chang, Eun Mee Kim, In-young Kim, Seung-Cheol Lee, Robert Liu, Sang-woo Nam, Kap Soo Oh, and Yong-Seok Park.

A second project meeting was held in La Jolla in October 2000. As with the first meeting, that workshop was deepened by the participation of a number of outsiders, including Young-Nahn Baek, Peter Beck, U Tak Chung, Tamio Hattori, Takeo Hoshi, Satoshi Koibuchi, Larry Krause, Chung Lee, Bill Mako, David McKendrick, Marcus Noland, Bee Roberts, James Shinn, Yoshiro Tsutsui, and Meredith Woo-Cumings.

All academic research depends on financing, and this project was no exception. Particular thanks are owed to the Korea Foundation for getting the ball rolling; without their initial support, the project would have been impossible. Ms. Young-Joon Min deserves a special note of thanks for the assistance she provided the project throughout.

KDI made the largest financial contribution to the venture, but even more importantly, freed the time of its researchers to work on this effort. The Korea Pacific Program at IR/PS contributed resources and we were fortunate to get financial and moral support from Peter Beck at the Korea Economic Institute (KEI) as well. KEI financed the attendance of several participants at the October 2000 workshop and Beck's comments and leads proved valuable at a number of points.

No project of this magnitude can work without administrative support, and Haggard and Kim would like to extend particular thanks to Kay-Marie Johns for her management of logistics and editing. Karen Johns also contributed to this task. Lim would like to thank Hyun-Ok Chung for taking care of the logistics of the workshop in March 2000. Jina Yu also contributed to the project.

As the project began to take shape, Haggard opened discussions with John Ravenhill, editor of the series on Asia-Pacific Studies, on bringing the project to press. John's encouragement played an important role in bringing the book to publication at Cambridge University Press. At the Press, the authors would like to thank Marigold Acland, Karen Hildebrandt, Paul Watt and Amanda Pinches, as well as Janet Mackenzie.

Two anonymous reviewers provided unusually detailed and useful comments; those comments spurred more revision of the manuscript than they might know.

Choongsoo Kim, President, Korea Development Institute
Lawrence Krause, Professor Emeritus, Graduate School of International Relations and Pacific Studies, University of California, San Diego

Contributors

Stephan Haggard is the Lawrence and Sallye Krause Professor of Korea-Pacific Studies at the Graduate School of International Relations and Pacific Studies at the University of California, San Diego. He is the author of *Pathways from the Periphery* (1990) and *The Political Economy of the Asian Financial Crisis* (2000), and co-author with Robert Kaufman of *The Political Economy of Democratic Transitions* (1995). He has written extensively on Korean political economy and is currently conducting research on globalization and social policy in East Asia, Latin America and Central Europe.

Wonhyuk Lim is a Research Fellow at the Korea Development Institute. An economic historian by training, he obtained a PhD in economics from Stanford University in 1993 and taught at the Korea Military Academy before joining the institute in 1996. His recent publications include *Privatization and Combined Heat and Power* (2000), co-authored with Il-Chong Nam and Hyehoon Lee, and *The Origin and Evolution of the Korean Economic System* (2000). He has advised the Korean government on privatization and *chaebol* reform and served as a consultant to the Asian Development Bank Institute. He is currently working on a book on the deregulation of network industries in Korea.

Euysung Kim is a member of the faculty of Yonsei University's Graduate School of International Studies. A specialist on trade theory, economic growth and Korean development, he received his PhD from Columbia University. His articles include "Trade Liberalization and Productivity Growth in Korean Manufacturing Industries: Price Protection, Market Power and Scale Efficiency" and "The Sources of East Asia's Economic Growth" (with Stephan Haggard). Professor Kim is currently working on the productivity performance of Korean manufacturing industries.

Myeong-Hyeon Cho is Associate Professor of Management at Korea University and Adjunct Professor at the Owen Graduate School of Management, Vanderbilt University. He has published numerous articles on corporate governance, including "Ownership Structure and

Corporate Value," in the *Journal of Financial Economics*. He has also served as a consultant to Bell South Co., Korea Telecom, Hanaro Telecom, Samsung, SDI, and POSCO. His research interests include corporate strategy and finance, with specific interests in corporate governance and corporate restructuring.

Joon-Ho Hahm is Assistant Professor of International Economics and Finance at the Graduate School of International Studies, Yonsei University. Before joining Yonsei, he was an Assistant Professor at the University of California at Santa Barbara and a fellow at the Korea Development Institute. Prof. Hahm has written extensively on financial market and macroeconomic issues. His articles have appeared in *Emerging Markets Review*, *Review of Economics and Statistics* and *Journal of Economic Dynamics and Control*. He was a member of Korea's Presidential Commission on Financial Reform and currently serves as an outside director for Hanvit Bank.

Sung Wook Joh graduated from Seoul National University and received her PhD in economics from Harvard University. She joined the Korea Development Institute as a research fellow after teaching at the State University of New York, Albany. Her research interests center on corporate governance and management incentives, and her articles have appeared in a number of journals including the *Journal of Financial Economics*. She is currently analyzing how institutions and market pressures change the behavior of firms.

Byung-Kook Kim is Professor at the Department of Political Science, Korea University, where he teaches party politics and comparative political theory. His publications include *Dynamics of National Division and Revolution: The Political Economy of Korea and Mexico* (1994), *State, Region, and International System: Change and Continuity* (1995), and *Consolidating Democracy in South Korea* (2000). In 1995, he received the Federation of Korean Industries Award for Distinguished Publication on Liberal Democracy and Market Economy. He is Executive Editor of the *Journal of East Asian Studies* and is currently editing a three-volume work, *The Park Era*, with Ezra Vogel.

Dong Gull Lee heads the Banking Team of the Korea Institute of Finance. He served as an expert member of the Presidential Commission on Financial Reform (1997), as an Assistant Secretary to the President for Economic Affairs and Policy Planning (1998), and as a member of the Task Force for Financial Supervisory Authority Reform (2000). He is currently a member of the Presidential Commission on

Policy Planning. He is the co-author of *Financial Reform in Korea* (1997) and *The Financial Supervisory Authority Reform in Korea* (2000), and has written numerous papers on financial and corporate reform.

Youngjae Lim is a Research Fellow at the Korea Development Institute. He received his BA and MA in economics from the Seoul National and a doctorate in economics from the University of Chicago. He has held positions as Fellow of Economics at Fitzwilliam College, Cambridge University, UK, and Research Associate at the National Opinion Research Center, University of Chicago. His research interests are in corporate bankruptcy systems, corporate governance and corporate finance. Recently he has published *Corporate Financing Sources and Firm Size in Korea: Micro-evidence* (2001) and *The Hyundai Crisis: Its Development and Resolution* (2002).

Jongryn Mo is Associate Professor of International Political Economy and Director of the Center for International Studies at the Graduate School of International Studies, Yonsei University. He received his PhD in business from Stanford University in 1992, taught for four years at the University of Texas, Austin, and was a national fellow at the Hoover Institution in 1995–96. He is co-editor of *North Korea after Kim Il Sung: Continuity or Change?* (1997) and *Democracy and the Korean Economy* (1999). His articles have appeared in leading academic journals, including *Journal of Democracy*, *Review of International Political Economy*, *Comparative Political Studies*, and *Journal of Conflict Resolution*. Professor Mo's current research examines the politics of economic policymaking in the post-developmental state era, the interaction of culture and institutions in East Asian development, and the use of sanctions and incentives as instruments of power.

Chung-in Moon is Professor of Political Science and Dean of the Graduate School of International Studies, Yonsei University. He has published eighteen books and over 150 articles in scholarly journals and edited volumes on Korea and East Asia. His most recent publications include *Korean Politics: An Introduction* (2001), *Economic Crisis and the Politics of Structural Reforms in South Korea* (co-authored with Jongryn Mo, 2000), and *Democracy and the Korean Economy* (co-edited with Jongryn Mo, 1999). He is currently writing a book on structural rigidity of the East Asian economy.

Kyung Suh Park is Associate Professor of Finance at the Business School, Korea University. He is the co-author of *The Origins and Policy Implications of the Asian Financial Crisis* (with Phil Sang Lee, 2000) and

Capital Crunch and Shocks to Small Enterprises: Korean Experience under Financial Crisis (2001, with Dongwon Kim). He has written extensively on corporate governance and restructuring issues in Korea, and is Associate Director of the Asian Institute of Corporate Governance at Korea University.

Kwangshik Shin is a senior adviser at the law firm of Kim & Chang. He has written a number of books and articles on Korean industrial organization and competition law and policy, and has been a consultant to a number of government agencies on Korean competition policy. His current research is on competition policy in the information-based economy.

Mikyung Yun is a Research Fellow at the Korea Institute for International Economic Policy. Her main research interest is industrial economics, including competition policy, intellectual property rights and foreign direct investment. She has published a number of papers on post-crisis restructuring, including "Foreign Direct Investment: A Catalyst for Change?" (2000), "The Role of Foreign Investment in Korean Privatization," *Journal of International Economic Policy Studies* (1999), *Bankruptcy Procedure in Korea: A Perspective* (1998), and with Kyung S. Lee, "A Primer on Korean Bankruptcy Law," *American Bankruptcy Institute Journal* (1999).

A Note on Usage

This book is about the *chaebol*: the conglomerate corporate form typical of the largest Korean groups. Given that this term is widely used and increasingly known outside Korean studies, we have chosen to retain it. In Korean *chaebol* can be either singular or plural, and we have followed that usage.

All dollar sums are in US dollars.

Abbreviations

BIS	Bank for International Settlements
CSIP	Capital Structure Improvement Plan
DLP	Democratic Liberal Party
EPB	Economic Planning Board
FDI	foreign direct investment
FEB	Finance and Economic Board
FSC	Financial Supervisory Commission
GATT	General Agreement on Tariffs and Trade
GNP	Grand National Party
HCI	heavy and chemical industry
IBRD	International Bank for Reconstruction and Development
IMF	International Monetary Fund
KAMCO	Korea Asset Management Corporation
KDI	Korea Development Institute
KDIC	Korean Deposit Insurance Corporation
KFTC	Korea Fair Trade Commission
M&A	mergers and acquisitions
MCIE	Ministry of Commerce, Industry and Energy
MOF(E)	Ministry of Finance (and Economy)
MOU	memorandum of understanding
MRFTA	Monopoly Regulation and Fair Trade Act
MTIR	Ministry of Trade, Industry and Resources
NBER	National Bureau for Economic Research
NBFIs	non-bank financial institutions
NICE	National Information and Credit Evaluation Inc.
OECD	Organization for Economic Cooperation and Development
SMEs	small and medium-sized enterprises
TFP	total factor productivity
ULD	United Liberal Democrats
WTO	World Trade Organization

1 Introduction: The Political Economy of Corporate Restructuring

Wonhyuk Lim, Stephan Haggard and Euysung Kim

The financial crisis that swept through Asia in 1997–98 had many roots, but one that has received increasing attention is the nature of the Asian business group (Pomerleano 1998; Claessens, Djankov and Lang 2000b; Rajan and Zingales 1998; Johnson et al. 2000; Johnson and Mitton 2001). These highly diversified, family-owned conglomerates have been the entrepreneurial engine of Asia's rapid growth over the last three decades. But at the same time they exhibited a number of troubling weaknesses, from high leveraging to weak corporate governance, lack of transparency and outright corruption.

In no country in the region is this ambivalence about the business group more pronounced than in Korea. Influential accounts of Korea's growth have put the Korean groups, or *chaebol*, at the very center of the country's economic transformation (Amsden 1989). Yet the *chaebol's* close and collusive ties with the government, increasing dominance of Korea's economy and oligopolistic practices also made them politically controversial (Cho 1990). These perceptions only strengthened with the financial crisis, for which many Koreans held the *chaebol* directly responsible.

This book offers a comprehensive overview of "the *chaebol* problem." We look at the economic and political origins of the *chaebol* as a corporate form, their performance, and the role they played in the financial crisis of 1997–98. That crisis provided a powerful stimulus for reform of the financial system, the regulatory environment, and the *chaebol* themselves. The economics and politics of these reform efforts are the central focus of this book.

This book makes a break from the pre-crisis literature by providing a comprehensive look at the evolution of the *chaebol* from a corporate governance perspective.[1] We define corporate governance as the entire set of institutions, both inside and outside the firm, through which the objectives of the company are set and executed and the performance of the firm is monitored. This book looks at both the internal and external dimensions of the *chaebol's* corporate governance and focuses on a number of significant changes that have reshaped the *chaebol* and redefined their relationship with the government since the 1980s.

After highlighting major features of the *chaebol* as a corporate form, we discuss internal governance problems that arise from the *chaebol's* ownership and control patterns. In particular, we emphasize that the *chaebol* form consists of subsidiaries rather than divisions. This multi-subsidiary structure may be exploited to advance the interests of the founder's family at the expense of other stakeholders (as well as efficiency) when countervailing legal measures are not available. Although the pre-crisis literature typically presumed the *chaebol* were characterized by concentrated ownership, we note that important changes have taken place in ownership patterns since the early 1980s.

We also show that the external dimension of the *chaebol's* corporate governance has undergone significant change as well. Democratization and liberalization increasingly shifted the balance of power from the government to the *chaebol*, but expectations for implicit government protection from bankruptcy continued to operate and distorted the resource allocation process (Hahn 2000). At least by the mid-1990s, the efficiency advantage of the *chaebol* was more presumed than real, and systemic risks were building up as Korea was caught between the old developmental state model and a market economy.

In this introduction, we begin by placing the *chaebol* in comparative perspective, focusing on both similarities and differences with business groups in other Asian countries. We then turn to theory, examining the role of market forces, corporate governance and politics in the emergence and operation of the *chaebol*; these two sections correspond to the first part of the book (Chapters 2–5). In the second part, we examine some of the causal links between corporate governance and the financial crisis of 1997–98. We also take a look at the role played by financial liberalization and lax supervision.

We then turn to the management of the crisis, beginning with the short-run management of "systemic distress": the simultaneous bankruptcy of large numbers of banks and firms (Chapters 6–8). We conclude by examining the longer-run institutional reform agenda: the reform of the bankruptcy system (Chapter 9), liberalization of rules governing foreign direct investment (Chapter 10), competition policy (Chapter 11), and corporate governance (Chapter 12).

1   The *Chaebol* in Comparative Perspective

Although the *chaebol* have a number of distinctive characteristics, the diversified family-based business group is a common feature of the industrial structure of many developing countries (Leff 1976, 1978; Granovetter 1995). The defining elements of this business group form – to which the Japanese *zaibatsu*, Korean *chaebol* and other Asian enterprises belong – are not easy to identify. Many of the main policy issues surrounding the Asian business groups do not have to do with the organizational features of the firm itself, but with the larger political and economic setting of which they are a part. For example, the problems associated with the *chaebol* are not limited to weak internal corporate governance, but to such factors as size, market dominance, a weak legal infrastructure, undue political influence and corruption.

We return to these problems below, but it is useful to begin with a more restricted definition that focuses on the group itself. Yasuoka's definition of the *zaibatsu* is a useful starting point: "a business group in which one parent company (holding company) owned by a family or an extended family controlled subsidiaries operating in various industries, with large subsidiaries occupying oligopolistic positions in the respective industries" (cited in Morikawa 1992: 250).[2] Note that, while this definition reflects the concerns about firm size and market dominance, it also encompasses three distinct *structural* elements: a *governance structure* of family dominance; an *organizational structure* of a holding company controlling legally independent firms (multi-subsidiaries rather than multi-divisions); and a diversified *business structure* encompassing a number of discrete products and services. Since the three elements of this definition are not categorical, however, the basic type exhibits important variations. Some of this variation may reflect differences in the economic and political environment in which firms operate, but some of it may reflect different stages in a common pattern of historical evolution.

With respect to the *governance structure*, recent studies by Claessens, Djankov and Lang (1998, 2000a, b) have examined the distribution of ultimate control and ownership rights in major corporations in Asia.[3] Japanese firms are now widely held. Southeast Asian business groups, by contrast, continue to show a pattern of concentrated family ownership; this appears to be the case with many Chinese groups in Taiwan and Hong Kong as well.[4] The *chaebol*, by contrast, are distinctive in that they combine effective family control with a relatively *low* concentration of ownership. As of the year 2000, the average ownership share of the thirty largest *chaebol* held by the *chaebol chongsu*, or boss, was only 1.5 percent, a level approached by some professional managers of widely held American companies.

This governance structure must be placed in historical perspective. Prior to the mid-1970s, the ownership and control of the *chaebol* was also characterized by a high degree of concentration. As Table 1.1

shows, after 1983 it declined steadily. These changes reflected the government's efforts to push the *chaebol* to go public in the mid-1970s and a stock market boom from the late 1980s to the mid-1990s that formally diluted ownership, although not, as we will show, control. Yet it may be too soon to tell whether this combination is in fact unique to Korea. Family-based business groups in Southeast Asia could follow a similar trajectory of declining family ownership with continuing control if stock markets expand in the absence of well-developed shareholder rights.

With respect to its *organizational structure*, the Asian business group combines the unified control of multi-divisional firms with the legal separateness of group firms (Granovetter 1995: 95–6). The *chaebol* broadly fit this model, typically consisting of legally independent affiliates that act like a single corporation under the control of the founder's family. The Chairman's Office serves as the command center for the whole group, often through meetings of a management committee that consists of the CEOs of the other firms in the group. An apparent difference in the Korean *chaebol* is the absence of pure holding companies, visible in the pre-war Japanese *zaibatsu* and in some Southeast Asian countries. The Korean government has subjected such pure holding companies to very restrictive conditions. Nevertheless, the *chaebol* typically use a lead or "flagship" business as the core company, and build a controlled pyramid structure that relies on in-group ownership of affiliates. Thus, in spite of superficial differences, the *chaebol* as a corporate form is closer to the *zaibatsu* than to the post-war Japanese business group (*kigyoshudan* or *keiretsu*), which is a much less hierarchical confederation of companies.

Taking Samsung as an example, Figure 1.1 shows how the founder's family uses a multi-subsidiary structure to maintain corporate control with only a small amount of its own equity. The Lee family has almost complete ownership of Samsung Everland, an unlisted firm operating an amusement park, and uses it as a *de facto* holding company. The family relies on the inter-subsidiary shareholdings of cash-cows such as Samsung Life Insurance and Samsung Electronics to establish exclusive family control over a great number of subsidiaries.[5]

Finally, with respect to *business structure*, Asian business groups typically engage in a wide variety of activities, in some cases reflecting the full range of a country's economic activities from agriculture to manufacturing to services.[6] One important difference across countries, however, has to do with the role of financial institutions in the group structure. The Japanese *zaibatsu* typically included financial institutions. Group-owned banks, trust companies, and insurance companies provided funding to non-financial subsidiaries. Family-based business groups in Southeast Asia also share this characteristic. By contrast,

Table 1.1 In-group ownership share for the top *chaebol* (%)

Chaebol	1983	1987	1989	1990	1991	1992	1993	1994	1995	1996	1997	1998	1999	2000
Top 30	57.2	56.2	46.2	45.4	46.9	46.1	43.4	42.7	43.3	44.1	43.0	44.5	49.6	43.4
Family	17.2	15.8	14.7	13.7	13.9	12.6	10.3	9.7	10.5	10.3	8.5	7.9	5.4	4.5
Subsidiaries	40.0	40.4	31.5	31.7	33.0	33.5	33.1	33.0	32.8	33.8	34.5	36.6	45.1	38.9
Top 5	n.a.	60.3	49.4	49.6	51.6	51.9	49.0	47.5	n.a	n.a	45.2	46.6	53.5	n.a
Family	n.a.	15.6	13.7	13.3	13.2	13.3	11.8	12.5	n.a	n.a	8.6	n.a	n.a	n.a
Subsidiaries	n.a.	44.7	35.7	36.3	38.4	38.6	37.2	35.0	n.a	n.a	36.6	n.a	n.a	n.a
Hyundai	81.4	79.9	n.a	60.2	67.8	65.7	57.8	61.3	60.4	61.4	56.2	53.7	n.a	n.a
Samsung	59.5	56.5	n.a	51.4	53.2	58.3	52.9	48.9	49.3	49.0	46.7	44.6	n.a	n.a
Daewoo	70.6	56.2	n.a	49.1	50.4	48.8	46.9	42.4	41.4	41.7	38.3	41.0	n.a	n.a
LG	30.2	41.5	n.a	35.2	38.3	39.7	38.8	37.7	39.7	39.9	40.1	41.9	n.a	n.a

Note: The in-group ownership share for a *chaebol* is calculated by obtaining the weighted average of the combined ownership share of the founder's extended family and subsidiaries for all subsidiaries.

Source: Korea Fair Trade Commission; Yoo (1999).

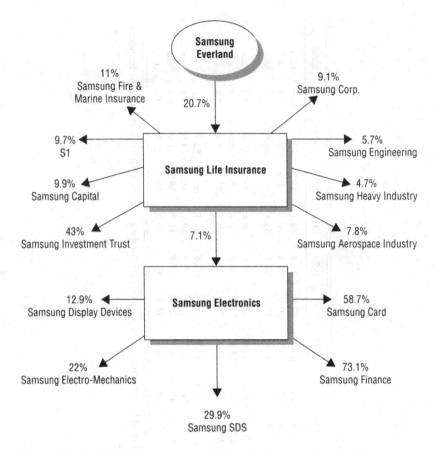

Figure 1.1   Multi-subsidiary structure of the *chaebol*: Samsung Group, 1999

Note: Figures represent inter-subsidiary shareholdings.

Source: Financial Supervisory Commission. Cited from *Chosun Ilbo*, August 19, 1999.

major commercial banks in Korea, having been nationalized in 1961, were not privatized until the mid-1980s and then only with restrictions on ownership. As a result, the Korean *chaebol* did not have banks in their business portfolios through most of the high-growth period.

However, this observation requires some qualification. The *chaebol* owned and operated commercial banks briefly after their privatization in the late 1950s, but the banking sector was renationalized under the military government in 1961. The government prohibited the *chaebol* from entering the banking sector and restricted licenses for non-bank financial institutions, but it never prohibited the *chaebol* from owning them. A number of *chaebol* established merchant banks, securities firms, and insurance companies in the 1980s and 1990s as the financial market was progressively liberalized.[7] The *chaebol's* increasing diversification into the non-bank financial sector suggests that the difference between the *chaebol* and other family-based business groups in Asia has diminished somewhat over time (see Chapter 4).

2   Theoretical Approaches to the *Chaebol*

If we set aside cultural approaches that focus on purported national or ethnic idiosyncrasies – common in the vast literature on Chinese business groups in particular – at least three different avenues exist for explaining the business group as a corporate form.[8] The first approach is an efficiency model that emphasizes profit-maximizing motives, especially in a context of underdeveloped or imperfect markets for inputs and services. A second approach focuses on principal-agent problems and the ability of owner-managers to exploit informational asymmetries to their advantage. The third explanation is political and emphasizes the role of business–government relations and policy in the evolution of the business group.

These three theoretical models are partly complementary.[9] But since they have important policy implications, we seek ways in which they might be tested against one another.[10] For example, if the *chaebol* is basically an efficient organizational form, then the appropriate reforms are those that guarantee that firms operate in a competitive setting through market liberalization and strengthened competition policy; Kwangshik Shin presents such an argument in Chapter 11 and it is implicit in Mikyung Yun's discussion of foreign direct investment in Chapter 10. If the *chaebol* operate primarily to advance the interests of the founder's family at the expense of other shareholders, then reforms in corporate governance are essential; Myeong-Hyeon Cho makes this case in Chapter 12. If, however, the *chaebol* are the creature of politics, then even more fundamental reforms of the business–government relationship may be required; these issues are addressed in Chapter 3 by Byung-Kook Kim and Chapter 6 by Jongryn Mo and Chung-in Moon.

The efficiency model

The economic theory of the firm looks at corporate form as a rational and efficient response to some set of constraints. The prevalence of the business group in developing countries can be explained by the imperfect or underdeveloped nature of the legal system and the markets for inputs, services, and managerial control itself (Khanna 2000).

The logic of this approach can be seen by considering three distinct types of business expansion: vertical integration, related horizontal diversification, and unrelated horizontal diversification.[11] In pursuing vertical integration, the firm is choosing to do more activities in-house instead of procuring from others; as Coase (1937), Williamson (1975) and others have noted, the firm's make-or-buy decisions critically depend on transaction costs that arise from uncertainty, asymmetric information, and incomplete contracting. The level of development for markets as well as legal and social institutions affects these costs.[12] As Wonhyuk Lim argues in Chapter 2, individual corporate histories of the *chaebol* contain numerous examples of vertical integration arising from precisely these considerations.

The decision to diversify horizontally – to enter a new line of business with which the firm has few forward or backward linkages – has a different logic. One motive is risk diversification. A firm – or more precisely the owner of a firm – may want to develop a range of businesses in order to reduce overall risks, especially in the absence of a well-developed capital market. A second efficiency motive for horizontal diversification is to utilize a common, essentially non-rival, factor of production across a variety of different economic activities. For example, a group may use overseas marketing information collected through a general trading company as a common factor of production and manufacture various products adapted to overseas customer needs. Related to this is the "internal markets" hypothesis. When capital and labor markets are underdeveloped, the *chaebol* form can exploit well-developed internal factor markets to diversify. Alice Amsden (1989) showed how *chaebol* growth was fueled not just by intra-group financial transfers but also by efficient use of the group's pool of managerial and engineering talent.

In short, the efficiency model argues that the business structure of the *chaebol* and other family-based business groups is a rational response to underdeveloped markets. Since this approach treats the firm as a monolith, however, it does better at explaining business structure than governance and organizational structure: the questions of how the founder's family maintains control or why the business groups choose the controlled pyramid structure over a multi-divisional one. Principal-agent models are better equipped to address such problems, and they reveal a number of internal inefficiencies that the efficiency approach misses.

The principal-agent model

The principal-agent approach focuses on conflicts of interest among the stakeholders of the firm, particularly the problem of incentive compatibility and asymmetric information between shareholders and professional managers. The high concentration of ownership, particularly in Southeast Asia's family-based business groups, should make this conventional corporate governance problem less relevant; owner-managers should be committed to maximizing the value of their own companies. For such companies, the main governance issue is not the internal one of how shareholders monitor professional managers but the external one of how – and whether – banks and capital markets can exert control over large inside shareholders who also occupy top management positions. As Joon-Ho Hahm shows in Chapter 4, this problem was particularly acute in Korea.

In fact, internal agency problems also abound in the *chaebol*, but as Myeong-Hyeon Cho shows in Chapter 12, they take a somewhat different form. As we have seen, the founder's family typically has only a *small* ownership stake; nonetheless, it exercises control by using extensive inter-subsidiary shareholdings. The members of the founder's family who take top managerial positions are similar to professional managers in that they do not have a significant ownership stake. Unlike professional managers, however, they have considerable control rights and cannot easily be removed. We call this the *entrenchment problem*. Unless checked by incentive and monitoring schemes to protect outside shareholders, the founder's family can expropriate shareholder value with impunity.

These observations allow us to revisit the efficiency approach with a less innocent eye. Suppose that a *chaebol* enters a line of business through a new subsidiary in order to lower the costs associated with monopolistic or oligopolistic suppliers. The new subsidiary provides intermediate inputs to the firm at marginal cost, but sells the same goods to outside customers at noncompetitive (oligopolistic) prices. In this case, the firm is not engaging in any wrongdoing; the real problem is noncompetitive market structure. The *chaebol* is simply using vertical integration to reduce cost and maximize joint profit.

However, the *chaebol* is not a multi-divisional firm but a group of nominally independent companies. Therefore the ownership structure of the new subsidiary can differ from that of others in the group. Important redistributive issues can thus arise. In the case just cited, the new subsidiary could make more money by selling to outside customers rather than within the group. Its shareholders should therefore insist on some form of compensation from the shareholders of other subsidiaries in the group. Because of the centralized control of group decisions by the chairman, such compensation does not necessarily occur; rather, the controlling family can exploit asymmetries in ownership, control and profitability in order to expropriate shareholder value.

The focus on expropriation allows us to understand cases that are wholly anomalous from the perspective of the efficiency theory, such as subsidiaries that provide intermediate goods or services to the existing organization at prices that are *higher*, rather than lower, than market prices. The motive for such transfers is to effect resource transfers for private gain, for example, by shifting profits from subsidiaries in which the controlling family has a low stake to those in which it has a high stake.[13] The mechanisms for effecting such transfers are multiple, and extend far beyond the pricing of intermediates and other inputs to inter-subsidiary lending and the extension of loan guarantees (see Chapters 2, 4 and 11). Inter-subsidiary sales of shares often reflected expropriation motives as well, most blatantly in the case of Daewoo (see Chapter 7). Transfers of technology, real estate and even labor among groups could also reflect effective cross-subsidization and expropriation.

In short, the principal-agent model provides a rather different view of the *chaebol* and other family-based business groups than does the efficiency model. Focusing on the conflict of interest among stake-holders, the principal-agent model offers a consistent explanation for the business, governance, and organizational structure of family-based business groups.

Political economy approaches

While the efficiency and principal-agent models focus on relationships between and within firms respectively, the political economy approach examines the exchange relations between the government and the private sector. This approach has many variants, but the central insight is a simple supply and demand model of politics.[14] Either the politician or bureaucrat extends a rent to the private sector and collects a bribe in return (personal corruption), or the rent is extended in return for some form of political support, such as money or the mobilization of votes, that maximizes the politician's longevity in office. Although the former type of exchange is typically proscribed – at least formally – the latter may be either legal (legitimate campaign contributions) or illegal (political corruption).

Despite its relatively mechanistic view of the political process, the rent-seeking approach is of use in understanding the historical origins of the *chaebol* and has entered into many accounts either implicitly or explicitly (S. K. Kim 1987; Jung 1988; Steers, Shin and Ungson 1989; Woo 1991; Fields 1995: ch. 2; Haggard, Cooper and Moon 1993; Kang 1996, ch. 6; E. M. Kim 1997; Kang 2001). Following the Korean War, the government of Syngman Rhee (in office from 1948 to 1960) pursued a classic import-substituting strategy. Rents associated with the privatization of vested properties, an overvalued exchange rate, high rates of protection, government procurement, and preferential credit all served to encourage the rapid growth and high profitability of favored private enterprises.

Following the student revolution of 1960 and military coup of 1961, however, the political relationship between the government and the private sector changed in ways that suggest limitations on a simple rent-seeking approach. The younger military officers who led the coup intervened precisely to root out the corruption that had prevailed during the Rhee period and to reorient the government toward the pursuit of economic growth (Haggard 1990; Huer 1989). At least initially, they also had less need for the types of *political* support from the private sector that the Rhee regime required (see, however, Kang 2001).

It is this transformation of politics that models of the "developmental state" seek to capture (Johnson 1982; Woo-Cumings 1999). In the rent-seeking state, politicians and bureaucrats maximize their personal or political fortunes by extending rents to the private sector, with the distributive implications and distortions that such an approach implies. By contrast, the "developmental state" is headed by a cohesive political leadership, supported by a bureaucratic planning apparatus. This "strong state" maximizes its political fortunes through the pursuit of aggregate growth and limitations on corruption (Shleifer and Vishny 1993). This growth model may rely in part on the market, but it may also involve targeted support for particular economic activities. If these activities are not undertaken directly by the government through state-owned enterprises, as they were for example in Taiwan and Singapore, private firms must be induced to comply with government objectives. This occurs by providing conditional support of various sorts. In Korea, the main instrument for doing this was the financial system. The military government nationalized the banks while providing repayment guarantees on foreign loans extended to private firms, most of which lacked the standing to raise capital on their own in the international financial market. In return for financial support, however, firms were expected to comply with the changing dictates of the plan (see Chapter 2).

During the 1960s, the government placed particular emphasis on the promotion of exports, not simply through devaluation and selective trade liberalization but through more direct means as well. The government used the performance of firms in competitive export markets as a selection criterion in extending credit; firms could get full financial support, including for imported inputs, against export orders.

In the 1970s, due in part to perceived security threats, the government launched the drive to expand heavy and chemical industry (HCI) and established a set of industrial priorities that were highly capital-intensive: petrochemicals, steel, non-ferrous metals, electronics, heavy machinery and shipbuilding. These activities provided incredible rents to a very small group of firms. Kang (2001) argues that this "mutual hostage" situation served to limit the extent of rent-seeking. But it also generated tremendous risks of moral hazard. The overcapacity and inefficiency in the HCI sectors, and the bailouts and restructuring required of them, led the government to re-examine its industrial policy and shift away from the targeting approach in the 1980s. Subsequent liberalization and democratization accelerated the dismantling of some, but by no means all, features of the developmental state (see Chapter 3).

An important contribution of the political economy approach is to highlight severe problems in the *external* corporate governance of the Korean *chaebol*, particularly with respect to the monitoring role of the financial sector. As Joon-Ho Hahm shows in Chapter 4, the combination of a *dirigist* industrial policy and state ownership of banks weakened the incentives of banks to monitor the behavior of the *chaebol* or to serve as a check on poor internal corporate governance. However, the privatization of the commercial banks and the gradual liberalization of the financial sector did not necessarily serve to restore external discipline either, because it failed to create conditions conducive to the growth of autonomous financial institutions.

The government continued to intervene in the banking system in a number of direct and indirect ways, from the vetting of bank presidents to the maintenance of ownership stakes in major banks, particularly the Korea Development Bank. At the same time, the liberalization of the non-bank financial sector could be captured to provide new opportunities for the expropriation strategies outlined in the previous section (Haggard 2000; Chapter 2). As Joon-Ho Hahm shows in Chapter 4, financial liberalization weakened the government's control over investment decisions and allowed *chaebol*-owned non-bank financial institutions to channel funding toward group subsidiaries. As Dong Gull Lee shows in his case study of Daewoo (Chapter 7), this type of intra-group financing continued to grow even *after* the financial crisis had struck.

The political economy approach also fills in some important missing links in the expropriation hypothesis. We have suggested that the risk of expropriation increased after the 1980s as the government encouraged the development of the equity market and ownership dilution took place without concomitant improvements in legal protections for minority shareholders. If this were apparent, why did Korean investors hold stocks at all? In fact, cross-national evidence on equity holdings suggests that the share of Korean household savings invested in stocks is, in fact, comparatively low.[15] If the Korean financial sector were autonomous, firms themselves would have supported reforms of internal corporate governance in order to reduce expropriation risk, signal their commitment to maximizing shareholder value, and thereby increase the ease of raising capital. But with banks and non-bank financial institutions under the control of either the government or the *chaebol*, inadequate protection of shareholder rights had little adverse effect on the overall level of investment.

The political economy approach also suggests how financial repression affects the ownership structure of Asia's family-based business groups and the *chaebol's* extraordinary leveraging. It is not surprising that family owners prefer to retain control while expanding their business empires. But much of the literature on modern business enterprise assumes that family-based firms tend to become obsolete as the economy develops (Leff 1978). In particular, family-based companies should face difficulty competing with publicly listed companies that can raise capital by issuing equity, which has the effect of diluting the concentration of ownership and control.

But if family-based companies can readily obtain debt financing, they will be able to expand with relatively little equity capital. Moreover, weak legal infrastructure may allow controlling shareholders of family-based companies to retain their control even as their ownership is diluted.[16]

The political economy approach underlines the critical role that government played in both the founding and diversification of the *chaebol*. Diversification was driven not simply by efficiency and expropriation motives, but – at different times – by corruption and the financial incentives and socialization of risk associated with industrial policy. Ownership structure, the preference for debt, and weak external monitoring of the firm also had political roots. To what extent were these factors implicated in the crisis of 1997–98?

3   The *Chaebol* and the 1997 Crisis

The crisis that hit Asia in 1997 is not a unique event in the history of the developing world. Latin America and Africa experienced severe debt crises in the 1980s, and in 1994–95 Mexico experienced another round of international financial distress. These incidents differed in many ways, for example in the size of external shocks countries faced and in the mechanism that triggered the crisis. But many seemed rooted in a fundamental inconsistency between domestic policies, particularly monetary expansion to finance budget deficits, and the attempt to maintain a fixed exchange rate in the face of increased foreign borrowing. Early models of financial crises focused on these macroeconomic fundamentals.

These models do not capture important aspects of Korea's difficulties. Korea's terms of trade deteriorated by approximately 20 percent in 1995–96, but the current account deficit had actually narrowed to less than 2 percent of GDP before the crisis. Although the gross savings rate was declining somewhat in the years preceding the crisis, it exceeded 30 percent. The real exchange rate was essentially flat prior to the crisis, the budget was roughly in balance in 1996 and 1997, monetary policy was relatively cautious, and inflation was less than 5 percent.

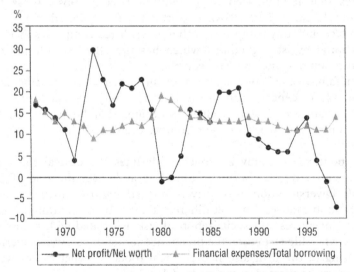

Figure 1.2   Profitability and cost of capital for the Korean manufacturing sector, 1967–97

Note: Total borrowing includes loans from financial institutions and corporate bonds issued by firms. It does not include non-interest-bearing IOUs in commercial transactions.
Source: Bank of Korea, *Financial Statements Analysis*, various issues; from Lim (2000: 49).

Moreover, Korea's currency crisis was only one element of a much broader domestic financial crisis that began *before* the collapse of the exchange rate in November 1997. The first and most general source of vulnerability to such a crisis – and one that has not been adequately underlined in the literature – is the historically weak performance of the Korean corporate sector. As Figure 1.2 shows, prior to the crisis of 1997 there were only two periods when the profitability of Korean manufacturing firms was significantly above the opportunity cost of capital. The first was from 1972 to 1978, when the corporate sector's debt burden was artificially reduced by the Emergency Decree of 1972[17] and the low interest rate policy during the ensuing HCI drive. The second was from 1986 to 1988, when the Korean economy enjoyed the "three-low" boom, characterized by low oil prices, low international interest rates, and a won that had depreciated sharply relative to the Japanese yen after the Plaza Accord of 1985. Whether compared with the United States and Japan or with other middle-income countries such as Taiwan, Korean firms consistently exhibit low profitability (Borensztein and Lee 1999).

The vulnerability associated with poor performance was compounded by the corporate sector's extraordinarily high leverage; Figure 1.3 traces the average debt-to-equity ratio for the Korean manufacturing sector from 1965 through the onset of the crisis. For the first half of the 1990s, it hovered around 300 percent. By the end of 1997,

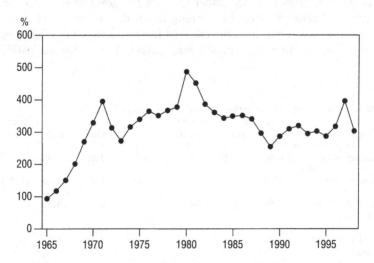

Figure 1.3   Average debt–equity ratio of the Korean manufacturing sector, 1965–98

Source: Bank of Korea, *Financial Statements Analysis*, various issues; from Lim (2000: 48).

the average debt–equity ratio had hit 400 percent. The ratio exceeded 500 percent for the thirty largest *chaebol* and reached 3000 percent for several large groups (Lee et al. 2000).

The other side of this combination of poor corporate performance and high leverage was Korea's severely weakened banking sector. Table 1.2 shows that the profitability of domestic commercial banks, as measured by the returns on assets and equity, was declining after 1994.[18] Moreover, bank profitability was declining even though the interest spread between bank loans and deposits had *widened* since 1993. Hahm and Mishkin (2000) conclude that the weakness of Korea's banking sector stemmed from deterioration in asset quality rather than increased competition in the financial sector. The root cause of the banking problem was in the deterioration of corporate fundamentals.

There are different interpretations as to how these vulnerabilities played into the onset of the crisis. Dooley and Shin (2000) argue that the crisis unfolded like a bank run. During the month of November alone, net capital outflow was over $15 billion, with the major component of this reversal coming from foreign borrowing rather than a shift in portfolio investment or foreign direct investment. In particular, foreign creditors ran from foreign branches of Korean banks, which were completely free from foreign exchange risk. This suggests that the reversal in capital flows was triggered as much by the anticipated bankruptcy of Korean corporations that threatened the solvency of the banking sector as by fears about currency depreciation. The currency crisis was merely a symptom of a deeper cause, exacerbated by the government's hopeless attempt to defend the won by running down the reserves. Even those explanations that seem to blame external factors for Korea's crisis (such as contagion, herding, and market manipulation) can only be justified

Table 1.2 Indicators of bank performance (end-year value, %, million *won*)

Indicator	1992	1993	1994	1995	1996	1997	1998
Return on assets	0.56	0.45	0.42	0.32	0.26	−0.93	−3.25
Return on equity	6.69	5.90	6.09	4.19	3.80	−14.18	−52.53
Operating income/ employee	28.6	31.7	52.1	39.1	40.2	26.8	
Loan-deposit rate spread	2.24	1.91	2.30	3.02	3.52	3.57	

Note: Average of 20 domestic commercial banks, including trust accounts.
Source: Hahm and Mishkin (2000: Table 4).

when the fundamentals are sufficiently weak. Financial crises do not happen just anywhere. Capital outflows were responding to real weaknesses in Korea's corporate and financial sector, weaknesses that had been revealed quite clearly by the bankruptcy of a number of large groups in the first half of 1997.

Yet if the corporate and financial sector weaknesses that we have talked about here and in the foregoing section have been long-standing features of Korea's growth, why did Korea not experience crises in the past? The short answer is that it did. As is evident from Figure 1.3, historical trends in the average debt–equity ratio demonstrate two prior peaks that coincide with major corporate and financial crises and government bailouts: the August 1972 Emergency Decree; and the 1979–81 "restructuring" of the HCI sectors.[19]

The 1972 Emergency Decree was clearly the most dramatic of past bailout exercises. As in 1997, corporate profits showed signs of weakness and the world economic recession made the situation worse. By 1971, the number of bankrupt enterprises that had received foreign loans climbed to 200. With warning from the business sector of further bankruptcies, the government announced an immediate moratorium on the payment of all corporate debt to curb lenders and the rescheduling of bank loans. With domestic curb lenders and bank depositors assuming the entire burden of the crisis, major bankruptcies were avoided (see Chapter 2).

The second crisis in 1979–81 came about following Park Chung Hee's assassination in 1979. Over-investment during the HCI drive began to take its toll on the economy. As Figure 1.3 shows, corporate leverage during this period was even higher than in 1997. With the second oil shock leading to a global recession, the accumulated total current account deficit during this period amounted to $14 billion. Korea was lucky because it did not have much trouble raising money from abroad.[20] Hence the government was able to patch over the corporate debt problem with interest rate reductions, debt rescheduling and tax cuts.

How was it possible that the government was able to muddle through these earlier crises without major corporate bankruptcies? One obvious difference is that much of Korea's external debt in 1997 was short-term (averaging more than 60 percent of total external debt during 1992–96). In contrast, short-term debt was no more than 20 percent of the total external debt during the 1972 crisis and 34 percent during the 1979–81 crisis. The financial opening of the 1990s liberalized the short-term capital market while maintaining controls on long-term financing. This sequence deserves some blame for increasing the vulnerability of the Korean economy to capital flight.

But it would be wrong to think that the Korean crisis could have been avoided if liberalization had not been pursued at all (Wang 2001). First, the liberalization of short-term capital was relatively modest. Neither firms nor banks could sell short-term debt instruments in domestic currency to foreigners; only trade-related financing and short-term foreign currency borrowing by banks were allowed. Second, the alternative of restricting short-term transactions of banks would have been just as costly. The fault was not short-term foreign borrowing but the virtual absence of prudential supervision of, and risk management by, both commercial and merchant banks.

The second difference from previous crises has to do with political economy. The authoritarian nature of past governments and the largely domestic nature of the crisis permitted the government to take quite decisive action, generally in favor of the *chaebol.* "Restructuring" was really little more than debt rescheduling designed to restore the basic terms of the government–business risk partnership (see Chapter 3). Corporate bankruptcies were avoided because creditors and taxpayers were forced to bear the burden. With democratization, the government could not avoid bankruptcies in the same way. Moreover, with the end of the Cold War, the Korean government was perhaps less able to find backing from its allies than in the past.[21] With limited options both externally and domestically, the government had no choice but to face the crisis head-on and make corporate reform a centerpiece of its recovery effort.

4   The Political Economy of Crisis Management

A distinguishing feature of the Asian financial crisis was systemic financial and corporate distress: the simultaneous insolvency of large numbers of banks and firms. The process of financial and corporate restructuring under such circumstances is both technically and politically difficult, since it involves the imposition – or more accurately, the recognition – of staggering social losses (Claessens, Djankov and Klingebiel 1999; World Bank 1998, 2000: ch. 3; Haggard 2000: ch. 4; Claessens, Djankov and Mody 2001). Although the Kim Young Sam government showed signs of hesitancy and delay in addressing these issues before the foreign exchange crisis broke in November 1997, the new Kim Dae-jung government was politically positioned to act decisively with respect to both short-term crisis management and longer-run corporate restructuring. The severity of the crisis, a fortuitously timed political honeymoon, and a political coalition and ideology that were supportive of reform of business–government relations all contributed to relatively decisive action (see Chapters 3 and 6).

Under conditions of systemic distress, the first tasks facing governments center on the financial sector: to decide which banks and other non-bank financial institutions need to be closed,[22] rehabilitating those that can be saved, and disposing of nonperforming assets.[23] The Kim Young Sam government began the process of setting aside funds to recapitalize the banking system and carving out nonperforming loans, and the new administration expanded these efforts dramatically, shutting down distressed banks and merging them with others under government direction. Kim Dae-jung quickly established a powerful regulatory agency – the Financial Supervisory Commission – to oversee these tasks. One result of the capital infusions and purchase of nonperforming loans was an effective nationalization of large parts of the banking system; this in turn had implications for the corporate restructuring process.

As with the management of the financial sector, the short-term corporate restructuring process centers on separating firms that are insolvent from those which are simply illiquid. Even during good times, this task is not always straightforward. During periods of highly volatile exchange rates, very high interest rates and a sharp contraction of demand, it is particularly difficult.

The government can address this problem in one of three ways. First, it could in principle rely wholly on court-led restructuring procedures. However, even countries with relatively strong bankruptcy laws are unlikely to be able to rely on this mechanism during periods of systemic distress. Second, the government can enforce capital adequacy and loan loss provisions rigorously while providing incentives for banks to engage in out-of-court settlements; this is the so-called London approach. This strategy requires that banks are financially sound enough to manage problem loans on their own.

A final strategy is for the government – or the government acting through the banks it effectively owns – to play an active role in the corporate restructuring process. Such involvement might range from coordinating intra-creditor and creditor–debtor relations and monitoring and enforcing agreements, to using various instruments to enforce financial and operational restructuring objectives.

Despite protestations that the government was following a London approach, Kyung Suh Park shows clearly in Chapter 8 that government involvement in corporate restructuring was deep. The government's approach was a three-tiered one that included a strategy for small and medium-sized firms.[24] In this volume, however, we focus on the first tier of the Big Five – Hyundai, Samsung, Daewoo, LG and SK – and the second tier of so-called "6–64" *chaebol.*

The Big Five posed the most daunting problems because they were both economically and politically important. The government dealt with them through the negotiation of informal, "voluntary" agreements that covered such controversial issues as inter-subsidiary loan guarantees and the reduction of excessive indebtedness. Capital Structure Improvement Plans signed with main creditor banks contained agreements on a variety of other restructuring measures as well, including asset sales to both domestic and foreign bidders, issuance of new equity, debt-for-equity swaps, and operational restructuring. One element of operational restructuring that came directly from the Blue House was the so-called Big Deals, under which the Big Five would swap major lines of business among themselves to consolidate excessive and duplicative investments while simultaneously achieving greater economies of scale. More than any other measure, the Big Deals reflected the directive nature of the government's approach to corporate restructuring.

Throughout 1998 and the first half of 1999, the government engaged in an ongoing public relations battle with the Big Five over their commitment to restructuring, particularly as it became clear that Hyundai and Daewoo had continued to take on more debt in 1998.[25] Daewoo proved the test case (see Chapter 7; Mako and Jung 2000). Dong Gull Lee shows in Chapter 7 that the government was slow in recognizing the scope of Daewoo's problems; that the ultimate restructuring plan agreed in August 1999 allowed for a number of units of the group to continue to operate; and that the government was forced to establish massive funds to support the investment trust companies which were big purchasers of Daewoo bonds. Despite these reservations, the fall of Daewoo must be seen as an important event in Korea's recent economic history: one of the country's very largest *chaebol* was allowed to fail.

The second tier of the corporate restructuring effort centered on the "6–64" *chaebol.* In mid-1998, 236 financial institutions signed and entered into the Corporate Restructuring Accord, which defined the informal workout procedure for these firms. A small number of lead banks would take responsibility for negotiating workouts of problem debts with the 6–64 corporate groups. Nominally this procedure would take place under so-called London rules, but the process was closely overseen by the Financial Supervisory Commission through the Corporate Restructuring Committee.

Kyung Suh Park argues in Chapter 8 that the program had a number of limitations. Park finds the greatest limitation of the restructuring effort in the weakness of the banks and the conflicts between the strengthening of bank supervision and bank incentives *vis-à-vis* their corporate clients. As the Financial Supervisory Commission strengthened capital adequacy requirements, banks shrunk their assets, contributing to the credit squeeze. Yet at the same time, the banks had neither the incentives nor (at least initially) the capabilities to actively lead the restructuring process. Park shows that contributions from shareholders and operational restructuring played a less central role than the restructuring of debt: rate reductions, deferrals of principal and interest, and conversion of debt into equity or convertible bonds. By the end of 2000, a "second round" of corporate and financial restructuring was required, including additional infusions of funds to the financial sector.

In sum, short-term corporate restructuring in Korea gets a mixed review. On the one hand, the Kim Dae-jung government must be credited for moving swiftly and comprehensively, and in facing down – albeit somewhat belatedly – even the largest *chaebol*. Certainly, the program looks ambitious when compared to other countries in the region.

Mo and Moon argue, in Chapter 6, that the speed with which the Korean government moved was bought by an exercise of directive powers that rested on a dubious legal foundation. A number of directive elements, such as the setting of quantitative targets and deadlines for achieving debt–equity ratios, might have been counterproductive. These measures also carried an important irony: they involved the Korean government more deeply in the micro-management of the corporate restructuring process. This new state intervention was partly the result of the dramatic expansion of the government's ownership of the banking system. However, it also reflected Kim Dae-jung's unusual political position as an outsider with few connections to the private sector and with a strong "progressive" or "populist" political base.

5   The Political Economy of Structural Reform

The short-run corporate restructuring effort did not precede the initiation of structural reforms; indeed, the new administration appeared more clear in its intentions with respect to these structural measures than it was with the financial restructuring program just outlined. These reforms focused squarely on corporate governance (see Chapters 6 and 12). Although they appeared to emanate from a consultative process between the president and the major *chaebol* leaders, Mo and Moon argue in Chapter 6 that the extent of private sector input to the process was probably minimal. The extensive legislative and regulatory program that evolved in the early months of 1998 predominantly reflected the preferences of the new administration, with input from the international financial institutions.

The five principles of corporate restructuring agreed on January 13, 1998 included enhancing transparency in accounting and management, resolving mutual debt guarantees among *chaebol* affiliates, improving firms' financial structure through a reduction of debt–equity ratios, streamlining business activities, and strengthening the accountability of *chaebol* bosses. On the occasion of Kim Dae-jung's National Liberation Day speech of August 15, 1999 – the high tide of the administration's skepticism about the *chaebol* – he announced three more principles, including regulation of the *chaebol's* control of non-bank financial institutions and inter-subsidiary equity investments, and prevention of irregular inheritance and gift-giving among *chaebol* owners.

Myeong-Hyeon Cho provides a detailed overview of these reforms in Chapter 12. His analytic starting point is what we have called the entrenchment problem: the difficulty of controlling owner-managers who have relatively low stakes in the firm but exercise control through in-group ownership. Many of the reforms clearly targeted this problem. Even more directive measures focused on the financial structure of the *chaebol* group and sought to cut through long-standing corporate practices that expropriated minority shareholders' value or shifted risk to the public sector (see section 2 above).

Cho's evaluation of the reforms is generally positive, particularly with respect to the reform of accounting procedures, transparency and disclosure, and shareholder rights. But Cho highlights a number of areas where owner-managers continue to evade effective oversight. For example, while the crisis led to a decline in the founding family's stake in its companies – a development Joh and Kim find adversely affects performance (Chapter 5) – the stake controlled by affiliated firms actually increased, potentially worsening entrenchment problems. Boards of directors have become more accountable, but questions remain about whether "outside" directors really enjoy independence.

Despite the importance of internal corporate governance mechanisms, the overall legal and market environment in which the *chaebol* function – including external corporate governance mechanisms – will probably have a greater influence on firm behavior in the long run. One of the most important of these environmental factors is the role of foreign direct investment in the economy. Korea has historically had a low level of foreign investment, but the Kim Dae-jung government dramatically accelerated the gradual opening process that had begun under his predecessors.

Mikyung Yun argues in Chapter 10 that concerns about the anti-competitive effects of foreign direct investment cannot be altogether dismissed; increasing foreign investment may simply trade concentrated *domestic* ownership for concentrated *foreign* ownership. However, Yun argues that such concentration may simply be the result of competitive processes. In a setting in which the market for corporate control is so weakly developed, opening the country both to more foreign investment and to cross-border mergers and acquisitions is likely to have a salutary effect on *chaebol* management and performance. In three case studies, she traces some mechanisms through which this might occur, including the effects of joint venture partnerships on internal corporate governance and the transfer of managerial technology.

The incentives to corporate restructuring are also powerfully affected by foreclosure and bankruptcy laws. If these laws or their implementation are weak, firms have incentives to delay restructuring debt and operations and even repayment. Reform of the bankruptcy process and clear enforcement of bankruptcy and foreclosure laws are important not only for managing actual firm failures, but also for providing incentives to creditors and debtors to reach out-of-court settlements.

Compared with Southeast Asian countries, bankruptcy procedures were somewhat stronger in Korea when the crisis hit. Implicit government guarantees against the bankruptcy of large *chaebol*, however, made these procedures less applicable than they appeared. When deciding whether to give a bankrupt firm a second chance, the law also effectively required the court to look beyond the firm itself and to consider the broader ramifications of the firm's failure for the local and national economy.

Using firm-level productivity data, Youngjae Lim shows in Chapter 9 that Korean bankruptcy procedures were biased toward rehabilitation rather than liquidation, even when the latter was warranted. Firms accepted into the rehabilitation-oriented bankruptcy procedures typically had lower than average productivity and continued to exhibit below-average productivity well after the initiation of the rehabilitation program. Even firms in structurally depressed industries, with little hope for a turnaround, were allowed to prolong their lives.

Since the crisis, the bankruptcy law has undergone two rounds of major reform in order to correct this bias and to expedite the process itself. It remains to be seen whether these changes, combined with corporate governance and financial sector reforms, will be sufficient to facilitate the orderly exit of nonviable firms.

The final component of the external environment that we examine is competition policy. In Chapter 11, Kwangshik Shin makes a strong argument that the fundamental problem posed by the *chaebol* is not conglomerate size, ownership concentration, nor even their propensity for "unfair" competition. Nonetheless, Shin shows that these perceptions have guided Korean competition policy and given it its particularly interventionist and directive character. Beginning with the Chun Doo Hwan administration, successive Korean governments initiated "*chaebol* policies" that attempted to impose various direct controls of investment and financing behavior on the large groups. These policies typically had little success in mitigating the problems they purported to address, particularly the level of concentration in the economy.

Shin argues that the *chaebol* created competition problems not because of conglomerate size *per se* but because of two broader problems. First, the combination of industrial policy, trade protection, limitations on foreign direct investment and a variety of formal and informal barriers to entry and exit shielded the *chaebol* from domestic competitive pressures. Second, extensive non-horizontal linkages associated with the *chaebol's* particular expansion strategies provided companies with a wider range of opportunities to exert market power and engage in anti-competitive practices. Shin argues that these discrete practices are the proper target of competition policy.

6   Conclusion: Whither Corporate Governance in Korea?

Despite the many successes of the Kim Dae-jung administration in initiating a reform of the corporate sector, all of the chapters in this volume express some reservations about the extent of the reforms. These shortcomings are in part political. The capacity to initiate reform is bounded by some political logic and, while the Kim Dae-jung government enjoyed a number of fortuitous conditions – including the vision of the president himself – all reformers must deal judiciously with such constraints. In the Korean case, these include the enormous social and political costs associated with corporate restructuring and the difficulties in maintaining reform momentum over time.

Yet a deeper note of caution is also in order. Many discussions of reform implicitly assume that there is an optimal reform path: a single way to initiate the range of policy and institutional changes discussed in this volume and a corresponding set of corporate, market and legal structures that will most fully tap the benefits of a well-regulated market economy. This expectation is a chimera, and for at least two reasons. First, it is clear that, within any given economy, firms adopt a variety of organizational forms, often in the same industry; there is more than one way to skin a cat. But second, it is clear that, at least in the past, the advanced industrial states have exhibited a wide array of different types of corporate governance, from the European corporatist and social

democratic models, to Japan's developmental state, to the more market-
oriented Anglo-Saxon model. To what extent is convergence in forms of
corporate governance occurring globally, and to what extent is Korea
part of that movement? We explore this question in the conclusion
(Chapter 13), examining the extent of change along a number of policy
and institutional dimensions.

Notes

1 See also Jang (1999) and Bae, Kang and Kim (2001).

2 The word *zaibatsu* is Japanese for the same two Chinese characters found in
   the word *chaebol*: *chae,* meaning wealth or finance, and *bol* meaning lineage,
   faction or clique, with a strong connotation of exclusivity. For analyses of
   the origins of Japanese groups, see Morikawa (1992); Okazaki (1999);
   Hattori (1989).

3 Ultimate ownership (cash-flow) rights and control (voting) rights are calculated as follows. Assume a family owns 40 percent of the stock of publicly
   traded firm A, which in turn owns 20 percent of the stock of firm B. The
   family only owns 8 percent of the cash-flow rights of firm B. But the
   relationship between ultimate control rights (as measured by the share of
   ultimate voting rights) and the degree of actual control is nonlinear. It may
   be possible to exercise control with an ultimate control stake of less than,
   say, 20 percent, since dispersed shareholders face collective action problems
   in monitoring management. Thus in this example the family could well
   control 20 percent of firm B, or even more. This gap between control and
   ownership rights is the source of agency problems (La Porta, Lopez-
   de-Silanes and Shleifer 1999).

4 According to Claessens, Djankov and Lang (2000b: 11), Thai corporations
   show the most concentrated ultimate cash-flow rights, followed by Indonesian and Malaysian companies. Among the middle-income countries in the
   region, Korean corporations have the least concentrated ultimate cash-flow
   rights. The concentration of ultimate control rights exhibits a similar pattern,
   with Thai and Indonesian companies having the highest concentration.

5 Although there is some evidence of cross- or interlocking shareholding (see
   Chapter 12), the practice does not seem to be prevalent in Korea
   (J. Kim 2000). For each *chaebol*, a few flagship subsidiaries typically make
   equity investment in other subsidiaries.

6 Of course, there are no natural thresholds with respect to this diversification
   criterion. Hyundai was a small family-owned construction company with an
   affiliate car-repair shop in the early 1950s. By the mid-1970s, the group had
   significant market share in the construction, engineering, shipbuilding and
   automobile industries. When did it cross the *chaebol* threshold?

7 Merchant banks or merchant banking corporations are wholesale financial
   institutions engaged in underwriting commercial paper, leasing, and short-
   term lending to the corporate sector. They fund themselves by issuing
   bonds and commercial paper and by borrowing from the inter-bank and
   foreign markets.

8 For parallel typologies, see Hamilton and Biggart (1988) and Granovetter (1995).

9 For example, when a *chaebol* establishes a new affiliate, it may do so in order to minimize transaction costs under imperfect market conditions; expropriate minority shareholders by exploiting asymmetries in ownership and control shares; and build a good relationship with the government by supporting its industrial policy.

10 An example of such a test is Claessens, Djankov, Fan and Lang (1999), who examine three hypotheses on corporate diversification: "an internal markets" hypothesis, in which firms diversify to utilize internal factor markets that are more cost-effective than external ones; a "risk reduction" hypothesis; and an "expropriation" hypothesis. The first and second are variants of the efficiency model we outline, the third is a principal-agent model. The authors find that diversification is associated with a statistically significant discount of firm value, but since this discount is less pronounced in less developed economies, they cannot reject the "internal markets" hypothesis. Larger divergence between control and ownership rights is associated with *more* diversification, especially at high control levels. This evidence casts doubt on risk reduction as the motive for corporate diversification and lends support to the expropriation hypothesis. Larger divergence should imply lower firm-specific risks for the ultimate owners, making it *less* necessary for them to pursue diversification.

11 Vertical integration refers to business expansion based on input–output linkages, while related horizontal diversification is based on technological or organizational relatedness.

12 For example, in countries where markets for intermediate goods and services are poorly developed, where the relevant prices for intermediate goods or services are difficult to discover, and where reliable on-time delivery is important, firms may pursue vertical integration. If the relevant markets for intermediate goods or services are dominated by monopolistic or oligopolistic producers, such a strategy may be particularly attractive.

13 The case of a scandal involving the subsidiaries of the SK Group provides an example. In 1994, Yukong sold its 700,000 shares in Daehan Telecom at 400 *won* per share to the eldest son of the SK Group's chairman. A year later, Sunkyung Construction sold its 300,000 shares in Daehan Telecom at the same price to the SK chairman's son-in-law. Yukong and Sunkyung Construction, both publicly listed companies, had originally bought Daehan Telecom shares at 10,000 *won* and thus incurred a loss of at least 9.6 billion won on these transactions (approximately $12 million at the prevailing exchange rate). Daehan Telecom, an unlisted SK subsidiary now completely owned by the chairman's eldest son and son-in-law, experienced a dramatic reversal of fortunes and reported a net profit of 11.8 billion *won* in 1997. SK Telecom, a leader in Korea's oligopolistic and highly lucrative cellular phone market, had apparently offered generous terms for services provided by Daehan Telecom. The motive for the pricing of these services seems to have been to expropriate shareholder value. SK Telecom was extremely profitable but was only partially owned by the founder's family; the high returns the company earned had to be shared with other stockholders. Daehan Telecom was a minor company, but closely held. By

exploiting asymmetries in ownership, control, and profitability across subsidiaries, SK's "ruling family" could siphon value toward itself.

14 Thoughtful introductions to the literature on rent-seeking in the context of
East Asian growth include Khan and Jomo (2000) and Kang (2001: ch. 1).

15 While American households invest more than 40 percent of their assets in
stocks, Korean households have only about 10 percent of their assets
in stocks. It seems Korean households invest in stocks primarily for short-
term capital gains.

16 Expropriation of minority shareholders will discourage households from
investing in stocks. Based on this observation, some argue that the government does not have to do much since investors will vote with their feet. This
argument is analogous to saying that the government does not have to do
much about crime-infested neighborhoods since residents will move out of
them. One of the most basic economic roles of the government is to protect
private property, and such protection has efficiency as well as redistributive
implications. The reluctance on the part of households to invest in stocks
pushes firms to rely heavily on debt financing. The highly leveraged financial structure of firms makes them vulnerable to external shocks, increasing
risks for the system as a whole. Moreover, if the financial sector is more
autonomous, such lack of property protection is likely to result in under-
investment.

17 Through the Emergency Decree, the government announced an immediate
moratorium on the payment of all corporate debt to curb lenders and the
rescheduling of bank loans (see Chapter 2.)

18 The seriousness of the banking sector weakness had not been readily recognized before the crisis because the officially released indicators of bank
balance sheets clearly did not reveal the truth about the underlying
problem. For example, the capital to total asset ratio and the BIS ratio in
1996 were reported to be above 4 percent and 9 percent, which according
to the US standard would have been considered more than "adequately
capitalized." The nonperforming loan ratio, as had been officially reported,
was actually falling during 1992–96! The unfolding of the crisis itself
revealed the highly suspect nature of these figures, leading us to suspect
even outright "evergreening."

19 Although not apparent in Figure 1.3, the Korean government undertook
major corporate bailout exercises also in 1969–70 and 1984–88 to ride out
recessions and avoid major financial crises (Cho and Kim 1997).

20 See Haggard (1994), Cho and Kim (1997) and Collins (1994).

21 According to Man-soo Kang, former Vice-Minister for Finance and
Economy, $4 billion in the Korea–Japan Economic Cooperation Fund
made available to Korea in 1983 from Japan would not have been possible
without strong urging from the Reagan administration. This fund served as
useful collateral for further external funding when Korea's credit standing
was quite poor. The greater exposure to external debt also meant that the
debt problem could not be simply written off as it had been in the past.

22 Once a bank is insolvent, managers have few incentives to run it on a commercial basis and looting can set in. Moreover, insolvent banks will pressure
the central bank to provide liquidity support and to issue guarantees, thus
prolonging the crisis.

23 To dispose of nonperforming loans, governments have typically opted either for liquidation or for more ambitious rehabilitation programs that seek to restructure the assets prior to sale (Klingebiel 2001); both present political challenges. A liquidation agency must have a clear mandate to dispose of assets, including to foreigners; if the assets are simply "warehoused," bank balance sheets are cleaned up but neither banks nor borrowers will have incentives to see that obligations are actually serviced. The government can also manage acquired assets aggressively to maximize value, but that too requires not only substantial administrative ability but also a clear mandate to maximize returns to the government.

24 Because of the administration's concern about the employment and equity consequences of failures of small and medium-sized enterprises (SMEs), and Kim Dae-jung's long-standing belief that SMEs have been slighted by government policy, the approach to this sector resembled a kind of corrective industrial policy. SME debts to the banks were initially rolled over for six months and then for a subsequent six months, and in 1999, the banks began to restructure SME debts. But the government has also restored liquidity to the sector through credit insurance funds, a central bank credit line, funding for trade finance, and four SME restructuring funds.

25 The call for explicit CSIPs was the first step in this process, followed by the government decision to halt credit to a number of small Big Five subsidiaries in June, and culminating in the public signing of financial pacts between the Big Five and their banks in December 1998 that included specific commitments to reduce the number of affiliates by target dates, including through the Big Deals; specific targets for the reduction of debt–equity ratios; an acceleration of the elimination of cross-guarantees between affiliates, and a reiteration of the commitment to reforms in corporate governance. The new agreements differed from the principles of a year earlier in their specificity and the monitoring that went along with them.

References

Amsden, Alice. 1989. *Asia's Next Giant: South Korea and Late Industrialization.* New York: Oxford University Press.

Bae, Kee-Hong, Kang, Jun-Koo, and Kim, Jin-Mo. 2001. "Tunneling or Value Added? Evidence from Mergers by Korean Business Groups." Paper presented at the First Asian Corporate Governance Conference, organized by the Asian Institute of Corporate Governance at Korea University, Seoul, December 14.

Borensztein, Eduardo, and Lee, Jong-Wha. 1999. "Financial Crisis and Credit Crunch in Korea: Evidence from Firm-Level Data." IMF Working Paper No. WP/00/25, International Monetary Fund.

Cho, Dong-sung. 1990. *A Study on the Korean Chaebol* (in Korean). Seoul: Maeil Economic Daily.

Cho, Yoon Je, and Kim, Joon Kyung. 1997. *Credit Policies and the Industrialization of Korea.* Seoul: Korea Development Institute.

Claessens, Stijn, Djankov, Simeon, Fan, Joseph, and Lang, Larry. 1999. "Corporate Diversification in East Asia: The Role of Ultimate Ownership Structure and Group Affiliation." Policy Research Working Paper 2089. Washington, DC: World Bank.

Claessens, Stijn, Djankov, Simeon, and Klingebiel, Daniela. 1999. *Financial Restructuring in East Asia: Halfway There?* Financial Sector Discussion Paper 3, Washington, DC: World Bank (September).

Claessens, Stijn, Djankov, Simeon, and Lang, Larry. 1998. "East Asian Corporates: Growth, Financing and Risks over the Last Decade." Unpublished MS, World Bank.

——. 2000a. "The Separation of Ownership and Control in East Asian Corporations," *Journal of Financial Economics*, 58 (1): 81–112.

——. 2000b. "East Asian Corporations: Heroes or Villains?" World Bank Discussion Paper No. 409. Washington, DC: World Bank (January).

Claessens, Stijn, Djankov, Simeon, and Mody, Ashoka, eds. 2001. *Resolution of Financial Distress: An International Perspective on the Design of Bankruptcy Laws.* Washington, DC: World Bank.

Coase, Ronald H. 1937. "The Nature of the Firm," *Economica*, 4 (16), November: 386–405.

Collins, Susan M. 1994. "Saving, Investment, and External Balance in South Korea," in Stephan Haggard, Richard N. Cooper, Susan Collins, Choongsoo Kim and Sung-Tae Ro, eds, *Macroeconomic Policy and Adjustment in Korea, 1970–1990.* Cambridge: Harvard University Press.

Dooley, Michael, and Shin, Inseok. 2000. "Private Inflows When Crises Are Anticipated: A Case of Korea," in Inseok Shin, ed., *The Korean Crisis: Before and After.* Seoul: Korea Development Institute.

Fields, Karl. 1995. *Enterprise and the State in Korea and Taiwan.* Ithaca: Cornell University Press.

Granovetter, Mark. 1995. "Coase Revisited: Business Groups in the Modern Economy," *Industrial and Corporate Change*, 4 (1): 93–130.

Haggard, Stephan. 1990. *Pathways from the Periphery: The Political Economy of Growth in the Newly Industrialized Countries.* Ithaca: Cornell University Press.

——. 1994. "From the Heavy Industry Plan to Stabilization: Macroeconomic Policy 1976–1980," in Stephan Haggard, Richard N. Cooper, Susan Collins, Choongsoo Kim and Sung-Tae Ro, eds, *Macroeconomic Policy and Adjustment in Korea, 1970–1990.* Cambridge: Harvard University Press.

——. 2000. *The Political Economy of the Asian Financial Crisis.* Washington, DC: Institute for International Economics.

Haggard, Stephan, Cooper, Richard, and Moon, Chung-in. 1993. "Policy Reform in Korea," in Robert Bates and Anne Krueger, eds, *Political and Economic Interactions in Economic Policy Reform.* Cambridge: Blackwell.

Hahm, Joon-Ho, and Mishkin, Frederic S. 2000. "Causes of the Korean Financial Crisis: Lessons for Policy," in Inseok Shin, ed., *The Korean Crisis: Before and After.* Seoul: Korea Development Institute.

Hahn, Chin Hee. 2000. "Implicit Loss-Protection and the Investment Behavior of Korean *Chaebol*," in Inseok Shin, ed., *The Korean Crisis: Before and After*, pp. 215–51. Seoul: Korea Development Institute.

Hamilton, Gary G., and Biggart, Nicole Woolsey. 1988. "Market, Culture and Authority: A Comparative Analysis of Management and Organization in the Far East," *American Journal of Sociology*, 94: S52–S94.

Hattori, Tamio. 1989. "Japanese Zaibatsu and Korean Chaebol," in Kae H. Chung and Hak Chong Lee, eds, *Korean Managerial Dynamics*. New York: Praeger.

Huer, John. 1989. *Marching Orders: The Role of the Military in South Korea's Economic Miracle*. New York: Greenwood Press.

Jang, Ha Sung. 1999. "Corporate Governance and Economic Development: The Korean Experience." Paper presented at the International Conference on Democracy, Market Economy and Development, Seoul, Feb. 26–27.

Joh, Sung Wook. 2000. "Does Shareholder Conflict Reduce Profitability? Evidence from Korea," in Inseok Shin, ed., *The Korean Crisis: Before and After*, pp. 185–213. Seoul: Korea Development Institute.

Johnson, Chalmers. 1982. *MITI and the Japanese Miracle*. Stanford: Stanford University Press.

Johnson, Simon, Boone, Peter, Breach, Alasdair and Friedman, Eric. 2000. "Corporate Governance in the Asian Financial Crisis, 1997–98," *Journal of Financial Economics*, 58: 141–86.

Johnson, Simon, and Mitton, Todd. 2001. "Corporate Governance and Corporate Debt in Asian Crisis Countries." Paper presented at the Conference on the Korean Economy and Recovery, Korean Institute for International Economic Policy, Seoul, May 17–19.

Jung, Ku-hyun. 1988. "Business-Government Relations in the Growth of Korean Business Groups," *Korean Social Science Journal*, 14: 67–82.

Kang, David. 2001. *Crony Capitalism: Corruption and Development in South Korea and the Philippines*. New York: Cambridge University Press.

Kang, Myung Hun. 1996. *The Korean Business Conglomerate: Chaebol Then and Now*. Berkeley: Institute of East Asian Studies, University of California, Center for Korean Studies Korea Research Monograph no. 21.

Khan, Mushtaq H., and Jomo, K. S. 2000. *Rents, Rent-Seeking and Economic Development: Theory and Evidence in Asia*. New York: Cambridge University Press.

Khanna, Tarun. 2000. "Business Groups and Social Welfare in Emerging Markets: Existing Evidence and Unanswered Questions," *European Economic Review*, 44: 748–61.

Kim, Eun Mee. 1997. *Big Business, Strong State: Collusion and Conflict in South Korean Development, 1960–1990*. Albany: State University of New York Press.

Kim, Jin-bang. 2000. "The Ownership Structure of the Chaebol: Statistics, Concepts, and Analysis," (in Korean) *Economic Analysis*, 48 (2): 57–93.

Kim, Seok Ki. 1987. "Business Concentration and Government Policy: A Study of the Phenomenon of Business Groups in Korea, 1945–1985." PhD dissertation, Harvard University.

Klingebiel, Daniela. 2001. "Asset Management Companies," in Stijn Claessens, Simeon Djankov and Ashoka Mody, eds, *Resolution of Financial Distress: An International Perspective on the Design of Bankruptcy Laws*. Washington, DC: World Bank.

La Porta, Rafael, Lopez-de-Silanes, Florencio, and Shleifer, Andrei. 1999. "Corporate Ownership Around the World," *Journal of Finance*, 54: 471–517.

Lee, Jong-Wha, Lee, Yong Soo, and Lee, Byung-Sun. 2000. "The Determination of Corporate Debt in Korea," *Asian Economic Journal*, 14 (4): 333–56.

Leff, Nathaniel. 1976. "Capital Markets in the Less Developed Countries: the Group Principle," in Ronald McKinnon, ed., *Money and Finance in Economic Growth and Development*. New York: Marcel Dekker.

———. 1978. "Industrial Organization and Entrepreneurship in the Developing Countries: The Economic Groups," *Economic Development and Cultural Change*, 26 (July): 661–75.

Lim, Wonhyuk. 2000. *The Origin and Evolution of the Korean Economic System*, Seoul: Korea Development Institute.

Mako, William, and Jung, Young Seok. 2000. "Financial Stabilization and Initial Corporate Restructuring." Unpublished MS, World Bank.

Morikawa, Hidemasa. 1992. *Zaibatsu: The Rise and Fall of Family Enterprise Groups in Japan*. Tokyo: University of Tokyo Press.

Okazaki, Tetsuj. 1999. *A History of Holding Companies: The Zaibatsu and Corporate Governance* (in Japanese). Tokyo: Chikuma Shinsho.

Pomerleano, Michael. 1998. "The East Asia Crisis and Corporate Finance: the Untold Micro Story." Unpublished MS, World Bank.

Rajan, Raghuram G., and Zingales, Luigi. 1998. "Which Capitalism? Lessons from the East Asian Crisis," *Journal of Applied Corporate Finance*, 11 (3): 40–8.

Shleifer, Andrei and Vishny, Robert. 1993. "Corruption," *Quarterly Journal of Economics*, 108 (August): 599–617.

Steers, Richard M., Shin, Yoo Keun, and Ungson, Gerardo R. 1989. *The Chaebol: Korea's New Industrial Might*. New York: Harper and Row.

Wang, Yunjong. 2001. "Does the Sequencing Really Matter? The Korean Experience in the Capital Market Liberalization," *Journal of the Korean Economy*, 2 (1): 35–67.

Williamson, Oliver. 1975. *Markets and Hierarchies*. New York: Free Press.

Woo, Jung-en. 1991. *Race to the Swift: State and Finance in Korean Industrialization*. New York: Columbia University Press.

Woo-Cumings, Meredith. 1999. "The State, Democracy and Reform of the Corporate Sector in Korea," in T. J. Pempel, ed., *The Politics of the Asian Economic Crisis*. Ithaca: Cornell University Press.

World Bank. 1998. *East Asia: Road to Recovery*. Washington, DC: World Bank.

Yoo, Seong Min. 1999. "Corporate Restructuring in Korea: Policy Issues Before and During the Crisis," KDI Working Paper No. 9903, Seoul: Korea Development Institute.

Part I
The Politics and Economics of the *Chaebol* Problem

2   The Emergence of the *Chaebol* and the Origins of the *Chaebol* Problem

Wonhyuk Lim

Since the Korean economic crisis broke in 1997, Korea's state-led model of economic development has come under heavy criticism. In particular, it has been argued that Korea's well-known triangular system connecting the government with big business and banks resulted in an inefficient financial sector and a highly leveraged corporate sector that lacked effective market discipline (IMF 1997). What is conspicuously missing in this line of criticism, however, is the recognition that the *same* system served as the backbone of the "rapid, shared growth" (World Bank 1993) which catapulted Korea from one of the poorest countries in the world into the ranks of the OECD countries in thirty years. No criticism of the Korean economic system would seem convincing without some explanation for its apparent success over those three decades.

This general observation on the rise and fall of the Korean economic system can be applied equally well to the *chaebol*, family-based business groups that dominate the Korean economy. The *chaebol* have long been a contentious issue in Korea (Cho 1990; Kang, Choi and Chang 1991), and in the wake of the economic crisis, it is tempting to issue a wholesale condemnation against them. This criticism of the *chaebol*, however, has to be reconciled with an appreciation of the role that they played in Korea's economic development (Amsden 1989).[1] Although the 1997 crisis undoubtedly provided an impetus for *chaebol* reform, the fact that the *chaebol* were widely blamed for the crisis does not, of and in itself, establish causality. Before claiming that "the *chaebol* problem" was the structural cause of the crisis, it seems not only necessary but also prudent to identify clearly the nature of this problem.

In order to provide a historical perspective on corporate restructuring efforts since the crisis, this chapter traces the origins and evolution of the *chaebol* and "the *chaebol* problem." Primarily relying on the political economy approaches as outlined in the introduction (Chapter 1), the chapter focuses on business–government relations and financial resource allocation mechanisms under different political and economic regimes.

The first section traces the emergence of the *chaebol* as a corporate form and analyzes the pattern of their growth. Section 2 analyzes the exchange relationship between the government and business under Syngman Rhee, who was the first president of the Republic of Korea from 1948 to 1960. Section 3 looks at changes in relations between business and government brought about by the Student Revolution of 1960 and the military coup of 1961. The new military government in effect formed a risk partnership with the *chaebol*, which it used as implementing agents in carrying out its economic development plans. The fourth section examines distortions in the government–business risk partnership introduced by the Emergency Decree of 1972 and the ensuing drive to develop heavy and chemical industry (HCI). The HCI drive aggravated moral hazard and resulted in an undue concentration of economic power, as the government pushed a select group of large *chaebol* to carry out specific investment projects with extremely generous financial support.

The chapter concludes with a brief discussion of the nature of "the *chaebol* problem" as of 1980, arguing that the conception of the *chaebol* problem as one of economic concentration fails to account for important developments that affected the *chaebol's* internal and external corporate governance in subsequent years. In fact, although the conception of "the *chaebol* problem" as one of corporate governance is a relatively recent development, it seems to provide a useful framework for understanding the 1997 crisis and the current corporate restructuring program.

1   The Origins and Evolution of the *Chaebol*: Stylized Facts

Although the *chaebol* have been at the center of economic policy debate in Korea for a long time, there is surprisingly little data-based literature on their history. Jones and SaKong (1980), S. K. Kim (1987), Hattori (1988), Amsden (1989), Cho (1990), Lee (1993), E. M. Kim (1997), Hwang (1999), and Lee (1999) are some of the exceptions that provide fairly comprehensive views on the development of the *chaebol*, but much more research needs to be done in this field.

To obtain facts on the history of the *chaebol*, one would ideally like to construct a data set incorporating the three structural elements that define the *chaebol* form (see Chapter 1): a governance structure of family dominance, an organizational structure of a holding company controlling formally independent firms, and a business structure of extensive diversification. Furthermore, one would like to set up the data in such a way that the efficiency, principal-agent, and political economy models of the *chaebol* might be tested against one another.

Data problems, however, make it extremely difficult to proceed in this fashion. It is possible – albeit time-consuming – to track changes in the organizational and business structure of individual *chaebol*, but it is nearly impossible to collect sufficiently detailed data on their governance structure. The distribution of cash-flow rights (ownership) and voting rights (control) may change more than a few times in a given year. If security laws impose strong disclosure rules, it may be possible to track changes in ownership stakes for publicly listed firms. For unlisted firms, however, it is impossible to collect such detailed information. Yet some of the most notorious examples of expropriation in Korea involve transactions between listed and unlisted firms.[2] Without detailed data on changes in the governance structure of unlisted firms, it is all but impossible to assess the full magnitude of the principal-agent problem in the *chaebol*. Consequently, in conducting hypothesis testing, it may be necessary to acknowledge considerable data limitations at the outset and work with a data set that is restricted in important ways. For empirical tests of the theoretical models of the *chaebol*, a limited sample of publicly listed firms over a period of only a few years may be the best option available.

Data

Instead of sacrificing data coverage to make empirical tests more feasible, this chapter takes the opposite approach. It forgoes rigorous hypothesis-testing in order to present stylized facts on the history of the *chaebol* based on a data set that is as comprehensive as possible. The data set used in this chapter is based on the individual corporate histories of the thirty largest business groups in Korea in the year 2000. Since 1987, the Korea Fair Trade Commission (KFTC) has annually designated the largest business groups in the country by asset size and imposed various restrictions on intra-group transactions in order to address the problem of economic concentration (see Chapter 11). The annual list is comprehensive in that it includes both listed and unlisted subsidiaries of each of the business groups under the effective control of the founder's family.

With the rank order based on total asset size, the 2000 cohort includes: Hyundai, Samsung, LG, SK, Hanjin, Lotte, Daewoo Co.,

Kumho, Hanhwa, Ssangyong, Hansol, Doosan, Hyundai Oil, DongA, Dongkuk Steel, Hyosung, Daelim, S-Oil, Dongbu, Kolon, Tongyang, Kohap, Cheiljedang, Daewoo Electronics, Hyundai Industrial Development, Anam, Saehan, Jinro, Shinsegye, and Youngpoong. Eight of these business groups have splintered off from their parent companies in recent years: Hansol, Cheiljedang, Saehan, and Shinsegye from Samsung; Hyundai Oil and Hyundai Industrial Development from Hyundai; S-Oil from Ssangyong; and Daewoo Electronics from Daewoo Co. The data set used in this chapter looks at the pattern of business expansion for the twenty-two original business groups from the year of their establishment.

In order to analyze the pattern of expansion for the twenty-two *chaebol* in the data set, newly established or acquired subsidiaries are grouped into three broad categories: related diversification, unrelated diversification, and vertical integration. As discussed in Chapter 1, vertical integration refers to business expansion based on links between input and output, whereas related diversification is based on technological or organizational relatedness.

In order to determine the type of business expansion, the industrial segment to which a new subsidiary belongs is compared with the existing business lines for a given business group. The business line for each subsidiary is ascertained from the company's annual report. The data set contains a total of 139 industrial segments. By comparison, Korea's three-digit standard industry classification, as revised in 1990, has a total of 71 segments. Although it would be ideal to code the business line of each company according to some standard industry classification scheme, significant changes in Korea's industry classification over the past several decades make it all but impossible to maintain consistency. In addition to this caveat, there is another important point to consider when assessing the relative weight of each type of business expansion. A business group may enter a new line of business either by establishing a new subsidiary or by setting up a new division within an existing subsidiary. With other things being equal, a business group is more likely to establish a new subsidiary in the case of unrelated diversification compared with related diversification or vertical integration. As a result, the relative importance of unrelated diversification may be overestimated when the pattern of *chaebol* expansion is analyzed based on data on the establishment or acquisition of subsidiaries. Although practical difficulties in ascertaining the establishment of divisions as opposed to subsidiaries may justify the methodology adopted here, this bias needs to be taken into account.

The pattern of *chaebol* expansion

Of the twenty-two business groups in the data set, Doosan is the oldest as it can trace its origin to the establishment of the Park Seung-jik Store in the 1890s. Six groups, including Hyundai, Samsung and LG, were founded during the period of Japanese colonialism, although they had little more than a local or regional presence at the time.[3] Eleven were established during the period of the American occupation (1945–48) and the Syngman Rhee government (1948–60). Four groups established in the 1960s, including Lotte and Daewoo, expanded rapidly enough in subsequent years to be included in the top 30 list in 2000.

Table 2.1 shows the pattern of business expansion for the twenty-two business groups since their founding dates. Today's top *chaebol* were little more than small, family-based enterprises until the 1940s – if they were around at all. As far as their individual corporate histories indicate,

Table 2.1   The pattern of *chaebol* expansion

Decade	Related diversification	Unrelated diversification	Vertical integration	Sub-total
1940s				
n	1	2		3
%	33.33	66.67		
1950s				
n	8	23	3	34
%	23.53	67.65	8.82	
1960s				
n	21	44	24	89
%	23.60	49.44	26.97	
1970s				
n	83	105	42	230
%	36.09	45.65	18.26	
1980s				
n	106	100	35	241
%	43.98	41.49	14.52	
1990s				
n	175	117	46	338
%	51.78	34.62	13.61	
Total				
n	394	391	150	935
%	42.14	41.82	16.04	

Source: Individual corporate histories.

they did not establish additional subsidiaries during the Japanese colonial period. They began to expand in earnest in the 1950s, responding to underdeveloped market conditions and rent opportunities. The number of newly established or acquired subsidiaries increased greatly in subsequent decades. While Kim (1997) and others have noted that the number of *chaebol* subsidiaries rose dramatically during the 1970s, primarily due to the HCI drive, the pace of expansion actually accelerated in the 1980s and 1990s, at least for this cohort. The table also shows that related diversification and unrelated diversification account for a roughly equal proportion of *chaebol* expansion, at slightly more than 40 percent, while vertical integration accounts for the rest. The relative weight of unrelated diversification has steadily declined since the 1950s.

The changing ranking of the *chaebol*

The data set used in the previous analysis of business expansion looks only at "births." While useful in illustrating the foundation and expansion of the *chaebol*, such data cannot show their changing fortunes over time. Table 2.2 shows the top ten *chaebol* over the past four decades. Four of the ten largest *chaebol* in 1960 went bankrupt in subsequent years, leading Chang (2000) to argue that there was little evidence of moral hazard in Korea. Such a conclusion, however, not only ignores the blanket bailout exercise engineered by the government through the Emergency Decree of 1972, but it also overlooks the fact that many of the largest *chaebol* in 1960 had become comparatively small and fallen out of the top ranks when they went bankrupt. The Kukje group did go bankrupt in 1985 when it was the seventh-largest *chaebol* in the country, but there was much speculation that the bankruptcy had as much to do with political reasons as financial weaknesses (Lee 1993: 312–15). In fact, the government was quick to assure the market that there would be no more massive bankruptcies when investors began to speculate that the financially vulnerable Daewoo Group would be next to fall in the wake of the Kukje bankruptcy.

Although data limitations make it impossible to carry out full-fledged empirical tests on the question of moral hazard, it is not too difficult to see that, until the fateful year of 1997, the bankruptcy of top *chaebol* became increasingly rare after the mid-1980s. In fact, since the bankruptcy of Kukje in 1985, none of the top thirty *chaebol* was allowed to fail until 1997, except for Woosung Construction in 1996 (No. 27 in 1995). Using firm-level data in the immediate pre-crisis period, Hahn (2000) shows that, compared with other firms, top-ranking *chaebol* tended to

Table 2.2   The top ten *chaebol*

Rank	Late 1950s	Mid-1960s	1974	1983	1990	1995	2000
1	Samsung	Samsung	Samsung	Hyundai	Hyundai	Hyundai	Hyundai
2	Samho	Samho	LG	Samsung	Daewoo	Samsung	Samsung
3	Gaepung	LG	Hyundai	Daewoo	Samsung	Daewoo	LG
4	Daehan	Daehan	Hanjin	LG	LG	LG	SK
5	LG	Gaepung	Ssangyong	Ssangyong	Ssangyong	SK	Hanjin
6	Tongyang	Samyang	SK	SK	Hanjin	Ssangyong	Lotte
7	Keukdong	Ssangyong	Hanhwa	Hanhwa	SK	Hanjin	Daewoo Co.
8	Hankook Glass	Hwashin	Daenong	Hanjin	Hanhwa	Kia	Kumho
9	Donglip	Panbon	Dong-Ah Construction	Kukje	Daelim	Hanhwa	Hanhwa
10	Taechang	Tongyang	Hanil Syn. Textile	Daelim	Lotte	Lotte	Ssangyong

Source: For the late 1950s, mid-1960s, 1974, and 1983, E. M. Kim (1997: 124); for 1990, 1995, and 2000, Korea Fair Trade Commission, "The Designation of Large-Scale Business Groups," each year.

maintain higher investment rates and increase investment when uncertainty rose. This investment pattern is consistent with moral hazard. A firm that expects the government to provide protection against bankruptcy would have a higher rate of investment and tend to increase investment when uncertainty rises because it discounts downside risks.

2   Crony Capitalism of the 1950s

The end of the Japanese colonial rule confronted Korea with the crucial tasks of reassigning property rights and re-establishing the external trade and foreign exchange regime of the country. Furthermore, given the lack of domestic capital and technology, policies designed to attract investment had to be implemented. Instead of formulating a comprehensive economic development program to address these policy challenges, however, Syngman Rhee, the first president of Korea, chose to use the discretionary allocation of state-controlled resources to secure and sustain his political supporters.

A case in point is the sale of vested properties ("enemy properties"), formerly Japanese-owned industrial properties taken over by the US military government and subsequently transferred to the new Korean government. The Rhee government set the conditions for the sale of these properties so as to preclude competitive bidding and to favor the interim plant managers as well as the politically well-connected. The Rhee government typically set the assessed value of the vested industrial properties at 25–30 percent of the market value. Moreover, it offered the new owners of these properties generous installment plans when the annual rate of inflation hovered around 30 percent.

In return for their windfall gains, the new owners of these properties provided kickbacks to Rhee's Liberal Party. For instance, Kang Jik-sun, a businessman who picked up Samcheok Cement Co., donated a 30-percent equity share in the company to the ruling Liberal Party (K. Kim 1990: 170–4). Certainly, not everyone who was privileged to pick up an industrial property at a fire-sale price had the entrepreneurial talent to build a business empire. But vested properties provided the initial base for many of the largest *chaebol*.[4]

The privatization of commercial banks in the 1950s provides another example of the irregularities in the disposal of state-owned properties. The government initially put banks up for sale in 1954. The sales included a number of provisions designed to address the concerns of economic experts who feared that ill-conceived bank privatization would distort resource allocation and place financial institutions under the control of industrial capitalists. When it turned out that no bids satisfied these provisions, however, the government drastically relaxed the requirements. The result was exactly what had been feared. Using political connections, top industrial capitalists borrowed money from the banks in order to make bids for the ownership of the same banks. When bank privatization was completed in 1957, all major commercial banks were under the control of industrial capitalists, as shown in Table 2.3. It goes without saying that the beneficiaries of bank privatization were major contributors to Syngman Rhee's Liberal Party.

In addition to these politically motivated privatization programs, Rhee also used the discretionary allocation of aid goods, import licenses, and government contracts as a means of consolidating his power base. The market exchange rate was at times nearly three times as high as the official rate. Rhee's reasoning was clear: The possession of foreign exchange and aid goods at less than their market value would create arbitrage opportunities, and it would allow him to distribute favors to businessmen willing to provide kickbacks to the Liberal Party (Haggard 1990).

Table 2.3 Largest shareholders of privatized banks (March 1957)

Bank	Largest shareholder's affiliation	Largest shareholder's equity share (%)
Chohung Bank	Samsung	55
Sangup (Commerce) Bank	Daehan Flour Milling	29
Heungup Bank	Samsung	83
Jeochuk (Savings) Bank	Samho	51

Source: Yoon et al. (1996).

US aid goods provided raw materials for the famous "three white" industries of the 1950s in Korea: sugar, cotton yarn, and wheat flour. Rhee's politically motivated "industrial policy" created huge profit opportunities. The cost of producing a sack of wheat flour was estimated at 350 *hwan*, but a select group of domestic manufacturers were able to charge 1200 *hwan* per sack, and shortages sometimes pushed prices to 5000 *hwan* (S. Kim 1965: 27-30). The top *chaebol* of the 1950s had a major presence in these industries. For instance, the sugar refinery industry was dominated by Samsung, Samyang, and Daehan.

In the end, what passed for an economic system in Korea in the 1950s was primarily shaped by Rhee's use of policy instruments to secure and sustain his power base. The sale of vested properties resulted in windfall gains for favored businessmen and undue concentration of economic power. The overvaluation of the Korean currency, designed to maximize arbitrage opportunities, had the effect of severely discouraging exports so that the export-to-GNP ratio was as low as 3 percent. This was a dramatic departure from the 1930s and the early 1940s when Korea's exports amounted to about 30 percent of GNP. The Rhee government's myopic policy was largely responsible for turning a trading nation into a nearly autarchic aid-dependent country (Lim 2000: 14-16).

3   The Formation of the Government–Business Risk Partnership in the 1960s

When a student protest in April 1960 finally put an end to the Syngman Rhee government, Korea was in a dismal state. It was an aid-dependent country whose per capita income was one of the lowest in the world.

After the April 1960 Revolution, prominent businessmen were accused of having grown rich through political connections with the Syngman Rhee regime. Taking over the task of dealing with these "illicit wealth accumulators," a new military government led by Park Chung Hee accused them of tax evasion and other illegal business practices, and confiscated their equity shares in commercial banks. This drastic measure paved the way for the government to exert direct control over commercial banks, in effect renationalizing the banks that had been privatized in the late 1950s.

Initially, the military government pursued an "industrial deepening" program, in which the government would carry out massive investment projects in basic industries financed by increased primary exports, foreign loans, and forced domestic savings and inflation. In the second half of 1962, however, the Park government was forced to abandon this strategy when the United States used its aid leverage to demand stabilization measures and also to press the military leaders to stick to their commitment to restore an elected regime by 1963. Determined to avoid being trapped in such a vulnerable position again, the Park government went far beyond the orthodox economic policies prescribed by the Americans, and adopted drastic measures to promote exports and increase economic independence (Mason et al. 1980).

First, the Park government accommodated the US demands and instituted a set of reforms designed to reduce distortions in such macroeconomic variables as the exchange rate and the interest rate. Second, the government took unprecedented steps to share the investment risks of the private sector. In particular, state-owned banks provided explicit repayment guarantees to foreign financial institutions on loans extended to Korean firms. Third, Park Chung Hee himself spearheaded an effort to boost exports, offering various incentives based on market performance. The resulting risk partnership between government and business, combining state-led financial resource allocation with export market orientation, defined the core of the Korean economic system.

By providing a state guarantee on foreign borrowing by the private sector, the Park government signaled that it was willing to form a risk partnership with business leaders, whether they had been "illicit wealth accumulators" or not. The guarantee system allowed the government to use its credibility to raise capital on the international market while controlling the allocation of financial resources to private firms. In effect the government *contracted out* the provision of goods and services to the private sector while acting as a guarantor and monitor of the loans. Export performance, in particular, provided the government with a relatively objective criterion to select private firms when it made its decision to extend repayment guarantees.

4   The Consolidation and Distortion of the Risk Partnership in the 1970s

The government–business risk partnership and high economic growth fueled what may be characterized as an investment explosion in the second half of the 1960s. In particular, in 1968 and 1969 investment increased at an average rate of nearly 50 percent per annum and domestic credit expanded at over 60 percent. The reckless investment boom inevitably produced a number of firms that could not meet their foreign debt obligations. Fearing that the bankruptcy of these firms would adversely affect Korea's credit ratings, the government took over managerial control of thirty such firms in May 1969 (C. Kim 1995: 256). Chonusa, one of the largest trading firms in Korea at the time, was included in this list. Concerned with the moral hazard implications of a blanket bailout, the government took a principled stance against insolvent firms and held the management of these firms accountable for their previous business decisions (Lee 1993: 222–38). After all, the government had guaranteed only the repayment of private sector foreign debt to the foreign lenders. It had never guaranteed the protection of governance rights to the incumbent owner-managers.

As the Korean economy showed signs of overheating near the end of the 1960s, the International Monetary Fund stepped in to prescribe a stabilization package. Under tight credit control, the commercial banks could not provide much relief to firms with heavy debt burdens. Financially strapped firms had to turn to the last available resort: the curb market. By the end of 1971, hundreds of firms could not meet their debt obligations, and the average debt–equity ratio for the manufacturing sector was close to 400 percent (Cho and Kim 1997: 80–5). Business leaders urged the government to take extraordinary measures. In a meeting with Park Chung Hee in June 1971, the president of the Federation of Korean Industries, representing big business interests, urged the government to reduce taxes, expand the money supply, *and* have the banks take over the "usurious" curb loans to relieve the debt burden of firms (C. Kim 1995: 263). Unlike in 1969, the government felt that it could no longer take a principled stance against insolvent firms because of systemic risks (C. Kim 1994: 66–70).

In the end, the Park government decided to bail out the debt-plagued corporate sector, and it issued the Presidential Emergency Decree for Economic Stability and Growth on August 3, 1972. The Emergency Decree placed an immediate moratorium on the payment of all corporate debt to the curb lenders and called for an extensive rescheduling of bank loans at a reduced interest rate. The moratorium was to last three years, after which all curb funds had to be turned into five-year loans at a 1.35 percent monthly interest rate, or an annual rate of 16.2 percent, when the prevailing market rate exceeded 40 percent (Bank of Korea 1973).

After the economy recovered, the government did try to make up for the excesses of the Emergency Decree by attempting to improve the corporate governance and financial structure of major private firms. The government believed that opening up family-owned enterprises to public shareholding would lead to the emergence of modern corporations characterized by dispersed ownership and professional management. The government also felt that public listing would allow firms to issue equity to finance their long-term investment and reduce their dangerous dependence on debt.[5] Until 1972, the year before the introduction of the Law on Facilitating the Opening Up of Corporations, only sixty-six firms had gone public since the opening of the stock exchange in 1956. From 1973 to 1979, more than three hundred companies went public (C. Kim 1994: 73–4).

In spite of this apparent success, however, the public listing of firms failed to produce the intended results. Because the government neglected to introduce institutions designed to reduce agency problems and protect the property rights of minority shareholders, the separation of ownership and control actually *worsened* the corporate governance of Korean firms. Entrepreneurs continued to prefer debt to equity as a means of raising capital. Although equity financing could reduce leverage, the owner-managers were not willing to share ownership and control with people outside the family (see Chapter 1). Moreover, the Emergency Decree of 1972 had shown that an excessive reliance on debt would not only go unpunished but might actually be rewarded by the government, as long as other companies also depended heavily on debt. In short, the Emergency Decree ushered in a new era characterized by the deepening of the government–business risk partnership.

The drive to expand heavy and chemical industry (HCI), officially launched in 1973, further consolidated the risk partnership. The idea of setting up a public sector holding company in the HCIs was briefly discussed in policymaking circles, but was rejected in favor of using established private firms with extremely generous government support. During the late 1970s, HCIs accounted for almost 80 percent of all fixed investment in the manufacturing sector, when their share in the manufacturing sector's output was around 40 percent. As a result, a myriad of small and medium-sized enterprises in the light manufacturing industries were in effect pushed aside by a select group of *chaebol* that expanded their business empires thanks to generous government support. During the HCI drive, the real interest rate on bank loans was negative. The Park government's relentless push for the HCIs was called

off only when serious macroeconomic imbalances and political problems forced it to adopt a comprehensive stabilization package in April
1979 (Stern et al.1995). The expansion of the large conglomerates at
the expense of smaller enterprises was also eroding political support for
Park Chung Hee's increasingly dictatorial regime.

The HCI drive in the 1970s transformed the government–business
risk partnership in favor of the *chaebol*. In contrast to the 1960s, government support during the HCI drive was not contingent on export
market performance and had a strong industry-specific bias. As only a
select group of large conglomerates were favored, the bias seemed
almost *firm-specific*. As Table 2.4 shows, the share of the top *chaebol* in
GDP greatly increased during the heyday of the HCI drive. This
increase in economic concentration was primarily a result of extremely
generous financial support provided by the government rather than a
by-product of market-based resource allocation.

Although Park Chung Hee might have felt that he could always
control the *chaebol* much as he did state-owned enterprises, he was in
fact creating behemoths that would come to dominate the Korean
economy. Having channeled massive resources into the *chaebol* to carry
out high-priority investment projects – sometimes over the initial
objection of their owner-managers – the government had to take
responsibility should these projects turn sour. Moreover, the gigantic
size and high leverage of the *chaebol* strengthened the case for the argument that they were "too big to fail" should a crisis strike.

These developments had a profound impact on the Korean economic
system. When the government was forging a risk partnership with
private firms in the 1960s by guaranteeing repayment on their foreign
borrowing, it certainly did not intend to guarantee the governance
rights of the incumbent owner-managers. Nor did it necessarily favor
large business groups. The Emergency Decree of 1972 and the HCI
drive, however, transformed the nature of the government–business risk
partnership and exacerbated moral hazard. The Emergency Decree set

Table 2.4 *Chaebol's* share of value added (%)

Chaebol	1973	1974	1975	1976	1977	1978	1979	1980	1981
Top 5	3.5	3.8	4.7	5.1	8.2	8.1	–	–	–
Top 10	5.1	5.6	7.1	7.2	10.6	10.9	–	–	–
Top 20	7.1	7.8	9.8	9.4	13.3	14.0	–	–	–
Top 46	9.8	10.3	12.3	12.3	16.3	17.1	16.6	19.5	24.0

Source: SaKong (1993).

a precedent that the government would take extraordinary measures to deal with a systemic crisis *without* holding the incumbent management of firms and banks accountable for their previous business decisions. Subsequently, the industrial targeting approach adopted during the HCI drive trapped the government in a vicious cycle of intervention, and the massive financial support extended to the top *chaebol* favored these family-based business groups.

5   The *Chaebol* Problem in 1980

Although the government called off its ambitious HCI drive in April 1979 in order to stabilize the economy, the second oil shock and the assassination of Park Chung Hee in October 1979 made things worse. A new military regime, led by General Chun Doo Hwan, came into power and introduced drastic measures to control inflation. In addition, the technocrats who were entrusted by Chun with the running of the economy advocated a transition to a more market-oriented system. They felt that excessive state intervention had produced serious moral hazard and driven the economy on the verge of a debt crisis (Jones and SaKong 1980).

Central to their concerns was "the *chaebol* problem." The technocrats were aware of social and political problems associated with the *chaebol*. The government's generous support of the *chaebol* raised equity issues and increased potential corruption. The economic power of the *chaebol* could be converted to political power, seriously distorting the political as well as the resource allocation process (Korea Development Institute 1979: 10).

Yet conspicuously missing from the technocrats' conception of the *chaebol* problem were corporate governance issues. In fact, the technocrats advocated policy measures designed to disperse ownership (Korea Development Institute 1979: 12). Apparently affected by the relatively concentrated ownership structure of the *chaebol* at the time (see Table 1.1), the technocrats felt that the dispersal of ownership would address the problem of economic concentration. They did not understand that, even with dispersed ownership, concentrated control could be maintained in the absence of institutional reform designed to protect the rights of non-controlling shareholders (see Chapters 1 and 1.2). Nor could they have foreseen the explosive growth of the non-bank financial institutions under *chaebol* control in the subsequent decades (see Chapter 4). In this regard, the conception of "the *chaebol* problem" in 1980 was rather different from that in the post-crisis period with its emphasis on corporate governance issues.

By contrast, even back in 1980, the technocrats clearly recognized the potential costs of moral hazard and the dilemma that the government faced. Since the collapse of large *chaebol* would bury the financial system in nonperforming loans, the government was more or less obliged to guarantee their stability. This implicit guarantee, however, encouraged the *chaebol* to undertake excessive investment. Expecting to be bailed out should a crisis strike, they would discount downside risks and invest wildly, unless restrained by the government. In order to maintain the stability of the economy, the government thus found itself having to intervene in the investment decisions of private firms.

The solution to this apparent dilemma would require that the government let market forces operate and allow a nonviable *chaebol* to go bankrupt, while simultaneously working to contain systemic risks. The government would also have to hold incumbent owner-managers accountable for their previous decisions and refrain from intervening in the investment decisions of private firms in the future. Autonomous financial institutions, free from the control of the government *and* industrial capitalists, would have to be allowed to make decisions on their own and bear the full consequences of their actions. The government would have to redefine its role and focus on competition policy and prudential regulation rather than the allocation of financial resources according to its industrial policy objectives. This series of decisive measures would serve as a credible signal that the regime had indeed changed.

By this time, however, the Korean economic system had produced a coalition of economic players who were interested in consolidating and maintaining the government–business risk partnership, which enabled the *chaebol* to prosper as a corporate form. Although some reform-minded policymakers advocated a transition to a more market-oriented system, the installed base of economic players with vested interests would impede reforms. As Byung-Kook Kim and Joon-Ho Hahm show in Chapters 3 and 4, reform-minded policymakers would be pushed aside by bureaucrats who were more willing to accommodate the wishes of entrenched interests. As a result, much of "the *chaebol* problem," encompassing both moral hazard and corporate governance issues, remained unsolved even as the economic crisis of 1997 approached.

Notes

1 Public attitude toward the *chaebol* in Korea is characterized by fundamental ambivalence. In 1991, three economists expressed this ambivalence in the form of a provocative question in the subtitle of their book: Is the *chaebol* the locomotive of growth or the personification of avarice? The authors did not bother to distinguish between *chaebol* firms and *chaebol* bosses, but their overall assessment of the *chaebol* was clearly negative. See Kang, Choi and Chang (1991).
2 See the discussion of the SK Telecom–Daehan Telecom case in Chapter 1.
3 During Japanese colonial rule, the two most prominent Korean-owned business groups were Samyang (centered on Kyungsung Spinning) and Hwashin (centered on Hwashin Department Store). The success of the two groups was, however, tainted by the collaboration of their owners with the Japanese regime (Lee 1999). In particular, Park Heung-sik, the owner of the Hwashin Group, actively supported Japan's war efforts during World War II. After Korea's liberation in 1945, Park became the first person to be arrested by the Special Commission on Anti-National Activities. Kim Yeon-su of the Samyang Group was also arrested, but both of them escaped punishment thanks to Syngman Rhee's politically driven strategy of courting the rich and the powerful – pro-Japanese or not. The collaboration of these prominent businessmen with the Japanese colonial regime tarnished the image of capitalists in Korean society (Cha and Lim 2000). It is, however, important to note that business groups such as Samsung, Hyundai and LG had only a regional presence during the colonial period. While McNamara (1990) and Eckert (1991) emphasize the colonial origins of Korean capitalism, few of the top *chaebol* today were significant corporate entities during the colonial period.
4 For instance, Choi Jong-keon, previously an employee at Sunkyung Spinning Co., took over the company and built the foundation of the SK Group. Other cases in point are Doosan, which acquired the Korean subsidiary of Showa Kirin Brewing Co., and Haitai, which took over Youngkang Confectionery.
5 When the firms that greatly benefited from the Emergency Decree of 1972 were slow to go public, Park Chung Hee instructed the cabinet in May 1974 to speed up the public listing of these companies, "warning family-owned conglomerates against their incessant expansion efforts via borrowing from the banks" (C. Kim 1994: 122–3).

References

Amsden, Alice H. 1989. *Asia's Next Giant: South Korea and Late Industrialization.* New York: Oxford University Press.
Aoki, Masahiko, Kim, Hyung-ki, and Okuno-Fujiwara, Masahiro, eds. 1997. *The Role of Government in East Asian Economic Development: Comparative Institutional Analysis.* New York: Oxford University Press.

Bank of Korea. 1973. *August 3 Emergency Economic Decree: Comprehensive Report* (in Korean). Seoul: Bank of Korea.

Cha, Dong-Se, and Lim, Phillip Wonhyuk. 2000. "In Search of a New Capitalist Spirit for the Korean Economy," in Kenneth L. Judd and Young Ki Lee, eds, *An Agenda for Economic Reform in Korea*, pp. 449–89. Stanford: Hoover Institution Press.

Chang, Ha-Joon. 2000. "The Hazard of Moral Hazard: Untangling the Asian Crisis," *World Development*, 28 (4): 775–88.

Cho, Dong-sung. 1990. *A Study on the Korean Chaebol* (in Korean). Seoul: Maeil Economic Daily.

Cho, Yoon Je, and Kim, Joon Kyung. 1997. *Credit Policies and the Industrialization of Korea*. Seoul: Korea Development Institute.

Eckert, Carter. 1991. *Offspring of Empire: The Ko'chang Kims and the Colonial Origins of Korean Capitalism, 1876–1945*. Seattle: University of Washington Press.

Haggard, Stephan. 1990. *Pathways from the Periphery: The Politics of Growth in the Newly Industrializing Countries*. Ithaca: Cornell University Press.

Hahn, Chin Hee. 2000. "Implicit Loss-Protection and the Investment Behavior of Korean *Chaebols*," in Inseok Shin, ed., *The Korean Crisis: Before and After*, pp. 215–51. Seoul: Korea Development Institute.

Hattori, Tamio. 1988. *Managerial Development in Korea* (in Japanese). Tokyo: Bunshindo.

——. 1989. "Japanese Zaibatsu and Korean Chaebol," in Kae H. Chung and Hak Chong Lee, eds, *Korean Managerial Dynamics*. New York: Praeger.

Hwang, Myong-Soo. 1999. *A Study on the History of Korean Entrepreneurs* (in Korean). Seoul: Dankuk University Press.

International Monetary Fund (IMF). 1997. "Korea – Memorandum on the Economic Program." December 3.

Jones, Leroy P., and SaKong, Il. 1980. *Government, Business, and Entrepreneurship in Economic Development: The Korean Case*. Cambridge: Harvard University Press.

Kang, Chul-Kyu, Choi, Jung-Pyo, and Chang, Ji-Sang. 1991. *The Chaebol: Locomotive of Growth or Personification of Avarice* (in Korean). Seoul: Bibong Press.

Kim, Chung-yum. 1994. *Policymaking on the Front Lines: Memoirs of a Korean Practitioner, 1945–79*. Washington, DC: Economic Development Institute of the World Bank.

——. 1995. *A 30-Year History of Korean Economic Policy: A Memoir* (in Korean). Seoul: Joong-Ang Daily News.

Kim, Eun Mee. 1997. *Big Business, Strong State: Collusion and Conflict in South Korean Development, 1960–1990*. Albany, NY: State University of New York Press.

Kim, Ky Won. 1990. *The Structure of the Economy During the U.S. Military Government Era – with a Focus on the Disposal of Vested Enterprises and Workers' Self-Management Movement* (in Korean). Seoul: Pureunsan.

Kim, Seok Ki. 1987. "Business Concentration and Government Policy: A Study of the Phenomenon of Business Groups in Korea, 1945–1985." PhD dissertation, Harvard University.

Kim, Seong-du. 1965. *Chaebol and Poverty* (in Korean). Seoul: Paekcheong Munhwasa.

Korea Development Institute. 1979. "The Problem of the *Chaebol* Firm" (in Korean). Mimeo, March.

Lee, Han-koo. 1999. *A History of the Formation of the Korean Chaebol.* (in Korean). Seoul: Bibong Publishing Co.

Lee, Jae-hyung. 1997. "The Current Picture and Performance of Korean Business Groups (*Chaebol*)." PhD dissertation (in Korean). Sungkyunkwan University, Seoul.

Lee, Jong-jae. 1993. *The Chaebol Resume* (in Korean). Seoul: Hankook Ilbo Publishing Co.

Lim, Wonhyuk. 2000. *The Origin and Evolution of the Korean Economic System.* Seoul: Korea Development Institute.

Mason, Edward S., Kim, Mahn Je, Perkins, Dwight H., Kim, Kwang Suk, and Cole, David C. 1980. *The Economic and Social Modernization of the Republic of Korea.* Cambridge: Harvard University Press.

McNamara, Dennis. 1990. *The Colonial Origins of Korean Enterprise, 1910–1945.* New York: Cambridge University Press.

O, Wonchul. 1995. *Korean-Style Economy-Building: An Engineering Approach* (in Korean). Seoul: Kia Economic Research Institute.

SaKong Il. 1993. *Korea in the World Economy.* Washington, DC: Institute for International Economics.

Stern, Joseph J., Kim, Ji-hong, Perkins, Dwight H., Yoo, Jung-ho. 1995. *Industrialization and the State: The Korean Heavy and Chemical Industry Drive.* Cambridge: Harvard Institute for International Development.

World Bank. 1993. *The East Asian Miracle: Economic Growth and Public Policy.* New York: Oxford University Press.

Yoon, Seok-beom, et al. 1996. *A Study of Korea's Modern Financial History* (in Korean). Seoul: Sekyungsa.

3 The Politics of *Chaebol* Reform, 1980–1997

Byung-Kook Kim

1 Kim Dae-jung's Triple Reform: The Background

"The bubble has finally burst," the editorial of a major newspaper, *Kyounghyang Sinmun*, exclaimed on December 1, 1997. Yet the great socioeconomic dislocation that accompanied the crisis also produced an outburst of reformist energy (B. Kim 2000b: 35–74). Initially forced by an agreement signed with the International Monetary Fund in 1997, reform soon won support from a wide spectrum of local political forces, and sentiment crystallized into a package which envisioned nothing less than a systemic transformation of the Korean economy.

Kim Dae-jung's era of systemic reform (1998–2003) was long awaited. Ever since a deep stagflation brought down Park Chung Hee (1961–1979), Korea's ruling political elite saw the *chaebol* as both a liability and an asset in its quest for economic growth and political legitimacy. The dissident (chaeya) movement had long accused the *chaebol* of causing social inequity and moral decay. But this ethical critique was increasingly joined by the pragmatic question of whether the *chaebol* way of doing business "worked." These moral and pragmatic criticisms, coming from vastly different ideological forces on both left and right, worked together to make the *chaebol* a "privileged issue."[1]

Many of Kim Dae-jung's "five-plus-three principles" (see Chapter 6) were alterations of his predecessors' reform policies. Despite such continuities, however, Kim Dae-jung's approach was fundamentally different from his predecessors'. For Kim Dae-jung, *chaebol* reform was part of a larger systemic reform to create a new democratic market economy, whereas for his predecessors, it was largely an instrument to reduce the built-in contradictions of Korea's existent developmental state model.

For Kim Dae-jung and his IMF advisers, the crisis of 1997 was systemic, its causes rooted in larger political and economic institutions. This distinctive institutional amalgam that took shape during the Park era included opaque corporate governance, bureaucratically driven financial institutions, and company unionism based on lifetime employment. The institutions of bureaucratically governed finance, imperial corporate governance structure centered on a single owner family,[2] and company unionism served Park's goal of making Korea a second Japan in his time.

As capital market liberalization occurred in the 1980s, however, Korea lost three prerequisites for the successful functioning of these institutions. The national consensus of "Growth First" broke down with the spread of distributional conflicts. Labor acquired organizational power and became ideologically contentious. And foreign capital flooded into banks and the *chaebol* on the assumption that the government had guaranteed repayment.

The remedy that Kim Dae-jung offered for these changed circumstances was a concerted program to reform the financial sector, the labor market and the *chaebol*. The three constituted an indivisible package and depended on one another for success (K. Kim, 1999: 165–82). To remold *chaebol* groups into competitive producers, banks had to make loans on the basis of objective assessments of borrowers' cash flow rather than politically motivated and administratively implemented guidance by state bureaucrats. The new regime for banks would not work without a simultaneous downsizing of the *chaebol*, which in turn required comprehensive labor reform. Without layoffs, *chaebol*

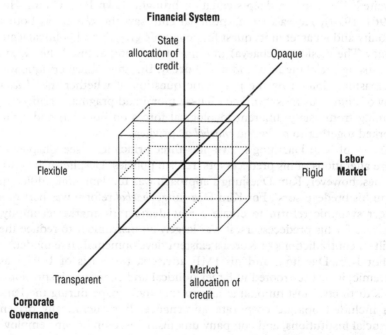

Figure 3.1   Three dimensions of the economic system

could not reduce surplus capacity, let alone exit from losing business ventures. Moreover, foreign investors would acquire and recapitalize insolvent banks only if excess employees could be fired and redundant branches closed down.

But these already formidable tasks of reform would fall short of fundamentally transforming business behavior unless Korea overhauled its opaque system of corporate governance. Banks can establish prudential supervision over big business only if accounts are clean and transparent, if majority shareholders are legally accountable for their decisions, and if inside trading among affiliated *chaebol* firms is dismantled.

Kim Dae-jung's predecessors considered one or another of these reform measures. But the fear of a vicious cycle of business failures, bank runs and political instability held them back from launching serious financial, labor or *chaebol* reform programs, let alone bringing all three together into one policy package. When one or another ministry's reform efforts reached a stage where complementary policy change in other issue areas was required, the other ministries as well as political parties typically scaled back – if not altogether discarded – the reform. In a pre-dawn session, the then ruling New Korea Party under Kim Young Sam (1993–98) railroaded a labor bill that trashed the idea of a grand compromise in January 1997. When the race for presidential elections began in earnest in July, both Kim Dae-jung and Lee Hoi Chang, the opposing contenders, visited the Kia Motors plant and pledged continued government support. To make the situation worse, Deputy Prime Minister Kang Kyung Sik sent out contradictory signals, allowing Jinro to restructure under composition (*hwaui*) while blocking a similar application from Kia.

The reasons for the change in policy direction under Kim Dae-jung are partly a result of economic necessity, partly a product of political beliefs. Among the thirty largest *chaebol* groups, eight went under during 1997 alone. Once state officials began to search for ways to reestablish confidence in the badly shaken financial system after 1997, reform necessarily spilled over into *chaebol* and labor problems. Only when all hopes of salvaging Korea's statist developmental model were crushed with large-scale business failures did policymakers begin to link and implement the three reform agendas systematically.

The lack of a vision of systemic transformation before 1998, however, did not imply policy inaction. On the contrary, "reform" became a catchword for all political forces after democratization in 1987, and even before. Many of Kim Dae-jung's reforms originated in long policy discussions within and outside the state bureaucracy over two decades. This explains how Kim Dae-jung – an outsider excluded from all positions of political authority over fifteen years – could assemble his triple reform in 1998; the ideas were already there, in the state bureaucracy and academia.

In the early 1980s, Chun Doo Hwan (1980–88) saw stabilization as Korea's first priority and initiated his own triple reform of "financial liberalization," company unionism, and "industrial rationalization." However, his reform never abandoned the idea of state leadership, and even his newly enacted Monopoly Regulation and Fair Trade Act was initially ineffective in promoting competition. Industrial policy considerations always prevailed over concerns on the lack of competition and compromised the effectiveness of the Act.

Roh Tae Woo (1988–93) and Kim Young Sam (1993–98), by contrast, took reform more seriously because of political democratization and increasing financial globalization. Facing labor unrest in a more open political environment, both sought one or another form of "grand compromise" under which workers acquired new political rights in return for accepting labor market flexibility. Their proposals were strikingly similar,[3] and met similar results after predictably fierce opposition. When the Ministry of Labor finally did act under strong pressure from Kim Young Sam in 1996, it committed the fatal political blunder of strengthening labor market flexibility while ignoring reciprocal concessions on workers' rights. The labor movement revolted and nullified Kim Young Sam's new labor legislation in the early months of 1997.

The history of financial reform was even more discouraging. Thoroughly dominated by the Ministry of Finance (MOF), and without significant public participation, financial reform never confronted the root of the problems. Not until 1997 did a presidential advisory commission consider a wide-ranging reform that included prudential regulation, central bank independence, resolution of nonperforming loans, mergers and acquisitions of state-owned financial institutions, and changes in bank ownership structure. The commission, belatedly launched in January 1997, submitted reports on financial reform in April, June, and October. But the MOF defined the task of reform narrowly as helping Korea's financial system survive rather than overhauling it and imposed new regulatory controls. Many experts, journalists, politicians and bureaucrats agreed, seeing financial issues strictly as a question of *administrative* reform, for example, how to make the central bank more autonomous from the MOF.

Given such a lack of substantive progress on labor and financial reform, it is not surprising that *chaebol* reform – if there was any before 1998 – was similarly weak. The Ministry of Trade and Industry thought mainly in terms of "industrial policy" when confronted with large surplus capacity in the manufacturing sector. Rather than allowing

ailing firms to go under, the ministry devised a policy of "specialization" whereby banks induced *chaebol* to focus on a few "core
businesses." Nor was corporate governance a salient issue before 1998.
The first time Korea's major newspapers carried an article on corporate
transparency was in 1996, and even then the political elite spoke of a
neutral "*chaebol* policy" rather than "*chaebol* reform" (Figure 3.2).

In sum, from 1979 through 1997, policymakers muddled through,
juggling complex regulatory policies and putting in place even more
controls, only to see financial problems re-emerge – if not worsened –
when economic growth slowed down. Once systemic reform was discarded as a viable option, it proved difficult to avoid new regulatory
controls.

Within this continuity of "muddling through," however, one finds a
subtle trend of increasing political tension and cognitive conflict over
the nature of "reform." This conflict arose because Korea progressively
became more democratic and financially open, both of which made
"reform" an even more politically contested term. As early as 1987,
68.2 percent of survey respondents accused *chaebol* firms of "earning

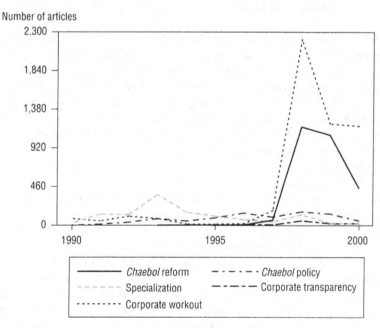

Figure 3.2   Media coverage of *chaebol* issues, 1990–2000

Source: Chosun Ilbo, Donga Ilbo, Joongang Ilbo, and Han'gyorae Sinmun.

profit through irregular means," including government assistance, wage controls, and tax evasion. Even after the explosion of labor disputes in 1987 and 1988 and dramatic wage increases, 85 percent still saw labor demands as legitimate. The managers of small and medium-sized firms likewise saw themselves as victimized by big business; in 1988 only 29.3 percent saw their relationship with *chaebol* firms as "complementary." The rest reported various damages inflicted by *chaebol*, including recurrent delays in payment for parts and components, expansion into unrelated business fields, and disruption of supplies of raw material (Cho 1990: 304–11).

This public discontent constituted a force propelling reform onto the national agenda, but the public remained moderate in its demands. Even with the sense of triumph that overtook society with Chun's downfall in 1987, only 18.1 percent supported "radical reform." This chapter details how this hope for incremental reform in the face of vested interests only worsened Korea's economic problems, contributing to the events of 1997–98.

2   The Heyday of Developmentalism under Chun Doo Hwan

In 1972, Park Chung Hee rescued ailing conglomerates through a moratorium on curb loans and an injection of liquidity (see Chapter 2). In spite of the massive state assistance, however, Korea found itself once again in a severe economic crisis by 1979. The *chaebol* sector was a major culprit. Expansion into uncompetitive businesses with bank subsidies had come to endanger macroeconomic growth and stability. Given their size and role in overall capital accumulation, the *chaebol's* financial problems became national ones.

By 1979, all political forces were calling for change. Searching for a way to legitimize his *coup d'état* after Park's death, Chun sided with this national sentiment and instituted a reform program. Despite his initial rhetoric of "social justice" and "economic liberalization," however, Chun's political rule proved to be an extension of developmentalism. Although some of his economic advisers had strong reformist tendencies, Chun never was what many observers then thought he was, a "neoliberal" with the goal of "dissolving" Korea's developmental state (Moon 1994: 142, 145), even if it risked conflict with the *chaebol* (E.M. Kim, 1997: 167–211). For Chun, 1979 was simply another case of "industrial rationalization" to help big business escape – however temporarily – from a liquidity crisis brought on by surplus capacity and excessive debt.

Chun did depart from Park in pursuing a conservative monetary policy. But when he faced a major business failure, Chun did not hesitate to fall back onto Park's old recipe of conferring fiscal privileges, financial subsidies, and licensing benefits to ailing businesses. Even after Chun scaled down the heavy and chemical industrialization drive and subsidized mergers and acquisitions with relief loans and loan write-offs in 1981, 11 percent of total loans of the five major commercial banks were still nonperforming in 1984. By 1985, 78 firms with a total debt of 9.8 trillion won (25 percent of the deposit money banks' loans and discounts) were failing. In the next two years, his regime generously rescheduled or wrote off 74 percent of the nonperforming loans, financed through special assistance of three trillion won from the central bank (Park and Kim 1994: 209). The market option of declaring ailing firms bankrupt was never seriously considered for fear of contagion effects on the financial institutions and other *chaebol*.

The picture of Chun as a neoliberal is misleading. The "monetarist" bent that he brought to macroeconomic management was not a product of his conversion to monetarism, but an effort to reduce the financial excesses and over-expansion of the late Park years. The old ways of doing business continued, with a subtle but critical shift in policy priorities. The Chun regime provided an ample supply of privileges and benefits to the *chaebol*, but within an overall framework of conservative monetary policy. This approach marked a change *within* Park's growth model, not a fundamental "neoliberal" overhaul of its financial and corporate governance structures.

The limits to Chun's reformism appeared even more clearly in his program for "financial liberalization." The early signs of change had already surfaced in 1974, with Park still in power. To establish greater oversight of lending, Park had assigned a "principal transaction bank" to each *chaebol*, with broad approval and monitoring authority over business activity (Park and Kim 1994: 208). Chun followed with a program of financial liberalization, first allowing four commercial banks to go part "public" by selling shares during 1981–83. The government began to relax state control on interest rates after 1984 and gradually loosened restrictions limiting competition among different types of financial institutions between 1981 and 1987.

In response to a major financial scandal implicating his family, Chun even played with the idea of establishing a "real-name financial transaction system." Disallowing financial transactions under false or borrowed names could potentially enlarge the tax base, further social justice by making interest income fully taxable, and refurbish state banks with underground funds fleeing the informal curb markets.

However, fearing capital flight, Chun's Democratic Justice Party refused to legislate the bill for a real-name financial transaction system in 1982 (*Donga Ilbo*, October 27 and November 1, 1982). The MOF, constrained by large nonperforming loans and jealously guarding its legal prerogatives, also ended interest rate decontrol in 1988 (Park 1994: 150; Park and Kim 1994: 191–2). Nor did the government reform the opaque corporate governance structure. To make it more transparent by establishing an effective auditing and accounting system would have risked not only business resistance but also financial panic, because it would only verify what many feared: *de facto* insolvency of many *chaebol* groups and banks. The creditor banks had to reduce loan risk by favoring larger firms with safe collateral such as real estate (Patrick 1994: 369).

The "privatization" drive, initially conceived as an integral part of "liberalization," met a similar fate. The privatization launched in 1981 was, in fact, a variant of the MOF's traditional dual strategy of state control over the major commercial banks – *chaebol* ownership was limited to 8 percent – and private ownership of provincial banks and non-bank financial institutions (NBFIs), including finance companies, insurance, and mutual saving banks. Chun could not or would not wander too far from this strategy on ownership, lest the commercial banks fell under *chaebol* control as well. The horizontal integration of the real and financial sectors under *chaebol* control would make prudential supervision even more difficult, since the commercial banks' clients would become their owners. The other option of allowing foreign entry was even worse because it would have seriously weakened the MOF's capacity for "administrative guidance" and the very basis of its political influence. The alternative of having institutional investors form a core shareholder group was never seriously contemplated.

The passing in 1980 of the Monopoly Regulation and Fair Trade Act apparently collided with Park's legacies by formally prohibiting unfair trade practices, including price discrimination, the obstruction of market entry by rival firms, and the formation of cartels. The law, however, entrusted regulatory power in the Economic Planning Board (EPB) – the pilot agency to promote growth – and gave it wide discretion over implementation. Affiliate firms could hold each other's shares "if the EPB Deputy Prime Minister deems it necessary for either industrial rationalization or international competitiveness." Likewise, cartels were not barred outright. They only had to be "registered" or "approved" by the EPB. The issue of which were the "market-dominant firms" in need of state supervision and monopoly regulation was also left open, with the EPB deciding more or less unilaterally. The penalties for noncompliance were also very light.[4]

The option of establishing a new regulatory agency with its organizational mission focused narrowly on ensuring market competition and fair trade was rejected, inevitably reducing monopoly regulation to a secondary issue in interministerial policy circles. The Korea Fair Trade Commission (KFTC) faced an uphill battle even within the EPB, which would side with it only when growth was assured, an unusual occurrence in financially overstretched Korea (see Chapter 11).

To stabilize without a complete overhaul of financial and corporate governance structures, Chun relied heavily on labor control. All pretensions of "corporatist" bargaining were jettisoned as he explicitly codified into law all informal practices and customs hitherto developed to weaken the power of labor unions. The labor laws as amended in 1980 barred workers from having more than one union, thus safeguarding the prerogatives of the official Federation of Korean Trade Unions and its affiliated industry federations from challenges by dissident labor activists. Mistrustful of even this submissive official labor movement, Chun banned "third parties" – including the Federation of Korean Trade Unions – from intervening in disputes between workers and their employers. Moreover, he prohibited labor unions from engaging in political activities, including election campaigning and political fundraising. These provisions – known as "*samkeum*" or three prohibitions – isolated labor federations from the working masses and further reduced the Korean labor movement to a fragmented force of company unions driven by narrow economic motives (Song 1991). Through such labor laws, Chun reaffirmed Park's strategy of using labor repression to make up for both capital market weakness and corporate sector rigidity in facilitating macroeconomic adjustment. Chun successfully stabilized Korea's economy by giving *chaebol* relief loans while repressing wages.

3   Paralysis under Roh Tae Woo

The Korean economy had found equilibrium based on continued state credit allocation, "flexible" labor markets, and an opaque corporate governance structure. However, precisely as Chun achieved stabilizing growth, two seeds for its demise rapidly began to take root. Under intense pressure for democratization, Chun reinstituted the political rights of "old" opposition politicians and *chaeya* leaders in 1984 and, in doing so, unleashed a powerful force of democratization that would culminate in the "June Revolt" of 1987. The other seed was sown in 1985 when Washington brokered the Plaza Accord, which revalued East Asian currencies and began the opening of the country's capital markets.

The next decade or so saw Korea struggle with the arduous task of adjusting its way of doing business to fit these two challenges of democratization and globalization. The two developments collided head-on with several policy assumptions undergirding Korea's growth, particularly labor market flexibility. Industrial peace broke down only a month after Chun pledged direct presidential elections in June 1987. Dissident labor leaders forged an alliance with radical *chaeya* activists, setting up "regional conferences" for unions in small vendor firms, "industry federations" for the service sector, and umbrella "councils" for *chaebol* unions by 1990. Democratization produced an intermediate level of labor organization, too powerful to be a mere price-taker in labor markets, but also too weak to bring a binding social contract for all major segments of the internally fractured labor movements. Consequently, real wages rose 8.3 percent annually between 1987 and 1996, 3.7 percentage points higher than between 1979 and 1986. *Chaebol* unions in heavy and chemical industries led the wage hikes.[5]

Labor activism undermined Korea's growth machine by making it difficult to adjust through labor repression. Previously, when inflationary pressures built up, the government forced tight wage restraint on workers.[6] This option of adjustment was no longer possible after 1987. *Chaebol* unions could disrupt the entire national economy through strikes, a power capability that constrained both state action and business calculations even when labor unions did not actively exercise it (J. Kim, 1992).

By 1987, the developmental state also saw state credit allocation challenged, if not undermined. Alarmed by Chun's 1981 plan to "decontrol" interest rates through a gradual reduction of policy loans, *chaebol* bought up security firms, insurance houses, and finance companies and acquired sizeable shares of the commercial banks (see Chapter 4). The combined share of ownership of the four largest *chaebol* in commercial banks rose very rapidly, averaging 19.2 percent for the Big Five and even reaching 33.8 percent for the Korea First Bank by 1984. The NBFIs – already under *chaebol* control before Chun's rise to power – continuously increased their market share by offering higher interest rates than the banks (Seo 1991: 106, 138 9). The thirty largest business groups received 40.1 percent of total short-term finance and accounted for 55.3 percent of the corporate bond market by 1987, far higher than their 33.7-percent share of deposit money banks' total lending (Kim and Hong 1993). Moreover, the ten *chaebol* security houses bought up their affiliate companies' bonds and guaranteed loans contracted by their affiliate companies (Securities Exchange Supervisory Commission 1989a).

Precisely as labor repression was becoming impossible, state control of capital markets began to break down. The Finance Ministry encountered an even greater difficulty in establishing prudential supervision over loan decisions. The largest *chaebol*, in fact, enjoyed the best of two worlds: they continued to have good access to loans from the banks at controlled interest rates while securing an independent source of capital in newly acquired NBFIs.

Rolling back capital market liberalization was not an option, however. With a huge trade surplus, Korea became a target of intense US pressure. The two nations had agreed to hold bilateral Financial Policy Talks in August 1989 and progressively lifted regulatory barriers.[7] Once foreign takeover of local financial institutions became a possibility, the MOF thought it could not but strengthen *chaebol* power over capital markets; they were, after all, the only local actor large enough to hold foreign financial institutions in check. The MOF began encouraging local securities houses to go abroad to directly raise funds in foreign capital markets in 1988. The *chaebol* responded with enthusiasm. Larger *chaebol* groups also rushed to establish merchant banks. Hyundai entered in 1988, followed by Hanjin in 1993, LG in 1994 and Samsung, Ssangyong and Hanhwa in 1996. By 1993 only Kia and Lotte among the ten largest *chaebol* did not have their own securities companies.

As Roh Tae Woo assumed presidential power in February 1988, then, two inexorable forces of change had been unleashed. On the one hand, labor militancy drove up real wages, preventing policymakers from adjusting through their old recipe of wage cuts. On the other hand, *chaebol* could raise money through their own NBFIs as well as issuing stock in both local and foreign capital markets, which seriously threatened state power over credit allocation. Labor militancy and *chaebol* power were new political constraints to which Roh had to adjust.

To build a new institutional formula for growth in such a radically transformed environment was difficult. Having conspired with Chun to launch a *coup d'état* in 1980, and been elected president with only 36.6 percent of the valid votes in 1987, Roh found that his power base rapidly dissipated. Only a month and a half after his inauguration, Roh lost his parliamentary majority, as regionalism replaced democracy as a primary political cleavage and fragmented his native Kyungsang region into northern and southern voter blocs. For the next eight months Roh struggled just to hold onto power, undermined by nationally televised Assembly hearings on his predecessor's illicit profiteering and brutal political repression.

To save his regime, Roh broke away from his lifelong friend and political patron, banishing Chun to a remote monastery in Solak and prosecuting his protégés on charges of abuse of power and illicit wealth accumulation. Chun's purge did not solve Roh's political problem; on the contrary, it worsened it. The National Assembly hearings indirectly implicated Roh in his predecessor's political wrongdoings, while making him a traitor in the eyes of his military friends. Roh lost old supporters without winning new ones.

To save his faltering regime, Roh joined forces with Kim Young Sam and Kim Jong Pil to establish a Democratic Liberal Party (DLP) in January 1990, but this too undermined rather than strengthened Roh's power base. With his eyes on the next presidential election, Kim Young Sam publicly broke his pledge to back a constitutional amendment to introduce parliamentary rule by October 1990 and challenged Roh's authority within the DLP. When the ruling party mended internal differences over constitutional change in May 1991, it was Roh who yielded (*Joongang Ilbo*, May 28, 1991). Before the presidential election scheduled for December 1992, all factional leaders deserted Roh in an unsuccessful attempt to forge a coalition against Kim Young Sam (*Joongang Ilbo*, April 7, May 29, July 10, August 6, November 11, and December 27, 1991).

The precipitous decline in the supply of political power notwithstanding, Roh saw an explosion of demand for structural reform. "The *chaebol* problem," in particular, became a "privileged issue," but different actors had different notions of what "the *chaebol* problem" was. The society defined the issue primarily in ethical terms, identifying *chaebol* as a major culprit in undermining the country's egalitarian social structure and moral integrity through shady political deals. The academic community criticized the *chaebol* as an outmoded form of business organization that lived off subsidized loans from state banks and monopoly profits from regulation, thus eroding the country's international competitiveness. For the MOF, *chaebol* reform was increasingly seen as both a precondition and an effect of financial reform. Only when the *chaebol* became efficient enough to pay back loans could the MOF carry out its pledge to decontrol interest rates.

Many reform measures adopted by Roh were replicas of Chun's. The ceiling on bank loans that Roh used to restrain *chaebol* from reckless empire building was originally introduced in 1984 (*Donga Ilbo*, August 22, 1984). A legal provision for regulations on cross-shareholding was also first included in the amended Monopoly Regulation and Fair Trade Act in 1984. Chun even ordered the *chaebol* to eliminate all cross-shareholding within five years in 1986 (*Donga Ilbo*, December 16, 1986). Similarly, Roh's idea of transforming *chaebol* into "specialized" industrial conglomerates with four or five "core areas" of production through swapping secondary "unrelated" businesses with other *chaebol* (Bedeski 1994: 86–8) could trace its origin to Chun's 1985 policy, which required *chaebol* to sell off unrelated businesses before entering a new product market. Moreover, the May 1990 measure prohibiting the purchase of large land parcels as well as entry into "unproductive" sectors (*Donga Ilbo*, May 9, 1990) echoed Chun's September 1980 measures (*Donga Ilbo*, September 27, 1980). And in 1987, in the middle of presidential elections, Roh pledged to outlaw financial transactions under false name, as Chun had done in 1982.

Despite a greater sense of urgency pervading key policy circles, the state actors remained within Park's paradigm and Chun's notion of reform to limit over-expansion, not to overhaul the entire developmental state model. Even the more radical "public concept" of land, which Roh introduced in 1991 to place a ceiling on land ownership by big business, to levy special taxes on "unearned incomes" from real estate speculation, and to order the sale of idle land with a threat of credit reduction, tax investigation, and expropriation, did not represent a paradigmatic shift in policy ideas on the *chaebol*. The public concept of land was introduced to hold down land prices and channel capital into more productive business fields (*Joongang Ilbo*, July 24, August 6, and October 28, 1991). As such, it only implied a strengthening of the traditional policy of forcing *chaebol* to focus on their main businesses, not a search for alternative forms of business organization.

However, Roh's initiative failed even before it was written into law in 1991. The driving force behind *chaebol* reform, EPB Deputy Prime Minister Cho Soon and Presidential Secretary on Economic Affairs Moon Hi Gap, were replaced by a conservative economic team in 1990 as a result of intense pressures from both party leaders and *chaebol*. With the reformers removed, their policy package became an orphan without a determined supporter inside the economic bureaucracy. These laws, administrative guidance, and directives were implemented more vigorously than during Chun's rule, but not vigorously enough to discourage *chaebol* from risky business behavior. On the contrary, Roh's capital market liberalization – without a prior bank restructuring, strengthened prudential regulation, and corporate governance reform – more than offset his policy directives on loan ceilings, cross-shareholding, real estate sales, and "industrial specialization." The *chaebol* could and did bypass Roh's regulatory regime simply by going abroad to raise new funds.

Roh was even more ineffective in reforming labor markets. Shaken by a sharp wage hike after the "Great Workers' Struggle" in July–August 1987, the Ministry of Trade and Industry proposed in 1990 that the Ministry of Labor amend labor laws to extend work hours, prohibit wage payments during labor strikes, allow the hiring of outside workers during strikes, and codify management as the exclusive prerogative of employers. But within four months, the government retreated before a threat of labor unrest (*Donga Ilbo*, March 27, 1990, and April 7 and *Han'gyorae Sinmun*, July 5, 1990). Thereafter, the Ministry of Labor pushed aside the Ministry of Trade and Industry and dominated labor policy talks. The "consolidated wage system" that the Ministry of Labor proposed in 1991 sought to deter employers from paying special allowances to satisfy union demands in excess of administrative guidance on wage increases. But this proposal was buried as well, when labor threatened to campaign against the DLP in the presidential and National Assembly elections (*Donga Ilbo*, November 9, 1991).

On April 24, 1992, with only eight months left before the presidential election, Roh established an "Inquiry Commission on Labor Laws". A tripartite organ with twelve members representing "public interests" and six others drawn from major employers' associations and labor federations, the commission opened – however timidly – a new era in Korean labor politics. Never had the Ministry of Labor brought both labor and business leaders into policymaking as equals. Nor had it given experts a central role in shaping overall labor policy. By giving the public interest representatives a majority of the seats at the commission, and also forming within it a "Basic Committee" with eight public interest members to draw up draft bills, Roh transferred the policy initiative from MOL to a more innovative expert group.

As initially planned in its "Administration Regulations," the Inquiry Commission on Labor Laws would work on the draft bills drawn up by the Basic Committee and "suggest" them for legislation. The discussion proceeded rapidly, with interest groups submitting specific demands for legal revision in May 1992. The Basic Committee convened eleven times through February 1993. But the commission ended up postponing its formal proposal to September 1993 because labor and capital deadlocked over the issue of labor market flexibility and workers' basic rights. Caught up in intense presidential election campaigns, both ruling and opposition political parties were in no position to deliberate on labor reform. Any new labor bills would have to be part of the next president's reform program (Choi, Chun, Lee and Yu 2000: 117–206).

By the end of the Roh government, then, neither state directives nor market signals effectively regulated and disciplined credit allocation. Structural rigidities in the labor markets also intensified and corporate governance structures remained opaque.

4   Kim Young Sam's Rhetoric of Reform

"There have been too many people living in others' shadow. They need to be consoled and relieved from anguish. The haves should concede. Those who are powerful should give. The freedom won should be a freedom for the community" (*Joongang Ilbo*, February 25, 1993). With those brave words, Kim Young Sam assumed presidential authority in February 1993. Despite such colorful rhetoric, however, he proved no reformer. He won presidential power through traditional means. The *chaebol* generously financed his election campaign in 1992, state agencies mobilized voters through dense client networks, and parastatal social groups waged a negative ideological campaign against rival opposition candidates.

Kim Young Sam assumed power with neither a detailed agenda nor a concrete action plan. This was so because policy had never been what politics was about in Yeouido's gray National Assembly building, where Kim Young Sam had spent his entire public life. The reformist spirit undergirding his inaugural speech reflected a desire for national renewal, but was unaware of the complex tradeoffs and serious political risks inherent in any politics of reform. Setting a detailed agenda and drawing a viable strategy for reform was a political task to be tackled after – not before – his swearing into office in February 1993.

Lacking any programmatic vision, Kim Young Sam defined reform primarily in a negative way in his early days of political rule: as a purge of legislators, bureaucrats and military officers who had illicitly accumulated wealth, abused power while in public office, or conspired in the *coup d'état* of 1980. The initial two hundred days of his administration saw ten National Assembly members resign, imprisoned or expelled from the DLP, as well as 32 military commanders discharged or indicted (Suh and Kim 1999: 29–33). These seven months were a moment of moral catharsis for society, finally holding its political and military elite accountable for past wrongdoing. The public approval rating for Kim Young Sam skyrocketed, reaching 84.2 percent by May 22 and hitting 86.1 percent on October 25, 1993 (Gallup Korea). The ruling party likewise won six of the eight seats contested in special National Assembly elections between April and August.

Kim Young Sam's courage dissipated, however, when confronted with proposals for more "positive" social and economic reforms. The showdowns with Chun's Hanahoi faction (The Society of One) in the armed forces and with morally compromised legislators were relatively easy because society was unaffected by them. Labor, *chaebol* and banking reform were different: adjustment costs were concentrated, while benefits were not only dispersed throughout society but also to be reaped only in the long run. Moreover, despite a visible slowdown since 1992, Korea's economy hardly looked as if structural reform were required. In 1992, GNP grew by 5 percent and inflation remained low. Labor, *chaebol* and bank reforms were accordingly judged as entailing unnecessary political and economic risks.

The debate over policy priorities within Kim Young Sam's inner circles lasted only a few weeks. After publicly denying the rumors of an impending *chaebol* reform in April 1993, Kim Young Sam launched an expansionary monetary policy, which by definition precluded reform.

Despite the continued emphasis on economic growth, one could still discern a subtle change in tone brought on by democratization. For example, the KFTC slowly began to exercise its power to fine for unfair trade practices (see Chapter 11). But it was not Kim Young Sam's intention to drastically increase those fines, nor to perform risky surgery on the underlying structural causes of those practices. Like his predecessors, he strove to build an orderly market of big businesses, albeit through a somewhat more "activist" Fair Trade Commission.

The new *chaebol* policy of "sectoral specialization" constituted an extension of Roh's previous policy of specialization by "main firms". To prevent *chaebol* entry into unprofitable, unrelated business ventures, Roh had the MOF encourage the thirty largest business groups to choose two or three main companies. The ministry would lift all restrictive regulations on bank loans for these firms in return for their restraint in issuing new loan guarantees for affiliate firms.

The policy failed dismally to improve the financial structure of *chaebol*. After three decades of extremely aggressive debt financing, *chaebol* could not be strengthened by merely prohibiting new intersubsidiary loan guarantees and shareholdings. The 76 firms chosen by the thirty largest *chaebol* as main companies in 1991 had already guaranteed loans worth 38.3 trillion *won* for affiliate companies – three times their own equity – when the MOF initiated its main company policy. More than half of those loan guarantees were held by thirteen main companies of the five largest *chaebol* (*Chosun Ilbo*, September 20, 1991). The ministry accordingly revised its policy to reduce all outstanding inter-subsidiary loan guarantees within four years, but because of the worries over a financial panic as well as the opposition from *chaebol*, the MOF could not even submit this plan for a cabinet review. Meanwhile, the MOF delivered on its other promise of exempting the main companies from financial regulation, which became an additional incentive for borrowing and aggressive investment (*Donga Ilbo*, August 3, October 10, and October 21, 1992).

Two years later Kim Young Sam announced a new sectoral specialization policy. Because the *chaebol* had abused the MOF by selecting as their main companies those in need of a large dose of debt financing rather than those with a potential for growth, the Ministry of Trade, Industry and Resources (MTIR) under Kim Young Sam called for reconceptualizing "core businesses" in terms of industrial sectors rather than companies. The objective was to create firms on a par with the leading multinational corporations. "The sectoral specialization policy departs from other *chaebol* policies by focusing only on international competitiveness," Trade, Industry and Resources Minister Kim Chol Su declared. "Neither restricting business concentration nor redistributing wealth and income constitutes a central objective of sectoral specialization" (*Han'guk Gyongjae Sinmun*, October 28, 1993). In such a spirit, the MTIR departed from the MOF's policy by reclassifying Korea's economy from 73 to 15 industrial sectors and allowing horizontal diversification and vertical integration within one's chosen sectors. Moreover, whereas the MOF's policy had allowed two or three main companies per *chaebol*, the MTIR designated two or three core sectors, with six or seven "leading companies" for each conglomerate. Lured by a promise of financial privileges, Korea's thirty largest *chaebol* had 112 companies registered as their "leading firms" by January 1994.

In sum, Kim Young Sam basically followed Park's policy rule of "big is beautiful." Moreover, when Samsung lobbied in December 1994 to establish an integrated passenger car plant in Pusan – the DLP's regional stronghold – Kim approved it over the MTIR's opposition; the president had his eye on winning the 1996 National Assembly election. With that decision, even the minimal restrictions that the MTIR set on the entry into non-core sectors collapsed rapidly.

This was most unfortunate because the president was pushing for capital market liberalization on the other policy front. In his expansionary "Plan for a New Economy" formally launched in July 1993, Kim Young Sam pledged to join the Organization for Economic Cooperation and Development by December 1996. This decision would profoundly change the basic parameters of economic policymaking by requiring extensive capital market liberalization.[8] To meet the OECD's requirement for capital market liberalization, Finance Minister Hong Jae Hyung announced a foreign exchange deregulation on February 4, 1994. In March 1995, as Korea formally applied for OECD membership, the MOF initiated another round of deregulation to satisfy OECD prerequisites in the areas of current invisible trade and capital movements. Sweepingly opening the capital markets, Kim Young Sam's advisers argued, would pressure financial institutions to undertake mergers and acquisitions to acquire international competitiveness and, through them, force the corporations to exit from insolvent business ventures.

This financial big bang could come only if new investors could close down excess branches and lay off workers. But Korea's legal system not only disallowed layoffs, but also prohibited hostile mergers and acquisitions. Moreover, even if the relevant laws were changed, the reform would be partial unless the *chaebol* downsized and became cost-conscious producers. Without a simultaneous downsizing of the *chaebol*, which in turn depended on labor reform for success, the new regimen for banks would not work. And if no labor, financial and *chaebol* reform followed, Korea would enter global capital markets with a real sector surviving on bank subsidies, plagued by labor market rigidities, and entrapped in an opaque corporate governance structure. That was what happened under Kim Young Sam. While his sectoral specialization policy inadvertently aggravated the *chaebol's* appetite for empire building and his capital market liberalization opened a way for the *chaebol* to satisfy that appetite with foreign capital, Kim Young Sam's labor reform only solidified the rigid divisions between capital and labor, as well as within the fragmented Korean labor movement.

When the Basic Committee of the Inquiry Commission on Labor Laws completed its draft bills on labor markets in June 1993, the Ministry of Labor refused to make them public because "many articles could instigate serious dissension" (*Han'gyorae Sinmun*, August 25, 1993). The expert group's draft bills showed a new but controversial thinking on labor issues. The Basic Committee's public interest representatives assumed a "neutral" position, proposing to lift the *samkeum* as demanded by labor in return for recognizing employers' right to flexibly allocate working hours. Then in August 1994, after another round of intense interministerial struggles, big business lobbying, and labor disputes, MOL again postponed the submission of new labor bills (*Donga Ilbo*, August 25, 1994). Delaying did not bridge the differences, however. When the Ministry of Labor decided in March 1995 not to push for any labor reform during Kim Young Sam's presidency (*Donga Ilbo*, March 6, 1995), the MTIR as a defender of business interests took up the issue and called for employers' right to lay off workers in times of economic distress and to bring in temporary outside workers on a contract basis (*Han'gyorae Sinmun*, August 29, 1995). But this, too, did not reach the cabinet because Kim Young Sam was preparing for National Assembly elections.

Nevertheless, labor reform remained a privileged issue, resurfacing with a greater strength after each defeat. This was not only because many employers and workers as well as expert groups saw reform as a project of moral rejuvenation or economic competitiveness, but also because the Basic Committee kept labor reform alive by developing a new discourse on the issue. To win business support for its plan for a "grand compromise" with labor unions, the Basic Committee progressively incorporated the employers' demand for labor market flexibility into the reform package. But it also sought labor backing by proposing to lift the Ministry of Labor's three prohibitions. The committee, however, was too weak to structure negotiations and ended up articulating a "neutral" document that only angered everyone. The ruling party as well as state ministries balked at implementing what the Basic Committee proposed. In 1993, amidst a major strike in Hyundai affiliate companies, the EPB and the MTIR openly challenged the call by the "progressive" Labor Minister, Rhee In Jae, to pay minimum salaries even during strikes (*Joongang Ilbo*, June 21–23, 1993). In 1994, with dissident labor unions coalescing into a Korea Confederation of Trade Unions, DLP leaders demanded that the Ministry of Labor not concede on its *samkeum* regulations on labor union activities (*Joongang Ilbo*, June 1, 1994).

With the opposition gaining force, in December 1994 Park Se Il, a key public interest representative on the Basic Committee, joined Kim Young Sam's presidential staff as Senior Secretary on Policy Planning. After a year of political frustration, Park Se Il persuaded Kim Young Sam to establish a staff on social welfare, with four state ministries directly under its jurisdiction: labor, education, environment, and health and social welfare. The office was established in December 1995 with Park as its head (*Joongang Ilbo*, December 21, 1995). From this office, Park launched a Presidential Commission on Labor Reform on May 9, 1996, with ten representatives drawn equally from labor and capital, and another twenty recruited from public interest and academic groups (Park 2000).[9]

The timing of reform was wrong, however, launched in the fourth year of Kim Young Sam's single nonrenewable, five-year presidential term. By then, the public approval rating of the president had plummeted to only 30.4 percent, while the political parties were positioning themselves for the coming 1997 presidential election. Kim Young Sam was on the verge of becoming a lame duck.

The difficulties started from within the Presidential Commission on Labor Reform. The commission members derailed reform by stubbornly defending old privileges. The representatives of business associations opposed any tampering with Korea's repressive *samkeum* while demanding their own rights (*samjae*). The leaders of labor federations defended Korea's traditional system of lifetime employment and seniority rules in promotion while calling for an immediate lifting of all three prohibitions.

The commission's failure to submit a compromise bill prompted Kim Young Sam to set up an interministerial committee on November 11, 1996 under leadership of Labor Minister Jin Nyum, a technocrat with barely disguised sympathies for business interests. The resultant government bill was then submitted for legislation on December 10, with both the Federation of Korean Trade Unions and the Korea Confederation of Trade Unions threatening a general strike, and opposition political parties staging a sit-in on the floor of the National Assembly. The bills underwent another major surgery in the National Assembly. On December 26, 1996, two presidential staffs on political and economic affairs joined the conservative bosses of the New Korea Party (NKP, the DLP's successor) to further strengthen employers' rights to lay off workers while delaying, for three years, the removal of the legal constraints on workers' rights to form multiple labor federations.

Severe labor unrest followed, forcing another round of labor law revisions, this time jointly by the governing and opposition political parties. On March 8, the new laws were promulgated. Essentially compromise bills, they suffered from internal contradictions, doing too little to deal effectively with the structural flaws of Korea's fragmented system of company unionism, but too much for both capital and labor to remain politically unruffled. The employers' right to lay off workers was recognized. However, to placate labor unions, it was subject to a tight legal constraint, only to be exercised under "acute" economic distress. The potentially explosive issue of removing union officers from the company payroll was similarly evaded with a provision that called for "financial independence of labor unions" through establishing a special company fund, to be financed jointly by employees and employers. The workers' rights to be represented by multiple unions were likewise permitted immediately at the level of the federation, but not at the level of company unions, which angered management as well as labor for different reasons.

The financial reform met a similar fate. Kim Young Sam established a Presidential Commission on Financial Reform in January 1997, precisely when his labor reform profoundly discredited his government. The initial talks of orchestrating a "big bang" in the financial sector quickly disappeared (*Joongang Ilbo*, January 10 and March 15, 1997). The president had lost all moral authority with the labor fiasco as well as the Hanbo scandal of January 1997 which revealed that corporate officials of the company were using bribes to secure bank lending.

Moreover, the Presidential Commission itself was a moderating force on reform. Thirteen of its thirty members were drawn from big business. As the primary beneficiaries of bureaucratically distributed bank loans, they had an interest in avoiding any "radical" solutions, especially on the issues of prudential regulation, governance structures, and hostile mergers and acquisitions. This was most unfortunate since any realistic solution on nonperforming loans could not but be radical – implemented as part of an integral measure on prudential regulation, governance structures, hostile mergers and acquisitions, and corporate downsizing – given their astronomical size, estimated as 14.3 percent of all outstanding loans (*Joongang Ilbo*, March 15, 1997). Only a program of corporate workouts, layoffs, bank privatization, and foreign takeovers could prevent a severe liquidity squeeze. But the Presidential Commission predictably focused on administrative reorganization instead, producing a proposal that would give the central bank effective control over monetary policy and place all regulatory powers over banks, security companies, and insurance firms under a new Financial Supervisory Commission (FSC) (*Joongang Ilbo*, May 16 and June 4, 1997).

Even this proposal did not survive subsequent bureaucratic struggles. The Finance and Economic Board (FEB, established in 1994) rebelled, successfully winning back most of its power over monetary policy from the central bank and supervisory authority over financial institutions. "The FEB will be responsible for the work of superior quality," a top presidential adviser said on June 14, 1997, "while FSC will look after strictly administrative work and simple repetitive tasks" (*Joongang Ilbo*, June 15, 1997). The FEB retained its power to prepare financial laws and distribute licenses and permits to set up bank and NBFI branches. The Monetary Policy Committee, formally the highest authority in monetary policy, was placed above rather than inside the central bank (in direct opposition to the Presidential Commission's proposal), with its chairperson subject to removal by the president upon the recommendation of the FEB Minister.

Even the FEB did not have the final say on financial reform. The National Assembly would not legislate its bills, with NKP leaders even calling for an indefinite postponement of financial reform as early as May 13 (*Joongang Ilbo*, May 16, 1997). The political parties adopted a strategy of ignoring the FEB's bills altogether. With only six months to the presidential election, it was difficult even to convene a National Assembly session. Entrapped in a devastating negative campaign after July 1997 and hit by massive business failures since January, all party leaders evaded making a choice on financial reform (B. Kim, 2000a: 173–201). The president meanwhile had become a lame duck, discredited by charges of corruption as well as incompetence. Even his own political party turned against him, promising on November 6 to hold a National Assembly hearing on economic mismanagement and irregularities if it won the election. Two days later, the party even forced Kim Young Sam to withdraw from the party.

Accordingly, reform drifted without a political supporter until Korea pleaded for an IMF bailout on November 21. Only then did Korea face reality, and financial reform became irreversible. As a precondition for providing a relief fund of over $55 billion, the IMF forced the country to restructure its financial institutions. The standards on capital adequacy of the Bank for International Settlements were put into motion and caused bank closures as well as mergers and acquisitions. Korea also pledged to overhaul the *chaebol* by disallowing loan guarantees between affiliate firms, as well as building more transparent corporate governance structures (see Chapter 12). Under intense IMF pressure, Korea allowed foreigners to own up to 50 percent of Korean companies and adopted a flexible exchange rate system (see Chapter 10).

The financial crisis made even Korea's evasive party politicians draw up a joint proposal for financial reform in a special steering committee on December 1, 1997, which resulted in the legislation of fifteen new laws thirty days later (*Joongang Ilbo*, December 2 and 30, 1997). The new laws allowed foreigners to hold up to 33.3 percent of bank stocks, removed the legal obstacles to hostile mergers and acquisitions, guaranteed the institutional autonomy of the central bank, lifted all regulations on interest rates, and empowered the FSC to order an extensive workout program for insolvent financial institutions (S. Kim 1999: 223–62). In February 1998, Kim Dae-jung, as the president-elect, pushed through a revision of the labor laws, allowing employers to lay off workers in cases of mergers and acquisitions and to bring in outside workers on a temporary contract basis.

5   Conclusion

The failure of reform in Korea was in the first instance a cognitive failure. The ruling political elite – whether authoritarian or democratically elected – never ceased talking of reform, but none fully grasped what it involved. Only briefly in 1996, among a few inner policy circles led by Park Se Il, was systemic reform seriously considered as an option for Korea, only to be defeated by concerted political opposition from the *chaebol*, organized labor, the state bureaucracy, and political parties.

However, even reformers' understanding of Korea's economic problems was incomplete and inadequate. They were unaware of the significance of corporate governance, transparency, and accountability, and focused on labor and financial reform only. The advocates of labor and financial reform, moreover, often found themselves opposed to one another.[10]

Before these belated and ultimately futile efforts at systemic transformation, "reform" was defined primarily as adjusting Park Chung
Hee's institutional legacies to changed political and economic conditions rather than leaping into a qualitatively different model of
growth. This was because Korea remained an essentially bureaucratic
polity in spite of increasing globalization and democratization. With the
National Assembly and political parties in utter disarray,[11] and labor
fragmented into two hostile blocs of "official" and "dissident" unions,
it was state ministries that defined the policy agenda, chose policy
instruments, and controlled implementation. They saw reform simply
as an extension of their previous efforts to prevent nonperforming
loans, wage hikes, and *chaebol* market power from weakening Korea's
international competitiveness.

The 1997 financial crisis demonstrated how wrong they were. But
although the crisis delegitimized Park's institutional legacies for good and
rapidly engendered a new national consensus for systemic reform, the
task of policy reformulation continued to reside with state bureaucrats
even after 1997, given the continuing weakness of the National Assembly,
political parties, and interest groups. The state became a reformer with
the task of overhauling an economic system it had helped establish and
maintain. This fact would profoundly affect the nature of systemic reform
Korea was to have after 1997, but that is another chapter.

Notes

1 On the concept of privileged problems, see Hirschman (1965: Part II).
2 See Dong Hoon Kim (1999: 65–104).
3 The "three prohibitions" (*samkeum*), barring multiple unions in the work-
   place, intervention by "third parties" in labor disputes, and political
   activities by labor unions, would be lifted. In return, capital gained "three
   systems" (*samjae*): to lay off workers in time of business difficulty; to hire
   workers on a temporary basis; and to flexibly allocate work hours.
4 Public officials found guilty of leaking confidential information on regulatory policy were fined a million *won* or less. Companies engaging in
   cross-shareholding and cartels without prior state approval were fined thirty
   million *won* or less. Likewise, obstructing a rival firm's market entry
   through unfair business practices met an imprisonment of less than a year
   or a fine of less than seventy million *won*.
5 The wage ratio between firms with fewer than thirty workers and companies with more than five hundred employees fell from 90 percent in 1986 to
   71 percent by 1991. See Kim and Lim (2000: 111–37).
6 In 1971, real wages grew by only 1.7 percent, after rising 12.9 percent
   annually for five years. Then, in 1980, they fell by 4.1 percent after growing
   16 percent per annum for four consecutive years.

7 See Securities Exchange Supervisory Commission (1989b).

8 The governing and opposition political parties did not take positions until Kim Young Sam sought National Assembly ratification for Korea's entry in October 1996.

9 To personally shape new labor laws, moreover, Park recruited four academic colleagues from his Basic Committee years. Bae Mu Gi became a Standing Member, Park Rae Young and Yun Seong Cheon chaired two committees, and Lim Jong Yul served as General Secretary for Yun's critical Committee on Labor Laws and Legal Institutions.

10 For example, Lee Seok Chae's Presidential Staff on Economic Affairs sabotaged Park Se Il's Staff on Social Welfare when Park drew up the bills to legalize multiple unions in return for recognizing the employers' right to lay off workers in time of economic difficulty. The economic staff wanted a labor law only to facilitate its plan for a "big bang" in the financial sector, which involved a series of mergers and acquisitions of the insolvent banks that caused massive layoffs. In Lee's view, legalizing multiple unions made bank restructuring more difficult by strengthening "radical" dissident bank unions.

11 The MOF allowed foreign securities companies to hold up to 40 percent of shares in securities companies in 1989, an increase of 30 percentage points. The ministry also allotted 10 percent of listed stocks for purchase by foreign individuals in 1992, albeit with an upper ceiling of 3 percent ownership for any single foreign individual. See Securities Exchange Supervisory Commission, *Capital Markets Annual* (in Korean; various issues); Ministry of Finance and Korea Development Bank (1993); and Korea Productivity Association (1996).

References

Bedeski, Robert E. 1994. *The Transformation of South Korea: Reform and Reconstruction in the Sixth Republic under Roh Tae Woo, 1987–1992*. Seoul: Routledge.

Cho, Dong Sung. 1990. *A Study on Korean Chaebol* (in Korean). Seoul: Maeil gyongjae sinmunsa.

Choi, Young Gi, Chun, Kwang Seok, Lee, Cheol Su and Yu, Bom Sang. 2000. *Labor Law Change and Worker–Employer Relations in Korea: The History of Labor Law Change since 1987* (in Korean). Seoul: Korea Labor Institute.

Hirschman, Albert O. 1965. *Journey Toward Progress*. New York: Doubleday.

Kim, Byung-Kook. 2000a. "Electoral Politics and Economic Crisis, 1997–1998," in Larry Diamond and Byung-Kook Kim, eds, *Consolidating Democracy in South Korea*. Boulder: Lynne Rienner Publishers.

——. 2000b. "The Politics of Crisis and a Crisis of Politics: The Presidency of Kim Dae-jung," in Kongdan Oh. Armonk, ed., *Korea Briefing, 1997–1999: Challenges and Change at the Turn of the Century*. New York: M. E. Sharpe.

——. 2000c. "Party Politics in South Korea's Democracy: The Crisis of Success," in Larry Diamond and Byung-Kook Kim, eds, *Consolidating Democracy in South Korea*. Boulder: Lynne Rienner Publishers.

Kim, Byung-Kook, and Lim, Hyun-Chin. 2000. "Labor Against Itself: Structural Dilemmas of State Monism," in Larry Diamond and Byung-Kook Kim, eds, *Consolidating Democracy in South Korea*. Boulder: Lynne Rienner Publishers.

Kim, Dong Hoon. 1999. "The Corporate Governance Structure of Korean *Chaebol*" (in Korean), in Dae Hwan Kim and Kim Kyun, eds, *The Theory of Chaebol Reform* (in Korean). Seoul: Nanam.

Kim, Eun Mee. 1997. *Big Business, Strong State: Collusion and Conflict in South Korean Development, 1960–1990*. Albany, NY: State University of New York.

Kim, Gi Tae, and Hong, Hyun Pyo. 1993. "The Characteristics and Meaning of *Chaebol*" (in Korean), in Gi Tae Kim, ed, *The Structure of Korea's Economy* (in Korean). Seoul: Hanul Academy.

Kim, Jang Ho. 1992. "The Recent Trends in Labor Economics and the Integral Wage System" (in Korean). Paper presented at a conference organized by the Labor Studies Institute, Korea University.

Kim, Kyun. 1999. "*Chaebol* Reform and the Future of Korean capitalism" (in Korean), in Dae Hwan Kim and Kyun Kim, eds, *The Theory of Chaebol Reform* (in Korean). Seoul: Nanam.

Kim, Sang Jo. 1999. "Financial Reform to Bring about *chaebol* Reform: The Direction and Tasks" (in Korean), in Dae Hwan Kim and Kyun Kim, eds, *The Theory of Chaebol Reform* (in Korean). Seoul: Nanam.

Korea Productivity Association. 1996. *The Management of the Korean Economy* (in Korean). Seoul: Korea Productivity Association.

Leipziger, Danny M. 1988. "Industrial Restructuring in Korea," *World Development*, 16 (1).

Ministry of Finance and Korea Development Bank. 1993. *Thirty Years of Foreign Capital Import in Korea* (in Korean). Seoul: Ministry of Finance and Korea Development Bank.

Moon, Chung-in. 1994. "Changing Patterns of Business–Government Relations in South Korea," in Andrew MacIntyre, ed., *Business and Government in Industrializing Asia*. Ithaca: Cornell University Press.

Park, Se Il. 2000. *Reforming Labor Management Relations: Lessons from the Korean Experience, 1996–1997*. Seoul: Korea Development Institute.

Park, Yung Chul. 1994. "Korea: Development and Structural Change of the Financial System," in Hugh T. Patrick and Yung Chul Park, eds, *The Financial Development of Japan, Korea, and Taiwan: Growth, Repression, and Liberalization*. New York: Oxford University Press.

Park, Yung Chul, Kim, Byung Joo, and Yun, Park Jae. 1986. *A Research on the Development of the Financial Sector* (in Korean). Seoul: Korea Development Institute.

Park, Yung Chul, and Kim, Dong Won. 1994. "Korea: Development and Structural Change of the Banking System," in Hugh T. Patrick and Yung Chul Park, eds, *The Financial Development of Japan, Korea, and Taiwan: Growth, Repression, and Liberalization*. New York: Oxford University Press.

Patrick, Hugh T. 1994. "Comparisons, Contrasts, and Implications," in Hugh T. Patrick and Yung Chul Park, eds, *The Financial Development of Japan, Korea, and Taiwan: Growth, Repression, and Liberalization*. New York: Oxford University Press.

Securities Exchange Supervisory Commission. 1989a. "The Materials

Demanded for National Assembly Audit" (in Korean). Seoul: Securities Exchange Supervisory Commission.

———. 1989b. *Capital Markets Annual* (in Korean). Various issues. Seoul: Securities Exchange Supervisory Commission.

Seo, Jae Jin. 1991. *The Capitalist Class of Korea* (in Korean). Seoul: Nanam.

Song, Ho Keun. 1991. *Labor Politics and the Labor Market of Korea* (in Korean). Seoul: Nanam.

Suh, Jin-Young, and Kim, Byung-Kook. 1999. "The Politics of Reform in Korea: Dilemma, Choice, and Crisis," in Suh and Changrok Soh, eds, *The World After the Cold War: Issues and Dilemmas*. Seoul: Graduate School of International Studies, Korea University.

4   The Government, the *Chaebol* and Financial Institutions before the Economic Crisis

Joon-Ho Hahm

To address the fundamental causes of the Korean financial crisis, it is essential to understand the nature of the relationship among the government, financial institutions, and *chaebol*. This relationship has critically affected the overall efficiency and performance of the economy. While there have been numerous studies on the role of state-controlled finance in the development era, the evolution of the credit allocation mechanism throughout the recent period of financial liberalization remains poorly understood.[1] This chapter focuses on the financing mechanism of the investment boom of this pre-crisis period and finds that the corporate financing pattern in the 1990s is characterized by two notable features: the rising volume of credit intermediated by non-bank financial institutions (NBFIs); and the increasingly shorter maturity structure of corporate debt, both domestic and foreign. Those features were in fact deeply connected with the nature of financial liberalization policies undertaken, and they reflected distorted incentives rooted in a legacy of implicit government guarantees.

Conventional wisdom emphasizes the role of commercial banks and their relationship with the government as a main culprit in the crisis. This chapter argues that distorted credit allocation channeled through the liberalized sector – NBFIs and direct financing – contributed to the vulnerability of the financial system. Hence, the root cause of the crisis can be traced to the mismanagement of the transition process to a truly operating market economy. Specifically, we examine the following hypotheses:

- Early attempts at financial liberalization in the 1980s implied a weakening of traditional relationships among the government, *chaebol* and banks. With bank privatization, tightened bank credit controls and a shift in government policy priorities to non-*chaebol* sectors, the pattern of bank credit flows changed.
- In response to these regulatory changes, the financing pattern of the *chaebol* also evolved. NBFIs and the capital market became

79

increasingly important sources of firm financing. *Chaebol* established their dominance in the non-bank financial sector by the early 1990s and influenced the agenda and sequencing of financial liberalization, which was accelerated after 1993. This structural shift implied the increasing independence of the *chaebol* in their major investment decisions.

- The government recognized the potential problems of *chaebol* dominance over NBFIs by the early 1990s. But no serious measures were subsequently undertaken to stem the risks, suggesting that policy choices in this liberalization episode were often captured by interest groups, most notably by the *chaebol* themselves.
- There is no evidence that the increasing financial independence of the *chaebol* helped raise efficiency in overall credit allocation. On the contrary, it is more likely that the market mechanism distorted incentives and failed to monitor credit flows to *chaebol*. Unbalanced financial liberalization combined with the legacy of implicit government insurance resulted in excessive supply of credit to *chaebol* and magnified overall financial risks in the economy.

In the following section, we characterize the structural evolution of the relationship among the government, the *chaebol* and the banks in the transition period of the 1980s, a period when the traditional tripartite regime began to collapse with early attempts at financial liberalization and the emergence of NBFIs. Section 2 describes the acceleration of financial liberalization and the dominance of *chaebol* over the non-bank financial sector after 1993. This section also reviews the adverse consequences of the increasing influence of *chaebol* over NBFIs and characterizes the financial liberalization process. Section 3 focuses on the efficiency and risk implications of this structural shift in the period after 1993. The absence of adequate financial supervision, coupled with the legacy of implicit insurance, enabled *chaebol* to engage in large-scale debt-financed investments, magnifying the structural vulnerability of the entire financial system.

1   Early Attempts at Financial Liberalization and Weakening of State Control over *Chaebol* Investment (1980–93)

Risk sharing between government and business was a core feature of Korea's development strategy in the 1960s and 1970s (see Chapter 1). The government played the role of Schumpeterian banker, which mobilized financial savings and allocated them to chosen strategic industries

(Yoo and Lim 1999). Lee (1992) characterized the government–*chaebol* relationship in this period as a "quasi-internal organization."[2] Limited amounts of financial resources available at subsidized interest rates and tight state controls over finance implied that competitive pressure existed among *chaebol* to be selected as beneficiaries. It also meant that the government was equipped with a tool to subordinate corporate incentives to its policy objectives.

Regardless of its contribution to rapid industrialization, extensive credit rationing produced an uncompetitive and distorted financial system. Controls on interest rates and selective credit allocation resulted in increasingly inefficient allocation of funds and mismanagement of financial institutions as the economy grew in size and became more diverse. Government-led development policies resulted in over-capacity in the heavy and chemical industries (HCIs) and the unbalanced growth of large firms relative to small and medium-sized enterprises (SMEs). The government subsequently adjusted its financial policy toward fewer credit controls and financial liberalization. The traditional relationship among the government, *chaebol* and banks changed accordingly. This structural change, reinforced by the shift in the regulatory environment facing banks, was accompanied by changes in the pattern of bank credit flows and *chaebol's* financing behavior.

Reprivatization of commercial banks and strengthening of bank credit controls

The first major attempt at financial liberalization was the reprivatization of commercial banks during 1981–83.[3] However, the negative experience of the 1950s led the government to insist on the separation of banking and commerce.[4] The sale of government-owned bank shares was carried out under the principle that an individual or enterprise could not purchase more than 5 percent of total bank shares issued. The Banking Act amendment of December 1982 also introduced an explicit ownership regulation that any individual or corporation could own only up to 8 percent of total shares issued.[5]

The separation of commerce from the banking system left the possibility that the government could indirectly control the *chaebol's* investment decisions through the banking sector. Indeed, while bank ownership was transferred to the private sector, the practice of government intervention and indirect controls over bank credit allocation continued.[6] Government intervention, including meddling in the appointment of chief executives, significantly undermined the autonomy and accountability of banking institutions and throttled their credit evaluation functions.

The bank credit control system was also strengthened in the 1980s.[7] The credit control system was formally incorporated into the revised Banking Act in 1982, and the Office of Bank Supervision was vested with the authority to set a ceiling on the share of *chaebol* in any bank's loans. This measure was to check the concentration of economic power and to ensure access to bank credit by SMEs. Bank credits to *chaebol* were tightly controlled to ameliorate the problem of loan concentration, and in 1987, the "basket" credit control system directly limited the share of bank loans going to the thirty largest *chaebol*.[8]

Industrial policies toward balanced growth and changes in bank credit flows

With the strengthening of controls over bank credit to the *chaebol*, the government's policy priorities also shifted during this period. In response to increasing social demands for equity, income redistribution and balanced growth, underdeveloped sectors, such as SMEs and agriculture, fisheries and mining, gained higher priority in bank credit allocation. *Chaebol*-related industries were gradually de-emphasized and the Bank of Korea reduced policy loans to large corporations. The government encouraged loans to SMEs by tightly monitoring the share of loans extended to them by commercial banks. A "specialization" policy for *chaebol* was reinforced in 1993 to induce them to refrain from excessive diversification and to stem the concentration of economic power (see Chapter 3).

This shift in government policy and the regulatory environment implied that the traditional bank–*chaebol* relationship was also changing. The availability of bank credits for *chaebol* was gradually limited as the government redirected policy priorities and strengthened the credit control system. Table 4.1 shows the trend in the ratio of bank loan shares allocated to each industry relative to its share of GDP. A ratio of one means that allocation of credit exactly mirrors the share of that activity in the economy; ratios higher than one imply biases in favor of the given sector, ratios lower than one biases against the sector. The data clearly show that the HCIs and overall manufacturing industry received less bank credit in the 1980s and 1990s relative to the 1970s, while a growing share of bank loans was allocated to the agriculture, fishery, and mining sectors and the service industries. Table 4.2 shows that SMEs received an increasing share of commercial bank loans while *chaebol* received decreasing shares. Table 4.3 shows trends in the basket control limits imposed and the actual bank loan shares for the top five *chaebol*. The limit and actual share of the top five *chaebol* in bank loans dropped substantially in the late 1980s.

All of this evidence suggests that *chaebol* increasingly needed alternative sources of finance.

Emergence of NBFIs and alternative financing sources for *chaebol*

The amount of bank credits intermediated to the *chaebol* is affected by a variety of supply-side and demand-side factors. As we have seen, an important supply-side factor was the change in the bank regulatory environment, especially direct regulations on asset allocation. Demand-side factors pertain to the availability of alternative financing schemes for the *chaebol*. At least three sources need to be considered in light of advances in financial liberalization: financing from the NBFIs; direct financing in domestic capital markets; and increasing access to foreign credit sources.

Table 4.1 Bank loan shares relative to GDP shares, by industry (%)

Industry	1970s	1980s	1990s
Agriculture, fishing, mining	0.45	0.48	0.69
Manufacturing:	2.16	1.81	1.51
Heavy Chemical	2.63	1.95	1.67
Light Industry	1.85	1.64	1.24
Power and construction	1.95	1.40	0.60
Service	0.65	0.54	0.88

Note: Share of bank loans allocated to the industry / GDP share of the industry.
Source: Bank of Korea, *Monthly Bulletin*, various issues; Korea Development Bank, *Monthly Bulletin*, various issues; re-cited from Cho and Kim (1997).

Table 4.2 Share of deposit money bank loans to small and medium-sized enterprises (SMEs) and *chaebol* (%)

Loans	1988	1989	1990	1991
To SMEs	48.1	50.1	55.5	56.8
To 30 largest *chaebol*	23.7	20.7	19.8	20.4

Source: Bank of Korea and Office of Bank Supervision; re-cited from Cho and Kim (1997).

Table 4.3 Bank credit basket controls and share of bank loans
to top five *chaebol* (%)

Year	Limit on loan shares	Actual shares
1987	18.6	15.3
1988	15.2	12.7
1989	8.6	7.2
1990	7.2	6.6
1991	5.8	5.8
1992	5.6	5.2
1993	6.2	4.9
1994	5.7	4.4
1995	5.3	3.6
1996	4.9	3.6

Source: Presidential Commission for Financial Reform, *Financial Reform in Korea* (1997).

As can be seen in Table 4.4, the market share of NBFIs increased rapidly during the 1980s, from 29.1 percent of total deposits in 1980 to 46.4 percent in 1985 and 59.0 percent in 1990. The same trend is observed if we investigate the composition of non-securities financial saving. Even if we exclude certificates of deposit and money trust accounts of commercial banks from the NBFI category, NBFIs still accounted for a substantial share of total financial savings, exceeding 30 percent as early as 1980. Moreover, this share increased rapidly during the 1980s, reaching 54.2 percent in 1990, while the share of bank accounts decreased steadily from 59.8 percent of the total in 1980 to 26.8 percent in 1990.

As the role of NBFIs continued to increase, the influence of *chaebol* on them did as well. In contrast to the banking sector, there was no outright ownership regulation for NBFIs; the ownership of NBFIs was indirectly regulated only by entry barriers. However, in the absence of transparent entry qualifications, the discretionary issuance of licenses resulted in increasing ownership of NBFIs by *chaebol*. For instance, during 1988–93, 22 new life insurance companies were established. *Chaebol* owned many of them. From the late 1970s to the mid-1980s, thirty-one investment finance companies were established; nineteen were owned by *chaebol*. The *chaebol* owned eleven securities companies by the end of 1981.

Table 4.4   Market shares of financial institutions in Korea (end of period, %)

Financial institution	1980	1985	1990	1995	1998
Deposits					
Commercial banks	42.8	31.2	25.5	19.9	22.6
Specialized banks	28.1	22.4	15.5	7.9	5.2
NBFIs	29.1	46.4	59.0	72.2	72.2
Loans and Discounts					
Commercial banks	38.8	34.2	29.3	23.9	27.9
Specialized banks	24.5	24.2	19.0	12.6	10.0
NBFIs	36.7	41.6	51.7	63.5	62.1

Source: Bank of Korea.

The increasing ownership of NBFIs by the *chaebol*, coupled with tight control of bank credits, allowed the NBFIs to emerge as an important alternative financing source for *chaebol*. The share of the top thirty *chaebol* in commercial bank loans decreased steadily throughout the early 1990s, from 23.7 percent in 1988 to only 13.9 percent in 1995. During the same period, the *chaebol's* share of NBFI lending increased from 32.4 to 38.4 percent. Given that the aggregate market share of NBFIs was increasing rapidly, the increasing share of *chaebol* in NBFI loans implies a substantial volume of credit was intermediated to *chaebol* through this alternative source.

Capital markets were also deregulated substantially in the 1980s, further increasing the availability of direct financing for *chaebol*. Table 4.5 shows trends in the financing of the corporate sector in Korea. Borrowings from NBFIs and direct financing both became increasingly important sources of corporate financing in the 1980s and early 1990s, while the share of foreign borrowing decreased during the same period. Table 4.6 shows trends in the composition of financial liabilities in the corporate sector. Borrowings from NBFIs increased substantially during the 1980s and the share exceeded borrowings from the banking sector by the early 1990s. Shares of commercial paper and corporate bonds outstanding also increased substantially in the late 1980s, which indicates that direct debt financing had become important for the corporate sector by the early 1990s. During this early liberalization period, the share of foreign borrowing actually *decreased* steadily.

The overall evidence indicates that financial liberalization during the 1980s weakened the traditional relationship among the government, *chaebol* and banks. The government retained control over the banking system despite privatization, and it indirectly controlled bank credit

Table 4.5 Structure of corporate financing in Korea (%)

Source of finance	1970	1975	1980	1985	1988	1990	1991	1992	1993
Indirect finance	39.7	27.7	36.0	56.2	27.4	40.9	41.8	36.3	32.8
Borrowing from banks	30.2	19.1	20.8	35.4	19.4	16.8	19.8	15.1	13.7
Borrowing from NBFIs	9.5	8.6	15.2	20.8	8.0	24.1	22.0	21.1	19.0
Direct finance	15.1	26.1	22.9	30.3	59.5	45.2	37.9	41.4	53.3
Commercial paper	0	1.6	5.0	0.4	6.1	4.0	-3.8	7.6	14.7
Corporate bonds	1.1	1.1	6.1	16.1	7.5	23.0	24.2	12.5	15.0
Stocks	13.9	22.6	10.9	13	40.6	14.2	15.1	15.9	16.5
Foreign borrowings	29.6	29.8	16.6	0.8	6.4	6.8	4.4	5.0	-2.3
Others	15.6	16.4	24.5	12.7	6.7	7.1	15.9	17.3	16.2

Note: External financing, based on flows. "Others" include government loans and trade credits among corporate firms.
Source: Bank of Korea, *Understanding of Flow of Funds in Korea*, 1994.

Table 4.6 Composition of financial liabilities in Korean corporate sector (%)

Liability	1970	1975	1980	1985	1990	1993
Borrowings from:						
Financial institutions	19.4	23.6	32.2	35.8	36.5	37.0
Banks	14.8	17.2	20.7	19.7	18.7	17.8
NBFIs	4.6	6.5	11.5	16.0	17.8	19.2
Securities issued	37.5	23.1	21.3	27.2	35.9	39.0
CPs	0.0	0.6	2.0	2.6	4.8	5.3
Corporate bonds	0.3	0.7	3.5	7.2	11.0	13.4
Stocks	37.2	21.7	15.0	16.4	18.3	16.5
Foreign borrowings	10.5	15.3	15.0	9.4	5.5	4.1
Others	32.6	37.9	31.4	27.6	22.1	20.0
Total	100.0	100.0	100.0	100.0	100.0	100.0

Note: Based on balances. "Others" include government loans and trade credits among corporate firms.
Source: Bank of Korea, *Understanding of Flow of Funds in Korea*, 1994.

allocation by tightening regulations. The *chaebol's* corporate financing behavior evolved in response to these changes, and the NBFIs and domestic capital markets emerged as important financing vehicles by the early 1990s. This structural change implied that the *chaebol* were gaining independence in their major investment decisions.[9]

2   Accelerated Liberalization and *Chaebol* Dominance of Non-Bank Financial Institutions (1993–97)

After 1993, *chaebol* established their dominance over the rapidly expanding non-bank financial sector. Progress in comprehensive capital account liberalization gave an additional degree of freedom to the *chaebol*. The further erosion of the traditional bank–*chaebol*–government risk-sharing scheme implied that *chaebol* became much more independent in their investment decisions. At the same time, it also meant that a new monitoring scheme based on market principles was urgently required. However, the government took few measures to strengthen prudential regulation and enhance the governance structure of financial institutions. In the absence of an effective monitoring and disciplining mechanism in deregulated financial markets, the legacy of implicit insurance significantly undermined the efficiency of credit allocation and led to structural vulnerability of the entire economy.

Increasing dominance of *chaebol* over NBFIs and its negative consequences

While the influence of the *chaebol* over the NBFIs increased steadily from the 1970s, their dominance peaked at the onset of the financial crisis. At the end of 1998, the seventy largest *chaebol* owned 140 non-bank financial institutions.[10] Table 4.7 shows the rapid growth in the market share of NBFIs owned by the top five *chaebol* in the late 1990s. The growing dominance of *chaebol* in the non-bank financial sector, especially in the absence of an effective supervisory and monitoring scheme, brought about serious conflicts of interest. The lenient supervisory standards and poor monitoring practices produced numerous incidents of illegal and unfair activities, where funds from affiliated financial institutions were exploited for the benefit of *chaebol's* ailing subsidiaries.

When the crisis broke, *chaebol*-affiliated NBFIs became private cash vaults for the *chaebol*. For instance, Korea (Daehan) Life Insurance, the third-largest life insurance company in Korea, extended credits of more than 3 trillion *won* (approximately $2.7 billion) to affiliated subsidiaries of its parent company during 1996–98, violating regulations on related party loans. By June 1998, the life insurance company was in a net debt position by more than 2 trillion *won*, and in August 1998, the financial supervisory authority ordered 100-percent write-offs of equity and injected public funds to nationalize it. Daehan Merchant

Bank and Dongseo Securities became insolvent in 1997 due to related party loans. In another case, Daewoo's affiliated NBFIs, Daewoo Capital and Diners Club Korea, purchased commercial paper of affiliated subsidiaries through Seoul Capital, which turned out to be a disguised or "camouflaged" subsidiary of Daewoo. There are also numerous cases of unfair, though not illegal, transactions of *chaebol*-affiliated NBFIs. For instance, Samsung Life Insurance purchased subordinated debt of commercial banks issued to raise their BIS capital ratios, and in return, the commercial banks purchased bonds issued by subsidiaries of Samsung at above-market prices.

The merchant banking industry deserves special attention in this regard.[11] In 1990 there were only six merchant banking corporations and all of them were foreign affiliated. However from 1994, entry barriers were lowered for the industry and the scope of business expanded. By the end of 1996 a total of thirty merchant banking corporations were in operation, undertaking most of the commercial paper issuing and discounting business in Korea. With the financial crisis, nearly all of the twenty-four newly licensed merchant banking corporations went bankrupt and were permanently closed.

The problems associated with the merchant banking industry highlight important aspects of the changing relationships between the government, the *chaebol* and financial institutions. Merchant banking corporations were not subject to ownership regulations, which resulted in the ownership of sixteen of them by *chaebol*. While maintaining relatively tight supervisory standards for commercial banks, the government applied much more lenient regulations to the merchant banking industry, which does not accept outright deposits.[12] Minimal supervision was applied, on the assumption that competition and resulting market discipline would correct potential problems. Regulations and guidance on interest rates were much more lenient, enabling merchant

Table 4.7 Market share of non-bank financial institutions (NBFIs) owned by the top five *chaebol* (year ended March, %)

% share owned by top five *chaebol*	1996	1997	1998	1999
Of NBFIs				
Deposits	17.6	18.6	29.6	34.0
Assets	–	22.5	30.4	34.7
Of financial sector				
Deposits	4.7	4.8	8.6	13.4
Assets	–	8.1	10.0	14.6

Source: Kim and Lee (1999).

banking corporations to compete with commercial banks by offering competitive quasi-deposit products. Nor were merchant banks subject to the tight capital adequacy regulations applied to commercial banks.

In the absence of effective supervision, merchant banking corporations engaged in increasingly risky business. The loan concentration to *chaebol* was relatively high, and they often borrowed short-term, at low interest rates from abroad and invested in long-term, high-yield assets in foreign currencies (such as Russian bonds), exposing themselves to substantial duration mismatch and currency risks. They even engaged in various off-balance-sheet transactions on risky offshore products. At the end of 1996, the nonperforming loan to capital ratio of the merchant banking corporations was as high as 31.9 percent, while the ratio was 12.2 percent in the commercial banking sector (Shin and Hahm 1998: 25, Table I.10). The deterioration in asset quality and balance-sheet soundness was much more severe in the NBFIs than the commercial banks.

These negative consequences resulted from the marriage between commerce and finance and were not limited to the merchant banking industry. Using micro-accounting data on corporate and financial firms from 1990 to 1997, Kim (1999) finds that, controlling for other variables, *chaebol* that owned NBFIs systematically borrowed more at lower borrowing costs than firms that did not own NBFIs. Kim interprets this as evidence of unfair fund-flows from the NBFIs to affiliated companies. More interestingly, as summarized in Table 4.8, Kim (1999) also found that during 1995–97 financial institutions affiliated with *chaebol* recorded systematically lower profitability as well as lower capital ade-

Table 4.8 Profitability and capital adequacy of non-bank financial institutions (averages of 1995–97, %)

	Chaebol-affiliated	Independent
Profitability (ROA)		
Merchant banks	0.67	0.81
Securities companies	–3.12	–0.63
Investment trust	–1.66	2.40
Capital adequacy		
Merchant banks		
(BIS capital ratio)	5.4	6.3
Securities companies		
(net operating capital ratio)	164.7	234.2

Note: ROA (ratio of ordinary income to assets) is an average of 1995–97 figures; and capital adequacy measures are at the end of March 1998.
Source: Kim (1999).

quacy compared with independent financial institutions. This finding indicates that the credit allocation of *chaebol*-owned NBFIs was much less efficient. This inefficiency was possibly due to the absence of an appropriate governance system, namely, the fact that they were being exploited as *chaebol's* private cash vault.

Unbalanced financial liberalization magnifies financial risks

Financial liberalization is often cited as the primary impetus for subsequent credit expansion and deterioration of asset quality in the financial sector. Hahm and Mishkin (2000) argue that, although financial liberalization might have not been critical to the lending boom in Korea, it did play an important role in increasing the structural vulnerability of the financial system. Moreover, political pressure from the *chaebol* has affected the speed and sequence of financial liberalization, which in turn had important consequences on the financial risks faced by the Korean economy as a whole.

In retrospect, the financial liberalization program in Korea was unbalanced. The first asymmetry came from the unbalanced interest rate regulation across commercial banking and NBFIs. The latter were allowed greater freedom in their management of assets and liabilities and, crucially, were permitted to apply higher interest rates on their deposits and loans than those of the regulated commercial banks. Relatively large differentials on deposit interest rates across commercial banks and investment finance companies persisted until the mid-1990s (see Table 4.9).

Table 4.9 Average interest rates on deposits (%)

Type of deposit	1991	1992	1993	1994	1995	1996	1997
Commercial bank time deposits (6–12 months) (A)	6.0	6.0	5.0	5.0	7.0–9.0	9.3	13.9
Investment finance co. cash management account (180 days) (B)	15.0	15.5	11.9	12.9	13.3	11.8	12.6
(B) – (A)	9.0	9.5	6.9	7.9	4.3–6.3	2.5	–1.3

Note: Investment finance companies were transformed to merchant banking corporations in July 1996.
Source: Bank of Korea, *Monthly Bulletin*, various issues.

This asymmetry contributed to the excessively rapid expansion of NBFIs in the late 1980s and early 1990s (see Table 4.4), substantially increasing financial risks for the entire system.

Financial risks for the system increased first because NBFIs were not adequately supervised and there was no effective market monitoring mechanism. Second, as noted by Lee et al. (2000), yields on short-term instruments of the NBFIs such as commercial paper were deregulated before bank deposit rates and corporate bond rates.[13] Given that funds intermediated by NBFIs were more short-term in nature, the resulting fund-flows associated with the NBFIs increasingly shortened the average maturity of corporate financing, thereby exposing the corporate sector to substantial liquidity and refinance risks.

Another asymmetry came from the unbalanced deregulation of the capital account in the period after 1993. In 1993, the Korean government expanded the purposes for which financial institutions could provide loans denominated in foreign currencies. Short-term foreign borrowing by financial institutions was allowed at the time, while the government maintained quantity restrictions on long-term foreign borrowing as a means of managing capital flows.

In addition, the number of financial institutions engaging in activities denominated in foreign currencies increased sharply with financial liberalization. The transformation of twenty-four investment finance companies into merchant banking corporations during 1994–96 meant a corresponding increase in the number of participants in the international financial market, because merchant banks were allowed to engage in foreign exchange transactions while investment finance companies were not. During the same period, Korean commercial banks opened twenty-eight foreign branches, which gave them greater access to foreign funds. As can be seen in Table 4.10, the result was a rapid increase in external liabilities of financial institutions and a dramatic increase in short-term foreign debt, exposing the economy to substantial foreign exchange liquidity risk.

"Ignorance" versus "capture" in the evolution of policy choices

Given the observations above, an important political economy question arises. Why did the government allow *chaebol* dominance over NBFIs and pursue financial liberalization in this haphazard manner? While it is quite plausible that policymakers in the initial financial liberalization episode of the 1980s were not fully aware of the potential problems associated with the dominance of industrial capitalists over the financial

Table 4.10 External liabilities of Korea ($100 million, percent)

	1992	1993	1994	1995	1996	1997	1998
Gross external liabilities[1]	629.0	670.0	887.0	1,197.0	1,643.4	1,580.6	1,493.5
(y-o-y growth rate)		(6.52)	(32.39)	(34.95)	(37.29)	(-3.82)	(-5.51)
Financial institution[2]	436.0	475.0	651.0	905.0	1,165.3	896.0	719.0
Corporations	137.0	156.0	200.0	261.0	417.5	462.0	410.0
External Liabilities/GDP	19.99	19.38	22.04	24.46	31.60	33.16	46.48
Short-term external liabilities/ Total external liabilities[3]	58 82	60.15	65.84	65.75	56.58	40.00	20.64
Short-term external liabilities/ Foreign exchange reserves[3]	215.69	198.89	227.48	240.58	279.75	309.82	59.24

Notes:
1. External liabilities include external debts as defined by the IBRD, plus offshore borrowings of Korean banks and overseas borrowings of Korean banks' overseas branches.
2. Financial institutions include foreign bank branches operating in Korea.
3. External liabilities and foreign exchange reserves are year-end values.
Source: Ministry of Finance and Economy.

sector or unbalanced financial liberalization, the policymakers in the 1990s seem to have been quite aware of the risks.

An interesting piece of evidence is the financial reform section of the "New Economy" blueprint of the Kim Young Sam government, released by the Ministry of Finance in July 1993. It reveals that policymakers clearly understood the potential risks of the dominance of *chaebol* over NBFIs. According to the blueprint, the government planned to introduce explicit ownership regulations, such as the ones applied in the commercial banking sector, to the NBFIs. They also tried to reinforce financial supervision to minimize the potential adverse consequences of this dominance. Political pressures may have played a non-trivial role in the failure to implement this plan.

Faced with the changing nature of the traditional relationship, *chaebol* were looking for an alternative source of financing which was not subject to government control and, naturally, financial liberalization was one such vehicle. Lee et al. (2000) argue convincingly that the unbalanced financial liberalization resulted from the endogenous response of *chaebol* which had established dominance in NBFIs. Hence the sequence of financial liberalization was designed to increase the scope of NBFIs and liberalize their related businesses first.

Another case in point was the Kim Young Sam government's imprudent interest rate and capital market deregulation for the benefit of the business sector and the delay in serious financial reforms until 1997. An extreme case of imprudent and politically captured liberalization policy was the licensing of merchant banking corporations (Haggard 2000). The government allowed nine investment finance companies to transform themselves into merchant banking corporations in 1994 and another fifteen in 1996. The licensing process was influenced by intense lobbying of bureaucrats and politicians. According to the investigation result of the Board of Audit and Inspection, three of the newly transformed merchant banking corporations in 1996 were actually insolvent at the time they were licensed (*Chosun Ilbo*, March 18, 1998). Fifteen out of the sixteen newly licensed corporations were finally closed down in the resolution process of the financial crisis.

3   Why Did the Market Fail to Monitor Credit Flows to *Chaebol*?

A closer look at corporate performance reveals that *chaebol* suffered from low profitability in the early 1990s (Table 4.11). The profitability picture for the smaller *chaebol* was particularly weak, even during the boom years of 1994–95.[14] The decrease in the profitability of the corporate sector implies that the efficiency of investment was deteriorating.[15] One commonly used aggregate measure of investment efficiency is the incremental capital–output ratio.[16] If the allocation of investments was efficient, output would grow faster with the same level of investment, and hence the ratio would be lower; rising ratios reflect declining efficiency. Figure 4.1 shows the trend in the incremental capital–output ratio computed from the previous five years' cumulative investments and output changes. It increased from 4 in 1986 to around 6 in 1992 and remained at that level with the onset of the crisis. Although this is an aggregate and imperfect measure of investment efficiency, when combined with deteriorating corporate sector profitability, it suggests that the efficiency of corporate investment may have seen a structural decrease in the 1990s relative to the 1980s.[17]

Why did the market fail to monitor and correct this structural misallocation of financial resources? Remember that a notable feature of credit allocation in the 1990s was the rapidly rising volume of NBFI-intermediated credit flows to *chaebol*. There are two important factors behind the rapid expansion of NBFI-intermediated credits. The first factor was the relatively high return on the NBFIs' financial products, which had partly resulted from the unbalanced financial liberalization discussed above. However, had the market correctly perceived implied risks, the rapid expansion of NBFIs would not have been possible. The second important factor was that the risk associated with the NBFIs *ex ante* was not so high, given the legacy of implicit insurance extended to *chaebol* from the development era of the 1960s and 1970s. Of course, the government did not voluntarily provide these guarantees implicitly or explicitly, in particular with respect to the NBFIs. However, the fact that there has been not a single bank failure since the 1960s reinforced the widely held presumption that such a guarantee still existed in the financial sector.

Table 4.11 Return on assets of the 30 largest *chaebol* (%)

Size of *chaebol*	1993	1994	1995	1996	1997
1st–5th	1.86	3.54	4.86	1.41	0.43
6th–10th	0.87	1.17	1.10	−0.49	−2.15
11th–30th	−0.40	−0.06	−0.08	0.08	−3.00
All 30	1.11	2.19	3.15	0.23	−2.13

Note: Simple averages of each *chaebol's* return on asset figures reported in Joh (1999).
Source: Hahm and Mishkin (2000).

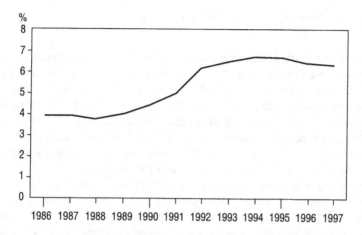

Figure 4.1   The incremental capital–output ratio, 1986–97

A source of moral hazard that helped produce deterioration in both financial and non-financial balance sheets was the government involvement in credit markets, which created the impression that the *chaebol* were "too big to fail."[18] We have already seen one important incident of large-scale corporate bailouts in August 1972 (see Chapter 2). Financial institutions kept lending to *chaebol* because they anticipated that the government would not allow these firms to go bankrupt, thus in effect guaranteeing their loans. Depositors and investors of NBFIs also behaved in this way, with no strong incentives to monitor them. As we have seen in Tables 4.7 and 4.8, the fact that *chaebol*-affiliated NBFIs enjoyed relatively faster growth despite their relatively poor performance could be interpreted as additional evidence of this distorted incentive on the part of depositors and investors based on the belief that they were "too big to fail."

Another impetus to excessive risk-taking on the part of Korean financial institutions was that foreign lenders were not given sufficient incentives to monitor Korean institutions because they assumed, rightly as it turned out, that they would suffer only minor losses if Korean financial institutions got into trouble. They would be protected from loss either by the Korean government or by international institutions such as the IMF which would provide the necessary funds to bail them out. In sum, the legacy of traditional government–*chaebol* relationships led to market failure.

4   Summary and Policy Lessons

The traditional tripartite relationship between the government, banks and *chaebol* in the 1960s and 1970s could be characterized as a government risk-sharing scheme. In return for government controls, implicit insurance was extended to the banking system. The resulting mobilization of credit in turn made the *chaebol's* aggressive investment possible. Indeed, the "insurance and moral hazard" aspect of the business–government relationship had been built from an early stage in the country's growth (Lee 1992; Yoo and Lim 1999).

Notwithstanding the effectiveness of government-directed credit policies in the early development era, the financial liberalization of the 1980s implied a fundamental shift in the traditional credit allocation mechanism. While privatizing the banking system in the early 1980s, the government tightened bank ownership and the credit control system in an effort to ensure the soundness of the banking system and to indirectly control bank credits toward the *chaebol*. However, financial liberalization also meant an additional degree of freedom for *chaebol* in terms of their financing sources. The emergence of NBFIs and opening of more direct and overseas financing opportunities enabled *chaebol* to become more and more independent in their major investment decisions.

Despite government efforts to liberalize the financial system and bring in market principles, the practice of indirect and occasional intervention continued, and the financial market was haunted by the legacy of the traditional government–*chaebol* risk partnership. Depositors and investors behaved as if the implicit guarantee had been extended to NBFIs, leading to the assumption that *chaebol* were "too big to fail." As a result, the investment boom of the early 1990s was aggravated and the efficiency of credit allocation undermined. Unbalanced financial liberalization, pursued in a haphazard manner under the influence of the *chaebol*, substantially increased the risks in the financial system.[19] The deterioration in the balance sheets of the corporate and financial sector created structural vulnerability for the entire Korean economy. As a result of large shocks in the terms of trade and contagion effects from Southeast Asian countries, financial crisis erupted in 1997.

We can draw several policy lessons from the Korean experience. The structural weakness of the Korean economy came from the failure to install an effective financial system operating on market principles and gradually replacing the traditional state-controlled mechanism of resource allocation. Three factors seem important in making this transition. First, it is critical to break the legacy of implicit guarantees. The distortion of incentives based on the expectation of future bailouts causes significant misallocation of resources for the entire economy. Early resolution of insolvent firms and financial institutions through transparent exit mechanisms is therefore critical. However, political considerations often lead to regulatory forbearance, which revives the implicit insurance. To minimize regulatory forbearance, it is important to have a politically independent supervisory system and the accountability of supervisory authorities needs to be strengthened. Opening up the actions of supervisors to public scrutiny makes regulatory forbearance less attractive, thereby reducing principal-agent problems and moral hazard. Transparency also reduces the incentives of politicians to lean on supervisors to relax their supervision duties.

The Korean case also highlights a second factor in a successful transition: the importance of strengthening financial supervision over NBFIs. Although many of the problems came from the ownership of NBFIs by *chaebol*, it is far less clear whether ownership regulations such as the one for commercial banks should be introduced for the NBFIs. An alternative policy direction for the NBFIs would have three components. First, it is important to establish market discipline by fostering competition among the NBFIs. Entry barriers need to be made transparent, and when lowering them, the "fit and proper" test for the qualification of large shareholders should be applied. In addition, exit barriers or implicit government protection against bankruptcy must be scrapped. Enhanced competition can help solve the problem of conflicting interests only when underlying market forces truly drive the competition. The government's previous attempt to introduce competition among NBFIs failed in part due to the lack of a proper information structure. Poor accounting standards made credit information worthless in evaluating the performance of NBFIs. An information infrastructure needs to be established to strengthen disclosure requirements and improve accounting standards so that the market will work on the basis of relevant and transparent information. Second, internal monitoring mechanisms for the NBFIs should be improved. The reform of governance is important to minimize conflicts of interest among large shareholders, minority shareholders and depositors of the NBFIs. Finally, as in the commercial banking industry, prudential regulations such as prompt corrective action need to be strengthened and strictly applied for the NBFIs.

A third issue in the transition is sequencing; financial liberalization needs to be designed and implemented in a more orderly manner. Based on the Korean experience, there appear to be advantages in allowing the presence of fully operating foreign financial institutions *before* fully liberalizing the capital account. In addition to the efficiency and spillover effects these firms bring, they support diversification, which is particularly important for emerging markets. The importance of strengthening prudential supervision while pursuing liberalization cannot be overstated. Prior to opening, financial institutions should be adequately capitalized at global standards. The risk management capability of both financial institutions and corporate firms should also be strengthened.

In many emerging market countries, financial liberalization brings about substantial exposure to interest rate and currency risks. These can lead to a full-blown financial crisis if a currency crisis hits the economy. Governments need to probe the full range of risks and design policies to counter them when financial liberalization programs are designed and implemented.

Notes

The author thanks Stephan Haggard, Takeo Hoshi, Euysung Kim and Wonhyuk Lim for helpful comments and suggestions.

1 On the relationship between financial policy and industrialization in Korea, see Amsden (1989), Cho (1989), Lee (1992), Cho and Kim (1997), among others.

2 Lee (1992) argues that policy implementation within a quasi-internal organization can be more effective than policy implementation through the market due to the sharing of information and economies in transaction costs.

3 Hanil Bank was privatized in 1981, the Korea First Bank and Seoul Trust Bank were privatized in 1982, and Cho Heung Bank was privatized in 1983.

4 The relationship between banks and commerce in Korea can be traced back to the mid-1950s, when the government, which had assumed ownership of commercial banks from the US Military Government in 1948, began to reprivatize the banking system. The privatization process ended in 1957. However the initial failure of privatization attempts during 1954–56 and the subsequent relaxation of eligibility for bank ownership resulted in the takeover of commercial banks by a few big businesses. The ownership of banks by *chaebol* was subsequently accompanied with various negative consequences such as concentration of bank loans to affiliated companies. Cho and Kim (1997) argue that the negative consequences of this first bank privatization provided a strong rationale for government control over banking for the next few decades.

5 The limit on nationwide commercial bank ownership was reduced to 4 percent of voting shares later in 1994.

6 According to Perkins (1997), the government's efforts to liberalize and privatize the financial system in the 1980s met with two major barriers; first, the large nonperforming assets of banks accumulated during the previous two decades of government-directed lending; and second, the

strength of the government bureaucracy itself, which did not want to give up control over banks.

7   The credit control system was originally introduced in 1974 to improve the capital structure of *chaebol* by encouraging them to minimize debt financing and use more direct financing. Also public listing in the stock market was encouraged to induce deconcentration of corporate ownership. These policies, however, were not actively enforced during the rest of the 1970s.

8   With the basket credit control system, equity investment regulation was introduced in 1987. Direct cross-shareholdings between subsidiaries within a big business group and establishment of pure holding companies were prohibited. The basket credit control system and the equity investment regulation became two major policy tools to stem concentration of economic power.

9   See Kim (1988), Moon (1994), Haggard (1994), Mo (1999) and Yoo and Lim (1999) for discussions on the political economy aspects of the government–business relationship in Korea.

10 The total number of NBFIs at the end of 1997 was 487, excluding leasing companies. These included: merchant banks, securities companies, investment trusts, life insurance and fire and casualty insurance companies, installment finance companies, mutual savings, venture capital companies, credit card companies and factoring finance firms.

11 Merchant banking corporations in Korea are wholesale financial institutions engaged in underwriting commercial paper, leasing, and short-term lending to the corporate sector. They fund themselves from issuing bonds and commercial papers and borrowing from the inter-bank and foreign markets.

12 Merchant banking corporations were supervised by the Ministry of Finance and Economy, while commercial banks were under the supervision of the Bank of Korea.

13 In the second half of 1991, in the first round of interest rate deregulation, the government lifted regulations on the yields and supply of commercial paper, whose main market makers were merchant banking corporations.

14 The improvement in profitability for the top five *chaebol* in 1994–95 was mainly due to a boom in semiconductor industries.

15 There are various factors behind this low corporate sector profitability and investment efficiency. One major factor is poor corporate governance practices. For instance, Joh (1999b) presents evidence that major shareholders pursued private interests at the expense of minority shareholders, and this resulted in low corporate profitability in Korea.

16 The incremental capital–output ratio is the ratio of investment to the change in output, usually measured as cumulative investments relative to the change in output over a period of five years or more. International financial institutions regard an ICOR on the order of five or less a "good" standing, while lending is viewed as dangerous if a country's ICOR is above that level.

17 Joh and Kim (Chapter 5) report that *chaebol*-affiliated firms showed significantly lower profitability and productivity relative to independent firms during 1993–97, which also indicates that the investment efficiency of *chaebol* was deteriorating in the 1990s.

18 Using micro-accounting data on corporate investments, Hahn (1999) presents evidence that *chaebol* in fact preferred riskier businesses

anticipating implicit loss protection from the government. Controlling other factors, which affect corporate investment, *chaebol* increased investment when the uncertainty associated with its future profitability was perceived to be larger.

19 Even without blaming the government or the *chaebol*, it is plausible to think that the sheer lack of skill and experienced personnel in light of Korea's extraordinarily rapid growth and liberalization themselves would cause problems. In that sense, the statement here may seem a bit harsh toward Korea. However, the haphazard, politically motivated capital account liberalization in the 1990s and the complete absence of supervision for NBFIs were problems that cannot be simply blamed on the lack of skill and expertise.

References

Amsden, Alice. 1989. *Asia's Next Giant: South Korea and Late Industrialization.* New York: Oxford University Press.

Cho, Yoon-Je. 1989. "Finance and Development: The Korean Approach," *Oxford Review of Economic Policy*, 5 (4), Winter.

Cho, Yoon-Je, and Kim, Joon-Kyung. 1997. *Credit Policies and the Industrialization of Korea.* Seoul: Korea Development Institute Press.

Haggard, Stephan. 1994. "Business, Politics and Policy in Northeast and Southeast Asia," in Andrew MacIntyre, ed., *Business and Government in Industrializing Asia.* Ithaca: Cornell University Press.

———. 2000. *The Political Economy of the Asian Financial Crisis.* Washington, DC: Institute for International Economics.

Hahm, Joon-Ho. 2000. "Interest Rate and Exchange Rate Exposure of Korean Financial Institutions: Implications for the Propagation of Financial Crisis." Mimeo, Yonsei University.

Hahm, Joon-Ho, and Mishkin, Frederic S. 2000. "The Korean Financial Crisis: An Asymmetric Information Perspective," *Emerging Markets Review*, 1: 21–52.

Hahn, Chin-Hee. 1999. "Implicit Loss-Protection and the Investment Behavior of Korean *Chaebol*: An Empirical Analysis" (in Korean), *KDI Journal of Economic Policy*, 21 (1): 3–52.

Joh, Sung-Wook. 1999a. "The Korean Corporate Sector: Crisis and Reform." Mimeo, Korea Development Institute August.

———. 1999b. "Profitability of Korean Firms before the 1997 Economic Crisis" (in Korean), *KDI Journal of Economic Policy*, 21 (2): 3–48.

Kim, Eun Mee. 1988. "From Dominance to Symbiosis: State and *Chaebol* in Korea," *Pacific Focus*, 3, Fall.

Kim, Joon-Kyung. 1999. "Policy Directions to Improve Ownership Structure of Financial Institutions" (in Korean). Mimeo, Korea Development Institute.

Kim, Se-Jin, and Lee, Dong Gull. 1999. "Agenda of Financial Restructuring" (in Korean). Paper presented at the Korea Money and Finance Association workshop on Improving Software in the Financial Industry, Seoul, June.

Lee, Chung H. 1992. "The Government, Financial System and Large Private Enterprise in the Economic Development of South Korea," *World Development*, 20 (2): 187–97.

Lee, Chung H., Lee, Keun, and Lee, Kangkoo. 2000. *"Chaebol*, Financial Liberalization, and Economic Crisis: Transformation of Quasi-Internal Organization in Korea." Mimeo, University of Hawaii.

Lee, Kyu Uck. 1994. "Ownership–Management Relations in Korea Business," L. J. Cho and Y. H. Kim, eds, in *Korea's Political Economy*. Boulder: Westview Press.

Mo, Jongryn. 1999. "The Microfoundations of the Developmental State and the Asian Economic Crisis." Paper presented at the annual meeting of the American Political Science Association, Atlanta, Geo., September.

Moon, Chung-In. 1994. "Changing Patterns of Business–Government Relations in South Korea," in Andrew MacIntyre, ed. *Business and Government in Industrializing Asia*. Ithaca: Cornell University Press.

Perkins, Dwight H. 1997. "Structural Transformation and the Role of the State: Korea, 1945–1995," in D. S. Cha, K. S. Kim, and D. H. Perkins, eds, *The Korean Economy 1945–1995: Performance and Vision for the 21st Century*. Seoul: Korea Development Institute Press.

Shin, Inseok, and Joon-Ho, Hahm. 1998. "The Korean Crisis – Causes and Resolution." Working Paper 9805, July. Seoul: Korea Development Institute.

Yoo, Seong Min, and Lim, Youngjae. 1999. "Big Business in Korea: New Learning and Policy Issues." Working Paper 9901, February. Seoul: Korea Development Institute.

5 Corporate Governance and Performance in the 1990s

Sung Wook Joh and Euysung Kim

Since the Korean economic crisis of 1997, corporate governance has become a subject of active academic and policy debate. Many have pointed out the deficiencies in the "Korean way" of corporate governance that led to weakened fundamentals and the poor economic performance of Korean firms. However, direct evidence on the effects of different governance systems on corporate performance and competitiveness is still sparse. This chapter provides empirical evidence on the link between corporate governance and firm performance in the 1990s.

A number of existing studies focus on the relationship between corporate governance and firm performance. Most studies are based on macro-level, cross-country comparisons that are rarely convincing because there is no single model of good corporate governance that holds across all countries.[1] The effectiveness of different corporate governance systems is influenced by history, culture and differences in legal and regulatory frameworks, as well as the structure of product and factor markets (Maher and Anderson 1999). Hence, it does not make much sense to debate whether the "Anglo Saxon model" is superior to the "Japanese model" or the "German model". Moreover, given that there are significant variations in corporate governance systems within each country, we cannot even be sure whether such countrywide comparisons are valid.

This study therefore joins the small but growing literature that focuses on firm-level data within countries. The search for good practice should be based on identification of what works within a given country. Lessons for Korea's corporate governance reform need to draw on Korean data.

Using firm-level data during the period leading up to the crisis (from 1993 to 1997), we examine the impact of corporate governance structure on two measures of corporate performance: profitability and productivity.[2] Profitability is an obvious measure of corporate performance from the shareholder's perspective. Most standard models of the firm are based on the premise that the firm's objective is to maximize profit. Our second measure, productivity, is not introduced as an alternative to profitability as a measure of a firm's performance; rather, it is one of the key *determinants* of profitability. We are interested in this particular source of firms' profitability because it best reflects efficient investment by all stakeholders of the firm and the potential for long-term growth.[3] In an era of global competition where technological superiority determines the competitiveness of firms and industries, it is crucial to understand the ways in which different systems of corporate governance affect innovative activities and the entrepreneurship of corporations.

The first section discusses the analytical linkages between corporate governance structure and firm performance, and the second covers the data and sources used. The third and fourth sections identify some facts about Korean firms' corporate governance structure and performance, focusing on ownership and capital structure respectively. The fifth section analyzes corporate performance prior to the 1997 economic crisis, and the sixth presents the estimation results of the relationship between corporate governance structure and firm performance.

1 Corporate Governance and Firm Performance

"Corporate governance" has many different meanings. According to Shleifer and Vishny (1997), corporate governance defines the ways in which the supplier of finance to corporations is assured of getting a return on their investment in a firm. A firm includes management, capital suppliers (including debt-holders, equity-holders and their representatives – that is, boards of directors), and other stakeholders such as employees. By defining the firm's rules, incentives and goals, these parties affect the mechanisms by which capital and resources are allocated, profits are distributed, and performance is monitored. While a number of different dimensions of corporate governance structure can be identified for the purpose of understanding their impact on firm performance, we emphasize two key aspects: ownership concentration and capital structure.[4]

A frequent question about the effect of corporate governance on a firm's performance is whether an owner-controlled (insider) system is better than a manager-controlled (outsider) system. Analytically, the answer is not obvious. Concentrated ownership provides better monitoring and is thus able to overcome the agency problem posed by misalignment of interest between shareholders and managers. But the controlling shareholder, with privileged access to management, might

be less concerned with total profit and more interested in the extraction
of private rents at the expense of minority shareholders. The question is
basically an empirical one as to which effect dominates.[5]

Another important dimension of ownership concentration that
relates more directly to the relationship between governance and
productivity is the effect of owner concentration on investment
horizons. In outsider systems, widely dispersed ownership offers
enhanced liquidity of stocks and better risk diversification for investors.
But from the firm's perspective, a governance system that allows high
investor turnover may encourage managers to focus excessively on
projects with short-term payoffs and provide weak incentives for stakeholders to make firm-specific investments (Mayer 1996). Projects with
long-term payoffs, such as research and development and firm-specific
human capital investments, may be undervalued as a result of stock
market myopia. This, in turn, would affect the firm's innovation, technological development and long-term growth.

In insider systems of corporate governance, concentrated ownership
typically implies lack of liquidity in secondary markets. For example,
investors may withhold funds because they fear exploitation by the
controlling blockholder. But this may help to encourage more long-
term relationships and commitment among stakeholders. The ongoing
nature of relations between various stakeholders, including banks,
suppliers, clients and the workforce, may promote greater investment in
firm-specific assets. This relationship is particularly important in high-
technology activities with highly specific assets.

The second major issue is the role of the capital structure in corporate
governance. Lee (1995) argues that the choice of the mix of debt and
equity in corporate financing can be interpreted as a choice for different
governance systems. Under certain conditions, a firm's debt–equity
structure will not affect the firm's value (Modigliani and Miller 1958).
But changes in debt–equity mix can have important effects on a firm's
behavior (Williamson 1988; Grossman and Hart 1986; Jensen 1986;
Stulz 1990). Since a rise in debt increases default risk, debt financing
could have a disciplinary effect on managers who fear bankruptcy. Bond
covenants specifying the manager's discretionary use of funds can
constrain management behavior. In general, a governance system based
on debt financing can be characterized as one functioning through strict
rules, while a governance system based on equity financing allows
greater flexibility and discretion.

These characterizations offer testable conjectures about the relationship between a firm's capital structure and its performance. If active
equity markets encourage innovative activity and entrepreneurship,
firms relying on equity financing should see higher profit and more

productivity growth. Debt financing, on the other hand, does not favor high risk: the innovative activities which could raise a firm's productivity and hence profit potential in the long run. This is because banks (or debt-holders) face an asymmetric risk. In the worst case, the bank can lose all the credit it has extended; but should the firm succeed, the best the bank can hope for is to be fully repaid with interest. The bank is thus excessively exposed to downside risk and would favor conservative projects.[6]

Despite their plausibility, the test of these hypotheses is not straight-forward. In Korea, one could argue that the government's implicit guarantee has virtually eliminated the default risk for the *chaebol*. Hence, *chaebol* with preferential bank financing could take more risks than non-*chaebol* firms with similar levels of debt financing. It would therefore be interesting to see whether capital structure has a different impact on the performance of *chaebol* and non-*chaebol* firms. Moreover, if the risk-taking made *chaebol* more innovative and entrepreneurial, their dependence on debt financing could be associated with *better* firm performance. On the other hand, if *chaebol's* risk-taking is better explained by the recklessness associated with moral hazard, then debt financing would have quite the opposite impact on their performance.

To test these two main hypotheses, we must control for a variety of other factors that can jointly affect corporate governance structure (measured in terms of ownership concentration and capital structure) and firm performance (measured as profitability and productivity). When using profitability as a measure of performance, we introduce a number of variables that are standard correlates of profitability: firm size (measured as the log of asset size), market share, R&D intensity (measured as R&D expenses over sales), advertisement over sales ratio, and export over sales ratio.[7]

In the case of productivity performance, some of the obvious candidates include exposure to trade (also measured as export-to-sales ratio) and R&D intensity. Firms' exposure to trade, in particular, would be important to include in the analysis because it might not only affect productivity performance but also have non-trivial effects on shaping firms' corporate governance systems. A growing body of literature suggests that the globalization of capital markets and liberalization of trade could force convergence of corporate governance systems (Shinn 1999). If true, the exclusion of trade could lead to classic omitted variable bias.

In several regression analyses, we include a separate *chaebol* (business group) dummy variable to test whether the performance of *chaebol* is superior to that of independent firms for reasons apart from differences in corporate governance structures. For example, *chaebol* might enjoy

higher profitability because of lower transaction costs, network external-
ities and the advantages of internal capital markets.[8] As for *chaebol's*
productivity performance, the typical argument is that their ability to
diversify risk allows them to be better innovators. With lower capital
costs, they are also better able to purchase technology from abroad.

On the other hand, there are also strong arguments suggesting that
chaebol's growth mostly resulted from crony capitalism and had little to
do with efficiency (see Chapter 1). In fact, their excessive diversification
into unrelated areas and monopolistic behavior caused *chaebol* to be
inefficient and unprofitable.

Finally, there might be other factors, such as industry-specific
characteristics (related to markets or products) or political and macroeconomic instability, which are important determinants of firms'
profitability and productivity. Because these factors are difficult to
measure on a firm-level basis, we employ a dummy variable. An
industry-specific dummy is introduced to capture the effects of all
omitted attributes that vary across industries but do not change over
time.[9] A time-specific dummy captures discrete productivity shocks specific to the period in which they occur but common to all firms (such as
macroeconomic and political shocks).

2   Data

This study employs detailed financial information on publicly traded
firms between 1993 and 1997, collected by National Information and
Credit Evaluation Inc. (NICE). Each firm reports its financial statement to the Korea Securities Supervisory Board. Upon receiving the
financial data from the board, NICE checks the integrity of the data. All
dependent and independent variables used in this chapter (with a few
exceptions such as price deflators) are based on NICE data. After
excluding financial institutions and state-controlled firms from the
analysis, our data set includes 1925 observations on manufacturing
firms, of which 552 observations belong to *chaebol*.

A few comments about some of the explanatory variables are in order.
Market share is calculated as a firm's share in industry sales measured at
the four-digit level. As for ownership information, the NICE data set
includes the names of large individual and institutional shareholders,
their family members and their shareholdings. After identifying all institutional owners and their shareholdings, we subtracted them from the
sum of large shareholders' ownership. Through this calculation for each
firm, we derived the controlling family's direct ownership stake.[10]

The selection of the thirty largest *chaebol* follows the classification of the Korea Fair Trade Commission (KFTC), which is based on the size of total assets. These groups are subject to several restrictions on bank lending and a ceiling on the groups' equity investment. We also identify forty additional *chaebol* based on the magnitude of their debt. Using debt size rather than asset size to choose *chaebol* results in nearly the same sample. In effect, the *chaebol* dummy includes firms that belong to the seventy largest *chaebol* groups.

As for dependent variables, we use the ratio of ordinary income to assets (ROA) as a measure of profitability. Profitability is an obvious choice as a measure of firm performance because payoffs to both creditors and shareholders are directly correlated with the firm's profits. Although the level of profit is a direct measure of profitability, it is related to the size of the firm; ROA is less affected by the firm size.

Our measure of productivity performance (total factor productivity, TFP) is estimated using a multilateral index approach originally developed by Caves, Christensen and Diewert (1982) and later extended by Good, Nadiri and Sickles (1996).[11] The index provides a measure of the proportional differences in TFP for each firm in each year relative to a hypothetical firm with average TFP in the base year. This multilateral productivity index is particularly useful in panel-data applications because it provides a consistent way of summarizing the cross-sectional distribution of firm productivity, using only information specific to that period and how the distribution moves over time. We analyze productivity changes over time and across firms by comparing their productivity with the productivity of the average hypothetical firm in the base year. We then try to account for these productivity differentials by looking at governance variables, industry-specific variables, and others.[12] Detailed information on data on output and inputs of capital, labor, and intermediate goods used to construct the index of TFP can be found in the Appendix.

3   The Ownership Structure of Korean Firms

The long-held convention about East Asian corporations had been that they have concentrated ownership structures (Rajan and Zingales 1998; La Porta et al. 1998a).[13] However, Korea (along with Japan) has been noted as an exception; both countries have a widely dispersed ownership structure (La Porta et al. 1998a, 1998b; Claessens et al. 1998).[14] Our data also confirm the view that control of Korean corporations can be achieved with significantly less than an absolute majority of the stock (see also Chapters 1, 2 and 12). For all firms in our sample, controlling family members owned 21.3 percent of their firms on average. However, this was only 12.7 percent for *chaebol* firms, and 24.7 percent for non-*chaebol* firms.

Our definition of *chaebol* firms includes the seventy largest business groups in Korea, so our finding is consistent with Claessens et al. (1998) and La Porta et al. (1998b) that size matters in explaining the distribution of ownership concentration. In most countries, these studies found that the share of family ownership was higher for smaller firms. Claessens et al. (1998), for example, show that only four of the largest twenty Korean firms in their sample had family ownership above 20 percent, while forty-eight of the smallest fifty companies had ownership exceeding 20 percent.

Family control with low ownership concentration is possible for a number of reasons. First, relatively weak laws protecting small shareholders allow controlling shareholders to maintain low ownership stakes. According to the Korea Stock Exchange, about 97 percent of the shareholders in listed firms are small individual shareholders. Small shareholders together owned 60 percent of total shares in the 1980s and 40 percent in 1997. With a wide dispersion of ownership among small shareholders, the free-rider problem in monitoring the controlling shareholder is severe. Moreover, during the 1993–97 period, Korean law required at least 5-percent ownership for a shareholder to exercise rights such as demanding convocation, inspecting account books and filing derivative suits.[15]

In Korea, the restriction on the voting rights of institutional investors in listed companies is an additional factor allowing effective control with low ownership stakes. For example, "shadow voting" regulations required institutional investors to cast their votes proportionately to other votes. Despite their significant ownership stakes in Korean corporations, institutional investors posed no threat to the controlling shareholder despite their low ownership stake.

Controlling families in *chaebol*-affiliated firms are also able to exercise control through interlocking ownership among subsidiaries. The patterns of institutional interlocking ownership found in *chaebol*-affiliated firms are complicated because of their need to circumvent regulations which prevent direct circular interlocking ownership (firm A owns firm B, and firm B in turn owns firm A).[16] Nonetheless, according to the KFTC, the average interlocking inter-subsidiary ownership exceeded 33 percent in the 1990s. Interlocking shareholdings imply that in-group ownership friendly to the controlling family could be quite high, making any challenges to management virtually impossible.

4   The Financing of Korean Firms

The financial crisis of 1997 revealed how vulnerable the Korean economy was to the high leveraging of its corporate sector. In 1997, the average debt–equity ratio for Korea was 396 percent, while the comparable figure for the United States was 154 percent, Japan 193 percent, and Taiwan 86 percent.[17] Although Korea's debt dependency increased somewhat during the crisis period, the debt–equity ratio had been high throughout its development history. Hence, it is not simply a change in the level of debt financing, a sudden credit expansion and lending boom, that caused the 1997 crisis.[18] Nor was it a simple liquidity crisis due to mismatched term structure in corporate debt financing. We want to know whether Korea's high reliance on a debt-based corporate governance system, as opposed to equity-based financing, can be linked to fundamental weaknesses in the Korean corporate sector.

Why did Korean corporations overwhelmingly choose a debt-based corporate governance structure instead of an equity-based one? Joh (1999) argues that the high level of debt is the outcome of past governments' policies, particularly subsidized credit in support of the government's industrialization drive. However, firms that received preferential finance were not always profitable and faced periodic financial distress.[19] In these instances, the government rescued troubled companies with favorable loans from government-controlled banks.

The practice of government bailouts continued long after policy lending had stopped, weakening banks and exacerbating moral hazard for firm managers. This problem of moral hazard was particularly severe for *chaebol* firms. The average equity ratio (equity divided by assets) of publicly traded firms in our sample was 34.4 percent. However, the ratio for the largest seventy *chaebol* was much lower (27.7 percent) than for the non-*chaebol* firms (37 percent).

Chaebol-affiliated firms were particularly capable of raising bank financing because of interlocking ownership and debt payment guarantees. The belief that they were "too big to fail" created incentives for firms

Table 5.1 Equity investment of the 30 largest *chaebol* (trillion *won*, %)

	1995	1996	1997
Equity investment (A)	1.13	1.36	1.69
Equity (B)	5.07	6.29	7.04
Ratio (A/B)	22.3	21.6	24.0

Source: Korea Fair Trade Commission.

Table 5.2   Debt payment guarantees of the 30 largest *chaebol* (trillion *won*)

Year	Equity (A)	Debt payment guarantees			Ratio (%)	
		Restriction (B)	No Restriction (C)	Sum (B+C)	B/A	(B+C)/A
1993	3.52	12.06	4.49	16.55	342.4	469.8
1994	4.28	7.25	3.82	11.07	169.3	258.1
1995	5.07	4.83	3.38	8.21	95.2	161.9
1996	6.29	3.52	3.23	6.75	55.9	107.3
1997	7.04	3.36	3.13	6.49	47.7	92.2

Note: The government imposed a ceiling on the debt payment to equity ratio depending on where firms borrowed. "Restriction" is the share of guarantees subject to this ceiling.
Source: Korea Fair Trade Commission.

to exaggerate their size to facilitate bank financing; this was particularly easy for *chaebol* engaged in intra-group inter-subsidiary transactions.[20] As seen in Table 5.1, the average equity investment ratio (equity investment divided by equity) exceeds 20 percent in the top thirty *chaebol*.

The widespread use of debt payment guarantees also made it possible for large *chaebol*-affiliated firms to gain easy access to bank credits. Debt payment guarantees can reduce information asymmetry when the firm that provides the guarantees has more information than creditors. However, debt payment guarantees can also lead to over-borrowing and chain bankruptcies. Table 5.2 shows that the amount of payment guarantees exceeded the level of equity.[21]

5   Performance of the Korean Corporate Sector Prior to the Crisis

As we saw from Figure 1.2, Korea's corporate sector showed very low profitability for ten years before the crisis. Firms did not even earn the opportunity cost of capital (roughly measured by the borrowing interest rate). The decade-long poor performance of the corporate sector is an obvious indicator of the fragility of the Korean corporate sector.

Using the methodology described in section 2, we have constructed indexes of total factor productivity (TFP) for the period from 1993 to 1997. Table 5.3 compares the productivity of firms at the 25th, 50th, and 75th percentiles with that of the median hypothetical firm in the

Table 5.3   Efficiency comparison with the average firm in 1993 (%)

Efficiency	1993	1994	1995	1996	1997
25th percentile	−34.66	−31.01	−32.06	−30.30	−26.33
Median	−0.03	1.75	−1.75	5.54	3.22
75th percentile	27.87	29.47	32.14	31.49	36.08

Note: The total factor productivity of firms at the 25th, 50th, and 75th percentiles each year is compared with that of the average hypothetical firm in the 1993 base year.

1993 base year. For example, the estimate of −1.75 for the median firm in 1995 means that the output performance of the median firm in 1995 was 1.75 percentage points lower than what the 1993 benchmark firm could have produced with the same factor inputs as the 1995 median firm. The median firm in 1995 was thus less efficient than the average hypothetical firm in 1993.

With respect to the changes in the shape of the distribution from year to year, there is no evidence of substantial widening or narrowing. The dispersion in the interquartile range stayed roughly the same. Productivity did increase over time. The cumulative productivity change for the median firm was about 3 percentage points, while firms at the 25th and 75th percentiles saw a change of about 8 percentage points between 1993 and 1995. As a result, the distribution became relatively more skewed to the right.

Focusing on the average productivity performance of the median firms, we find substantial variation within the four-year period. The median firm's productivity differential of 3.22 percentage points in 1997 translates into less than one percentage point annual average increase over 1993–97. However, it represents a *decline* of 2.32 percentage points from the median firm's productivity differential for the previous year of 5.54 percentage points. In sum, relatively low productivity growth came about in the midst of relatively large variations in productivity performance. The question we address is whether any portion of this trend movement and fluctuations in productivity performance can be attributed to changes in the corporate governance structure of Korean firms.

6   Empirical Tests and Results

The call for corporate governance reform in Korea is rarely based on a solid empirical foundation. Simple cross-country benchmark

Table 5.4   Impact of corporate governance on firm-level profitability

	Dependent variable	
	Rate of return on assets (1)	Rate of return on assets (2)
Corporate governance variables		
Ownership	0.0755	0.0774
concentration	(8.93)	(8.40)
Equity ratio	0.0743	0.0741
	(7.40)	(7.50)
Control variables		
Chaebol dummy		−0.9110
		(−2.15)
Log (Assets)		0.0735
		(0.32)
R&D expenditure/		0.0667
sales		(0.77)
Export/sales		0.0166
		(2.34)
Advertisement/sales		0.1784
		(1.96)
Market share		0.0298
		(2.55)
Industry and time dummies included	Yes	Yes
Number of observations	1925	1925
Adjusted R^2	0.1745	0.1824

Note: Numbers in brackets are t-values controlling for White's heteroskedasticity.

comparisons serve as the bases for policy recommendations without any consideration of the context under which different governance systems operate. In this section, we evaluate the relationship between corporate governance structure (as characterized by each firm's ownership concentration and capital structure) and firm performance in a sample of publicly traded manufacturing firms.

Table 5.4 presents the estimated impact of corporate governance on firm performance (using profitability as the dependent variable). The first model regresses corporate profitability on corporate governance variables. The results show that both ownership concentration and equity ratios (equity divided by assets) have a significant and positive impact on profitability. With each percentage point increase in ownership and in the equity ratio, the rate of return on assets rises by an average of 0.076 and 0.074 percentage points, respectively. The magnitude of this change may not be as small as it appears. A doubling of the current equity ratio in Korean firms (which was about 34.4 percent during the period for our sample) would lead to an increase of 2.55 percentage points in profitability. If Korean firms had moved their equity ratios closer to other advanced countries, the profitability would have been more than twice the actual rate of return on assets of 2.51 percent during 1993–97.

The second model estimates the impact of corporate governance indicators on firm profitability along with the control variables outlined above. The regression results show that the coefficients on the corporate governance variables are quite robust to the change in specification. The *chaebol* dummy variable (associated with the top seventy business groups) is quite significant, showing that the profitability of *chaebol* is on average less than non-*chaebol* firms. One hypothesis was that firms affiliated in *chaebol* groups would have lower transaction costs, lower capital costs, and other advantages that non-*chaebol* firms do not share. According to our analysis of the 1993–97 period, the inefficiencies in the *chaebol's* way of doing business (possibly due to excessive diversification, crony capitalism, or other factors) were more serious than the presumed advantages.

It is worth noting here that our results also contradict Chang and Choi (1988), who found that *chaebol* performed better than independent Korean firms, using data from 1975 to 1984. One possible explanation for the difference is that the period underlying their results overlaps with Korea's heavy and chemical industry drive of 1973–79, in which *chaebol* in favored industries enjoyed oligopoly rents and received preferential policy loans at subsidized interest rates. These government-induced *chaebol* advantages in fact continued until the Industrial Development Act and the Monopoly Regulation and Fair Trade Act were enacted in the 1980s. Hence, the conclusion drawn by Chang and Choi (1988) that group-affiliated firms show superior performance because such structure reduces transaction costs arising from organizational failure must be seriously questioned.[22] Given the unique status of *chaebol* in the Korean economy, one could presume that the corporate governance system in *chaebol* firms works quite differently from that of non-*chaebol* firms. Table 5.5 checks the robustness of the previous result by running the same regression on the sub-sample of *chaebol*-affiliated firms.

The results reported in Table 5.5 are qualitatively the same as those reported in Table 5.4. The coefficients on corporate governance variables are now somewhat smaller, but both are still significant. As for

Table 5.5 Profitability of *chaebol*-affiliated firms

	Dependent variable	
	Rate of return on assets (1)	Rate of return on assets (2)
Corporate governance variables		
Ownership	0.0493	0.0667
concentration	(2.97)	(3.67)
Equity ratio	0.0600	0.0653
	(3.61)	(3.84)
Log (Assets)		1.3269
		(3.35)
R&D expenditure/		–0.2668
sales		(–1.84)
Control variables		
Export/sales		0.0359
		(2.72)
Advertisement/sales		0.0747
		(0.36)
Market share		–0.0304
		(–1.85)
Industry and time dummies included	Yes	Yes
Number of observations	552	552
Adjusted R²	0.1287	0.1991

Note: Numbers in brackets are t-values controlling for White's heteroskedasticity.

control variables, the coefficient on the export/sales variable is now larger and still significant. The size of assets is also now a significant variable explaining *chaebol's* profitability. The market share variable, on the other hand, is no longer significant at the 5-percent level.

As a next step, we employ the relative productivity differences of Korean firms as a measure of corporate performance. Again, regression is estimated without control variables for the purpose of comparison. Again, we report results from the full sample (Table 5.6) and from the sub-sample of *chaebol*-affiliated firms (Table 5.7). The results are essentially the same. Hence we restrict our discussion to the estimates reported in Table 5.6.

Table 5.6 Impact of corporate governance on firm-level productivity differences

	Dependent variable	
	Rate of return on assets (1)	Rate of return on assets (2)
Corporate governance variables		
Ownership	0.0040	0.0018
concentration	(7.49)	(3.31)
Equity ratio	0.0003	−0.0007
	(0.52)	(−0.98)
Chaebol dummy		−0.1101
		(−4.15)
Control variables		
R&D expenditure/		−0.0201
sales		(−3.18)
Export/sales		−0.0002
		(−0.63)
Industry and time dummies included	Yes	Yes
Number of observations	1925	1925
R^2	0.2506	0.3046

Note: Numbers in brackets are t-values controlling for White's heteroskedasticity.

Unlike the previous case, where firm performance was measured in terms of profitability, productivity is significantly and positively related only to ownership concentration. With the average controlling shareholder's ownership being 21.3 percent for this sample, we expect the productivity for firms with average ownership to exceed that for firms with negligible family ownership by about 0.8 percentage points. The impact of the concentration of controlling shareholder's ownership on corporate performance (regardless of the measures used) is robust.

We had expected the equity ratio to have a significant and positive impact on productivity performance, given the presumption that an equity-based governance structure is more conducive to innovative activities than a debt-based governance structure. However, the result shows that the equity ratio loses its significance when performance is measured by productivity.

However, it is important to note that the *chaebol* dummy is again highly significant and negative. The common presumption that *chaebol's* cost advantages and ability to diversify risk make them better innovators and acquirers of technology turns out to be wrong; *chaebol* underperform non-*chaebol* firms with both profitability and productivity as the performance measure.[23]

Table 5.7 Relative productivity performance of *chaebol*-affiliated firms

	Dependent variable	
	LnTFP (1)	LnTFP (2)
Corporate governance variables		
Ownership	0.0042	0.0027
concentration	(3.01)	(1.92)
Equity ratio	0.0008	0.0004
	(0.75)	(0.40)
Control variables		
R&D		−0.0266
expenditure/		(−2.39)
sales		−0.0006
Export/sales		(−0.74)
Industry and time dummies included	Yes	Yes
Number of observations	552	552
R^2	0.2281	0.2697

Note: Numbers in brackets are t-values controlling for White's heteroskedasticity.

7   Conclusion

This chapter has examined the relationship between corporate governance structure, measured by controlling shareholder's ownership concentration and financial structure, and performance. With panel data of publicly traded Korean firms from 1993 to 1997, we have identified a robust relationship between ownership concentration and profitability and productivity. Higher ownership concentration is associated with stronger firm performance. We interpret this result to confirm the hypothesis that higher ownership concentration leads to greater convergence of interest between the controlling shareholder and other shareholders, which in turn leads to better corporate performance. The equity ratio retains its significant and positive impact on firm performance only when performance is measured with profitability (ROA).

In addition, we found a significant and negative impact of *chaebol* affiliation on corporate performance. Despite many possible *chaebol* advantages, this study shows that *chaebol*-affiliated firms have inferior performance when compared to non-*chaebol* firms in terms of both profitability and productivity.

Our findings suggest that the problems with Korean *chaebol* are that their controlling shareholders have too little ownership stake in the firms and their capital structure relies too much on debt financing. When controlling shareholders own large stakes in the company, their incentive to expropriate from minority shareholders is checked by the fact that too much expropriation would negatively affect the total profit of the company. The controlling shareholders in Korean *chaebol* do not have adequate ownership stakes in the companies they control, so the incentive for expropriation is greater. Although there are no simple solutions to problems in Korea's corporate governance system, it seems that the most crucial reform must be directed at the laws and practices that allow unchallenged management control in *chaebol* firms despite relatively minor ownership stakes of the controlling family.

There are, however, a number of reasons to be cautious about taking these conclusions too far. This chapter has not dealt with several important issues that might help us better understand the importance of corporate governance. Our ownership data are limited in that they only account for direct ownership by the controlling shareholder. Our results might change if one could get at the "ultimate" ownership data. Also, we have not explored the possibility that the relationship between corporate governance data might be nonlinear or more importantly, endogenous. Corporate performance might determine corporate governance structure.

Appendix: The Measurement of Firm-Level Total Factor Productivity

Measurement of firm-level productivity performance requires data on output, intermediate, capital, and labor input, and factor shares (see Haggard and Kim 1997). For manufacturing firms listed in Korea's stock exchange, detailed financial information included in the NICE data set provides most of the data required for the measurement of productivity index. We have constructed estimates of TFP indexes for the period from 1993 to 1997, for which we have matched ownership data.

Firm output is defined as total sales deflated by a wholesale price index at the two-digit industry level. As for labor inputs, we used the total number of both production and non-production workers, adjusted by annual changes in average work hours per day in the manufacturing sector and by two digit-level average monthly workdays. The measure of capital input is the book value of capital stock of the firm. Following Aw, Chung and Roberts (1998), we have adjusted the book values for yearly price changes in addition of new capital equipment. The measure of material input includes raw materials and manufacturing costs (such as electricity, water, fuel and subcontracting costs), and it is deflated by an intermediate input price index. All price indexes used come from the Bank of Korea's yearly publication of price statistics.

For factor shares, labor income share is measured as total salaries (including retirement benefit payments) to total workers divided by the value of output. The intermediate share is measured as the expenditure share of intermediate input in the value of output. Applying the standard assumption of constant returns, the capital income share is obtained as a residual by subtracting labor share and intermediate input share from one. Kim (2000) actually showed that constant returns are a reasonable assumption in the Korean case.

Using the data on Korean firms, the index of the proportional difference in TFP for plant f in year t relative to the hypothetical plant in the base year can be calculated using this equation (following Aw, Chung and Roberts 1998):

$$\ln TFP_{ft} = (\ln Y_{ft} - \overline{\ln Y_t}) + \sum_{s=2}^{t} (\overline{\ln Y_s} - \overline{\ln Y_{s-1}})$$

$$- [\sum_{i=1}^{n} \frac{1}{2}(S_{ift} + \overline{S_{it}})(\ln X_{ift} - \overline{\ln X_{it}})$$

$$+ \sum_{s=2}^{t} \sum_{i=1}^{n} \frac{1}{2}(\overline{S_{is}} + \overline{S_{is-1}})(\overline{\ln X_{is}} - \overline{\ln X_{is-1}})]$$

where Y_{ft} is the output of firm f in year t; X_i is the input i; and S_i is the factor income share of input i. The overbars denote the average value over all firms in year t.

Notes

1 See Gugler (1999) for a survey.
2 Several previous studies of Korea are related to this issue. For example, Chang and Choi (1988) focus on the impact of transaction costs on firm performance and Chang and Hong (1998) focus on performance consequences of resource sharing among group-affiliated firms. Joh (2000) examines the relationship between firm profitability and corporate governance.
3 There is a strong theoretical presumption in both traditional and new growth theories that the main engine of sustained long-run economic growth is productivity growth. The new endogenous growth theories in particular show a number of different ways in which productivity advances can occur: learning by doing, human capital accumulation, R&D. If the corporate governance system affects any of these mechanisms, it would be an important factor in determining the rate of technological progress.
4 Other features of governance often emphasized include the market for corporate control and the role of boards of directors.
5 Previous analyses based primarily on US and UK data have suggested that "owner-controlled" firms significantly outperform "manager-controlled" firms. See Leech and Leahy (1991), Prowse (1992), Agrawal and Knoeber (1996) and Cho (1998). But these results are specific to the country in which the study is conducted; the question is, given Korea's legal and institutional context, whether insider systems dominate outsider ones.
6 Carlin and Mayer (1999) suggest that debt-financed firms may be effective in earlier stages of accumulation-based growth, whereas equity-financed firms may be effective in later, more "mature" stages of productivity-based growth that requires R&D.
7 See Gale (1972) and Martin (1993) for a summary of these linkages.
8 See Leff (1978) for arguments along these lines.
9 A study by Zeckhauser and Pound (1990), for example, found that owner-controlled firms outperform manager-controlled firms in industries with

relatively low asset specificity (e.g. machinery and paper products) but found no difference in industries with relatively high asset specificity (e.g. computers). Hence there might be some interactive relationships, which also should be explored.

10 Because it is not always possible to identify whether an individual shareholder identified in the NICE data is related to the controlling family, our approach can be considered an upward estimate of the overall controlling family's direct ownership.

11 The approach has been used recently by Aw, Chung and Roberts (1998) to estimate TFP of Taiwanese and Korean plant-level data and this study follows the same methodology to calculate the Korean firm-level TFP estimates.

12 Good, Nadiri and Sickles (1996) provide a detailed discussion on methodology.

13 Most recent studies show that a highly concentrated ownership is quite common throughout developed countries as well (Demsetz and Ricardo-Campbell 1983; Shleifer and Vishny 1986; Morck, Shleifer and Vishny 1988; and La Porta et al. 1998a).

14 Among 356 publicly traded Korean corporations in their sample, Claessens et al. (1998) find that less than 4 percent of the firms were controlled by families that own at least 40 percent of the shares, while 20 percent of all firms were controlled by families with less than 30 percent of the shares. Families with at least 10 percent of the total shares controlled more than 67 percent of Korean firms. La Porta et al. (1998a) studied a sample of the ten largest non-financial corporations from a cross-section of 49 countries and found that the average ownership by the three largest shareholders in Korean corporations was 23 percent, much lower than the ownership concentration of 46 percent found for the whole sample.

15 The minimum ownership requirements for shareholders' rights have been lowered since 1998.

16 Moreover, holding companies were not allowed in Korea until 1998.

17 The Taiwanese figure is based on 1996 data.

18 The portion of short-term debt in the overall debt portfolio did rise significantly and exposed the Korean corporate sector to term structure risk. But, analytically there is no reason to presume that this change in term structure would lead to fundamental weakness in corporate performance. Our focus, however, is on whether a debt-based corporate governance structure is intrinsically worse than equity-based corporate governance in terms of performance.

19 The Korean corporate sector faced extreme difficulties in 1972, following the second oil shock in 1979, and during the 1984–88 recession in the overseas construction, shipping, textile, machinery, and lumber industries.

20 For example, through interlocking ownership, firm A invests its assets in an affiliated firm B. As a result, the sum of the assets of firm A and firm B can exceed the total assets of the group. At least 60 percent of firms subject to external auditing report that they have legally affiliated firms. See Joh (1999).

21 It is quite likely that the level of debt payment guarantees is higher than indicated in Table 5.2. The amount of payment guarantee reported does not

include guarantees for money borrowed abroad and prevalent interlocking ownership among affiliated firms exaggerates much of the equity in the same group. In many of the recent cases of *chaebol* bankruptcies, firms failed because they had overextended debt guarantees.

22 Nam (1979) calculates that SMEs have debt-financing costs (after-tax annual interest costs) that are more than 5 percentage points higher than large firms. This shows the extent of government subsidy on large firms. Moreover, according to Chang and Choi's (1988, Table III) own regression results, the coefficients on *chaebol* dummies are basically insignificant for profit after taxes but before interest. In other words, their claim is not robustly supported by the evidence.

23 The R&D ratio was found to have a significant and negative impact on productivity in both the full and *chaebol* samples. This is a quite puzzling outcome, perhaps due to a specification problem. Regression (1) in Table 5.6 is in reduced form; we do not specify the precise mechanism through which corporate governance impacts productivity performance. But if ownership and capital structure affect productivity performance by encouraging firm-specific investments such as R&D, then measuring the impact of R&D on firm performance, apart from what is already captured by corporate governance variables, as in regression (2), may produce a spurious result.

References

Agrawal, Anup, and Knoeber, Charles R. 1996. "Firm Performance and Mechanisms to Control Agency Problems between Managers and Shareholders," *Journal of Financial and Quantitative Analysis*, 31 (3): 377–97.

Aw, Bee Yan, Chung, Sukkyun, and Roberts, Mark J. 1998. "Productivity and the Decision to Export: Micro Evidence from Taiwan and South Korea." National Bureau for Economic Research, Working Paper No. 6558.

Carlin, W. and Mayer, C. 1999. "Finance, Investment and Growth," CEPR Discussion Paper No. 2233. London: Centre for Economic Policy Research.

Caves, Douglas W., Christensen, Laurits R., and Diewert, Erwin W. 1982. "Multilateral Comparisons of Output, Input, and Productivity Using Superlative Index Numbers," *The Economic Journal*, 92 (365): 73–86.

Chang, H. J., Park, Hong-Jae, and Yoo, Chu Gyue. 1998. "Interpreting the Korean Crisis: Financial Liberalization, Industrial Policy, and Corporate Governance," *Cambridge Journal of Economics*, 22 (6): 735–46.

Chang, Sejin, and Choi, Unghwan. 1988. "Strategy, Structure and Performance of Korean Business Groups: A Transactions Cost Approach," *Journal of Industrial Economics*, 37 (2): 141–58.

Chang, Sejin and Hong, Jaebum. 1998. "Economic Performance of Korean Business Groups: Intra-Group Resource Sharing and Internal Business Transaction." Mimeo.

Cho, M. H. 1998. "Ownership Structure, Investment and the Corporate Value: An Empirical Analysis," *Journal of Financial Economics*, 47 (1): 103–21.

Claessens, Joseph, Fan, P. H., and Lang, Larry. 1998. "Ownership Structure and Corporate Performance in East Asia." Mimeo, World Bank.

Demsetz, Harold, and Ricardo-Campbell, Rita. 1983. "The Structure of Ownership and the Theory of the Firm," *Journal of Law and Economics*, 26 (2): 375–93.

Edwards, S. 1998. "Openness, Productivity and Growth: What Do We Really Know?" *Economic Journal*, 108 (447): 383–98.

Gale, Bradley T. 1972. "Market Share and Rate-of-Return," *Review of Economics and Statistics*, 54 (4): 412–23.

Good, David H., Nadiri, M. Ishaq, and Sickles, Robin C. 1996. "Index Number and Factor Demand Approaches to the Estimation of Productivity." National Bureau for Economic Research, Working Paper No. 5790.

Grossman, Sanford J., and Hart, Oliver D. 1986. "The Costs and Benefits of Ownership: A Theory of Vertical and Lateral Integration," *Journal of Political Economy*, 94 (4): 169–219.

Grossman, Sanford J., Hart, Oliver D., and Maskin, Eric S. 1983. "Implicit Contracts Under Asymmetric Information," *Quarterly Journal of Economics*, 98 (3): 123–56.

Gugler, K. 1999. "Corporate Governance and Economic Performance: A Survey." Mimeo, University of Vienna, Austria.

Haggard, Stephan, and Kim, Euysung. 1997. "The Sources of East Asia's Economic Growth," *Access Asia Review*, 1 (1): 31–63.

Jensen, Michael. 1986. "Agency Costs of Free Cash Flow, Corporate Finance and Takeovers," *American Economic Review*, 76 (2): 323–9.

———. 1988. "The Takeover Controversy: Analysis and Evidence," in J. Coffee, L. Lowenstein, and S. Rose-Ackerman, eds, *Knights, Raiders, and Targets: The Impact of the Hostile Takeover*, pp. 314–54. New York: Oxford University Press.

Joh, Sung Wook. 1999. "The Korean Corporate Sector: Crisis and Reform." KDI Working Paper no 9912, Seoul: Korea Development Institute.

———. 2000. "Does Shareholder Conflict Reduce Profitability? Evidence from Korea," in Inseok Shin, ed., *The Korean Crisis: Before and After*. Seoul: Korea Development Institute.

Kim, Euysung. 2000. "Trade Liberalization and Productivity Growth in Korean Manufacturing Industries: Price Protection, Market Power, and Scale Efficiency," *Journal of Development Economics*, 62 (1): 55–83.

La Porta, Rafael, Lopez-de-Silanes, Florencio, Shleifer, Andrei, and Vishny, Robert W. 1998a. "Law and Finance," *Journal of Political Economy*, 106 (6): 1113–55.

———. 1998b. "Agency Problems and Dividend Policies around the World." Mimeo, Harvard University.

Lee, Young-Ki. 1995. "Corporate Governance: The Structure and Issues in Korea." Mimeo, Seoul: Korea Development Institute.

Leech, D., and Leahy, J. 1991. "Ownership Structure, Control Type Classifications and the Performance of Large British Companies," *Economic Journal*, 101 (409): 1418–37.

Leff, N. 1978. "Industrial Organization and Entrepreneurship in the Developing Countries: The Economic Group," *Economic Development and Cultural Change*, 26 (4): 661–75.

Maher, M. E. 1997. "Transaction Cost Economics and Contractual Relations," *Cambridge Journal of Economics*, 21 (2): 147.

Maher, Maria, and Anderson, Thomas. 1999. *Corporate Governance: Effects on Firm Performance and Economic Growth*. Organization for Economic Cooperation and Development.

Martin, Stephen. 1993. *Advanced Industrial Economics*. Oxford: Blackwell.

Mayer, C. 1996. "Corporate Governance, Competition and Performance," *OECD Economic Studies*, 27: 7–34.

Modigliani, Franco, and Miller, Merton H. 1958. "The Cost of Capital, Corporation Finance, and the Theory of Investments," *American Economic Review*, 48: 261–97.

Morck, Randall, Shleifer, Andrei, and Vishny, Robert W. 1988. "Management Ownership and Market Valuation: An Empirical Analysis," *Journal of Financial Economics*, 20 (1–2): 293–315.

Nam, S. W. 1979. "Hankook Kiupui Chaemoo Koojowa Chabon Cost [Financial Structure and Capital Cost of Korean Companies]." *Hankook Gaebal Yunkoo*. Seoul: Korea Development Institute.

Prowse, S. D. 1992. "The Structure of Corporate Ownership in Japan," *Journal of Finance*, 47 (3): 1121–40.

——. 1994. "Corporate Governance in International Perspective: A Survey of Corporate Control Mechanisms Among Large Firms in the United States, the United Kingdom, Japan and Germany." BIS Economic Papers, no. 41.

Rajan, Raghuram G., and Zingales, Luigi. 1998. "Financial Dependence and Growth," *American Economic Review*, 88 (44): 18–19.

Randlesome, Collin, and Myers, Andrew. 1998. "Cultural Fluency: The United Kingdom versus Denmark," *European Business Journal*, 10 (4): 184–94.

Shinn, James. 1999. "Bringing the State Back in to the Boardroom: Corporate Governance Convergence in Japan and Korea?" Mimeo, Princeton University.

Shleifer, Andrei, and Vishny, Robert W. 1986. "Large Shareholders and Corporate Control," *Journal of Political Economy*, 94 (3): 461–88.

——. 1997. "A Survey of Corporate Governance," *Journal of Finance*, 52 (2): 737–83.

Stulz, R. M. 1990. "Managerial Discretion and Optimal Financing Policies," *Journal of Financial Economics*, 26 (1): 3–27.

Von Thadden, E. 1995. "Long-Term Contracts, Short-Term Investment and Monitoring," Review of Economic Studies, 62 (213): 557–75.

Williamson, O. E. 1975. *Markets and Hierarchies*. New York: Macmillan.

——. 1985. *The Economic Institutions of Capitalism*. New York: Free Press.

——. 1988. "Corporate Finance and Corporate Governance," *The Journal of Finance*, 43 (3): 567–91.

Zeckhauser, R., and Pound, J. 1990. "Are Large Shareholders Effective Monitors? An Investigation of Share Ownership and Corporate Performance," in R. Hubbard, ed., *Asymmetric Information*, Corporate Finance and Investment. Chicago: University of Chicago Press.

Part II
The Political Economy of Crisis Management

6 Business–Government Relations under Kim Dae-jung

Jongryn Mo and Chung-in Moon

The Korean economic miracle is often attributed in part to the symbiotic nature of the relationship between business and government (E. M. Kim 1997; Moon 1995). The state cultivated and patronized the private sector under broadly defined developmental objectives, while private firms, especially *chaebol*, served as the agents of economic growth and transformation. Unity of purpose as well as dense, organic networks between the public and private sectors fostered economic growth by mitigating uncertainty, expediting the flow of information, and reducing transaction costs.[1]

The 1997 economic crisis and subsequent structural reforms have radically restructured the political-economic terrain of business–government relations. Neoliberal reforms shattered the organic and symbiotic ties between the two, pitting the state against business. While the state was blamed for excessive intervention and poor monitoring, the private sector, especially the *chaebol*, did their part with poor corporate governance, reckless corporate expansion and high leveraging. The collusive ties between business and government were seen as the source of the rent-seeking, corruption and moral hazard that aggravated the economic downturn (Haggard and Mo 2000; Moon and Mo 2000; Yoo 1999, 2000; Jang 1999).

President Kim Dae-jung, who took office in February 1998, had a mandate to manage the economic crisis through sweeping corporate reforms. The International Monetary Fund (IMF), which had coordinated a rescue financing of $57 billion in November 1997, sought extensive corporate reforms, including transparency and accountability in corporate governance, improved corporate financial structure, and overall corporate restructuring. In addition, there was a widely shared understanding that economic recovery was inconceivable without radical reform of the *chaebol*.

The reform measures resulted in an unprecedented realignment of business–government relations. In a race to hunt down scapegoats for the crisis, previous business–government ties were frayed and it was even hinted that the *chaebol* should be dismantled. Despite an expanded space for political maneuver generated by democratization, the companies were relatively defenseless, and the government was thus able to formulate and implement an array of new laws and institutions to restructure the corporate sector.

This chapter traces the changing patterns of business–government relations since the economic crisis. The first section presents a brief overview of corporate reforms. The second section looks at the impact of these reforms on business–government relations: The changing patterns of state intervention, the shifting balance of power between the public and private sectors, and the political and economic implications for transparency, accountability, rent-seeking and corruption. The third section examines some of the determinants of these corporate reform efforts: The interplay of the crisis environment, the political preferences of Kim Dae-jung and his supporters, and external influences. The last section outlines prospects for business–government relations, and suggests some theoretical, comparative and policy implications.

1   Economic Crisis and Corporate Reform: An Overview of the "Five plus Three Principles"

In the wake of the 1997 financial crisis, the corporate sector came under heavy attack from all sides, and the *chaebol* became everyone's favorite political scapegoat. Their excessive investment, heavy leveraging, dominance of the domestic economy, lack of transparency and exclusionary corporate governance structures were singled out as causes of the financial crisis (Yoo 1999, 2000; KDI 1999). The IMF and the Korean government both placed top priority on structural reforms in the corporate sector.

Corporate reforms were guided by the "five plus three" principles agreed between the government and the private sector, particularly the big business sector which is the focus of this chapter (see Table 6.1). The five principles of corporate restructuring, agreed on January 13, 1998 between President-elect Kim and *chaebol* leaders, included enhancing transparency in accounting and management, resolving mutual debt guarantees among *chaebol* affiliates, improving firms' financial structure, streamlining business activities, and strengthening managers' accountability. The three supplementary principles, announced in President Kim's National Liberation Day speech on

August 15, 1999, included regulation of *chaebol's* control of non-bank financial institutions and circular equity investment by *chaebol* affiliates, and prevention of irregular inheritance and gift-giving among family members of *chaebol* owners.

Corporate transparency and the reliability of Korean firms' accounting practices became an issue because firms were bypassing restrictions on investment and transfer pricing and thus discouraging foreign investment (see Chapter 12). In response, the Kim Dae-jung administration pushed for the revision of the Act on External Audit of Stock Companies, which the National Assembly passed in February 1998. This law accelerated the adoption of combined financial statements. Combined financial statements would provide more accurate information about the *chaebol's* overall financial condition by showing internal transactions among *chaebol* subsidiaries, including inter-subsidiary shareholdings and debt payment guarantees. The government also strengthened the role of outside auditors by having them selected by a committee of shareholders and creditor banks rather than by controlling shareholders alone, and by increasing the penalty that the outside auditors had to pay for any wrongdoing.

The government moved to resolve the issue of debt payment guarantees among subsidiaries by prohibiting the new issuance of such guarantees among the *chaebol's* subsidiaries beginning on April 1, 1998 and requiring the *chaebol* to phase out existing ones by March 2000. Such authority was granted to the government by the revision of the Monopoly Regulation and Fair Trade Act on February 14, 1998 (see Chapter 11). To induce corporations to reduce their debts, the government directed banks to negotiate financial restructuring agreements with their debtor companies, Capital Structure Improvement Plans (CSIPs; see Chapter 8). A total of 64 conglomerates or debtor groups were directed to this program. The five largest *chaebol* were asked to reduce their debt ratios below 200 percent by the end of 1999. These agreements between banks and *chaebol* were nominally voluntary, but there was no doubt that the government was deeply involved. To discourage corporate over-borrowing, the government revised the corporate tax law on February 14 to disallow tax deductions of interest payments on "excessive" borrowings, beginning in 2000.

The government also relied on the banks to close insolvent firms and force the *chaebol* to streamline their business activities by liquidating and consolidating subsidiaries. This included "swaps" of subsidiaries among the *chaebol* (the so-called Big Deals) and other restructuring measures.[2] On June 18, the banks announced a list of 55 insolvent firms, including 20 *chaebol* subsidiaries, which were to close. Other firms, judged to be troubled but not insolvent, were required to enter into "workout" plans with their main creditor bank under which the troubled firms could receive additional financial support in return for restructuring efforts. The workout plan was applied to the smaller *chaebol*, those ranked sixth or below in total sales.

The fifth and last principle of corporate restructuring was to hold owner-managers accountable for their decisions. Although the *chaebol's* owner-managers had exercised effective control over their subsidiaries, they held positions with questionable legal status, such as "group chairman," and were not legally liable for their actions (see Chapter 12). To address this problem, the government forced *chaebol* to abolish the office of group chairman and appoint owner-managers to the board of at least one of the member firms. To enhance outside monitoring of corporate decision-making, the government required listed firms to appoint outside directors by revising the regulations for listing on the stock market in February 1999. The government further strengthened minority shareholders' rights in May 1999 by lowering the minimum share requirement for filing a derivative suit (from 1 to 0.01 percent). This change made it easier for investors to sue management for malfeasance.

These government efforts were enhanced by a grassroots movement, led by a non-governmental organization, People's Solidarity for Participatory Democracy, to protect the rights of minority shareholders (Jang 1999). These changes in corporate governance allowed citizen groups, acting as representatives of minority shareholders and even foreign investors, to uncover questionable transactions in several prominent *chaebol* firms, including SK Telecom and Samsung Electronics. Foreign shareholders, whose numbers are growing, have also started demanding accountability and board representation.

In addition to the "five principles," President Kim Dae-jung also announced three supplementary measures to strengthen regulation of corporate governance on the occasion of the National Liberation Day on August 15, 1999. The first supplementary measure lowered the cap on the share of NBFIs' stock-holding in a subsidiary belonging to the same business group. For instance, Group A's investment trust company could not hold more than 7 percent (previously 10 percent) of shares in Group A's affiliated subsidiary. The measure was designed to prevent a fusion of industrial and financial capital. The second principle prohibited subsidiaries of the top 30 *chaebol* from making equity investment in excess of 25 percent of their net assets. This limitation sought to block *chaebol's* octopus-like corporate expansion through pyramid equity investment. The last supplementary principle tightened monitoring of irregular practices in inheritance and gift-giving among family members of *chaebol* owners.

As Table 6.1 demonstrates, the Korean government has been successful in implementing corporate reforms, and their effects have been
pronounced (Moon and Mo 2000). From 1999, the top 30 *chaebol* were
required to prepare combined financial statements of all affiliated firms.
External auditors and corporate accounting officers are now subject to
stiffer penalties. Minority shareholder rights have been significantly
improved, and listed companies are now required to fill one-fourth of
their boards of directors with outsiders.

There were also major changes in inter-subsidiary relations within
groups. Debt payment guarantees and equity investment among
affiliates, which served as principal vehicles for *chaebol* expansion, were
either prohibited or restricted. Investigation of inter-subsidiary transactions led to the imposition of large fines (by Korean standards) on
such *chaebol* as Samsung, Hyundai, and LG. In addition, the new
corporate tax system will prohibit the deduction from taxable income of
interest payments on any debt exceeding four times the level of equity
capital. Substantive corporate restructuring has also taken place. The
top four *chaebol* met the deadline for reducing their debt–equity ratios
to 200 percent or less by the end of 1999 (Moon and Mo 2000: 57).

The most drastic reforms involved the bankruptcy and dismantling of
weak *chaebol* (see Chapters 7–9). By the end of 2000, seventeen of the
top thirty *chaebol* in 1997 had entered court receivership, composition,
or workout programs, reshaping the entire business landscape in Korea.
The most dramatic was the collapse of the Daewoo Group, then the
third-largest business group in Korea (see Chapter 7). Frequently in
trouble over the years, the Daewoo Group was viewed as "too big to
fail"; the government's handling of the group's financial difficulties was
thus seen as a test of its commitment to corporate restructuring. Grave
political and economic risks notwithstanding, the government did in
the end not bail out Daewoo.[3] By letting some *chaebol* go bankrupt, the
Kim Dae-jung government demonstrated its political commitment to
corporate reforms.

An industrial restructuring program, known as the Big Deals, was
also undertaken to realign the core industries of the top *chaebol*. The
government's initial intervention took the form of informal administrative guidance by the executive and was reminiscent of the restructuring
under Chun Doo Hwan. The criticism of the program delayed the
business swaps, but as the government disengaged from its brokerage
role, the *chaebol* expedited the swaps on their own.

Of seven industrial sectors targeted through the Big Deals, six swaps
were completed by the end of December 1999 (Lee 2000; Yoo 2000).
Despite criticisms, most of the swaps appeared to go well, with the
exception of the petrochemical sector. Kia Motors went to Hyundai

Table 6.1 Five plus Three Principles: an overview

	Principles	Institutions and policy	Implementation	*Chaebol's* position
Five Principles (Jan. 13, 1998)	Enhanced transparency	Consolidated financial statements Outside directors (50 percent) Protection of small shareholders/ collective litigation	In effect since 2000 In effect since 2000	Critical of collective litigation
	Control intra-group transactions	Ban on inter-subsidiary debt payment guarantees	Completed by the end of 2000	Improvement of overseas local loans
	Improved financial structure	Reduction of debt–equity ratio to 200 percent	Completed by the end of 1999	Preferred flexible application by business line
	Streamlining business lines	Separation and sale of non-specialized affiliates	In progress	
	Stronger accountability	Accountability provisions for CEOs	Completed	
Three Principles (Aug. 15, 1999)	Improve management structure of secondary financial institutions	Limits on cross-equity holding at 7 percent	Completed	
	Limit on *chaebol's* equity investment	Cap on total amount of equity investment of 25 percent of net assets	Effective in 2001	Remove or relax caps
	Prevention of irregular inheritance and gift-giving	Amendment of related laws	Completed	
30 Group Designation System	Prevention of economic concentration	Ban on debt payment guarantees Ban on cross-investments	Yearly review by KFTC	Limited to four or five groups

Source: Adapted from *Joongang Ilbo*, May 16, 2001.

Motors, while Renault took over Samsung Motors. Aerospace affiliates of Hyundai, Samsung and Daewoo merged into the new Korea Aerospace Industries, whereas power plant components of Samsung Heavy Industry and Hyundai Heavy Industry were transferred to Korea Heavy Industries & Construction (Hanjung). Hyundai Semiconductor absorbed LG Semiconductor. The oil refinery and rolling stock sectors were also streamlined without major upheaval (Yoo 2000: 80–2).

It is interesting to note that most of the legal and institutional framework essential for corporate restructuring was formulated and implemented *before* the formal inauguration of the Kim Dae-jung government (Haggard, Pinkston and Seo 1999). Once the basic principles of corporate restructuring were agreed on February 6, 1998, the next task was to translate them into laws and other binding agreements. The corporate restructuring measures consisted of two types: long-term institutional reforms for changing *chaebol* organization; and short-term policy remedies for improving the financial condition of the Big Five and the other *chaebol*. Since institutional reforms required extensive legislative change, the president-elect, in cooperation with the outgoing Kim Young Sam government, introduced necessary legislation on February 14, only a week after the government and the *chaebol* had agreed on the basic plans. The efficiency of the legislative process continued after this first round of reform. Although some bills were held up in the National Assembly in the fall as a result of inter-party conflicts over other issues, there were few controversies over the bills' content.

2   The Limits to Reform

The achievements of the Kim Dae-jung government in corporate reform should not be underestimated. As Byung-Kook Kim details in Chapter 3, previous governments had launched corporate reforms in order to limit economic concentration and improve competitiveness. Regardless of regime type, however, such efforts proved less than successful (Moon 1988, 1995). The authoritarian Chun regime undertook a major political offensive to restructure the *chaebol* system after the 1979–80 crisis, but it eventually failed. Since the democratic transition in 1987, both the Roh Tae Woo and Kim Young Sam governments staged extensive policy efforts to limit economic concentration. As with the Chun regime, their efforts were only marginally successful (see Chapter 3). But the Kim Dae-jung government was able to implement a great deal of the unfinished corporate reforms within less than a year, reforms that represented a radical departure from previous government policies.

Such achievements notwithstanding, corporate reform under Kim Dae-jung was not without its limits. The *chaebol* have been able to tap into a large pool of capital outside the banking system, such as the corporate bond and trust fund markets, and some of the apparent improvement in their finances can be attributed to asset revaluation (see Chapter 13).

Table 6.2 shows that production capacity in major industries also continued to rise throughout the crisis period. Except for industries in structural decline, such as textiles, only machinery and equipment and fabricated metal products have experienced a decrease in capacity. Such trends can be attributed in part to rapid economic recovery. But the government's continuing support for ailing firms, including some *chaebol*, has also contributed.

The ultimate test of corporate reform is whether or not firms are subject to market discipline, and one such indicator is whether or not the government allows insolvent firms to fail. While the government did

Table 6.2 Production capacity indices in key manufacturing industries, 1995–99 (1995 = 100)

During	Manufacturing	Food products & beverages	Textiles	Chemicals & chemical products	Non-metallic mineral products
1995	100.0	100.0	100.0	100.0	100.0
1996	108.3	102.4	95.5	107.1	113.6
1997	113.6	102.3	90.7	116.2	118.5
1998	119.1	101.0	86.0	128.6	118.8
1999	129.2	100.7	84.9	131.8	117.3

	Basic metals	Fabricated metal products	Machinery & equipment n.e.c.	Radio, TV & communication equipment	Motor vehicles & trailers
1995	100.0	100.0	100.0	100.0	100.0
1996	104.5	102.7	105.3	130.9	107.2
1997	108.7	106.2	107.0	144.4	118.5
1998	121.2	103.0	100.5	184.5	126.7
1999	127.8	97.6	98.6	255.5	136.0

Source: Bank of Korea, *Monthly Bulletin*, March 2000 (National Statistics Office).

allow failed *chaebol* such as Kia, Hanbo, Samsung Motors and Daewoo to go bankrupt, some of their subsidiaries with questionable economic merits are still operating (see Chapters 8 and 9). Moreover, the government has kept some nonviable, smaller *chaebol* alive with workout programs instead of letting them go bankrupt, which, in turn, may have contributed to the onset of another credit crunch in 2000.

Another problem area is corporate governance. Despite extensive measures to ensure transparency and accountability, *chaebol* owners still exercise control disproportionate to their level of share ownership. Stumbling blocks to reform in this area include the owners' control of affiliates through holdings in non-listed firms that, in turn, hold majority shares in affiliates. It is suspected that owners also still control nominally "outside" directors and auditors. Inheritance schemes and gift-giving among *chaebol* family members as well as illicit internal trading among affiliates of *chaebol* have also posed ongoing challenges to the Kim government's corporate reform efforts.

Although more than half of the top thirty *chaebol* went bankrupt in the wake of the economic crisis, the reforms have also achieved limited success in coping with the problem of economic concentration. Although *ownership* concentration was reduced after the economic crisis, overall *business* concentration presents a somewhat different picture. The relative weight of the top thirty *chaebol* in the national economy increased after the economic crisis. In 1996, for instance, the top 30 *chaebol* accounted for 39.3 percent of total sales, 37 percent of total value added, 44.7 percent of tangible fixed assets, and 17.6 percent of total employment. These figures rose to 43.3 percent, 41.2 percent, 46.5 percent, and 19.9 percent respectively in 1998 (Choi 2000).

Despite these reservations, one cannot deny that President Kim Dae-jung made remarkable progress in the area of institutional reform. Even if it is still too early to make any definitive assessment of corporate reforms in Korea, it is worth analyzing the political dynamics of the successes and limits of reforms to date.

3   Shifting Patterns of Business–Government Relations

Relations between business and government in Korea have undergone a complex evolution since 1945 (Moon 1995; Kim 1997). The predatory state of the 1950s was reorganized under the military. Park Chung Hee supported big business through both command and control measures and selective incentives through the 1960s and the 1970s. As the private sector became larger during the government-led heavy and chemical industrialization drive of the 1970s, the business–government relationship was gradually transformed from one of state dominance to symbiosis (Kim 1997).

Since the democratic transition in 1987, however, the terms of engagement between the state and business have changed once again. The *chaebol*, the very symbol of concentration of economic power and collusive ties with government, became a major political liability. At the same time the forces of democratization and globalization significantly enhanced business freedom of maneuver. Chairman Chung Ju Young's effort to form his own political party and his bid for the presidency in 1992 testified to this trend of growing political independence. Choi Jong Hyun, chairman of the powerful Federation of Korean Industries, similarly declared that business support for parties and candidates would be selective and tied to perceived benefits (Moon 1994). Globalization and gradual liberalization also implied a reduction of the government's direct policy leverage through instruments such as preferential credit.

The corporate reforms of the Kim Dae-jung government have brought about unexpected consequences in business–government relations, reversing the privileged position of big business. The first and most visible sign of change is the increasingly adversarial relationship between the government and business. Since the government of Chun Doo Hwan, a change of government always coincided with anti-*chaebol* rhetoric; but such rhetoric was quickly discarded and collusive ties between state and business resurfaced (Moon 1994; Haggard and Moon 1990).

The Kim Dae-jung government was different. Critics argued that two phrases summarized the Kim government's *chaebol* policy: *chaebol chaekimron* (blame *chaebol*) and *chaebol haichairon* (dismantle *chaebol*). According to some critics, these slogans reflected the view that the *chaebol* were responsible for the 1997 economic crisis, and that they should therefore be broken up (Yoo 2000). In his 1999 National Liberation Day address, President Kim emphasized the importance of *chaebol* reform in the following words: "We cannot complete economic reform without reforming the structure of the *chaebol*, the most critical problem of our economy." Kim Tae-dong, who served as the first senior economic secretary to President Kim, reflected even more critical views within the administration. He argued that the *chaebol* had become too powerful and that their dismantling was essential for successful economic reforms. Critics claimed public sentiment echoed these views (Yoo 2000).

The second important change was a revival of state power. As noted before, state power over the private sector had gradually eroded in the

process of democratization and globalization. While forces of democratization enhanced private firms' political leverage, the process of
globalization deprived the state of its traditional policy tools to
command, control, and discipline the private sector. Moreover, bilateral
pressures from the United States and multilateral pressures from the
WTO and the OECD forced the Korean government to discard its
industrial and defensive trade policies. Pressures for deregulation also
deprived the Korean government of its capacity to intervene and
manipulate the private sector (Mo and Moon 1999a). Economic liberalization and deregulation weakened state power while enhancing the
power of the private sector.

In the wake of the economic crisis of 1997 and subsequent corporate
reforms, however, power shifted back to the state. It is ironic that the
Kim Dae-jung government's neoliberal reforms, which were designed
to curb the interventionist developmental state, ended up being quite
interventionist, even domineering in the early stages.

Such interventionism was justified in the name of "ordo-liberalism"
(Government of the Republic of Korea 1999: 32–3). Ordo-liberalism
was originally proposed by Walter Eucken, a German scholar who
attributed the rise of Nazism to the failure of the free market system
during the Weimar Republic. Eucken argued that the failure to establish
a viable institutional framework for the market arose from vested
interests and monopoly powers that distorted free competition through
extensive entry and exit barriers. In such settings, aggressive intervention may be justified because the market cannot restore competitive
order on its own.

Although the Kim Dae-jung government intervened using this logic,
the original idea of transitional, strategic intervention was soon for-
gotten and the government went well beyond the role of a neutral
rule-maker and rule-enforcer. In fact, critics claimed that the state
under Kim Dae-jung became more powerful and micro-managing than
under his predecessors, even dictating the survival and demise of
individual firms.

The exercise of such power does not necessarily lead to compliance
by private firms, however; as the case of the Big Deals shows, the new
order left room for negotiation. The Big Deals were initially the centerpiece of the government's restructuring plan for the Big Five. Informal
negotiations with the *chaebol*, however, did not go smoothly because
President Kim Dae-jung and his advisers hesitated in the face of
domestic and international criticisms of the plan. Economists and
international lenders objected to the government's actions in brokering
private transactions relating to mergers and acquisitions and opting to
merge insolvent firms with healthier ones rather than just liquidating

them. The Big Deals were not popular with liberal activists either, because they feared the deals would give too many benefits to the *chaebol*, including tax reductions, debt-for-equity swaps and debt write-offs. Some *chaebol* also fiercely resisted the government's plans.

Once the government announced on July 4, 1998 that the Big Deals would be arranged on a voluntary basis, however, the *chaebol* became more cooperative and negotiated actively with the government to win more favorable terms. By the second round of government–business dialogue in August, the government and the Big Five agreed to pursue intra-sector, not cross-sector, Big Deals.

As the evolution of the Big Deals shows, the Big Five were able to incorporate some of their demands into the CSIPs. Among more than fifty legislative proposals that the *chaebol* made, the government accepted several, including clearer rules on mergers, new tax incentives for mergers and acquisitions, and stronger asset protection for companies filing for court protection. Through their dialogue with the government, the *chaebol* were also able to win financial subsidies such as higher discounting ceilings on trade bills and lower interest rates on export loans. The debate on whether to change the law to allow the formation of holding companies also came out of the government–business consultations.

Although the Kim Dae-jung government has freely exercised state power, its modes of intervention in the market proved radically different from the past. The most intriguing aspect of the Kim administration is the increasing use of *informal executive guidance*. But the crisis situation and personal expertise in economic affairs propelled Kim Dae-jung directly into negotiations with business. Informal arrangements such as the Tripartite Committee and involvement in the Big Deals through private meetings with *chaebol* leaders are examples of such direct executive guidance. Such informal executive guidance became an important arena for consensus-building and negotiation, more important than the National Assembly.

Despite the significance of direct executive involvement, administrative guidance also played a role in the crisis. It is often believed that such intervention was by and large dismantled as the Korean government globalized the economy and gave up its practice of industrial policy. But such intervention did not wither away under Kim Dae-jung, even if it became much more indirect. The Capital Structure Improvement Plans (CSIPs) are a case in point. CSIPs were nominally private arrangements between *chaebol* and their primary creditor banks. However, because most of the creditor banks were owned or controlled by the government, CSIPs became instruments through which the government forced the private sector to comply with its mandate for corporate reforms. Unlike the past, when government agencies and most notably the Ministry of Finance were directly involved in disciplining corporate behavior, the Kim Dae-jung government turned *chaebol's* pledges into binding action programs through bank-led CSIPs (see Chapter 8).

What factors account for the shift? One is closely related to institutional changes arising from the crisis. The government used its control of banks through the newly created Financial Supervisory Commission to force the *chaebol* to improve their financial structure and streamline their business activities. Banks had enormous power over the *chaebol*; as their main creditors, they could bankrupt firms by cutting off credit. But the life and death of banks was in turn dependent on the deliberations of the Financial Supervisory Commission, which was under government control. As Haggard, Pinkston and Seo (1999) explain:

> existing law was inadequate to manage problems of systemic distress – the simultaneous insolvency of large numbers of banks and corporations – and indeed could even have perverse effects in the short run. For example, some features of Korean bankruptcy procedures allowed firms court protection and continued access to credit. Moreover, it was difficult to craft legislation that would address the underlying problems of excessive corporate leverage.

Indirect administrative guidance through the CSIPs proved effective. CSIPs were instrumental in inducing the Big Five to comply with the government's corporate reforms.[4] However, CSIPs were not without drawbacks. Admittedly, the banks have a role to play in the management decisions of the firms to which they lend, particularly if loans are non-performing. However, it was not appropriate for the banks to threaten to withhold credit to force debtors to give up business lines or reduce debt ratios when the debtors were not formally in default. It is especially troubling given that the *chaebol* could not turn to other banks in the face of such demands from their main creditor bank. No bank was in a position to do business against the wishes of the government.

Indirect administrative guidance through CSIPs revealed several other problems. First, it is not clear whether informal talks between government and business provided the Big Five with a meaningful opportunity to participate. *Chaebol* and their industry association, the Federation of Korean Industries, complained that the government used the talks as a mechanism for winning the *chaebol's* endorsement for its own plans rather than for negotiating in good faith. The *chaebol* were often pressured to sign an agreement that the government had already prepared, especially during the fourth round of government–business talks. Second, it was ironic that the government negotiated directly with the Big Five through an official arrangement like the government–business talks to produce CSIPs, which were essentially private contracts between the *chaebol* and their banks.

The evolution of business–government relations under Kim Dae-jung also raised a broader set of issues that remain the topic of intense political debate. First, are these relations more transparent, less prone to corruption and rent-seeking, and more subjected to law than in the past? Second, is a kind of societal corporatism emerging? And finally, does business operate more openly through parties and politicians than before? Let us address each question in turn.

In theory, business–government relations should be more transparent under Kim Dae-jung. When he was an opposition leader, Kim Dae-jung was opposed to close relations with business and did not draw much support from the private sector, leaving few political debts for him to pay after winning the election. Moreover, his all-out effort to improve transparency and accountability alienated the *chaebol*. As accounting standards strengthened, it also became technically difficult for companies to make informal political contributions.

However, public perceptions of business–government relations do not appear to have improved. According to Transparency International, the perceived level of corruption in Korea has not improved since 1997; Korea's score was 4.2 in 2001 on a scale of 1–9 (9 being the most transparent), little changed from its 1997 score of 4.3. Like previous administrations, the Kim Dae-jung government has been mired in a series of scandals involving key government officials and party leaders. The government has also been criticized for favoring companies owned by people from its regional base, Cholla, while discriminating against companies based in certain regions like Kyungnam.

What about the prospects for tripartism? Despite early promises, the future of societal corporatism is also in doubt. The Kim Dae-jung government attempted to create social corporatist arrangements to replace the old state corporatism that had survived the transition to democracy. The tripartite talks during the early days of the administration were an example of such an effort. The government–business dialogues, which were instrumental in enacting and implementing the CSIPs, represented another effort to create organic working relations between the government and business.

But corporatist arrangements have become less effectual over time. There is doubt as to whether the Kim Dae-jung government allowed all stakeholders to participate in the policymaking process. Especially with regard to the *chaebol* and *chaebol* policy, the government has been, by and large, exclusionary. Although Kim Dae-jung tried to project an appearance of consensus by announcing five principles of corporate reform after meeting with *chaebol* leaders, negotiations were informal and closed; it is not clear whether the *chaebol* leaders had any real input. The Tripartite Committee also ran into difficulties following its early successes with labor market reform. The committee gained formal legal status in 1999, but it has acted mainly as a mediator in several high-profile labor disputes and has not been effective as an ongoing arena for debating or deciding broad economic policies. Hard-line labor unions such as the Korea Confederation of Trade Unions have refused to participate in the committee, calling it a mechanism for forcing concessions on labor. In labor's view, Kim Dae-jung's dream of creating social corporatism has fallen far below expectations.

The question of whether the National Assembly and political parties play a more active role in policymaking is also difficult to assess. Both ruling and opposition parties have been catch-all parties without any specific party ideology and platforms. Even the conservative Grand National Party has at times taken anti-*chaebol* policy stances, not only because of overall public mood but because of policy initiatives of its own liberal wing. In addition, the tradition of an imperial presidency and executive dominance has continued under Kim Dae-jung, severely undercutting the power and influence of political parties and the National Assembly.

4   Accounting for Changing Business–Government Relations

If we agree that the Kim Dae-jung government's *initial* corporate reforms were relatively successful and had profound implications for business–government relations, what factors account for this success? Several appear important, including initial conditions, the preferences and coalitional dynamics of the Kim Dae-jung administration, and external influences.

Initial conditions: Opportunities and constraints

The 1997 financial crisis shocked Korea out of traditional policy patterns, disorganizing the interest groups that had previously vetoed policy reform and generating pressure on politicians to change failed policies. All three main vested interests – the *chaebol*, labor unions, and bureaucrats – were heavily criticized for their role in contributing to the crisis, and none could openly resist initial reform efforts. The *chaebol*, in particular, were singled out as villains by the media and politicians, and their influence on the political process weakened considerably, especially in the first several months of the Kim Dae-jung government. The economic crisis also helped the public to see economic reform in a more positive light since the cost of maintaining the status quo was much higher than previously thought. In short, a collective learning process had taken place.

While the crisis served as the catalyst for corporate reforms, inertial factors posed several constraints; not all of the initial conditions were propitious for reform. First, the very size of the *chaebol*, especially the Big Five, severely limited the government's options. The government's threat of credit sanctions was also weakened by the *chaebol's* increasing ability to raise money in capital markets. In short, the *chaebol* maintained a significant amount of leverage against the government despite the crisis. As a result, a certain degree of forbearance characterized the government approach to the Big Five; for example, the resolution of their insolvency through formal bankruptcy procedures was not a politically feasible option in 1998.

Second, Korean policymakers had to find solutions to the crisis under conditions of weak market and legal institutions. In particular the absence of secondary debt markets and the weakness of securities markets made it difficult to restructure large, heavily indebted companies. Controversies over the rule of law arose in part because the government simply did not have time to build the necessary legal infrastructure to support the restructuring of distressed assets and firms, let alone to change informal norms and practices. At the initial stage of the crisis the government had little choice but to respond with *ad hoc* command-and-control measures while working to develop the longer-term legal and market framework for corporate restructuring.

Lastly, the government itself was politically constrained and had to respond to public pressure for *chaebol* reform. Right or wrong, the government had to show tangible results early. For example, public pressure helps explain why the government was preoccupied with the Big Deals and with administrative reduction of debt–equity ratios. Although these two measures were questionable from an economic point of view, they were politically attractive because they were measurable and visible.

Policymakers under the Kim Dae-jung government aggressively exploited the opportunity arising from the crisis, even though a number of constraints continued to operate. On balance, however, even if the crisis environment was an important spur to reform, much depended on politics as well, including the policy preferences and political interests of the new president.

Leadership choice and coalitional dynamics

Unlike previous presidents, Kim Dae-jung brought with him surprisingly strong credentials as an economic expert. He was one of the few Korean politicians who came to office with a distinctive vision for the Korean economy. Earlier in his career he had embraced a populist economic agenda with emphasis on government intervention, participation and social justice. The title of one of his early books was *Mass-Participatory Economy* (Kim 1985). Over the years, however, Kim Dae-jung cultivated a more conservative image, supporting private enterprise and market competition. His stay in Britain in the early 1990s seems to have affected his thinking. Moreover he was constrained by the neoliberal mandate of the IMF and other international lenders. Thus while the political right, including the *chaebol*, was suspicious of President Kim's sincerity, his background as a supporter of social justice gave credibility to the idea that economic reform was socially desirable.

His efforts to combine these two seemingly incompatible policy lines were also a reflection of his coalitional base. Kim Dae-jung and his party represented a labor constituency and an underdeveloped region (Cholla) and were thus strongly opposed to close business–government relations, at least as they had worked in the past. Therefore, it is not surprising that President Kim placed the blame for the economic crisis squarely on the Korean corporate sector, and to a much lesser extent on bureaucrats, labor, and domestic or international financial institutions.

But as the leader of a coalition government, President Kim could not ignore the policy preferences of his partners, the United Liberal Democrats (ULD). The ULD was the most conservative of all parties in ideological orientation, in effect a reincarnation of the technocrats of the Park Chung Hee period. ULD legislators and advisers dominated the initial formulation of the administration's *chaebol* policy through their presence on the Emergency Economic Committee. Park Tae-joon, Kim Yong-hwan, Lee Hon-jae and Lee Kyu-sung, who were in charge of the initial management of the economic crisis, were all lieutenants of the economic miracle of the Park period. Their thinking influenced a number of critical initiatives, including the Big Deals.[5]

Forging an alliance with the ULD and its leadership to manage the economic crisis entailed sharp internal conflicts within the ruling coalition from the very beginning. For a long time prior to his election, President Kim Dae-jung had been assisted by the *Junggyonghoi*, an economic study group whose members included academics and activists with a leftist orientation. The ULD advisers and the *Junggyonghoi* members had quite opposing views of *chaebol* reform. The ULD technocrats believed that the *chaebol* reform should be undertaken prudently, since dismantling the *chaebol* would be tantamount to dismantling the Korean economy. *Junggyonghoi* members argued the *chaebol* were the source of many contradictions in the Korean economy and that it could not recover without overhauling the entire *chaebol* system.

As key economic posts were filled with ULD legislators or those recommended by the ULD, *Junggyonghoi* members were excluded from critical policy decisions. This pattern continued into 2001; *Junggyonghoi* members lost battles first with ULD advisers and later with bureaucrats. By mid-2001, none of its members was serving in the Kim Dae-jung government.

The opposing Grand National Party did not pose any significant challenge to the corporate reforms. The GNP was the ruling party when the economic crisis broke, and it came under heavy attack for its economic mismanagement. The GNP was thus not in a position to oppose legislation on corporate reform, even more so because of its close association with the *chaebol*. During its reign, the GNP was the largest beneficiary of *chaebol's* political contributions, and any move to patronize the large groups would have precipitated a public outcry. The GNP was also internally fragmented. The party absorbed liberal and even radical politicians in the 1990 three-party merger, and it was therefore difficult for it to produce a unified position on *chaebol* reform. In the absence of any coherent opposition, the new government's legislation sailed through the National Assembly.

Because the incumbent government of Kim Young Sam was so completely discredited, Kim Dae-jung enjoyed a strong honeymoon effect even before he was formally inaugurated. This gave him and his transition team freedom from domestic political constraints while enjoying widespread support from the public and media. The incoming government appeared to have the moral authority to reverse the policies of the outgoing regime, and the public and media did not challenge the adjustment program imposed by the IMF. The *chaebol* and labor unions may have opposed the reform measures, but they were not in a position to demand anything either. Moreover, a series of public interest groups strongly backed the government's efforts for *chaebol* reforms, particularly the People's Solidarity for Participatory Democracy, which was instrumental in bringing public attention to the problem of corporate governance. In short, Kim Dae-jung faced few domestic political constraints in the first months in office.

The government used the media effectively in persuading the public and building a political coalition for the corporate reforms. This effort began with a move to control the mass media; the government appointed its supporters to lead government-owned media organizations such as the Korea Broadcasting System and Yonhap News Service. It has also been rumored that the government sought to tame private media and newspapers. Many feel that traditionally conservative newspapers like the *Chosun Daily*, *Joongang Daily* and *Donga Daily* have been pressured to moderate their criticisms of the administration. But the crisis drove the mass media in the same direction as the public at large: to support the government's efforts by publicizing the importance of economic reform.

In sum, despite some internal divisions, Kim Dae-jung was successful in building a political coalition for corporate reform. The opposition GNP, bureaucrats, big business, and labor were neutralized by their role in the economic crisis, and the government was able to garner immense public support even from the left. Lack of domestic political opposition, immense public support, and skilled exploitation of a honeymoon all contributed to the government's early successes.

More generally, it appears that democracy itself gave legitimacy and credibility to the government's reform efforts. The problems commonly associated with democracy, such as the influence of special interests and legislative gridlock, were largely absent during Kim Dae-jung's first year (Mo and Moon 1999b). Where vested interests did matter, the president encouraged them to participate in the policymaking process. The Tripartite Committee was created to gain labor's support for labor market reform, and the president used a similar method in dealing with *chaebol* leaders. This inclusive democratic approach helped the government to forge a social consensus on contentious issues.

External pressures

A final cluster of influences was external. Outside pressures and the formation of transnational coalitions played an important role in paving the way for corporate reform and changing business–government relations.

In its standby agreements with the Korean government of December 5 and 24, 1997, the IMF emphasized the importance of two provisions of corporate restructuring: transparency of corporate governance (such as implementation of international accounting standards) and reduction of debt payment guarantees between affiliates within a single business group. The World Bank followed with more refined recommendations on corporate governance and competition policy when it signed structural adjustment loan agreements with Korea in February and October 1998.

The February 1998 agreement focused on ways to enhance accounting transparency and financial disclosure and improve corporate governance through better monitoring.

To a large extent, the Korean government had no choice but to implement a comprehensive reform program because IMF demands were themselves comprehensive. But the scope of economic reform became even larger when the IMF mandates were combined with President Kim Dae-jung's own plans for transforming the Korean economy. Although there are different interpretations of Kim's model, it is clear that he sought to dismantle the monopolistic structure of the Korean market and make advances in areas that had received less attention from previous governments, such as social welfare, small and medium-sized enterprises, and economic justice.

Although it appears that the IMF and World Bank played an important role in putting corporate reform on the agenda, it is debatable whether these ideas originated from the two international organizations alone. Korean negotiators wanted to incorporate at least some of these reform measures into the agreement, implying that the IMF and the IBRD did not insist on them. We are sympathetic to this hypothesis of "Korean instigation." IMF conditionality and pressures from international lending agencies may have helped the Kim Dae-jung government in pushing for corporate reform, but its acquiescence was not grudging. The government actively sought foreign help and advice.

Such help was necessary in part because Korea was in desperate need of foreign capital. The extent to which Kim Dae-jung favored foreign investors even prompted the *chaebol* to complain about "reverse discrimination." Kim Dae-jung's open embrace of the Western model of democracy and a market economy reflected more than the need to attract foreign capital; it rested on deep conviction. Nonetheless, foreign pressure and support helped in pushing the reforms through.

5   Conclusion: Prospects for Business–Government Relations

The economic crisis of 1997 unleashed powerful forces of change into the Korean economy and business–government relations. Although it is still early to fully evaluate the impact of the reforms, it is not unrealistic to expect Korea to become a truly market-oriented economy. The bases for our optimism are three.

First, there have been sufficient institutional changes to form a basis for further reforms. By their nature, institutional reforms are slow to take root. Already, however, there are signs that the basic "rules of the game" have changed. Companies can no longer pay lip-service to shareholder rights, transparent accounting standards, and value maximization; initial reforms have already affected the way businesses are run. Despite excessive state intervention in the early stage of building a new economic order, there is no reason to believe that the state cannot ultimately assume the more neutral role of rule-maker and rule-enforcer.

Second, the Korean economy is undergoing a structural change as a result of the information revolution. Unlike other crisis countries, Korea has a vibrant high-tech sector that is growing by leaps and bounds. High-tech start-ups, which are officially designated as "venture firms," account for only about 3 percent of value-added and employment at the moment. But as more money, management and engineering talent continue to enter the high-tech sector, the dominance by the *chaebol* will gradually weaken. In addition, the reduction in transaction costs brought about by electronic commerce weakens the relative merit of conducting internal transactions within a business group.

The last major change agent is foreign capital (see Chapter 10). Foreign investors already hold more than 30 percent of Korean shares, and their influence is particularly strong in commercial banking. Major banks in which foreigners have majority or major stakes include Korea First Bank, Korea Exchange Bank, and Kookmin Bank. Manufacturing has also received large amounts of foreign investment in recent years. Multinational companies have already acquired dominant market shares in chemicals, paper, and some consumer products. Although some areas of reform are frustratingly slow, the forces of change represented by high-tech and foreign firms will push the process along.

Beneath this optimistic outlook lie three countervailing concerns. First is the newly emerging tension between the global standard and "Asian capitalism." Discourse on convergence to global standards prevailed over "Asian capitalism" in the wake of the economic crisis, but support for the idea of Asian capitalism, including the *chaebol* system, lingers among conservative thinkers (Moon and Mo 2000: 65). Second, the increasing fragility of Kim Dae-jung's political coalition as his term drew to a close heightened concerns about the sustainability of corporate reform. His failure to win a legislative majority in the general election of April 2000 dampened the reform drive, and his lame-duck status made it difficult to steer corporate reform efforts through the GNP-dominated National Assembly in the last year of his administration. Finally, complacency and reform fatigue increasingly undercut the push for corporate reform. Thus, even if long-term prospects for corporate reform and business–government relations seem positive, it is not surprising that the reform momentum slowed in the late Kim Dae-jung years, leaving some unfinished tasks for the next government.

Notes

1 For theoretical analysis of the relationship, see Evans (1995) on "embed-dedness" and Chung H. Lee (1992) on business–government relations as a "quasi-internal organization."

2 The Big Deals were designed to avoid duplicative investment, surplus capacity, and excessive competition in seven business areas (refining, semi-conductors, rolling stock, aircraft, power plants, ship engines, and petrochemicals) by inducing voluntary swaps among chaebol's affiliates.

3 Some of its affiliates, including Daewoo Motors, Daewoo Electronics, and Daewoo Construction, survived through workout plans. But one cannot say that they were politically motivated, since many claimed that their going-concern values were higher than liquidation values.

4 In their December 1998 CSIPs, the Big Five agreed to: focus on four or five core businesses; reduce the number of subsidiaries and affiliates from 264 to 130: reduce their total debt-to-equity ratio to below 200 percent by the end of 1999; eliminate inter-subsidiary debt payment guarantees; and improve their corporate governance and enhance transparency. To meet the target debt–equity ratio, the chaebol indicated their plans to raise about 13 trillion won through new rights issues in 1999 and attract $13.6 billion in foreign capital, including $6.5 billion in FDI. These plans were subject to quarterly review by creditor banks. The FSC was to monitor progress and hold creditors accountable for the failure to enforce the agreements.

5 Kim Dae-jung's recruitment of these conservative technocrats was not simply a result of power sharing with the ULD. Kim also assigned ULD members to key economic posts in order to overcome the initial distrust of his populist line at home and abroad.

References

Chang, Ha-Joon. 1999. "The Hazard of Moral Hazard: Untangling the Asian Crisis," World Development, 28 (4): 775–88.

Cho, Yoon Je and Kim, Joon-Kyung. 1995. "Credit Policies and the Industrial-ization of Korea." World Bank Discussion Paper No. 286. Washington, DC: World Bank.

Choi, Seung-no. 2000. Korea's Large Business Groups 2000 (in Korean). Seoul: Free Enterprise Center.

Evans, Peter B. 1995. Embedded Autonomy: States and Industrial Transformation. Princeton: Princeton University Press.

Financial Supervisory Commission. 1999. "Bank-led Corporate Restructuring: A New Financial Control by the Government?" (in Korean). FSC Working Paper. Seoul: FSC.

Government of the Republic of Korea. 1999. DJnomics: A New Foundation for the Korean Economy. Seoul: Ministry of Finance and Economy.

Haggard, Stephan, and Mo, Jongryn. 2000. "The Political Economy of the Korean Economic Crisis," Review of International Political Economy, 7 (2): 197–218.

Haggard, Stephan, and Moon, Chung-in. 1990. "Institutions and Economic Policy: Theory and a Korean Case Study," *World Politics*, 17 (2): 210–37.

Haggard, Stephan, Pinkston, Daniel, and Seo, Jungkun. 1999. "Reforming Korea Inc.: The Politics of Structural Adjustment under Kim Dae-jung," *Asian Perspectives*, 23: 201–35.

Jang, Ha Sung. 1999. "Corporate Governance and Economic Development: The Korean Experience." Paper presented at the Korea Development Institute – World Bank Conference on Democracy, Market Economy and Development, Seoul, February.

Kim, Dae-jung. 1985. *Mass-Participatory Economy: A Democratic Alternative for Korea*. Cambridge: Center for International Affairs, Harvard University.

Kim, Eun Mee. 1997. *Big Business, Strong State: Collusion and Conflict in South Korean Development, 1960–1990*. Albany, NY: State University of New York Press.

Korea Development Institute. 1999. *Economic Restructuring in Korea: An Overview of Reforms Since the Crisis*. Seoul: Korea Development Institute.

Lee, Chung H. 1992. "The Government, Financial System and Large Private Enterprise in the Economic Development of South Korea," *World Development*, 20 (2): 187–97.

Lee, Young-Ryol. 2000. *The Big Deal Game: DJ versus the Chaebol* (in Korean). Seoul: Joongang Ilbo J&P.

Mo, Jongryn. 2002. "Political Culture and Legislative Gridlock: Politics of Economic Reform in Pre-Crisis Korea." Forthcoming in *Comparative Political Studies*.

Mo, Jongryn, and Moon, Chung-in, eds. 1999a. *Democracy and the Korean Economy*. Stanford: Hoover Institution Press.

——. 1999b. "Korea after the Crash," *Journal of Democracy*, 10 (3): 150–64.

Moon, Chung-in. 1988. "The Demise of a Developmentalist State? Neoconservative Reforms and Political Consequences in South Korea," *Journal of Developing Societies*, IV: 67–84.

Moon, Chung-in. 1994. "The Dynamics of Business–Government Relations in South Korea," in Andrew MacIntyre, ed., *Business and Government in Industrializing Asia*. Ithaca: Cornell University Press.

——. 1995. "Business–government relations in South Korea," in Andrew MacIntyre, ed., *Business–government Relations in Industrializing Asia*. Ithaca: Cornell University Press.

Moon, Chung-in, and Mo, Jongryn. 2000. *Economic Crisis and Structural Reforms in Korea: Assessments and Implications*. Washington, DC: Economic Strategy Institute.

Williamson, John, and Haggard, Stephan. 1993. "The Political Conditions for Economic Reform," in John Williamson, ed., *The Political Economy of Policy Reform*. Washington, DC: Institute for International Economics.

World Bank. 1998. *East Asia: Road to Recovery*. Washington, DC: World Bank.

Yoo, Seong Min. 1999. "Corporate Restructuring in Korea: Policy Issues Before and During the Crisis." KDI Working Paper No. 9903. Seoul: Korea Development Institute.

——. 2000. *Are the Chaebol the Real Culprits of the Economic Crisis?* (in Korean). Seoul: Korea Development Institute, Bibong Press.

7   The Restructuring of Daewoo

Dong Gull Lee

Among the most frequent characterizations of the Korean economy are rapid growth, state-led industrialization, export-oriented policies and, since the Asian financial crisis, over-expansion, moral hazard, poor corporate governance, government bailouts and restructuring. The Daewoo crisis combines all these elements and underscores the importance of corporate reform for future economic growth.

Corporate reform of the top *chaebol* has been one of the nation's top priorities since the 1997 economic crisis. Daewoo, however, failed to comply with government reform efforts, and the government and creditors failed to force Daewoo's hand. The result was the biggest bankruptcy in Korean history, one that caused a serious setback in Korea's recovery. This chapter shows how and why Daewoo collapsed, and how Daewoo, its creditors and the government behaved during the crisis.

Although most *chaebol* in Korea followed a similar path of expansion based on borrowed money, Daewoo carried this strategy to the extreme. Kim Woo Choong, Daewoo's chairman, might also have believed in the myth of "too big to fail," and overestimated his political influence. Daewoo's borrowing binge during 1998 did substantial damage to the already ailing giant, and by 1999 the group's collapse was unavoidable.

Creditor-led restructuring of Daewoo proved a "mission impossible" because creditors were squeezed by their own problems. Only the government could take the primary responsibility for Daewoo's restructuring. However, the Capital Structure Improvement Plan (CSIP) between Daewoo and its creditor banks and government limits on borrowing were half-hearted. Nor did the Financial Supervisory Commission seem strongly committed to real progress in restructuring the group.

The government continuously underestimated the seriousness of the Daewoo problem and allowed Daewoo's outrageous accounting gimmicks and forgery to go unchecked. For a number of reasons, the government shied away from strong action, including fear of the impact on the nation's economy, the astronomical costs of a clean-up, and incentives in the bureaucracy toward inaction. The relationship between Daewoo and the government under Kim Dae-jung, bureaucratic abhorrence of disclosing relevant information to the public, and the absence of a core team of dedicated experts also contributed to delay.

The first section gives a brief account of Daewoo's history and the distinctive features of its growth strategy. The second section examines Daewoo's overall performance until 1997; the third, its financial status during 1997–98. The fourth section explains how Daewoo responded to the crisis. The fifth looks at what its creditors and the government did in dealing with the company, what should have been done, and why they did not take the necessary steps. The sixth section evaluates the post-bankruptcy management of Daewoo by the government and creditors. The conclusion assesses the implications of the Daewoo crisis and the lessons that can be learned from it.

1   Rise of the Daewoo Group: Strategies for Growth

Daewoo was founded in 1967 as a small textile trading company with an investment of $18,000 and four employees. Daewoo's reputation as a producer of high-quality, low-priced merchandise brought it international customers like Sears and Roebuck, J. C. Penny and Montgomery Ward. By 1972, the company held 30 percent of the total US import quota for textile products (Steers et al. 1989).[1]

Building on this success, Daewoo expanded into new business fields after 1973, mainly through acquisitions of struggling companies and joint ventures. The group diversified into finance, construction, heavy and electrical machinery, shipbuilding and automobiles, the strategic industries emphasized by Park Chung Hee's plan to develop heavy and chemical industry (HCI). Since these sectors required huge capacity in technology, capital, manpower and organization, large firms were favored over smaller ones. Daewoo actively supported the government's industrialization policies and reaped first-mover advantages in new industries as well as various tax and financial benefits (Kang 1996). With favorable market conditions and government support, Daewoo had become one of Korea's largest *chaebol* by the late 1970s.

In the early 1980s, many companies that had been established or expanded during the state-led HCI drive of the 1970s faced difficulty and even insolvency. The government undertook an Industrial Rationalization Policy in the mid-1980s. Major *chaebol* acquired ailing firms at preferential prices with tax benefits and financial assistance. Daewoo took over one company and received preferential loans.

From the late 1980s, globalization became the new watchword and Daewoo attempted to adjust to the new environment by internationalizing its businesses. In a quest to become a global automotive giant, Daewoo invested heavily in car plants in Poland, India, the Ukraine, Romania, Uzbekistan and Vietnam. By the end of the decade, Daewoo Motors' global capacity reached 3.3 million units (*Business Week*, August 30, 1999).

The Daewoo Group was structured as one big company, with group-wide plans with respect to funding, manufacturing, exports and sales. On top was Daewoo Corporation, the *de facto* holding company or control tower. It exported products manufactured by other subsidiaries and provided them necessary financing. Financial subsidiaries acted as the front office in raising funds for the group.

At the end of 1998, Daewoo had forty-one subsidiaries and employed over 75,000 people domestically. Internationally, it owned 589 foreign subsidiaries and had offices in over 130 countries. Its main lines of business were trade (Daewoo Corporation), automobiles (Daewoo Motors, Ssangyong Motors, the mini-car division of Daewoo Heavy Industries and Daewoo Motor Sales), electronics (Daewoo Electronic, Daewoo Electronics Components, Orion Electronics and Daewoo Telecom), shipbuilding (Daewoo Heavy Industries) and finance (Daewoo Securities and Daewoo Capital). In 1998, these units accounted for over 95 percent of the group's total sales of 61.7 trillion *won* and its total asset value of 71.7 trillion *won*.

This brief history suggests three central components of Daewoo's growth strategy: close cooperation with the government; expansion through acquisitions; and high financial leveraging. First, Daewoo's growth strategies were always formulated to reflect government policies. When the government initiated policies to promote light industries in the 1960s, Daewoo began to aggressively export textiles. When the government launched the HCI drive in the 1970s, it acquired various companies to begin Daewoo Heavy Industries, Daewoo Shipbuilding and Heavy Machinery, and Daewoo Motors. When the government called for policies to promote high-tech industries in the 1980s, Daehan Home Electronics was acquired and became Daewoo Electronics. When the government sought to globalize the Korean economy from the late 1980s and 1990s, Daewoo built up a "global management network" of hundreds of foreign subsidiaries and offices.

The reason for such cooperation was simple. As long as Daewoo complied with government policy and showed good overall performance, it got preferential policy loans, tax credits, subsidies, protection and even bailouts when it got into financial trouble. For example, Daewoo took over Okpo Shipyard in 1978 at the government's request. In return, the government provided all the financing needed to complete the shipyard. The government also negotiated with the United States so that repair and maintenance jobs for the US Navy's Seventh Fleet could be done in Korea, and gave this monopoly to Daewoo, and assisted in building a mammoth machine industry complex in the surrounding Okpo area.

Daewoo's acquisition of Kyungnam Enterprise in 1986 provides another example of the group's ties to the government. The firm was on the verge of bankruptcy, and a deal was made to take it over as a part of the HCI rationalization policy. Daewoo received 200 billion *won* ($232 million) of preferential loans and the Korea Development Bank invested 50 billion won in Daewoo Shipbuilding, which was itself experiencing serious financial distress. This money, an astronomical amount at the time, was reportedly used to expand Daewoo Motors' production capacity (Lee 1993).

These cases suggest a second feature of Daewoo's history: the role of acquisitions. Daewoo began as a trading house with scanty capital and no production base. It acquired three companies before 1972, two textile producers and one leather processor, but gained momentum in 1973 thanks to profits from the US textile import quota. In that year, it acquired eight companies.[2] Hankook Machinery was acquired to become Daewoo Heavy Industries in 1976; Okpo Shipbuilding became Daewoo Shipbuilding and Heavy Machinery; and Saehan Motor Company became Daewoo Motor Company in 1978. By the end of 1978 the group had 41 companies, and only a handful of them had been built up from scratch. Among the major companies, Daewoo Corporation was the only one that was founded by Kim Woo Choong, the "Acquisition King."

The global network built during the 1980s and 1990s mirrored the domestic one. For example most of the car plants in Eastern Europe, built during the socialist era, were acquired at bargain prices.

Daewoo's expansion would have been impossible without high leveraging. Daewoo's start-up capital was negligible, and profits from existing businesses were inadequate to purchase new companies, some of which were bigger than existing ones and required extensive renovations of production facilities. Daewoo's financial skill thus played a vital role in its acquisition drive, giving Kim Woo Choong another nickname: "Financial Wizard."

The "Financial Wizard" and the "Acquisition King" were two sides of the same coin. The best example is the so-called "one-hundredth strategy" in Daewoo's foreign investments. Although the name was no doubt exaggerated, it implied that Daewoo needed only one-hundredth of the total capital of any foreign investment project. The strategy involved complex schemes of joint investment with local investors, preferential policy loans from the host country, loans given by local banks under the direction of the government, loans that other Daewoo subsidiaries secured elsewhere, and inter-subsidiary debt payment guarantees and equity investment.

Daewoo's financial subsidiaries[3] played an important role in financing investment projects. For instance, Daewoo Securities acquired a local bank in Poland in the early 1990s, which was a vital part of Daewoo's expansion in the transitional economies of Eastern Europe. And as we will see in more detail below, Seoul Investment Trust Company purchased 2.9 trillion *won* of bonds and commercial paper issued by various Daewoo subsidiaries in 1998 and 1999.

It is still impossible to find out how leveraged Daewoo was because past accounting data were later found to be highly unreliable. However, cash-flow statements shed some light on the extent of Daewoo's leveraging. Table 7.1 shows the top five *chaebol's* cash-flow statements from 1994 to 1997. The Daewoo Group's total net cash inflow from operations for the four-year period was 1.9 trillion won, only 13 percent of the total cash outflow of 14.1 trillion *won* for investment for the same period. In other words, about 87 percent of Daewoo's investment during this period was funded by loans.[4] This compares to 50 percent for SK, 41 percent for Samsung, 31 percent for LG, and 20 percent for Hyundai.

The growth strategy, based on close cooperation with government, acquisitions and high leveraging, was to some extent typical of all the major *chaebol*. What made Daewoo stand out was, first, the relentless and particularly unfocused nature of its acquisitions. Second – except for Daewoo Corporation, the parent of the group, and some peripheral subsidiaries – not a single major company in the Daewoo Group was built from scratch. Since Daewoo has always expanded through acquisitions, it has rarely gone through the agonizing process of developing, acquiring or even stealing new technology. By contrast, other leading *chaebol* in Korea founded many of the firms in their major business fields, and utilized acquisitions and financial assistance from the government during their expansion phase. Perhaps as a result, Daewoo subsidiaries' technological capabilities have always lagged behind their peers.

Third, and more generally, although Daewoo became one of the top commercial groups in terms of size, it has always been in the second class in almost all other aspects. Compared to its peers, the quality of goods it produced was low, technology lagged, productivity was poor, and profitability was disappointing. Other leading *chaebol* in Korea periodically sacrificed expansion to concentrate on improving technology

Table 7.1 Cash-flow statements of the top five *chaebol*, 1994–97 (billion *won*)

Source of cash flow	1994	1995	1996	1997	Total
Hyundai					
Operations	1,750	2,780	838	251	5,619
Investment	–3,470	–6,456	–8,378	–9,588	–27,892
Finance	2,182	3,735	7,559	10,684	24,160
Samsung					
Operations	3,853	5,118	2,509	3,540	15,020
Investment	–6,426	–9,229	–10,382	–10,918	–36,955
Finance	3,163	5,057	7,679	8,177	24,076
Daewoo					
Operations	622	251	1,828	– 850	1,851
Investment	–1,444	–3,329	–3,500	–5,826	–14,099
Finance	1,208	3,358	1,211	7,238	13,015
LG					
Operations	1,784	2,654	1,938	412	6,788
Investment	–2,570	–6,068	–6,394	–6,579	–21,611
Finance	1,273	4,022	4,398	8,139	17,832
SK					
Operations	459	939	1,818	2,066	5,282
Investment	–1,757	–2,040	–3,711	–3,123	–10,631
Finance	1,269	1,104	1,840	2,094	6,307
Total					
Operations	8,468	11,742	8,931	5,419	34,560
Investment	–15,667	–27,122	–32,365	–36,034	–111,188
Finance	9,095	17,276	22,687	36,332	85,390

Source: Choi (1998).

and product quality in order to gain dominant positions in domestic – and in some cases international – markets. However, Daewoo was negligent in such efforts, and thus remained in the second or third position in the domestic market in almost all the major items it produced.

Fourth, although Daewoo's corporate structure looks similar to other Korean groups, it is in fact distinctive. The typical *chaebol* structure has centered on the flagship company, many manufacturing subsidiaries and a separate trade house for exports (see Chapter 1). The flagship company is, in most cases, the major manufacturing firm which is the cash-cow of the group and hence acts both as the major holding company and funding source for other subsidiaries. If a new subsidiary becomes big and profitable enough, it becomes the second flagship and

they lead the group together or, in some cases, a new one takes over
flagship status from the older one. However, in Daewoo's case, there
was no cash-cow. The flagship, Daewoo Corporation, was a trading
house. Its profits were quite limited even in successful years. Nonetheless it had to find enough funds for subsidiaries' investments, operations
and export finance. Daewoo Corporation thus became the focal point
for international borrowing. In the domestic financial market, Daewoo
financial subsidiaries acted as the channel for funds. In sum, the
Daewoo Group was built around a "borrowing cow" rather than a
"cash-cow," and remained that way till the end.

2   Daewoo's Performance and Financial Situation before the Crisis

Daewoo's past performance was an undeniable success insofar as
growth is concerned. Under the partnership between Daewoo and
General Motors, Daewoo Motor Company was transformed from a
bankrupt assembly plant into one of Korea's leading automobile manufacturers. Okpo Shipyard was turned around to become one of the most
profitable shipyards in the world. Daewoo also showed great advances
in the high-tech fields of electronics and telecommunications and in
other industries through joint ventures. Daewoo formed partnerships
with General Dynamics and Boeing to manufacture fuselages and
equipment, with Caterpillar to produce forklifts and construction
equipment, and with Northern Telecom to produce optical fiber, cable
and telephone switching systems.

However, Daewoo's growth strategy also had costs. The interlocking
relationships between various companies combined with the high rate
of corporate borrowing increased the risk of financial difficulties for the
group as a whole. For example, when Daewoo Shipbuilding experienced financial distress in 1988–89, the consequences were felt by
Daewoo Heavy Industries, Daewoo Corporation, and the government's
Korea Development Bank, all of which had substantial investments in
shipbuilding (Steers et al. 1989). This incident, and others like it, indicated what was to come during the Asian financial crisis.

Daewoo's international operations also rested on business practices
that were highly risky. Daewoo Motors, one of Daewoo Group's
primary operating entities, is the prime example. In 1993, Daewoo was
given rights to assemble cars in Vietnam, a booming economy of
70 million people. But ten additional competitors entered the market.
The Vietnamese economy stalled, and demand for its cars plunged to

only 423 vehicles in 1998. Selling at a loss to gain share, Daewoo refused to retreat despite the fact that its total investment of $33 million was not paying off. Daewoo was also reported to be losing more than $30 million a year in India. Sales in Britain spurted to 30,400 units in 1998, but growth was unsustainable because of cut-rate pricing (*Business Week*, August 30, 1999; Clifford 1999). Daewoo Motors threw salt on its wounds in 1997 when, in the midst of economic crisis, it acquired troubled Ssangyong Motors and added more capacity.

Official accounting data did not reveal Daewoo's disappointing performance. For example, the Daewoo Group's official debt–equity ratios were not bad compared to other *chaebol* until 1997, and most Daewoo subsidiaries, including Daewoo Corporation and Daewoo Motors, reported substantial profits both in 1997 and in 1998. However, there is evidence that Korean investors have long discounted Daewoo's reports regarding profits and overall financial soundness. Such suspicions were reflected in the stock prices of Daewoo subsidiaries. Table 7.2 shows the ratio of market value to book value for the top five *chaebol* and other listed companies in April 1997, before the onset of the crisis. This is an important market measure of how profitable the company is and how efficiently capital is used. The ratio of the listed Daewoo entities was barely over 1, compared to 6.0 for Samsung, 6.6 for SK, 3.0 for LG, and 3.7 for Hyundai.

Table 7.2   Market value of the top five *chaebol*, April 1997

Chaebol	Number of listed companies	Capital (million won)	(%)	Market value (million won)	(%)	Market to book value of capital
Hyundai	20	2,036,618	4.69	7,462,136	6.12	3.66
Samsung	16	2,211,161	5.09	2,372,956	10.14	6.00
Daewoo	10	3,590,794	8.27	4,003,980	3.28	1.12
LG	12	2,262,931	5.21	6,780,909	5.56	3.00
SK	6	732,450	1.69	4,851,544	3.98	6.62
6th – 30th chaebols	121	7,900,897	18.19	16,184,718	13.27	2.05
Other listed companies	578	24,706,375	56.87	70,320,024	57.56	2.85
Total	763	43,441,226	100.00	121,976,267	100.00	2.81

3   Daewoo's Financial Situation in 1997–98

Table 7.3 shows some important items in the official accounting data of eight major Daewoo subsidiaries that account for over 95 percent of the sales of the Daewoo Group. Their total losses in 1998 were reported to be 510 billion *won*, a substantial drop from the previous year's net profit of 225 billion *won*. Daewoo reported that these huge losses were mainly due to one-time write-offs at Daewoo Telecom and the newly acquired Ssangyong Motor Company, whose combined losses were 885 billion *won* in 1998. Six other companies were supposedly in the black, generating net total profit of 375 billion *won* in 1998. This is quite an astonishing performance during a severe economic slump. Daewoo Corporation and Daewoo Heavy Industries posted sizeable net profits of 126 billion *won* and 209 billion *won* respectively in 1998; even Daewoo Motors allegedly earned 18 billion *won* during 1998.

The group's aggregate debt–equity ratio dropped from 486 percent in 1997 to 369 percent in 1998, still high but not bad for a *chaebol* group in its first year of restructuring. If asset revaluation is excluded, however, the result was more disappointing; excluding asset revaluation, the debt–equity ratio of eight companies was 562 percent in 1997, and 488 percent in 1998.[5] Daewoo Corporation and Daewoo Telecom showed some deterioration in their capital structure, but according to Daewoo this was mainly due to active trade financing to expedite exports in the case of Daewoo Corporation, and one-time write-offs of accounts receivable in the case of Daewoo Telecom. Daewoo also reported that total sales of these eight Daewoo companies increased by 12 trillion *won* in 1998, up 26 percent from the previous year. Aggregate operating income showed no decrease at all in 1998, again an astonishing performance during the recession.

In sum, the message Daewoo conveyed to the authorities, creditors and the public was that, although there was restructuring to be done, and several companies required special efforts to turn around, Daewoo was doing fine. The group had experienced some liquidity problems, but mainly caused by "groundless and malicious rumors" and aggravated by "unfriendly creditors" who tried to withdraw financing. Several major companies in the Daewoo Group improved their capital structures and most Daewoo companies earned profits on rapidly increasing sales; and all of this during the most severe economic recession and highest interest rates Korea had ever experienced.

Unfortunately, this unbelievable business performance was just that: unbelievable. First, profits were exaggerated and the group's actual losses amounted to over 4 trillion *won* in 1998 instead of the 0.5 trillion

Table 7.3   Daewoo's balance sheet: major operating units, 1997–98 (billion *won*, %)

	Daewoo Corp.		Daewoo Heavy Industries Ltd		Daewoo Electronics Co.	
	1997	1998	1997	1998	1997	1998
Assets	14,222.3	26,734.5	11,807.1	14,234.7	4,063.6	5,871.7
Current Assets	7,861.8	19,060.4	5,533.3	5,634.6	1,932.3	3,157.6
Fixed Assets	6,360.5	7,674.2	6,273.8	8,600.1	2,131.3	2,714.2
Investment in Securities	2,387.3	4,259.5	682.5	2,219.0	687.1	933.7
Tangible Assets	1,339.8	1,627.2	4,197.6	5,217.3	798.8	1,090.8
Liabilities	11,470.8	22,843.3	8,979.8	10,235.4	3,249.1	4,807.4
Borrowings & Bonds Payable	7,735.2	17,988.8	6,911.3	8,103.5	2,726.0	4,204.6
Capital	2,751.5	3,891.2	2,827.4	3,999.3	814.5	1,064.3
Asset Revaluation	433.1	682.7	359.1	1,423.6	–	224.8
Debt/Equity Ratio	416.9	587.1	317.6	255.9	398.9	451.7
(excl. asset Revaluation)	(494.8)	(712.0)	(363.8)	(397.4)	(398.9)	(572.7)
Sales	24,009.2	36,894.1	5,576.7	6,213.9	3,857.7	4,699.5
Operating Income	776.2	788.3	693.4	255.5	548.0	558.6
Non-operating Income	1,277.8	4,166.5	646.8	1,849.6	186.8	574.7
Interest Revenue	270.0	362.7	75.5	201.1	18.1	44.7
Gains from Asset Sales	4.7	1,995.9	–	1,054.0	4.3	297.7
Non-operating Expenses	1,970.6	4,809.1	1,198.4	1,878.2	676.3	1,121.6
Interest Expenses	880.3	1,930.1	573.6	1,049.3	339.1	490.4
Income before Income Taxes	65.5	126.0	131.6	208.7	52.3	8.2

Note: Continued next page.
Source: Financial Supervisory Commission.

won reported. Second, most of its capital, allegedly 15.4 trillion *won* as of end 1998, was fictitious; actual capital was near zero or even negative. Third, its debt–equity ratio in 1998, alleged to be 369 percent (488 percent excluding asset revaluation), was 2000 percent at best. It is apparent that, by the end of 1998, the Daewoo Group was already bankrupt, far beyond any hope of a turnaround.[6]

Table 7.3   (continued) Daewoo's balance sheet (billion *won*, %)

	Daewoo Motor Co.		Daewoo Motor Sales Co.		Ssangyong Motor Co.	
	1997	1998	1997	1998	1997	1998
Assets	8,513.4	15,863.6	1,778.4	1,961.6	3,968.3	3,793.0
Current Assets	4,075.1	3,550.3	1,079.2	767.0	1,031.1	953.3
Fixed Assets	4,438.4	12,313.3	699.3	1,194.7	2,955.2	2,839.7
Investment in						
Securities	129.4	5,903.6	36.8	169.1	58.5	11.7
Tangible Assets	2,931.6	4,126.9	247.1	812.3	2,382.5	2,358.6
Liabilities	7,474.1	11,790.6	1,616.5	1,241.4	4,137.2	2,746.8
Borrowings						
& Bonds						
Payable	5,343.4	9,181.1	266.4	659.9	3,401.9	2,380.0
Capital	1,039.4	4,072.9	162.0	720.2	−150.9	1,046.2
Asset						
Revaluation	295.2	786.6	–	516.4	–	–
Debt/Equity Ratio	719.1	289.5	997.8	172.4	(N.A.)	262.6
(excl. asset						
revaluation)	(1,004.3)	(358.8)	(997.8)	(609.1)	(N.A.)	(262.6)
Sales	5,797.7	5,119.1	3,681.1	2,109.9	1,441.6	794.2
Operating Income	636.8	980.6	−5.3	53.8	24.7	36.9
Non-Operating						
Income	611.8	888.0	67.9	131.8	132.5	140.7
Interest Revenue	104.6	700.6	60.2	103.5	15.7	18.8
Gains from						
Asset Sales	–	47.9	–	0.0	0.6	0.0
Non-operating						
expenses	997.5	1,851.1	48.1	179.1	468.4	423.3
Interest Expenses	557.8	1,448.6	40.6	143.0	289.1	237.3
Income before						
Income Taxes	252.1	17.6	15.0	5.1	−310.2	−499.8

Note: Continued next page.
Source: Financial Supervisory Commission.

First, profits. Daewoo Corporation, Daewoo Heavy Industries and Daewoo Electronics posted net profits of 126 billion *won*, 209 billion *won*, and 8 billion *won* respectively in 1998, a sizeable increase from their 249 billion *won* profits in 1997. These profits can be traced to the item termed "gains from asset sales" (Table 7.3), which amounted to 3348 billion *won*, equivalent to about $3 billion. However, these profits

Table 7.3   (continued) Daewoo's balance sheet (billion won, %)

	Orion Electronics Co.		Telecom Ltd Co.		Total	
	1997	1998	1997	1998	1997	1998
Assets	1,525.4	1,752.8	1,475.3	1,979.0	47,371.8	72,190.9
Current Assets	469.1	431.3	1,016.9	1,344.2	22,998.8	34,898.7
Fixed Assets	1056.3	1,321.5	458.4	634.8	24,373.2	37,292.5
Investment in						
Securities	268.7	309.6	171.5	271.0	4,421.8	14,077.2
Tangible Assets	545.1	883.5	137.3	222.2	12,579.8	16,338.8
Liabilities	1,211.9	1245.0	1,152.2	1,903.0	39,291.6	56,812.9
Borrowings						
& Bonds						
Payable	897.6	924.6	811.5	1,582.9	28,093.3	45,025.4
Capital	313.4	507.8	323.0	76.0	8,083.3	15,377.9
Asset						
Revaluation	2.9	95.1	–	–	1,090.3	3,729.2
Debt/Equity Ratio	386.7	245.2	356.7	2,503.9	486.3	369.4
(excl. asset						
revaluation)	(390.3)	(301.7)	(356.7)	(2,503.9)	(561.9)	(487.7)
Sales	964.4	1,176.1	1,150.2	1,412.1	46,478.6	58,418.9
Operating Income	58.5	111.9	192.8	142.2	2,925.1	2,927.8
Non-Operating						
Income	108.2	113.1	27.4	136.6	3,059.2	8,001.0
Interest Revenue	16.4	31.9	3.3	81.6	563.8	1,544.9
Gains from Asset						
Sales	–	6.0	1.8	6.2	11.4	3,407.7
Non-operating						
expenses	158.1	214.7	206.8	606.1	5,724.2	11,083.2
Interest Expenses	60.6	122.3	111.0	272.1	2,851.1	5,693.1
Income before						
Income Taxes	8.0	9.1	11.1	–385.2	225.4	–510.3

Source: Financial Supervisory Commission.

were fictitious, created through transactions among Daewoo sub-sidiaries. The scheme was as follows. Subsidiary A sold assets to Subsidiary B at inflated prices. Subsidiary B, in return, paid in stock or other assets, also at ballooned prices. Not only did Subsidiary A appear to earn profits from asset sales, but A's assets also increased from assets transferred from Subsidiary B. Subsidiary B also earned accounting profits if it gave its assets to A at exaggerated prices, or its capital increased if it gave newly issued stock to A. These transactions were nothing more than asset swaps among Daewoo subsidiaries at exaggerated values. If we correct for these fictitious profits, these three firms lost 3 trillion *won* altogether in 1998, and the entire Daewoo Group 4 trillion *won*.

Second, assets and capital. Daewoo reported assets of 72.2 trillion *won* and capital of 15.4 trillion *won* in 1998. But these were also fictions, as can be seen by looking at two items in Table 7.3: investment in securities and tangible assets. Investment in securities increased by 9655 billion won and tangible assets increased by 3759 billion won in 1998.[7] Daewoo's investment in securities and tangible assets thus increased by 13,414 billion *won* (approximately $12 billion) during a single year of severe recession, despite the fact that there were no major investments or acquisitions during the year. Most of the increase in tangible assets was due to asset revaluation and most of the increased investment in securities was due to asset swaps among Daewoo subsidiaries at exaggerated values. If we subtract this fictitious increase in asset values, Daewoo's assets *fell* from 72.2 trillion *won* to 58.5 trillion *won*, and its capital from 15.4 trillion *won* to 2 trillion *won*. Moreover, if the fictitious profit of 3348 billion *won* from asset sales among subsidiaries is subtracted from its capital, Daewoo's capital stood at *minus* 1.3 trillion *won* at the end of 1998.[8]

Third, debt–equity ratios. For Daewoo subsidiaries and the group as a whole, actual capital levels were negative in 1998. Contrary to the official 1998 debt–equity ratios shown in Table 7.3 (either including or excluding asset revaluation), Daewoo's *actual* ratios for most of the individual companies and for the group as a whole were either negative or, at best, extraordinarily high if one takes a very generous view toward Daewoo's investment in securities and tangible assets (Table 7.4). Even the debt–equity ratio of Daewoo Heavy Industries, the best among Daewoo subsidiaries, reached 2630 percent.

From these facts, it is clear the Daewoo Group was already bankrupt in 1998. The asset values of most Daewoo companies and the group as a whole fell far short of liabilities, and hence their net values were negative. But the Korean government and creditors only acknowledged Daewoo's bankruptcy in the due diligence audits completed in August 1999. We examine this failure below, but first look in more detail at Daewoo's response to the crisis.

Table 7.4 Assets and liabilities of Daewoo's 12 affiliates, 1999 (billion *won*)

Company	Daewoo report (June 1999)			Due diligence audits (August 1999)			(B – A)
	Assets	Liabilities	Capital (A)	Assets	Liabilities	Capital (B)	
Daewoo Corp.	29,203.0	26,590.9	2,612.1	17,458.6	31,994.4	–14,535.8	–17,147.9
Daewoo Telecomm Ltd.	3,294.1	2,985.2	308.9	2,260.3	3,159.3	–899.0	–1,207.9
The Diners Club of Korea	1,399.5	1,267.6	131.9	886.0	1,217.6	–385.6	–517.5
Daewoo Electronics Co.	8,230.1	7,655.3	564.8	5,046.7	7,729.0	–2,682.3	–3,247.1
Daewoo Electronics Components Co.	395.1	276.0	119.1	365.0	292.6	72.4	–46.7
Daewoo Heavy Industries Ltd.	13,974.1	10,661.4	3,132.7	12,028.3	11,009.3	1,019.0	–2,113.7
Daewoo Motor Co.	20,646.2	15,560.2	5,086.0	12,935.9	18,638.3	–5,702.4	–10,788.4
Daewoo Motor Sales Co.	2,130.2	1,367.3	762.9	1,397.3	1,215.6	181.7	–581.2
Ssangyong Motor Co.	3,347.6	2,976.9	370.7	2,762.2	3,097.8	–355.6	–706.3
Keangnam Enterprises Ltd.	1,087.1	851.7	235.4	626.4	696.8	–70.4	–305.8
Orion Electronic Co.	1,087.1	1,363.1	438.6	1,897.4	1,719.5	177.9	–260.7
Daewoo Capital Co.	6,564.4	6,202.0	362.4	3,566.8	5,993.8	–2,427.0	–2,789.4
Total	91,893.1	77,767.6	14,125.5	61,230.9	86,818.0	–25,587.1	–39,612.6

Source: Financial Supervisory Commission.

4   Daewoo Responds to the Crisis

Daewoo's response to the crisis came straight out of its old playbook: cooperate with the government, acquire failed companies to expand, and continue to borrow. The main cases in point include the acquisition of the Ssangyong Motor Company, the "Big Deals" with Samsung, and the attempt to purchase the Korea First Bank. At the same time, Kim Woo Choong signed a Capital Structure Improvement Plan that he had no intention of keeping and advised other *chaebol* to minimize layoffs.

The acquisition of Ssangyong Motors was initially regarded as a good deal both to the creditors and Daewoo. After 1.7 trillion won (about $1.5 billion) had been forgiven by the creditors, the company's balance sheet looked better than that of Daewoo Motors, the acquiring firm. Although it added no economic value to Daewoo Motors, whose production capacity was already far larger than its sales, it seemed to fit well into Daewoo's expansion. At the same time, the creditors and the government might have thought the deal a good way to solve the Ssangyong group problem, of which Ssangyong Motors was the focal point. Daewoo might have also thought that it would be rewarded for taking care of a failed company.

The Big Deals with Samsung, although they did not happen in the end, could be interpreted in the same context. It was not known whether Daewoo really wanted to sell Daewoo Electronics to Samsung, or whether Samsung really wanted to take it over. But Samsung clearly wanted to get rid of Samsung Motors and Daewoo seemed eager to take it over. The deal did not proceed well because Daewoo allegedly asked for 2 trillion *won* in cash from Samsung as the price for taking over all the debts of Samsung Motors. The deal fell through when Daewoo's problems began to surface in April 1999. However, this deal, too, seemed to fit Daewoo's old playbook: help the government get rid of a problem company, get financial assistance, and use that money to overcome its own financial difficulties through further acquisitions and expansion.

The failed attempt to take control of the Korea First Bank also fit into Daewoo's old strategy. Korea First Bank was supposed to be sold to a foreign bank, but only if the government made big concessions to the purchaser. Many in the government, as well as the general public, felt somewhat uneasy because of the cost and delay. Some simply opposed the idea of selling a major bank to foreigners, and Daewoo suggested that a consortium of Korean businessmen purchase Korea First Bank. Daewoo might have thought this an easy, quick solution to help the government, in return for which it could get the controlling rights of a major bank and a secure source of funds.

While pursuing this strategy, Kim Woo Choong, as the chairman of Daewoo group as well as the president of the Federation of Korean Industries, argued for the necessity of maintaining jobs. The government had developed various policies to lessen unemployment, and he thus might have thought that the government had no serious intention to hold *chaebol* to their Capital Structure Improvement Plans (CSIPs). As long as Daewoo *appeared* to meet targets, the government could save face and the company could escape punishment. As we will show, there were in fact some early indications that the CSIP was not regarded seriously as a vehicle to push *chaebol* reform.

In this context, it is easier to understand why Daewoo borrowed so much – 17 trillion won during 1998 – and why it cooked its books in such outrageous ways. Accustomed to surviving on borrowed money, Kim Woo Choong seemed to think that Daewoo would be safe as long as it could borrow. The government would not play the dangerous game of forcing Daewoo to bankruptcy because of the problems it would cause. Although some financial institutions reduced their loan exposure to Daewoo, most investment trust companies were eager to purchase Daewoo corporate paper and bonds because of the high returns they offered. They chose these high-return investments on the belief that the government would not let Daewoo go bankrupt. Seoul Investment Trust Company, which was under Daewoo's control, purchased most of this debt, but it was not alone. Daewoo had no problem in borrowing in the market until late October 1998, when the restrictions on the issue of corporate paper and bonds began. The group issued over 17 trillion *won* of corporate bonds and commercial paper in 1998.

Could Daewoo have saved itself? The answer is yes and no. By 1999, Daewoo could not be saved by any measures because so much damage had been done. However, if Daewoo began its restructuring in late 1997 when the crisis erupted, or in early 1998 at the latest, then it might have been possible to survive, although it would have been a difficult job.

As of August 1999, the due diligence audit found the difference between actual capital (that is, capital at market value) and book capital to be 43 trillion *won*. Of this difference, 23 trillion *won* was due to fraud and 20 trillion *won* due to decreased asset values.[9] Daewoo could easily have prevented a substantial portion of this 20 trillion *won* loss. For example, it could have saved about half of the group's actual losses in 1998, about 4 trillion *won*, if it had not acquired Ssangyong Motors, if it had not pursued a money-losing sales drive, and if it had cut its payroll and closed some unprofitable operations. It could have saved another 10 trillion *won* if it had not wasted money on senseless sales promotions that resulted in a tremendous accumulation of account receivables. And if it had pushed its restructuring plans harder, its subsidiaries' values could have been higher and hence the value of inter-subsidiary share-holdings would have been higher. All these combined would not have turned Daewoo around, but some subsidiaries could have become saleable. For example, Daewoo Heavy Industries, Daewoo Electronics, and Daewoo Telecom could have been sold at positive prices. Even for the companies that could not be sold as a whole, like Daewoo Corporation, some assets or business divisions could have brought in sizeable amounts of cash.

Because of the complicated links among subsidiaries through interlocking shareholdings and debt payment guarantees, as well as large hidden debts, one might argue that it was practically impossible for Daewoo to sell its subsidiaries. But this is not true. A firm can be divided and sold in many different ways. It can be sold as a whole, both assets and liabilities together. Or its asset side can be sold, leaving liabilities behind, or some part of its assets can be sold. It would not have been difficult for Daewoo to sell some part of its subsidiaries, leaving behind the complicated equity links, cross-loan guarantees, and hidden debts. If Daewoo did not sell its assets or subsidiaries, it was either because it did not want to sell them or because its asking prices were too high. Even though it might have been unable to get out of trouble

Table 7.5   Daewoo's fraudulent accounting (trillion *won*)

	Capital (August 1999) Daewoo's official accounting (A)	After due diligence (B)	Amount of Difference (B − A)[1]	fraudulent accounting[2]
Daewoo Corp.	2.6	−17.4	20.0	14.6
Daewoo Motors	5.1	−6.1	11.2	3.2
Daewoo Heavy Industries	3.1	1.0	2.1	2.1
Daewoo Electronics Co.	0.7	−3.0	3.7	2.0
Daewoo Telecom	0.3	−0.9	1.2	0.6
Sub-total	11.8	−26.4	38.2	22.5
Seven other subsidiaries	2.5	−2.2	4.7	0.4
Total	14.3	−28.6	42.9	22.9

Notes:
1. As of end August 1999.
2. As of end December 1999.
Source: Financial Supervisory Commission.

altogether, Daewoo could have reduced the possibility of complete breakup.

Consider also the reduction in payroll. Daewoo could easily have saved up to 1 trillion *won* every year by cutting 10 to 15 percent of its payroll. Under such a scenario, it might have recovered completely within five years.

Why were such steps not taken by Daewoo? For Daewoo to survive, Kim Woo Choong had to drastically downsize and transform it into a much smaller company. Such a transformation might not have been personally acceptable to him. Kim, who was used to huge windfalls from the acquisition of ailing companies, seemed to think he could secure windfalls from the sale of his own ailing companies. In fact, he had little to sell, not because he lacked saleable assets, but because his asking prices were too high. We do not know whether the early talks with General Motors and a Saudi businessman for asset sales were sincere or just gimmicks, but there are few who thought these deals could be struck.

Kim Woo Choong also seemed to think the new government's policy of *chaebol* reform would taper off as the three previous governments' had. Until late 1998 at least, he had every reason to believe this to be the case. First, huge amounts of cash continued flowing into Daewoo coffers, at least until October 1998 when the issuing of corporate bonds was restricted. Daewoo had no liquidity problems until then. Second, he also seemed to think he had enough political clout to protect himself and the group. Rumors about the special relationship between the new government and Kim Woo Choong had circulated in Korea from the time the new government won elections in December 1997. True or not, the impact of these rumors on the mindset of government officials, creditors and the general public should not be underestimated, particularly given the fact that the government did practically nothing until October 1998 to force Daewoo to reform.

Finally, Kim Woo Choong seemed to think he could fend off pressure by creditors and the government to drastically downsize because Daewoo was big enough to derail Korea's fledgling recovery and reignite the financial crisis. Daewoo had over 75,000 employees in Korea, a massive supplier network, and creditors that included trust companies holding nearly $18 billion in junk bonds (Clifford 1999). The impact would also be global as investigations later revealed; Daewoo owed more than 140 banks from 100 countries some $50 billion (*Business Korea*, August 1999). Even up to July 1999, when he announced a new restructuring plan and his intention to step down after Daewoo's restructuring was completed, Kim seemed to think the Daewoo group would be bailed out by the government and the creditors.

5   The Government and Creditors Respond to the Crisis

An important debate surrounds the question of when the government and creditors became aware of Daewoo's problems. They were brought to public light when Nomura Securities published a report in late 1998 on Daewoo's liquidity problems and their potential fallout. Rumors of Daewoo's bankruptcy began to surface as concerned investors withdrew existing loans. In mid-July 1999, Fitch IBCA and Standard & Poor's downgraded Daewoo Corporation to a CCC rating, which indicates "default is a possibility." By mid-1999, therefore, a consensus was forming in the market regarding Daewoo's prospects.

When did the government and the creditors become aware of the depth of the problem? They seemed to know in late 1998 that the group was in serious trouble, and that by March or April 1999 the situation had become dangerous. But up to the last minute they did not seem to realize that collapse was inevitable, and clung to the belief that the worst outcome could be avoided.

Daewoo's borrowing binge began right after the economic crisis hit Korea in December 1997 (Table 7.6). Roughly 2 trillion *won* worth of corporate paper and bonds were issued every month until September 1998, at which point the group had become the nation's number-one debtor. During the nine months from January to September 1998, its total debt increased from 29.7 trillion won to 44.8 trillion *won*, up over 40 percent. Government officials and creditors were alarmed by the rapid increase in Daewoo's debt level, particularly given the fact that interest rates were as high as 20 percent a year, falling to 13 percent over the course of the year. Daewoo's annual interest costs were estimated to be over 6 trillion *won*, a burden even healthier *chaebol* could not survive.

Alarmed by Daewoo's debt problem, the government began to pay greater attention to *chaebol* restructuring. In December 1998, top *chaebol*, including Daewoo, were ordered to submit new restructuring plans and revise their CSIPs with the main creditor banks. The Big Deals were pushed harder.

Daewoo's new restructuring program of December 1998 involved cutting the number of group companies from forty-one to ten, reducing its debt by 18.8 trillion *won* (about $17 billion), and lowering its debt–equity ratio to below 197 percent on average by the end of 1999. Progress in restructuring was to be monitored by the main creditor bank every quarter, and if Daewoo failed to meet quarterly targets, the main creditor bank was supposed to punish Daewoo by withdrawing existing loans.

Table 7.6 Loans and bonds outstanding for the top five *chaebol*, 1997–98 (trillion won, %)

	Hyundai	Samsung	Daewoo	LG	SK	Total
Loans						
End 1997(A)	15.5	15.5	8.8	10.2	4.1	54.2
Sept. 1998(B)	9.8	9.1	6.4	5.7	2.7	33.8
B – A	–5.7	–6.4	–2.4	–4.5	–1.4	–20.4
Commercial paper (CP)						
End 1997(A)	13.6	7.6	11.4	7.1	2.8	42.4
Sept. 1998(B)	14.3	7.8	17.5	7.3	3.9	50.8
B – A	0.7	0.2	6.1	0.2	1.1	8.3
Bonds						
End 1997(A)	11.7	10.4	9.5	10.3	4.2	46.1
Sept. 1998(B)	18.6	15.2	20.8	14.2	6.9	75.8
B – A	6.9	4.8	11.3	3.9	2.7	29.6
Total						
End 1997(A)	40.9	33.5	29.7	27.6	11.0	142.8
Sept. 1998(B)	42.8	32.1	44.8	27.2	13.5	160.3
B – A	1.9	–1.4	15.1	–0.4	2.5	17.5

Source: Financial Supervisory Commission.

Reducing the number of legal entities to ten had no significance in reducing actual operational assets, as had been shown in previous restructurings. Each *chaebol* was ordered to concentrate on three or four core competencies. Daewoo chose trade and construction, automobiles, heavy industries and finance and services, which covered all the previous business areas except electronics; at that time, Daewoo hoped it could get Samsung Motors in exchange for Daewoo Electronics. The debt–equity target, while relatively meaningless in terms of solvency given the absence of consolidated statements and the generous paper revaluation of group companies' equities, was viewed as overly optimistic.

But the most serious pitfall in the revised restructuring plan was that Daewoo was allowed to do practically nothing during the next three quarters, saving all important actions for the fourth quarter of 1999. The main creditor bank that was supposed to monitor its progress and respond if it failed to meet its quarterly targets had nothing do.

Although alarmed by Daewoo's rising debt, the government and creditor banks clearly underestimated the seriousness of the Daewoo problem. In 1999 they began to realize that Daewoo was far slower than its *chaebol* peers in restructuring, as Table 7.7 shows. Daewoo's debt–equity ratio increased from 527 percent to 588 percent during the first

Table 7.7   Debt–equity ratios of the top five *chaebol*, 1998–99 (trillion *won*, %)

	Hyundai	Daewoo	Samsung	LG	SK
Debt					
End 1998(A)	61.5	59.9	44.7	36.4	22.5
1st Half 1999(B)	64.9	61.8	39.3	35.2	21.4
(B – A)	3.4	1.9	–5.4	–1.2	–1.1
Debt–equity ratio					
End 1998(A)	449.3	526.5	275.7	341.0	354.9
1st Half 1999(B)	340.8	588.2	192.5	246.5	227.3
(B – A)	–108.5	61.7	–83.2	–94.5	–127.6

Source: Financial Supervisory Commission.

half of 1999, while its peers showed significant improvement. Even Hyundai, the other major *chaebol* in trouble, showed a significant drop in its debt–equity ratio.

Daewoo was feeling immense pressures in the market. It was getting harder for Daewoo to revolve corporate paper and bonds, and Daewoo unveiled a revised restructuring plan in April. But Daewoo's problems got deeper and in July, Kim Woo Choong made a final proposal. He would put all his personal wealth as collateral, concentrate on the management of the automobile group and retire after it was stabilized. In return creditors would provide 4 trillion *won* of emergency loans to Daewoo.

According to a government document, the government knew at that point that "Daewoo should be put into a workout because it cannot be saved by short-term emergency loans." But it seemed to think it could "devise the second best policy and implement it" to prevent the economy-wide shocks caused by a Daewoo workout. The second-best policy mentioned in the document was the above-mentioned July plan, which was later discarded. At the end of 2000, the government was still saying that the collapse of Daewoo was "an unanticipated event."

The general course of government policy is reviewed in Chapters 6 and 8 and can be summarized briefly here. On January 13, 1998, about six weeks before the inauguration, President-elect Kim Dae-jung met with the chairmen of four top *chaebol*[10] and agreed upon the five principles of corporate reform. The government changed almost all related laws and decrees during 1998, and *chaebol* were ordered to make restructuring plans and draw up CSIPs with their main creditor banks.[11]

However, the agreements proved to be an ineffective vehicle for *chaebol* reform. As Kyung Suh Park argues in Chapter 8, creditor banks, which were supposed to lead *chaebol* reform, had neither the will nor the power to enforce the agreements because they themselves were the targets of reform. Second, the government decided that *chaebol's* restructuring plans would remain secret to protect them from the potential damage that would be incurred if their business secrets were known to their foreign rivals. However, since the plans were not disclosed to the public, there was no way to monitor if restructuring was being carried out as planned.[12] Third, the Financial Supervisory Commission sent the wrong signal in late April 1998 when it said the top five would restructure on their own,[13] while the smaller *chaebol* would be put into workout programs. The commission later restructured merchant banks and securities houses by allowing (in fact, inviting) *chaebol* to put new money into their ailing financial subsidiaries instead of closing them.

Hence, it is not surprising that the government achieved practically nothing through the CSIPs except the endless rewriting of the restructuring plans for the Big Five and press releases to explain them to the public. Some reform-minded *chaebol* did in fact seek to restructure themselves. But the CSIPs had no teeth to force the hand of those resistant to reform, namely Daewoo and Hyundai.

Daewoo also exploited a critical loophole in the deposit insurance scheme by selling bonds guaranteed by the government. At the onset of the crisis in November 1997, the Ministry of Finance and Economy, worried about massive bank runs, made the critical mistake of covering insurance companies' guarantees of corporate bonds.[14] Given this coverage, insurance companies provided guarantees to Daewoo bonds indiscriminately, an extreme example of moral hazard. The total amount of guarantees provided to Daewoo bonds amounted to 7.2 trillion *won* when this arrangement was finally stopped in July 1998. Many financial institutions, especially investment trust companies, had purchased these guaranteed bonds.

The only significant action taken by the government, although belatedly, was the restriction on the issue of corporate paper and bonds by the *chaebol*. The primary targets of this action were Daewoo and Hyundai, and the government acted out of both alarm and frustration. It was alarmed because Daewoo and Hyundai might eventually go bust if borrowings went unchecked, and frustrated because they showed no sign of restructuring as long as they had access to finance.

In June 1998, talks on restricting Daewoo's issue of corporate paper and bonds began inside the government.[15] Despite opposition from the Ministry of Industry, Trade and Energy, the government decided to restrict the issuing of corporate paper beginning in July 1998. However, the decision on bonds was postponed indefinitely because of divided opinion. On one side were those who thought the restriction on bond issue would cause a severe liquidity problem for Daewoo and consequently lead to its collapse and a huge economic shock. On the other side were those who thought delay would cause bigger problems. In the meantime, Daewoo's bond issue increased rapidly, and it became the biggest debtor in the nation by September 1998 (see Table 7.6). Frustrated by the lack of progress in the talks among different branches and offices inside the government, Kim Tae Dong, Senior Secretary for Policy Planning, unilaterally announced the restriction on corporate bonds in late October.

But it was too late to turn Daewoo around: by then, its debt was too big to be serviced by normal operational income. The end came in July 1999, when 19.2 trillion *won* of corporate paper came due. Daewoo's bankruptcy was therefore not an intended outcome of a government plan.[16]

Why were the necessary steps not taken by the government and creditors? It was quite obvious to many in the market as well as in the government that Daewoo was in extreme financial difficulties and its collapse was inevitable. In retrospect, anyone could have recognized the seriousness of Daewoo's problem only by looking at its balance sheet and income statements. Why did the government and creditors not take the necessary steps to prevent its collapse?

As for the creditors, the answer seems quite simple: they were faced with their own problems. Table 7.8 shows the estimated losses of financial institutions due to Daewoo. It is quite clear that Daewoo's collapse would cause the bankruptcy of its major creditor banks, and that they could therefore neither force Daewoo to adopt drastic measures nor declare it bankrupt. As Kyung Suh Park shows in Chapter 8, creditor-led restructuring of Daewoo was a "mission impossible" from the beginning.

As in other countries, the government was the only actor who could have stopped the Daewoo collapse or at least minimized the costs by intervening swiftly once the insolvency of Daewoo became apparent. What were the necessary steps the government should have taken? The answers are very simple: set the rules, enforce them, punish those who break them, but help those who follow them honestly. That does not necessarily mean that the government should have intervened directly or resorted to non-market actions. But by setting the financial supervisory rules regarding problem loans and problem debtors, the government could have led creditors to force Daewoo to restructure.

The financial supervisory authority in Korea had the legitimate power to order creditors to reduce their exposure to Daewoo, which for many creditors was already over the supervisory limit. At the same time, the financial supervisory authority could have stopped financial institutions' reckless purchase of Daewoo corporate paper and bonds that were regarded as risky. Squeezed by creditors, Daewoo would have had no other options but to take drastic measures to downsize. If necessary,

Table 7.8   Estimate of losses of creditor financial institutions due to Daewoo

Creditor	Loans and Daewoo bond holdings (trillion *won*)	(%)	Estimated losses (trillion *won*)	Loss ratio (%)
Banks	22.0	(38.6%)	12.5	56.8
ITCs	18.6	(32.6%)	10.4	55.9
Seoul Guarantee Insurance Co.	7.2	(12.6%)	3.4	47.2
Merchant banks	2.9	(5.1%)	1.8	62.1
Insurance companies	1.1	(1.9%)	0.6	54.5
Securities firms	1.1	(1.9%)	0.7	63.6
Other non–bank financial institutions	4.1	(7.3%)	1.8	43.9
Total	57.0	(100%)	31.2	54.7

Source: Financial Supervisory Commission.

the government could have provided creditors with public funds to recapitalize them; otherwise, they too would have gone bankrupt. Public funds were being infused into the financial industry to refurbish it in any case, and these funds could be used to solve the Daewoo problem.

One way to enforce such a plan was the so-called Capital Structure Improvement Agreement between Daewoo and its creditors. By making a contract between creditors and the problem debtor, Daewoo in this case, the creditors could force Daewoo to restructure. The financial supervisory authority could monitor the progress of the agreement and, if necessary, punish creditors when progress was found to be unsatisfactory. The regulations had the authority to order financial institutions to handle problem loans appropriately. As we have seen, however, the government did not have the will to push Daewoo to restructure.

Why? First, the fear of the effects of Daewoo's collapse on Korean financial markets and the nation's economy was nearly universal among government officials. Some thought the Daewoo problem should be tackled as early as possible, not because they underestimated its magnitude but because they thought it would only get bigger over time. But the majority held the view that taking on the Daewoo problem prematurely would be costly. In retrospect, they misjudged both the seriousness of the issue and the inevitability of Daewoo's bankruptcy.

Second, bureaucratic concern about market instability also contributed to inaction. The economic bureaucracy often intervenes in the market to maintain the status quo in the name of "stability" rather than accept temporary instability, even if it is unavoidable to address some problems.[17] Given this bureaucratic tradition, it is almost impossible to expect the government to have acted before the problem broke out.

Third, the incentives in the Korean bureaucracy also caused inaction. Bureaucrats are often punished if things go wrong when they act, but not when they act after things go wrong. Since the tenure of most of the top bureaucrats is short, they tend to postpone necessary actions in the hope that problems will not occur during their tenures.

Fourth, Korean bureaucrats abhor the disclosure of relevant information to the public. They have tended to believe, out of elitism, that financial markets would be unduly destabilized if information were publicized, and as a result much information is deemed "sensitive" and withheld. As a result of such secrecy, the market did not have enough information to put pressure on Daewoo to restructure earlier.

Fifth, there has been no core team of dedicated experts in the government to devise, implement and monitor policy for *chaebol* reform. Powers were divided among various branches and offices, and opinions were often divided among them, resulting in stalemate and inaction. Showing impatience, the president would from time to time try to jump-start *chaebol* reform in the cabinet; the Big Deals might be understood in this light. An impatient president, without deep knowledge of financial markets and corporate management, was vulnerable to the ill-conceived advice that the Big Deals were an easy and quick way to undertake *chaebol* reform.

Sixth, Daewoo's special relationship with the government, whether true or not, was another important factor in understanding government behavior. Ever since Kim Dae-jung was elected as president in December 1997, there had been rumors about the special relationship between him and Kim Woo Choong. Only a handful of people can confirm or deny this relationship, but the rumor itself had some effects because it gave many top government officials the impression that Daewoo could not be pushed around. Kim Woo Choong seemed to have considerable political clout through other channels too, which he and other Daewoo managers and employees sought to exploit. At the same time, Daewoo used public relations gimmicks to avoid pressure. For example, Daewoo circulated news about negotiations with foreign investors to sell its subsidiaries, and said its restructuring would be derailed if the deals were interrupted by government intervention.[18]

6   Post-Bankruptcy Management

On July 19, 1999, Daewoo finally disclosed that it could not meet its debt payments. But the attempt to save Daewoo by the government, its creditors and Daewoo itself continued until August 26. The administration initially resorted to government-backed credit to bail out Daewoo. Korean banks allowed Daewoo to roll over existing loans, and issued additional loans to the company totaling 4 trillion *won* ($3.5 billion). In exchange, Daewoo was expected to put up 10 trillion *won* ($9 billion) in new collateral[19] and adopt some drastic measures for restructuring. On August 16, Daewoo announced yet another new plan to sell all its subsidiaries except Daewoo Motors and five other automobile-related companies, and made a "Special" Agreement for Capital Structure Improvement with its creditor banks. But these efforts did not calm the turmoil in the financial markets. On August 26, twelve Daewoo companies were put into workout and Kim Woo Choong was finally removed. It thus took six weeks for the administration to accept the bankruptcy of Daewoo after its announcement of *de facto* bankruptcy on July 19, 1999.

The workout plan agreed upon among creditors was nothing more than a default-postponement agreement (Table 7.9). Of 56 trillion *won* of existing loans (that is, not counting new ones), only 10 percent were swapped for equity. The rest either was swapped for convertible bonds, or interest was reduced or exempted.

Through early 2001 the sale of Daewoo companies had not proved successful, either. After Ford decided not to buy Daewoo Motors, creditors began new negotiations with General Motors. Negotiations to sell Daewoo Electronics, Daewoo Heavy Industries, and some divisions of Daewoo Corporation did not go well either. The administration and the creditors should have accepted that large losses were inevitable and moved to sell them quickly since carrying costs are high.

7   Conclusion

Daewoo's fall was caused by a string of bad investment decisions in a never-ending drive for expansion. These decisions went unchallenged because corporate governance simply did not exist. First of all, there was no distinction between ownership and management. The owner-dominated process of decision-making is a common characteristic of all *chaebol*, yet it was most distinct at Daewoo. The uncontested decision-making power of the chairman, despite his relatively small shareholdings, enabled Kim Woo Choong to make high-risk investments that aimed at

Table 7.9   Daewoo loan restructuring under workout (billion *won*)

	Interest reduction and exemption	Swaps Debt for equity	Swaps Debt for CBs	Other	New loans	Total
Daewoo Corp.	6,044.2	2,000.0	16,700.0	251.1	1,908.7	26,904.0
Daewoo Motor Co.	6,752.0	1,468.3	1,878.7	_	2,042.0	12,141.0
Daewoo Heavy Industries Ltd	7,556.1	1,349.2	_	_	147.5	9,052.8
Daewoo Electronics Co.	3,689.2	394.7	1,065.3	1,148.3	_	6,297.5
Daewoo Telecom Ltd	1,054.1	200.0	1,145.1	18.1	316.7	2,734.0
Ssangyong Motor Co.	1,586.9	130.0	_	18.9	264.0	1,999.8
Daewoo Electronics Components Co.	116.8	_	_	_	5.0	121.8
Kyungnam Enterprises Ltd	92.2	134.0	_	217.6	10.0	453.8
Orion Electronics Co.	1,229.8	_	_	_	38.0	1,267 8
Daewoo Motor Sales Co.	538.7*	_	_	_	_	_
Total	28,121.3	5,676.2	20,789.1	1,654.0	4,731.9	60,972.5

Note: CBs are corporate bonds.
* Redemption deferred.
Source: Maeil Economic Daily, November 27, 1999.

growth over profitability. These decisions were taken without checks from boards of directors, shareholders or creditors, who never held management accountable for its poor performance or wrongdoing. Second, the methods chosen to finance these projects excluded raising new equity capital in order to maintain the chairman's control.[20] Excessive reliance on debt financing eroded the profitability of projects and resulted in a financial structure with high debt–equity ratios (Jang 1999). As a result, Daewoo was quite vulnerable to external shocks such as recession, interest rate hikes, and credit crunches.

Third, cross-loan guarantees allowed Daewoo to enter into new businesses without accurate evaluation, and weak siblings were allowed to survive on borrowed money. This only aggravated the cash-flow problem of the group and induced sequential failures among affiliated companies (Jang 1999).

Fourth, diversification into dozens of different business lines, which had provided a safety net to Daewoo in the form of unfair transactions among affiliated companies, became an obstacle to focusing on core competencies (Jang 1999). This failure, in turn, left Daewoo with its outdated strategy of relying on low-priced, low-quality products and decreased its competitiveness in the market.

Fifth, a tradition of opaque and undisciplined accounting allowed Daewoo to hide its real financial picture for too long. Lack of transparency discouraged foreign and domestic investors from investing in Daewoo. Their inability to monitor and scrutinize corporate performance created distrust, making it impossible for the market to discipline Daewoo properly.

Creditors did not do their job, either. Creditors are supposed to evaluate and monitor debtors and act swiftly to minimize losses if debtors are found to be unable to service loans. Liberalization and deregulation of the financial sector without proper regulatory mechanisms brought lax government supervision and accounting standards that enabled lending institutions to discard financial prudence and provide loans to debt-ridden *chaebol*.

The government was also responsible because it did not abide by its own rules and principles. Its lax and inconsistent enforcement of laws and regulations sent conflicting signals to the *chaebol*, financial institutions and the market. Administrative disinclination to disclose information only compounded the managerial non-transparency of *chaebol*.

The lessons from the Daewoo case are quite clear. The five principles of corporate reform set by the government should be kept not only to overcome the current economic crisis but also to change the behavior of Korean corporations. Managerial transparency and accountability should be firmly established. Financial supervision should be strengthened. The government should enforce the laws and regulations firmly, and thus become a role model for a disciplined market economy.

Notes

1 In order to get a generous portion of the total quota, which was based on past shipments, Daewoo shipped a substantial amount of textile products to its own US subsidiaries. Such practices were very common among Korean exporters during the 1970s and 1980s to get preferential policy loans and to meet export targets. Daewoo resorted to similar tactics again in 1998.

2 One investment company, one securities house, one machine manufacturer, one construction company, one electric appliance manufacturer, two trading companies, and one textile manufacturer.

3 Daewoo Group's financial subsidiaries were Daewoo Securities, Daewoo Capital, Diners Club Korea, Daewoo Venture Capital, and Daewoo Investment Advisory Service. In addition, Seoul Investment Trust Company, although not formally a Daewoo subsidiary, was under Daewoo's control from the late 1980s.

4 Cash flow from finance in the statement includes loans as well as stock issues. As will be explained later, however, Daewoo's stock issues have been negligible for the past several years.

5 According to Daewoo's official accounting report, Daewoo Motors' debt–equity ratio dropped from 719 percent in 1997 to 290 percent in 1998 (from 1004 percent to 359 percent, excluding asset revaluation), Daewoo Motor Sales' ratio dropped from 998 percent to 172 percent (from 997 percent to 609 percent, excluding asset revaluation), and Daewoo Heavy Industries' ratio dropped from 318 percent to 256 percent (but increased from 364 percent to 397 percent, excluding asset revaluation).

6 This conclusion was initially drawn in April 1999 by the author from the official accounting data posted by Daewoo Group and reported to the various government authorities such as the Blue House and the Ministry of Finance and Economy. But the government, as far as the author knows, did not take any substantive remedial actions until Daewoo declared bankruptcy. The Financial Supervisory Commission confirmed in September 2000 that Daewoo had hidden debts and ghost assets that amounted to 22.9 trillion won.

7 Ssangyong Motors was officially included in the Daewoo Group from January 1, 1998. However, the increase in tangible assets is not due to the inclusion of Ssangyong which was counted both in 1997 and 1998.

8 If we do the same calculations for individual subsidiaries, Daewoo Heavy Industries had capital of 389 billion *won* at the end of 1998, but Daewoo Motors and Daewoo Corporation both had liabilities that exceeded assets. Daewoo Corporation saw a huge increase in current assets in 1998 due to the increase in receivables. Forty-six percent of Daewoo Corporation's total assets were account receivables at the end of 1998. Only the special audit can give us the explanation, but the author's conjecture is that most of account receivables were either goods "shipped and stored abroad" or pure fiction.

9 According to the Financial Supervisory Commission, the shortfall of 20 trillion *won* could not be regarded as the result of outright illegal accounting fabrication. Rather, they found it was mainly due to the differ-

ence between the cost method and market value method in valuing assets, or the difference between conservative and liberal valuations.

10 Kim Woo Choong, the chairman of the Daewoo Group, did not attend the meeting on the excuse of meetings with foreign investors. Daewoo had already announced its plan to seek strategic alliances with leading foreign companies or sell some of its affiliates to foreign investors, but none of these plans materialized.

11 The deadline for submitting the plan was the last day of February for the top five *chaebol*, the last day of March for the rest of the top thirty *chaebol*, and the last day of April for smaller *chaebol*.

12 The government decided in May 1998 to disclose the top five *chaebol's* restructuring plans. This decision was made by one senior secretary in the Blue House in order to expedite *chaebol* reform through public pressure on the *chaebol*, their main banks and the government itself. The Financial Supervisory Commission initially opposed disclosure but conceded in the end. No business secrets were revealed, only unrealistic target numbers without any substantive plans to achieve them.

13 When the 55 companies were chosen to be closed in June 1998, there were 20 subsidiaries of the top five *chaebol* on the list. But none of them was of any significant size.

14 Officials might have thought that issuing corporate bonds indirectly guaranteed by the government was necessary for the *chaebol* to secure funding since direct government bailouts or financial assistance were impossible under the terms of IMF and IBRD agreements.

15 The Financial Supervisory Service was ordered to track the new issue of corporate paper and bonds by the top five *chaebol* and report to the Blue House every month.

16 Some policymakers and advisers, inside as well as outside the government, strongly suggested in mid-1998 that the government initiate one well-planned bankruptcy of a *chaebol*, chosen from a list of already bankrupt ones, to show the will of the government in the market. Even though these companies were a lot smaller than Daewoo, the government could not do it.

17 When the government addresses problems in the financial market, they are often labeled "stabilization" policies: Financial Market Stabilization Policy, Capital Market Stabilization Policy, Stock Market Stabilization Policy, Bond Market Stabilization Policy, and so on.

18 There was also widespread concern about the extremely complicated nature of Daewoo's assets and debts, and a belief that no one except Kim Woo Choong could understand the web of undisclosed cross-guarantees, hidden assets and debts, and secret agreements. Many officials in the government and in other influential positions believed that if Kim Woo Choong were to be removed from Daewoo, it would collapse immediately.

19 Its market value was estimated to be far below 10 trillion *won*.

20 Another reason might be that new equity issue was not easy since stocks of Daewoo companies were not popular in the Korean stock market, as shown by low the market-to-book-value ratio of capital in Table 7.2.

References

Anon. 1999. "Rating Reflects Daewoo's Dire Straits," *Business Korea*, (8): 16.
Choi, Sung-No. 1998. *Korea's Large Business Groups in 1998* (in Korean). Seoul: Center for Free Enterprise.
Clifford, Mark L. 1999. "Daewoo's Boss is Playing a Dangerous Game," *Business Week*, August 16, p. 8.
Financial Supervisory Commission (FSC). Internal Documents.
Jang, Ha Sung. 1999. "Corporate Governance and Economic Development: The Korean Experience." Paper presented at the International Conference on Democracy, Market Economy and Development, Seoul, Feb. 26–27.
Kang, Myung Hun. 1996. *The Korean Business Conglomerate: Chaebol Then and Now*. Berkeley: University of California, Institute of East Asian Studies, Center for Korean Studies.
Kim, Eun Mee. 1997. *Big Business, Strong State: Collusion and Conflict in South Korean Development, 1960–1990*. Albany, NY: State University of New York Press.
Lee, Dong Gull. 1999. "Daewoo and Hyundai Restructurings: Evaluation and Suggestions." Unpublished MS. Seoul: Korea Development Institute.
Lee, Jong Jae. 1993. *Chaebol's Resume* (in Korean). Seoul: Hankook Daily Press.
Lim, Hyun Chin. 1985. *Dependent Development in Korea, 1963–1979*. Seoul: Seoul National University Press.
Ministry of Finance and Economy, Republic of Korea. 2000. *Daewoo-Related News*, various issues.
Rhee, Jong-Chan. 1994. *The State and Industry in South Korea: The Limits of the Authoritarian State*. Routledge: New York.
Song, Il. 1997. "Global Process and Strategy of Korean Conglomerate: Case Analysis of the Globalization of Daewoo Group," *Journal of Economics and Business*, 16 (1): 161–82. Seoul: Research Institute for Economics and Business Administration, Hankuk University of Foreign Studies.
Steers, Richard M., Shin, Yoo Keun, and Ungson, Gerardo R. 1989. *The Chaebol: Korea's New Industrial Might*. New York: Harper & Row Publishers.

8   Bank-led Corporate Restructuring

Kyung Suh Park

As a vicious credit crunch continued into early 1998, the Korean government started to implement an ambitious corporate and financial restructuring program. Understanding that moral hazard and high leveraging played a key role in the crisis, the goal of the restructuring was not only recovery, but also a market system in which shareholders, creditors, management and employees assumed certain responsibilities. Restructuring included efforts to improve the financial soundness of firms through the redeployment of corporate assets and subsidiaries, but also efforts to enhance the managerial transparency of corporations and new corporate governance systems. In contrast to the restructuring of the 1970s and 1980s, the restructuring of the 1990s included not only rehabilitation programs for individual firms and financial institutions but also efforts to change the institutional structure of the economy.

In the corporate sector, the Korean government adopted different approaches to restructuring, depending on firm size (see Chapters 6 and 7). For the largest five *chaebol*, the so-called Big Deals program called on firms to exchange business lines for the purpose of streamlining their business and focusing limited corporate resources on a few core activities. For the 6th through 64th *chaebol* and other independent firms, "workout" programs were applied where firms committed to implement a series of restructuring measures in return for debt rescheduling and reduction. In these cases, firms were subject to exit if they failed to successfully implement restructuring measures.

Another notable feature of the restructuring program was establishment of two new financial supervisory authorities: the Financial Supervisory Commission and the Financial Supervisory Service. A major problem with the financial supervisory authorities, however, was that they sometimes had incentives to emphasize the short-term stability of the financial markets at the expense of long-term corporate viability. One good example of this problem was the case of Daewoo (see Chapters 6 and 7). Daewoo had initially been included in the Big

Deals under the presumption that the survival of its affiliated firms was assured. However, it was later transferred to the workout program. Delayed application of a restructuring program to the Daewoo Group increased the size of the bad loans of the financial institutions, weakened the financial sector and hurt the credibility of the government.[1]

The most serious problem with the intrusive involvement of the government was its effect on the behavior of financial institutions. Paternalistic government intrusion rendered financial institutions passive in the corporate restructuring process. Instead, the supervisory authorities and the Corporate Restructuring Coordination Committee, a special committee established to oversee and coordinate the workout process, played a major role in the selection and termination of workout companies. The reliance on these agencies was partly due to the weak financial status of the creditor banks, which were also under their own restructuring programs. The role of commercial banks did change over time, however, and they gradually took a more active role in the workout process. Such a transition, even though still incomplete, can be ascribed to the changing environment of management for financial institutions in Korea.

This chapter deals with two important issues: corporate restructuring and the role of banks in the workout process. First, it reviews the restructuring process, including the workout program for mid-sized *chaebol* and independent companies. Second, it focuses on the incentives of banks, which were supposed to lead the overall corporate restructuring process but at the same time were fighting for their own survival; this fact greatly distorted the overall direction of corporate restructuring. In June 1998, the Financial Supervisory Commission announced a financial restructuring program that included the closing of five failing banks. Cornered by both regulatory authorities and the market, Korean commercial banks inevitably chose to shrink their assets by reducing the size of loans to the corporate sector. However, these moves adversely affected their clients, resulting in a vicious circle of corporate failures and mounting bad loans. This chapter analyzes the incentives of credit banks during the financial crisis and shows that the strict capital adequacy requirements imposed on them as a criterion for bank restructuring may have worsened the credit crunch, which was particularly devastating for small and medium-sized firms.

The Korean case clearly shows that successful corporate restructuring can only be implemented with the support of a healthy and responsible financial sector. Otherwise, extreme forms of moral hazard on the part of both firms and creditor banks can seriously distort the overall restructuring process.

1   The Workout Program: An Overview

Months after the financial disaster of December 1997, the Korean government introduced a workout program to restructure mid-sized *chaebol* and independent firms that were in financial distress. Officially called the "corporate rehabilitation program," it was similar to the London approach that Britain pursued in the 1990s, an informal corporate restructuring in which the Bank of England played the role of arbitrator. Close relationships among management, creditors and regulators were used to resolve disagreements among stakeholders. However, Korea's workout program was more intrusive than the London approach in that the supervisory authorities played a decisive role in setting the direction of workout programs for individual firms.

Workout programs are differentiated from court receivership or composition (see Table 8.1). Under a workout program, credit banks lead the overall process while the court, according to the Corporate Reorganization Act or the Composition Act, administers the latter. Workout programs are more flexible in their operation compared with court-led restructuring procedures, and therefore reduce the time for rehabilitation of failing firms. Remedy measures can be agreed upon in private negotiations between creditors and subject firms. Outside arbitrators get involved in the process only when the creditors and firms cannot reach agreement. Credit banks can also increase the retrieval rate of their loans through value-increasing restructuring, since a workout firm can continue its business without being disturbed in its relationships with business partners.

On the other hand, workouts do not have as much legal force. Court-led restructuring procedures can enforce a rehabilitation program even without an agreement from stakeholders. This lack of legal authority in workout programs can delay the overall rehabilitation process and increase the potential costs of financial distress. In workouts, for example, conflict among creditors, especially between large and small creditors, can be a source of inefficiency. In Korea, even though the Corporate Restructuring Coordination Committee played the role of arbitrator between creditor banks and debtors, it did not have legal means to enforce agreements, and could not adjudicate the conflicting interests of creditors and debtors, which sometimes delayed the implementation of restructuring measures.

Workouts can also be differentiated from the bailouts of the past in that the latter simply extended the life of failing firms through interest forgiveness and extension of new credit, without substantive restructuring. Loss sharing among shareholders, management and creditors, and voluntary business restructuring – including transfer of control

Table 8.1 Workout, court receivership and composition in Korea

	Workout	Court receivership	Composition
Applier	Firms, creditors	Firms, creditors, shareholders	Individuals, firms
Credits suspended	Credits specified in the agreement	All credits from commercial transactions (No recourse)	Credits specified in composition
Effective date for suspension	Call for creditors' meeting	Court decision for receivership	Court decision for composition
Shareholder rights	Capital reduction and debt–equity swap	More than half the shares effaced	No capital reduction
Control rights	Depends on creditors' decision	Management ousted	Control maintained by present management
Quorum and decision	Approval of more than 75% of creditors	More than 75% (66% for no–recourse credits) of the creditors	Presence of more than half of the creditors and approval of more than 75%
Repayment of debts	3–5 years	10 years at maximum	No limit but usually 10 years at maximum

Source: Park et al. (2000: 282).

rights – were rarely components of bailouts, while creditors in workouts actively pursue them in order to retrieve credits.

The workout program officially started in May 1998 when banks established the Committee for Corporate Insolvency Evaluation, which investigated 313 firms with potential financial problems. The main criteria for a workout included: expectations that the subject firm would have a higher value as a going concern; its workout program would be implemented and superior to other programs such as court receivership; and fairness among interested parties could be secured.[2] The initial workout program included sixteen out of the fifty-nine *chaebol* ranked 6th through 64th in size. Daewoo, the fourth-largest *chaebol* at the time, was included in August 1999. Fifty-five companies were selected initially, and the number was increased to 104 as more firms faced financial distress. Out of these, ninety-six firms were finally put into the workout process. Eight firms dropped out of the procedure since they could not agree with their creditors with regard to equity write-offs or loss sharing.[3] Another forty *chaebol* were later allowed to pursue their own restructuring programs while three were already under court receivership (see Table 8.2).[4]

In June 1998, a Management Monitoring Team was established in each bank to oversee the workout process of firms and to report directly to the president of the bank.[5] In addition, outside advisory groups consisting of consortia of international investment banks, accounting firms and law firms were employed to support the credit banks in the evaluation of workout programs and foreign investment.

The reason why the government used size as a criterion for inclusion in the workout program was that medium-sized *chaebol* would not cause too much of a shock to the economy even if they defaulted during the restructuring process. On the other hand, the five largest *chaebol* were judged to be too large to be restructured by the commercial banks and thus were excluded from bank-led restructuring programs.

Tables 8.3 and 8.4 list the workout firms; Table 8.5 compares them with other firms.[6] Out of the total of 644 listed firms, seventy-three went through the workout process. As of the end of 1997, the average asset size of workout firms was smaller than that of non-workout firms (698.1 billion *won* versus 801.2 billion *won*). Not surprisingly, their debt dependency was higher (359.5 percent versus 250.0 percent). Workout firms utilized more bond financing than non-workout firms, and their revenue sources were more oriented toward foreign exports. The higher dependency on direct financing might reflect the lack of monitoring by bondholders and managerial inefficiencies. In terms of governance, the average ownership of the largest shareholder and his relatives was smaller for workout firms (18.3 percent versus 25.0 percent), suggesting a potential for agency problems on the part of management and dominant shareholders. Creditor banks' share ownership of workout firms tended to be larger (11.2 percent versus 7.8 percent).

Table 8.2   Corporate restructuring of the 6th–64th *chaebol*, May 1998

Restructuring procedure	Groups
Workout (16 groups)	Ssangyong, Gohap, Dong-Ah, Anam, Shinho, Kabool, Tongkook Trading, Geopyung, Woobang, Byucksan, Jindo, Shinwon, Kangwon Industry, Sepoong, Shindongbang, Taegu Department Store
Court receivership or composition (18 groups)	Hanil, Tongil, Haitai, Kia, Hanbo, Sammi, Hanshin Engineering, Daenong, New Core, Soosan Heavy Industry, Hanlla, Chunggu, Jinro, Nasan, Keukdong Construction, Doore, Bosung, Hwaseung

Table 8.3   *Chaebol* workout firms and their main banks

Creditor banks	*Chaebol*	Affiliates	Selection date
Chohung	Geopyung	Geopyung Chemicals, Geopyung Iron, Geopyung Sygnetics	16.6.98
	Sepoong	Sepoong, Sepoong Construction	18.7.98
	Kangwon Industry	Kangwon Industry, Sampyo Trading, Sampyo Industry, Sampyo Heavy Industry	18.7.98
	Anam	Anam Semiconductor, Anam Electronics, Anam Environment	24.10.98
	Ssangyong	Ssangyong Construction, Namkwang Engineering	3.11.98
Hanbit	Kabool	Kabool, Kabool Spinning	14.7.98
	Byucksan	Byucksan Construction, Byucksan, Tongyang Trading	6.8.98
	Kohap	Kohap, Korea Chemicals, Korea Composite Chemicals, Kohap Trading	6.7.98
Korea First	Shinho	Shinho Paper, Shinho Chemicals, Dongyang Steel Pipe	9.7.98
	Tongil	Tongil Heavy Industry, Ilsung Construction, Ilshin Stone, Korean Titanium	20.7.98
	Tongkook	Tongkook Trading, Tongkook Spinning, Tongkook Compound	7.10.98
Seoul	Jindo	Jindo, Jindo Trading, Jindo Construction	14.7.98
	Woobang	Woobang	16.7.98
	Dong-Ah	Dong-Ah Construction	21.8.98
Korea Exchange	Shinwon	Shinwon, Shinwon JMC, Shinwon Marketing	18.7.98
Taegu	Taegu Department Store	Taegu Department Store, Taebak Shopping	1.9.98

Source: Financial Supervisory Commission.

Table 8.4 Non-*chaebol* workout firms and their main banks

Creditor banks	Groups	Firms	Selection date
Chohung	Donghwa Duty Free	Yoojin Travel, Donghwa Duty Free, Donghwa Development	18.8.98
	Dongbang	Dongbang, Dongbang T&C, Dongbang Metal	15.9.98
	Choongnam Spinning	Choongnam Spinning, Choongbang	4.11.98
Korea Commercial	Shinwoo	Shinwoo, Shinwoo Industry, Shinwoo Telecom	11.11.98
	–	Peerless Cosmetics	17.8.98
	–	Zetex	28.10.98
	–	Sungchang Inc.	16.10.98
Korea First	Ildong Medicine	Maxon Electronics, Ildong Medicine	31.7.98 9.9.98
Seoul	Mijoo Trading	Mijoo Trading, Mijoo Iron, Mijoo Metal, Mijoo Steel	24.12.98
Korea Exchange	–	Youngchang Instrument	19.9.98
	Shinsong Foods	Shinsong Foods, Shinsong Industry	30.12.98
Shinhan	–	Korea Computer	29.9.98
Korea Housing	Dongbo Construction	Dongbo Construction, Dongbo Development	1.10.98
Busan	Hanchang	Hanchang, Booil Telecom, Hanchang Papers, Seoul Tread Club, Hanchang Chemical	24.8.98 3.9.98
	–	Seshin	14.9.98
Kyungnam	–	Moohak	10.10.98
Taegu	–	Seohan	9.11.98
	–	Hwasung Industry	17.11.98
Korea Industrial	Kyunggi Chemicals	Kyunggi Chemicals, Daljae Chemicals	12.9.98
	–	Samil Industrial	9.9.98
	–	Namsun Aluminium	11.9.98
	–	Daekyung Steel	14.9.98

Source: Financial Supervisory Commission.

Table 8.5 Summary statistics of listed workout firms, end 1997

	Workout firms (73 firms)	Non-workout firms (571 firms)	t–test of difference (p value)	Wilcos z–test of difference (p value)
Total assets (billion *won*)	698.1	801.2	0.5301	0.4210
Debt ratio	359.5%	250.0%	0.0047	0.0001
Bank credit to total debt	0.304	0.344	0.0210	0.0353
Bond issues to total debt	0.278	0.198	0.0002	0.0001
Exports to sales	0.398	0.314	0.0456	0.0383
Largest shareholder ownership	18.34%	25.03%	0.0003	0.0001
Bank ownership	11.17%	7.84%	0.0022	0.0011
Foreign ownership	4.35%	4.88%	0.4464	0.2427
Stock holding period return (Jan. 1996– Nov. 1997)	–91.6%	–35.2%	0.0001	0.0001
Stock holding period return (Dec. 1997– Dec. 1999)	34.3%	80.8%	0.0001	0.0001

Source: KIS Data, Korea Credit Rating Company.

Interestingly enough, the holding period returns of the stocks of workout firms were much lower *before* as well as after the crisis. From January 1996 to November 1997, the average holding-period return[7] of the stocks of workout firms was minus 91.64 percent, which is well below the minus 35.21 percent for non-workout firms. This implies that the stock market accurately reflected the deteriorating financial status of those firms. The same thing happened after the crisis broke. The average holding-period return for workout firms from December 1997 to December 1999 was 34.3 percent, while that for non-workout firms was 80.8 percent.

In all, 210 financial institutions participated in the workout program, which included banks, merchant banks, insurance companies, securities companies, investment trust companies and other credit institutions. Finance companies and foreign financial institutions were excluded mainly due to the small size of credits. The participating financial institutions came up with the Agreement on Corporate Restructuring that prescribed the general obligations of the creditors. The workout programs included swaps of debt for equity or for convertible bonds, adjustment of interest and principal repayments, debt payment guarantees, new credits, capital infusion by shareholders, and asset sales.

In May 2000 the Financial Supervisory Service, in cooperation with the Corporate Restructuring Coordination Committee, investigated the overall workout program and advised credit banks to expedite the process and increase the amount of debt forgiveness for eighteen workout firms. The management of thirteen firms also was replaced. Such an adjustment was necessary because the original estimates of the financial status of workout firms provided by accounting firms and credit banks were found to be too optimistic. On the other hand, thirty-two workout firms were ultimately recommended for an early completion of the program mainly due to their good performance (eighteen firms), and the restructuring schedule for the remaining forty-four workout firms was finalized in November 2000 (see Table 8.6).

Initially, the workout program was to be finished by the end of 1999, but in consultation with the World Bank, it was extended beyond the original schedule. However, no new firms have been allowed into the program since July 2000. As of October 2001, out of the 104 companies initially selected, twenty dropped out of the program due to disagreement on loss sharing between creditors and firms or because liquidation was later deemed more appropriate. Seventeen merged with other companies. Thirty-six companies successfully completed their restructuring and graduated from the program. The remaining thirty-five were still under workout programs, of which eighteen were chaebol-affiliated firms and seventeen were independent firms.

Officially, three institutions participate in a workout: creditor banks, the Corporate Restructuring Coordination Committee, and the finan-

Table 8.6 Status of workout firms, August 2000

	Selected (A)	Dropped	Finished Early completion	Merged	Sub-total (B)	Outgoing (A – B)	MOU exchanged
Chaebol	61	5	9	12	26	35	33
Non–chaebol	43	3	8	3	14	29	29
Total	104	8	17	15	40	64	62

Note: "Dropped" refers to four affiliates of Tongil group, Anam Electronics, Kyunggi Chemical, Daljae Chemical, Samhyup Development.
Source: Financial Supervisory Commission.

cial supervisory authorities.[8] The main bank, or the credit bank that has the largest amount of credits, administers the overall workout process. A workout firm is selected through consultation with its main credit bank, which calls for a creditors' meeting after consulting the Coordination Committee. The main bank prepares a restructuring program and a memorandum of understanding, operates the Management Monitoring Team, and then reports monitoring results to creditors. The creditors' meeting consists of all financial institutions that agreed to participate in the workout program and drafts the Agreement on Corporate Workout among creditors. The creditors' meeting approves, with more than 75 percent of total credits, the selection and termination of a workout firm and its restructuring program.[9]

The Corporate Restructuring Coordination Committee was established by credit institutions and consists of seven experts in corporate restructuring with supporting staff. It advises credit banks, arbitrates between creditors and debtors, and imposes penalties for breach of contract. In consultation with the Financial Supervisory Commission, it has the ultimate power to decide the destiny of a workout firm. Credit banks welcomed the operation of the Coordination Committee since it played the role of the arbitrator not only *vis-à-vis* workout firms, but also *vis-à-vis* any outside parties, including the government.

Financial supervisory authorities also participate in the overall process to maintain the financial stability of the credit banks involved and the financial markets more generally. They advise credit banks in the area of debt rescheduling and other workout processes and provide institutional support by amending related regulations on debt-for-equity swaps, tax exemptions, securities investment, and other measures.

2   The Workout Process

As already mentioned, a workout process is initiated by a firm in financial distress or by its main credit bank. Once the restructuring is deemed necessary between the bank and the firm, the firm officially requests a workout and the bank calls a meeting of creditors. Any credit exercise is suspended for six months at maximum with the call for the creditors' meeting. The workout process begins with the approval of three-fourths of the credit institutions on the basis of their credit amounts.

Once the workout process is initiated, a corporate restructuring plan based on an evaluation by a third party is proposed and subjected to negotiations between creditors and then with the firm. If creditors fail to agree upon the plan, the Corporate Restructuring Coordination Committee steps in and arbitrates. Ultimately, credit banks and the firm reach an MOU, which prescribes the restructuring program to be implemented by both parties as well as penalties in case of nonfulfilment. The main credit bank in general monitors the observance of obligations through a dispatch of administrators, regular reports, and through the Committee for Management Evaluation, which consists of credit bank representatives.

The workout process ends when the subject firm completes the program. For firms that graduate early from a workout program, the existing MOU is withdrawn and the existing management resumes its full control of the firm. The normal relationship between creditors and the firm is also resumed. However, if there is any possibility of deterioration in the firm's performance in the future or a request for debt payment by creditors that could seriously affect the performance of the firm, the MOU still holds and the workout turns into a private composition.

Workout programs are implemented both through debt restructuring based on the MOU exchanged between a workout firm and creditors, and through voluntary business restructuring. Debt restructuring includes debt forgiveness, swaps of debt for equity or convertible bonds, and the infusion of new credits. Some firms also undertake voluntary restructuring programs, which are not covered in the MOU but are implemented as a way to show their commitment to survival. These programs include sales of assets and subsidiaries, infusion of foreign capital, and changes of management. In practice, in order to expedite the restructuring process, buy-back options were sometimes given to large shareholders, or taxes related with sold assets were exempted until 1999.[10]

An important objective of the workout program is to decrease the dependency of insolvent firms on debt. To improve the financial stability of workout firms, an extensive range of debt restructuring was implemented that usually covered three to five years of cash flow. As of the end of June 2000, 85.6 trillion *won* of debt was restructured, 86.8 percent of which was forgiven interest payments. Straight debt forgiveness was extensively utilized, while more sophisticated measures such as debt-for-equity swaps were used as a secondary tool of restructuring. For example, swaps of debt for equity or convertible bonds amounted to 3.4 trillion *won*, much smaller than debt forgiveness and representing only 21.6 percent of the original plan. The delay in the schedule for swaps was mainly due to disagreement between creditors and firms on conversion rates, and especially to existing managements' concern about ownership and control.

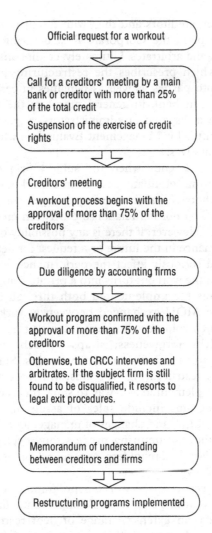

Figure 8.1 A workout procedure

Another important feature of the workout process was that twelve affiliates of the Daewoo Group accounted for more than 75 percent of the total amount of restructured debt (see Table 8.7). There was also a big change in the nature of Daewoo's debt restructuring that reflected its changing financial status. Loans for interest forgiveness increased from 36.0 trillion *won* at the end of 1999 to 53.1 trillion *won* as of June 2000 while that for debt-for-equity swaps decreased from 26.6 trillion *won* to 8.6 trillion *won*, reflecting the dire financial status of the group.

Table 8.7   Debt restructuring plans and implementation, June 2000 (100 million *won*, %)

Classification	Debt restructuring					New
	Debt rescheduling		Debt–	Others[2]	Total	credit[3]
	Interest forgiveness	Normal interest rates	equity swap[1]			
Total firms						
Planned	722,918	59,838	158,250	44,736	985,742	67,092
Implemented	702,440	46,515	34,238	72,848	856,041	48,522
(%)	(97.2)	(77.7)	(21.6)	(162.8)	(86.8)	(72.3)
Daewoo Group (12 firms)						
Planned	533,641	11,888	85,849	34,389	665,767	56,110
Implemented	530,744	11,888	5,666	35,257	583,555	37,209
(%)	(99.5)	(100.0)	(6.6)	(102.5)	(87.7)	(66.3)

Notes:
1. Including convertible bonds.
2. Loan–deposit offset, repayment and normal transactions.
3. Including debt payment guarantees.
Source: Financial Supervisory Commission.

In parallel with the debt restructuring imposed on debtors, voluntary business restructuring sought to increase the operating efficiency of related firms. The scale of voluntary restructuring proved smaller than debt restructuring (see Table 8.8). By the end of June 2000, the total amount of business restructuring by workout firms amounted to 5.4 trillion *won*, which included 407 billion *won* from the Daewoo Group. The pace of this restructuring was as scheduled for most of the workout firms except the affiliates of the Daewoo Group, which achieved only 46 percent of the original schedule due to delays in selling affiliates.

Asset sales, including the sale of real estate, were the main component of the voluntary program, amounting to 3.5 trillion *won*. Infusions of new capital, both from domestic and foreign investors, also contributed to the restructuring efforts of the workout firms. 1.13 trillion *won* of new capital was raised, about 50 percent of which was from foreign sources. Dominant shareholders also donated their private wealth as compensation for their mismanagement.[11]

On the other hand, sales of subsidiaries were not very successful as can be seen in the low implementation ratio of 14.1 percent. The main reason for the delay was firms' reluctance to sell affiliates showing better performance and inability to find buyers for affiliates with poor performance.

Table 8.8   Voluntary business restructuring, 2000 (100 million *won*, %)

Classification	Asset sales		Foreign	Sales of	New	Others	Total
	Sub-total	Real estate	capital induced	affiliates	capital		
Total (68 firms)							
Planned	29,944	24,225	3,490	12,491	4,085	4,284	54,295
Implemented	35,081	29,915	5,700	1,764	5,616	6,239	54,401
(Ratio, %)	(117.2)	(123.5)	(163.3)	(14.1)	(137.5)	(145.6)	(100.2)
Daewoo Group (12 firms)							
Planned	2,204	1,223	–	5,383	–	1,271	8,858
Implemented	2,049	1,294	–	754	–	1,271	4,074
(Ratio, %)	(93.0)	(105.8)	(–)	(14.0)	(–)	(100.0)	(46.0)

Note: "Others" includes donations by large shareholders, management improvements, etc.
Source: Financial Supervisory Commission.

A final component of the workout program was change in ownership and management. In the case of Dong-Ah Construction and Tongkook Trading, professional managers replaced the owner-managers. Ssanyong Construction of Ssanyong group, Dongyang Trading of Byucksan group, and Jechul Chemical of Geopyung group were separated from their business groups and/or sold to other *chaebol*. In the process, the incumbent management usually gave up their dominant shareholding position through reduction of capital. The transition in management was not without conflicts; some dominant shareholders resisted and tried to hold on to their ownership.

3   An Evaluation of the Workout Program

Despite positive aspects of the workout program, it also had several problems. From the beginning, the program was misunderstood as a way to delay the exit of failing firms. The program was very similar in spirit to the Bankruptcy or Default Suspension Agreement (DSA) that was applied to failing companies such as Kia and Hanbo in 1997, before the onset of the crisis.[12] The DSA program was criticized for delaying the exit of those conglomerates, thus enlarging the size of bad loans and contributing to the Korean economic crisis. Political considerations also influenced the selection process of workout firms. Affiliates of Daewoo Group were not included in the program initially since the government was worried about the side-effects of their inclusion.

A second criticism of the program was that it acted as a signal that the subject company was in financial distress; once in the program, firms could not obtain credits from the market and faced difficulties in maintaining their business. Actually, half the workout firms that were initially included in the program were already receiving forgiveness from their main banks. The program only confirmed such conjectures. Those companies that could not survive without financial support from credit banks were those who tended to apply for the program. However, some companies delayed their application until they were in serious trouble, thus increasing bad loans for their creditors.

Rather than the program being too harsh, it continued to generate moral hazard. Since the program usually allowed management to maintain control, managers had leeway to pursue their own benefit. The management of workout firms purposely overestimated their business prospects in order to maintain their control even at the expense of debt forgiveness. They sometimes refused to implement restructuring programs as agreed upon in the MOU, and would not share capital losses, hurting the credibility of the whole workout program.

Other examples of management misconduct included: sales of property owned by dominant shareholders to an affiliate at an above-market or below-market price; appropriation of corporate funds by dominant shareholders for private use; refusal by dominant share-holders to donate private capital as committed under the MOU; refusal to resign from their positions despite commitments to do so; use of corporate capital without prior approval of creditors during the workout process; and maintaining subsidiaries in disguise. In some cases, debt forgiveness was exploited in order to engage in price competition with competitors.

Perhaps the most controversial problem with the program, however, was the role of creditor banks. Creditor banks did not have the capability to lead restructuring programs, partly due to their own governance and incentive problems. There are many reported cases in which creditors did not faithfully fulfill their due diligence, did not take proper measures to force workout firms to meet restructuring schedules, and were unwilling to make critical decisions. They were even reluctant to initiate workout programs at all since including a corporate customer in a workout program meant increased loan loss amortization, which resulted in decreased operating profit. The bank-restructuring program of the Financial Supervisory Commission, based on the capital requirements of the Bank for International Settlements (BIS), aggravated such reluctance[13] (see Chapter 13).

The passiveness of credit banks stems mainly from their relationships with the government. The supervisory authorities have long intervened in the management of commercial banks in Korea. They controlled interest rates, regulated the business scope of banks, and even specified their manpower, branch networks and capital. Even after going through an extensive financial reform process in the 1990s, regulations still maintained their influence through implicit guidance channels.

This sort of intervention is partly ascribed to incentives of the bureaucrats in the supervisory authorities. They benefit from controls and red tape while in office, and even after retirement they can safely land management jobs at the credit institutions they used to supervise. The financial institutions find it necessary to hire those retired officials for maintaining good relationships with the supervisory authorities. It is therefore not surprising that the financial reforms implemented during the 1990s were less than thorough.

In some cases, the Management Monitoring Teams representing creditors did not faithfully fulfill their responsibilities. For example, they failed to demand management accountability for misconduct. An evaluation of the performance of workout firms was often superficial, and the measures taken to correct mismanagement were not appropriate. Securing the actual control of workout firms through debt-for-equity swaps was one way to accelerate the workout process, but credit banks proved reluctant to take the responsibility and passed final decisions over to the Corporate Restructuring Coordination Committee.

The problems were compounded by the fact that even the outside directors of workout firms were filled with ex-employees of credit banks. In some cases, existing management maintained control of working capital in clear violation of the workout rules, and sometimes they appropriated it. The operation of the monitoring team itself was not efficient and the selection of the heads of the teams was found to be improper in many cases.

The nature of the workouts is also vulnerable to criticism. Credit banks mostly focused on supplying liquidity through debt restructuring without seeking fundamental changes in the troubled firms' operations. Thus workout firms will remain a burden on credit banks. In order to make sense of the problems inherent in the *corporate* workout programs, we need some understanding of the *bank*-restructuring process.[14]

4   Bank Reform and Its Effect on Corporate Restructuring

Even though Korean commercial banks were supposed to lead the corporate restructuring and workout process, they could not properly do so, partly because they themselves were also under intense pressure. The government first announced its financial restructuring program, including the one for the banking sector, in November 1997. The financial supervisory authorities then imposed BIS capital adequacy requirements and threatened to close any banks that could not satisfy the 8 percent rule. Selecting corporate customers for workout was clearly not the top priority of the creditor banks, since it immediately hurt their capital position. In June of 1998, the Financial Supervisory Commission closed five failing banks either through mergers or purchase and assumption. The first stage of bank restructuring was completed by September 1998 as the five banks were merged with other banks and put into normal operation.

During this process, depository banks in Korea had three alternatives to meet the capital requirement: raise new capital, downsize, or adjust their portfolios. The first option was not viable because the domestic capital market was still in deep trouble. Foreign capital was not interested in the shaky domestic banks even though the market prices of bank shares were well below their face value.[15] Cornered by the regulatory authorities and the market, Korean commercial banks inevitably chose to shrink their assets and to change the composition of their portfolios.

Korean commercial banks sharply reduced their credits to meet the 8 percent BIS ratio requirement at the end of 1997 (see Table 8.9). The total assets of the deposit banks increased by 5.1 trillion *won* during the fourth quarter of 1997, 3.1 trillion *won* during December alone. But their loans decreased by 2.9 trillion *won* and 8.4 trillion *won* respectively during the same periods.

The proportion of loans to total assets of the deposit banks did not show any changes until November 1997 (see Table 8.10). However, it dropped from 50.9 percent at the end of November to 45.6 percent at the end of December. The proportion edged up slightly during the first half of 1998, but dropped to 41.6 percent again by the end of September 1998. On the other hand, the proportion of risk-free securities[16] jumped from 5.4 percent in November 1997 to 7.8 percent in December 1997 and to 9.2 percent in September 1998, while the proportion of risky securities such as corporate bonds remained at the level of 11.0 percent during the period. It increased sharply, however, from June 1998 when the five merged banks began to replace risky loans with risky securities. By the end of December 1998, risky securities accounted for 17.8 percent of banks' assets.

In absolute amounts, won-denominated loans decreased by 4.7 percent from December 1997 to September 1998, while securities investments increased by 81.8 percent. The decrease in domestic loans

Table 8.9 Deposit bank asset portfolios and corporate defaults, 1997–98 (billion *won*)

	Third quarter 1997	Fourth quarter 1997	All 1997	First quarter 1998	Second quarter 1998	Third quarter 1998	Fourth quarter 1998
M3 Loans	14,316.7	11,630	−1,986.1	1,514.3	−16,895.0	−18,591.6	−26,316.7
Securities	6,863.5	7,436.8	−73.6	5,819.9	1,839.7	17,593.3	22,000.9
Deposit banks' assets	16,628.0	51,559.1	30,823.7	46,413.0	−733.1	35,498.9	2,680.7
Loans	9,095.6	2,953.6	−8,392.5	10,714.2	−3,518.0	−8,696.8	1,899.6
(Small & medium firms)	(1,035.7)	(3,502.6)	(−5,461.9)	(−2,465.7)	(−4,528.4)	(−11,613.4)	(−3,496.3)
Securities	3,525.7	11,776.5	11,656.3	4,989.9	6,899.1	31,017.4	13,752.7
Number of default firms	3,834	6,101	3,197	9,449	6,357	4,221	2,801
Default amount	5,922.0	22,294.3	15,118.8	14,247.3	10,060.6	9,928.9	4,697.6
Default rate (%)	0.25	0.80	1.49	0.54	0.43	0.41	0.17

Table 8.10   Composition of deposit bank assets (% of domestic assets)

Period	Loans and discounts	Securities		
		Risky	Risk–free	Total
Dec. 1996	49.2	(8.4)	(6.9)	15.3
June 1997	52.1	(9.7)	(6.9)	16.6
Nov. 1997	50.9	(10.6)	(5.4)	16.0
Dec. 1997	45.6	(9.7)	(7.8)	17.5
Mar. 1998	47.5	(10.0)	(8.4)	18.4
June 1998	46.8	(11.0)	(8.9)	19.9
Sept. 1998	41.6	(15.7)	(9.2)	24.9
Dec. 1998	41.7	(17.8)	(9.7)	27.5

Source: Bank of Korea, Money and Banking Statistics, May 1999.

was mainly from those banks with BIS ratios below 8 percent, whose loans showed a much lower growth rate of 4 percent during the first half of 1998 compared with 7.5 percent in 1997. In 1998 sixteen out of twenty-one commercial banks in Korea recorded a decrease in the share of loans in total assets, while all banks boosted their securities investments. The five merged banks showed the biggest change in their asset composition as they increased the proportion of securities by 12.7 percent while reducing that of *won*-dominated loans by 4.2 percent out of the total assets.

Comparison of the loan activities of deposit banks also sheds some light on the effect of the bank-restructuring program. Between December 1997 and September 1998, the overall domestic assets of deposit banks increased by 16.8 percent. However, their asset growth rates significantly differed depending on their BIS ratios. The nine banks that did not satisfy the BIS criteria as of the end of 1997 recorded an increase of 4 percent in assets on average. The banks with BIS ratios of over 8 percent recorded loan growth rates of 11.7 percent, still much lower than the 17.6 percent of 1997.

There is substantial debate on whether there was in fact a credit crunch in Korea. However, it does appear that the portfolio adjustments of deposit banks seriously damaged the production activities of manufacturing firms, which were already under liquidity pressure due to decreasing sales. During the early period of the crisis, the corporate default rates increased sharply. The Bank of Korea responded by encouraging deposit banks to extend credits to small and medium-sized firms by expanding the supply of its low-cost discount window funds as well as by using window (informal administration) guidance. An increase in bank loans was observed in the first quarter of 1998, but mounting corporate defaults left the deposit banks to pursue their own interests at the expense of the corporate sector, and total loans decreased again during the second quarter of 1998 up until the third quarter. Larger firms were able to avoid the shock of the credit crunch due to their capability to resort to the capital markets for equity or for bond financing.

One notable outcome was a clear difference between large firms and small and medium-sized firms in their debt repayment schedules. Table 8.11 shows how small and medium-sized firms were under more financial pressure than large firms. The repayments of the former were on average 257 percent of their funds raised during 1998, while those of large firms were only 119 percent. Repayment ratios of over 100 percent imply that investment activities of the related firms had been seriously affected.

The industrial production statistics also confirm the differential effect of the credit crunch on corporate activities. The production index for small and medium-sized firms dropped sharply from 101.9 in 1997 to 72.4 in 1998.

Table 8.11 Sources of funds of manufacturing firms, 1998

Source of funds	Large firms	Small and medium–sized firms
Owner's equity	109.77	773.21
Debts	–9.77	–673.21
Long–term borrowing	33.56	13.30
Loans	–37.83	57.43
Corporate bonds	78.75	–70.17
Others	–7.36	26.05
Short–term borrowing	–65.12	–229.63
Loans	–119.07	–257.36
Long–term debt with maturities less than 1 year	54.08	–18.87
Others	–0.13	46.61
Payables	–20.07	–463.90
Others	41.86	7.02
Total	100.00	100.00

Source: Bank of Korea, Financial Statement Analysis for 1998.

The credit crunch problem, which was felt more severely by small and medium-sized firms, subsided from the fourth quarter of 1998 when the infusion of public funds into commercial banks began to restore their financial status. The Korean case clearly shows that a sound corporate restructuring in a crisis economy can be pursued only when its banking sector remains healthy.

5   Policy Implications and Conclusions

As economic growth slowed and Korean financial markets continued to show serious signs of turmoil, the Korean government and supervisory authorities announced a "second stage" of corporate and financial restructuring in September 2000. It sought to accelerate the exit of failing firms and financial institutions, and additional public funds amounting to nearly $40 billion were mobilized to aid failing financial institutions. Accordingly the reorganization of failing firms, including Daewoo affiliates and those in the workout process, was expedited. Woori Financial Group, the first of its kind in Korea, was established, which has four commercial banks and one merchant bank as its subsidiaries. In addition, corporate and securities laws were revised to further strengthen the rights of minority shareholders and the accountability of corporate directors and auditors.

New reform measures were also introduced to address problems observed in the workout process. A major change was the introduction of a "pre-packaged" bankruptcy system, similar to one used in the United States. This system is a modified version of court receivership, where the court automatically approves a pre-arranged deal between creditors and firms so that the rehabilitation process can be expedited with legal support.[17] In addition, if creditors cannot reach consensus on a workout program, they can turn to a pre-packaged bankruptcy system with the approval of only 50 percent of the creditors.

Another measure adopted to improve the workout system is the establishment of Corporate Restructuring Vehicles. These firms specialize in purchasing the assets of credit banks to workout firms. They will help banks liquidate bad assets by creating a market for them, and thus expedite the overall workout process.

Newly adopted forward-looking criteria for credit evaluation, which emphasize cash flow and the debt payment capability of firms, are also expected to improve the overall restructuring process. Banks have been reluctant to initiate workout processes for corporate customers mainly because it would bring increased losses under past loan classification.

However, with the forward-looking criteria, expected losses are faithfully reflected in the financial statements of banks, thus removing banks' incentives to shrink bad loans. The selection of workout firms in the future will be based on survivability and early exit of failing firms.

However, the most important change needed is to improve the relationship between banks and the government. As the selection process for the workout program shows, political considerations can be detrimental to any corporate restructuring program. In hindsight, the overall restructuring program was not aggressive enough and the government was too concerned about short-term stability. Fear of large-scale bankruptcy and political concerns about labor opposition produced a restructuring program that tended to overemphasize financial restructuring. The weak incentives of banks facing their own survival problems contributed to an incomplete overhaul of the economy. Many firms included in the workout program should have been allowed to go bankrupt. The case of Daewoo Group shows how an exception to this rule can undermine the whole restructuring process.

At least in the short run, the government should have provided the banks with stronger incentives to lead the corporate restructuring effort without having to worry about their own survival. In the long run a more meaningful corporate restructuring requires fundamental change in the governance of Korean commercial banks to attend to shareholder value and to provide due diligence.

Notes

1 During the period of delay, Daewoo raised capital through bond issues that amounted to 19 trillion *won* (about $1.7 billion), most of which was assumed by investment trust companies. A substantial part of raised capital was used to pay foreign debt or disappeared through secret accounts in the United Kingdom.
2 Regular interest rates were applied to the evaluation of insolvent companies.
3 In addition to the selected companies, 195 companies that were related to them also went through a similar process of corporate restructuring. 144 non-*chaebol* firms of larger size were also reviewed for workout possibilities, and 53 firms agreed to the program.
4 Fifteen *chaebol*, including Kia Motors and the Hanbo group, that went bankrupt before the crisis broke out were already under court receivership or composition.
5 In addition to the workout teams, credit banks also operated separate task force teams that dealt with the Big Deals among the five largest *chaebol*.
6 Only listed firms are analyzed.

7 Holding period return equals (stock price at the end of the period *minus* stock price at the beginning of the period) *divided by* (stock price at the beginning of the period).

8 At the end of 2000, the Corporate Restructuring Coordination Committee was replaced by the Corporate Restructuring Accord Implementation Committee.

9 Creditors also formed a Subcommittee for Due Diligence to check that the due diligence work by accounting firms was reasonable.

10 In the case of the sale of real estate for debt repayment, the special value-added tax was exempted. The transfer tax was exempted if shareholders sold their own assets and donated the money to their company for debt repayment. If assets were transferred as part of mergers or business transfers, 50 percent of the transfer income tax or special value-added tax was exempted. If a company purchased real estate that was on sale for restructuring purposes and resold it in five years, 50 percent of transfer income taxes or special value-added taxes were exempted. Special profits due to debt reduction as a result of early repayment under court receivership or composition were also not added to operating profit.

11 For example, the dominant shareholders of Byuksan Construction, Dong-Ah Construction, Ildong Medicine, and Hwasung Industry, donated 35 billion *won* during 1999.

12 Failing companies with more than 250 billion *won* of bank credit fell under the Default Suspension Agreement program, which suspended the exercise of credit rights for two months from the call for the creditors' meeting.

13 Credits to workout firms were classified as "substandard" and 20 percent of the loan needs to be amortized.

14 As of June 2000, the amortization ratios for potential loan losses for workout firms were about 15 percent for non-Daewoo firms and 43 percent for Daewoo firms, still below international standards.

15 Only the Exchange Bank of Korea succeeded in capitalizing with foreign capital during the first half of 1998.

16 Assets with zero weights in the calculation of the BIS capital adequacy requirements.

17 Under court receivership, the preparatory stage takes about thirteen months, while it can be shortened to four months under the pre-packaged bankruptcy system.

References

Bank of Korea. 1999. *Money and Banking Statistics*. Seoul: Bank of Korea.
—— Monetary Analysis Team. 1999. "Analysis on Credit Crunch after the Foreign Exchange Crisis in Korea." Mimeo.
Berger, N. Allen, and Udell, Gregory F. 1994. "Did Risk-Based Capital Allocate Bank Credit and Cause a 'Credit Crunch' in the United States?" *Journal of Money, Credit and Banking*, 26: 587–633.
Kim, Dongwon, and Park, Kyung Suh. 2000, "Capital Crunch and Shocks to

Small Enterprises: Korean Experience Under Financial Crisis," *Korean Journal of Finance*, 14 (2).

Nam, Kang and Kim. 1999. "Comparative Corporate Governance Trends in Asia." Paper presented at OECD conference on "Corporate Governance in Asia: A Comparative Perspective," Seoul.

Park, Young Chul, Kim, Dongwon, and Park, Kyung Suh. 2000. *Unfinished Reform: Corporate and Financial Restructuring in Korea*. Seoul: Samsung Economic Research Institute.

Part III
Reform and Restructuring

9 The Corporate Bankruptcy System and the Economic Crisis

Youngjae Lim

After the economic crisis broke in 1997, Korea undertook a reform of the corporate bankruptcy system in 1998–99.[1] These reforms were not sweeping but piecemeal, maintaining the existing legal framework intact. What, if anything, did the reforms achieve? Two years after the reforms, debate on reforming the corporate bankruptcy system continued; by the end of 2001, another round of bankruptcy reform was still pending. What weaknesses did the bankruptcy laws and procedures have to prompt another round of reform?

In discussing these issues, we focus on whether rehabilitation procedures targeted the right firms. Rehabilitation programs should target firms that go bankrupt because of temporary bad luck, but have a high potential for recovery. If firms do not meet this criterion, then rehabilitation programs are doomed from the start. Another related issue is the timing of filing for bankruptcy procedures. If ailing firms file for bankruptcy procedures too late, prospects for recovery are damaged.

In order to assess the effectiveness of bankruptcy procedures, we look at firm-level data on productivity, a major indicator of corporate performance (see Chapter 5). The information on corporate bankruptcy was gathered from such sources as the courts, the Financial Supervisory Service and the Bank of Korea. We analyze both the cross-sectional distribution of corporate bankruptcy and the time series of ailing firms' productivity before and after bankruptcy, using data on externally audited firms.[2] We also compare the productivity distribution of ailing firms for different rehabilitation procedures with an eye on the changes in laws and procedures introduced in 1998 and 1999.

This chapter does not elaborate on the workout program, the informal out-of-court bankruptcy process introduced after the crisis, which is examined in detail by Kyung Suh Park in Chapter 8. However, it must be emphasized that the formal in-court bankruptcy process would work better if informal out-of-court processes work efficiently, and *vice versa*. It is especially the case where, as in Korea, the scale and scope of corporate insolvency reaches levels that pose systemic risks.

The first section explains recent developments in the court corporate bankruptcy system. The second section shows the empirical relationship between *chaebol* restructuring and the corporate bankruptcy process from 1997 to 1999. The third section evaluates the effects of the 1998–99 reforms of the corporate bankruptcy system. The conclusion provides an evaluation of the 1998–99 reform effort and discusses the agenda for future reforms.

1   Recent Developments in the Corporate Bankruptcy System

Before the economic crisis of 1997, most ailing firms did not use the bankruptcy procedures overseen by the courts. The debt of bankrupt firms was usually collected on an individual basis under the Civil Procedure Act. Most assets of the bankrupt firms were already subject to mortgage or to security, and little was left for unsecured creditors. Additional procedures for the collection of debt were not needed.

Although most bankrupt firms were effectively liquidated on a non-judicial basis, some bankrupt firms were periodically bailed out by the government through various "rationalization" measures; for example, such measures were undertaken in the mid-1980s. These measures also undercut the use of formal bankruptcy procedures.

One technical hurdle to the use of judicial bankruptcy procedures was the Act on Special Measures for Unpaid Loans of Financial Institutions. The Act gave the Korea Asset Management Corporation (KAMCO) the authority to hold auctions of the assets of bankrupt firms before court procedures began. It stopped the Corporate Reorganization Act from operating in practice, since the auction of assets by KAMCO effectively pre-empted the corporate reorganization process. In 1990, the Constitutional Court declared this provision unconstitutional, paving the way for the wider use of judicial bankruptcy procedures.

By enacting the Rule on Corporate Reorganization Procedure in 1992, the Supreme Court began to move in the direction of improving judicial bankruptcy procedures. Among other things, the new rule established the conditions for the initiation of corporate reorganization proceedings. These included high social value, financial distress, and possibility of rehabilitation; interestingly, economic efficiency was *not* a requirement for corporate reorganization.

Several episodes of abuse of the corporate reorganization procedure by the controlling shareholders of ailing firms led the Supreme Court to amend the 1992 Rule in 1996. In particular, the court argued that the shares of controlling shareholders responsible for a firm's failure should be wiped out. This revision produced an unanticipated outcome: the owners of ailing firms looked for other possibilities that would allow them to maintain their control. They found such an alternative in the composition procedure. This was originally designed for small and medium-sized firms with simple capital structures, but there was no explicit limit on firm size until the law was revised in 1998. Composition required advance agreement with creditors before the court officially considered an application. A court-provided stay under the composition procedure applied only to unsecured creditors; secured loans could be collected. But what made the composition procedure popular was the fact that existing management maintained control.

Table 9.1 shows the resulting flight to the composition procedure. Filings for composition exploded from nine cases in 1996, to 322 cases in 1997, to 1,343 cases in 1998. In the first three quarters of 1997, before the onset of the crisis, many large firms facing bankruptcy sought to file for the composition procedure. Among these firms, the case of Kia Motors deserves special mention since it played an important role in the unfolding of the crisis in mid-1997. The debtor and the creditors initially wanted to apply for different procedures: Kia initially filed for composition, but shortly thereafter creditors chose to file for corporate reorganization. When both procedures are filed in this way, the filing for corporate reorganization overrides the one for composition. In the end, the court accepted Kia Motors into corporate reorganization, but the uncertainty and delay in dealing with ailing firms such as Kia clearly added to the uncertainty in the economy before the crisis broke out.

The economic crisis of 1997 put the existing corporate bankruptcy system, both judicial and non-judicial, under great strain. The number and scale of bankruptcies soared. Table 9.1 shows that the filings for judicial bankruptcy procedures rose dramatically in 1997. This internal

Table 9.1 Bankruptcy filings, 1995–99

Bankruptcy procedure	1995	1996	1997	1998	1999
Reorganization	79	52	132	148	37
Composition	13	9	322	728	140
Liquidation	12	18	38	467	733
Total	104	79	492	407	910

Note: Liquidation cases include both corporate and individual cases.
Source: Supreme Court of Korea.

pressure on the system was a driving force for the changes in laws and procedures that followed in 1998 and 1999, although the International Monetary Fund (IMF) and the International Bank for Reconstruction and Development (IBRD) also demanded an improvement in the corporate bankruptcy system as a condition for the bailout package.[3]

The revision of 1998 represented the most substantial change in the system since the enactment of the corporate bankruptcy laws in 1962. But pressed for time in the wake of crisis, the government did not succeed in initiating a fully comprehensive revision, which accounts for the second round of reform in 1999.

Through these two revisions, the role of the courts in the corporate bankruptcy process increased significantly; if it were not for the workout procedure introduced as an out-of-court settlement process in 1998, the role of the courts would have even been larger. In this process, the relative weight of court settlement and out-of-court settlement and the optimal size of firms participating in court settlement remain among the most important issues for future reform. This is especially the case given that the delayed process of financial sector restructuring is likely to put the out-of-court procedure under the influence of the government, the controlling shareholder of several major banks (see Chapter 8).

To improve the court settlement process, the 1998 revision introduced new provisions into the bankruptcy laws while maintaining the existing framework.[4] Most importantly, the new law introduced an economic efficiency criterion to qualify for judicial bankruptcy procedures instead of one based on high social value and prospects for rehabilitation. A comparison of the value of a distressed firm as a going concern with its liquidation value is now required for the initiation of all judicial bankruptcy proceedings. Another important change was to speed up proceedings. Time limits were introduced for the critical steps in the proceedings such as the decision on stay, the report of debts and equities, the approval of a reorganization plan, and other steps.

To induce a more active role for the creditors, the reform also established a creditors' conference. To enhance the capacity of the court to deal with bankruptcy cases, the court receivership committee was introduced as a special adviser on the critical steps in the proceedings. The process of wiping out the shares of controlling shareholders was also strengthened and made more transparent.

To prevent the abuse of the composition procedure, some critical changes were also made to the Composition Act. Large firms with complicated capital structures were not allowed to enter composition. Table 9.1 shows the impact of this change: the number of composition filings decreased sharply, from 728 in 1998 to 140 in 1999.[5]

Despite these changes, the 1998 revision left room for further reform.[6] To some extent, in fact, the 1999 revision filled the gap between initial reform proposals and what was finally passed in the 1998 revision.[7] In the 1999 revision process there was initially debate on the inclusion of an automatic stay in the new law. Under an automatic stay, the debtors' assets are automatically protected on filing from the creditors' rush to secure their claims. The pros and cons of the automatic stay were both strong. The final compromise sped up the initiation of proceedings to within one month of the filing.

Automatic stay can contribute to the rehabilitation of ailing firms after bankruptcy. On the other hand, the debtor might use the court to avoid a formal default and thereby evade criminal punishment under the Illegal Check Control Act. According to this Act, the managers or owners of ailing firms who issued bad checks are criminally liable. This was developed to overcome the informational asymmetry between the debtor and the creditors. Dealing with highly unreliable accounting information, creditors would be much less willing to lend money to debtors without such recourse. The debtors are in effect forced to make a credible commitment to repayment by risking incarceration in case of default.

The new revision also facilitated an efficient transition between corporate reorganization and liquidation. After the initiation decision, the court must compare the going-concern value of the firm with its liquidation value. If the liquidation value turns out to be larger than the going-concern value, the court *must* declare the liquidation of the firm.[8] Dong-Ah Construction was the first large firm to go down this path; the company was liquidated in early 2001.[9] This change could be regarded as one that contributes to an efficient working of the market mechanism.[10]

2   Corporate Bankruptcy and *Chaebol* Restructuring

If we look at the size distribution of firms in the economy over the 1990s, the shape of the distribution gets more skewed to the left over time: the number of very large firms – those with assets over a trillion won – grows, but overall, we find relatively more small-sized firms over time (Lim 2001). The crisis of 1997–98 had a more serious impact on these small firms.

Table 9.2 shows the proportion of insolvent firms belonging to the *chaebol* category from 1997 to 1999.[11] The table shows the relative share of solvent and insolvent firms, weighted by the size of assets. The insolvent firms in a given year include only those that went bankrupt in

Table 9.2 Assets of insolvent and solvent firms by *chaebol* size (trillion *won*, %)

Firms	1997			1998			1999		
	Solvent	Insolvent	Total	Solvent	Insolvent	Total	Solvent	Insolvent	Total
1st–30th largest *chaebol*	277.4 (96.37)	10.44 (3.63)	287.9 (100)	321.6 (98.24)	5.769 (1.76)	327.4 (100)	345.9 (99.01)	3.455 (0.99)	349.3 (100)
31st–60th largest *chaebol*	21.71 (99.14)	0.19 (0.86)	21.90 (100)	26.33 (82.17)	5.713 (17.83)	32.05 (100)	26.18 (97.81)	0.586 (2.19)	26.76 (100)
61st–300th largest *chaebol*	60.34 (71.94)	23.54 (28.06)	83.88 (100)	65.98 (74.83)	22.19 (25.17)	88.17 (100)	71.81 (81.71)	16.08 (18.29)	87.88 (100)
Small *chaebol* and independent firms	221.8 (94.25)	13.53 (5.75)	235.4 (100)	240.2 (96.56)	8.551 (3.44)	248.7 (100)	249.9 (90.10)	27.45 (9.90)	277.4 (100)

Note: Numbers in brackets denote share of total assets in each size category.
Source: Author's calculation for all the firms in the NICE data.

that year for the first time, and do not include those that went bankrupt in other years; hence, the table tells us the incidence of new bankruptcies in the various *chaebol* categories. "Solvent firms" are those that have not gone bankrupt in any year from 1997 to 1999.

Of the top thirty *chaebol* that went bankrupt, most did so in 1997; the scale of bankruptcy decreases over time. The other *chaebol* categories behave more or less like the top thirty.[12] On the other hand, independent[13] firms show their highest incidence of bankruptcy in 1999.

Once firms go bankrupt, they can enter into either court-administered or out-of-court settlements, including corporate reorganization, composition or workout. But not all firms undergo these rehabilitation programs; some simply remain bankrupt for a prolonged period of time. Most credit is shut off for these firms, and transactions thus take place in cash.

Table 9.3 shows the relative share of different types of settlement for new *chaebol* bankruptcies from 1997 to 1999. The firms that went bankrupt in 1997 show a clear pattern. For the top thirty *chaebol*, the majority (94 percent in terms of total assets) entered into the corporate reorganization procedure, whereas only a fraction (6 percent in terms of assets) went into the composition procedure. On the other hand, quite a significant proportion of small *chaebol* entered into the composition program. A substantial portion of the independent firms (and a less substantial portion of small *chaebol*) did not qualify for *any* rehabilitation program after bankruptcy.

In 1998, the government introduced an out-of-court workout procedure. Table 9.3 shows that, for large *chaebol*, the workout program was the main form of settlement. Even for independent firms, the workout program played an important role. By 1999, the role of the workout program had gotten much bigger, and most of the new bankruptcies (in terms of assets) were handled by this out-of-court procedure.

Figures 9.1–9.3 show the size distribution of the year bankruptcy cohorts and how that distribution has evolved over time. By focusing on the year cohorts, we can control for various year-specific effects and single out the relationship between the various rehabilitation settlements and the size factor over time. In the figures, we put together the size distribution of the top thirty *chaebol* as a reference point.

In 1997, the size distributions of the two types of court settlement cases are close to each other, although the size of firms undergoing corporate reorganization is a bit larger than those undergoing composition. This pattern changed in 1998 and 1999; the size of firms undergoing corporate reorganization became much bigger than those in composition. The changes in laws and procedures in 1998 and 1999 had a clear effect on the size distribution of court settlement cases. In the first year

Table 9.3 Insolvent firms' procedure by *chaebol* size (trillion *won*, %)

Firms	1997			1998				1999			
	No procedure	Com-position	Corporate reorg.	No procedure	Com-position	Corporate reorg.	Workout	No procedure	Com-position	Corporate reorg.	Workout
1st–30th largest *chaebol*	0.35 (3.38)	0.61 (5.80)	9.48 (90.82)	0.10 (1.73)	0 (0.00)	0 (0.00)	5.67 (98.27)	0 (0.00)	0 (0.00)	0 (0.00)	3.46 (100)
31st–60th largest *chaebol*	0 (0.00)	0 (0.00)	0.19 (100)	0 (0.00)	0 (0.00)	0 (0.00)	5.71 (100)	0 (0.00)	0 (0.00)	0 (0.00)	0.589 (100)
61st–300th largest *chaebol*	3.18 (13.51)	7.69 (32.66)	12.67 (53.84)	0.79 (3.54)	1.56 (7.03)	6.795 (30.62)	13.05 (58.81)	0 (0.00)	1.081 (6.73)	0.29 (1.78)	14.71 (91.50)
Small *chaebol* and independent firms	3.95 (29.16)	1.32 (9.73)	8.27 (61.11)	2.09 (24.44)	1.64 (19.16)	1.47 (17.18)	3.35 (39.22)	0.46 (1.69)	0.90 (3.29)	0.40 (1.47)	25.68 (93.55)

Note: Numbers in brackets denote share of total assets in each size category.
Source: Author's calculation for all the firms in the NICE data.

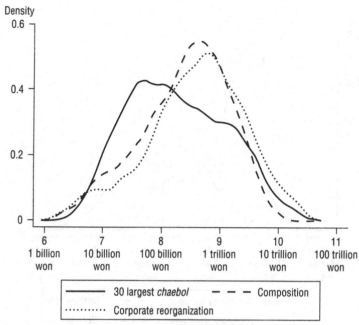

Figure 9.1   Size of the 1997 bankruptcy cohort (log of assets), 1997

Source: Author's calculation for all the firms in the NICE data.

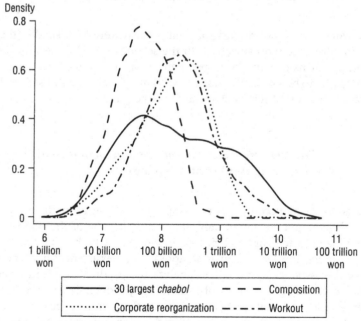

Figure 9.2   Size of the 1998 bankruptcy cohort (log of assets), 1998

Source: Author's calculation for all the firms in the NICE data.

216   Youngjae Lim

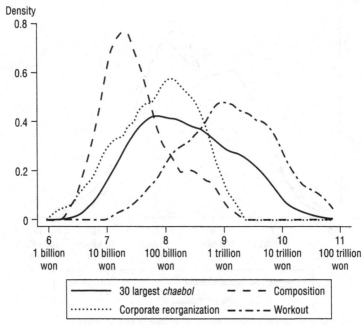

Figure 9.3   Size of the 1999 bankruptcy cohort (log of assets), 1999

Source: Author's calculation for all the firms in the NICE data.

of the workout procedure, firms in that process were a bit smaller than those in corporate reorganization. In the second year, however, the size of workout firms gets much bigger than those in corporate reorganization. This fact shows clearly that the workout program was used as an out-of-court bankruptcy mechanism for large *chaebol*.

3   The 1998–99 Reforms and the Performance of the Corporate Bankruptcy System

Firms go bankrupt because they cannot pay their debts. From the perspective of designing a corporate bankruptcy system, one of the important issues is how to tell (or to elicit information on) whether the financial distress of the insolvent firm is temporary or persistent. One way to resolve this issue empirically is to analyze the productivity of insolvent firms. We construct measures of total factor productivity for the firms in our data set and analyze them to evaluate the performance of the corporate bankruptcy system in place after the economic crisis. We analyze both the cross-sectional distribution of corporate bankruptcy and the time series of ailing firms' productivity before and after bankruptcy. We also compare the productivity distribution of ailing firms for different rehabilitation procedures with an eye on the changes in laws and procedures introduced in 1998 and 1999.

Industry distribution of corporate bankruptcy

Table 9.4 shows that the incidence of corporate bankruptcy is not evenly distributed across industries.[14] Instead, it is clustered in some industries, such as textiles, apparel, footwear, motor vehicle manufacturing, furniture, construction and wholesale trade, many of which are structurally depressed. This suggests that many bankruptcies that followed the economic crisis were not cases of temporary bad luck. Rather, many firms went bankrupt because of persistent and industry-specific difficulties.

Table 9.4   Insolvent and solvent firms by industry, 1997–99 (weighted by asset size, %)

Industry (the Korean Standard for Industrial Classification, 2 digits)	Solvent	Insolvent
Agriculture	96.19	3.81
Forestry	100.0	0.00
Fishing	96.13	3.87
Mining of Coal, Crude Petroleum and Natural Gas, Uranium and Thorium Ores	97.65	2.35
Manufacture of Food Products and Beverages	80.06	19.94
Manufacture of Tobacco Products	100.00	0.00
Manufacture of Textiles, Except Sewn Wearing Apparel	71.11	28.89
Manufacture of Sewn Wearing Apparel and Fur Articles	72.24	27.76
Tanning and Dressing of Leather, Manufacture of Luggage and Footwear	75.35	24.65
Manufacture of Wood and of Products of Wood and Cork, Except Furniture; Manufacture of Articles of Straw and Plaiting Materials	91.24	8.76
Manufacture of Pulp, Paper and Paper Products	83.27	16.73
Publishing, Printing and Reproduction of Recorded Media	98.50	1.50
Manufacture of Coke, Refined Petroleum Products and Nuclear Fuel	100.00	0.00
Manufacture of Chemicals and Chemical Products	90.11	9.89
Manufacture of Rubber and Plastic Products	98.35	1.65
Manufacture of Other Non–metallic Mineral Products	90.70	9.30
Manufacture of Basic Metals	81.04	18.96
Manufacture of Fabricated Metal Products, Except Machinery and Furniture	81.08	18.92
Manufacture of Furniture, Manufacturing of Articles n.e.c.	70.65	29.35
Manufacture of Computers and Office Machinery	92.11	7.89

Continued next page.

Manufacture of Electrical Machinery and Apparatuses n.e.c.	96.27	3.73
Manufacture of Electronic Components, Radio, Television and Communication Equipment and Apparatuses	82.53	17.47
Manufacture of Medical, Precision and Optical Instruments, Watches and Clocks	98.30	1.70
Manufacture of Motor Vehicles, Trailers and Semitrailers	47.34	52.66
Manufacture of Other Transport Equipment	91.73	8.27
Manufacture of Furniture, Manufacturing of Articles n.e.c.	70.65	29.35
Recycling	95.81	4.19
Electricity, Gas, Steam and Hot Water Supply	99.92	0.08
General Construction	68.25	31.75
Special Trade Construction	95.66	4.34
Sale of Motor Vehicles and Motorcycles, Retail Sale of Automotive Fuel	63.84	36.16
Wholesale Trade and Commission Trade, Except of Motor Vehicles and Motorcycles	60.45	39.55
Retail Trade, Except Motor Vehicles and Motorcycles	80.59	19.41
Land Transport, Transport Via Pipelines	99.91	0.09
Water Transport	99.44	0.56
Air Transport	100.00	0.00
Supporting and Auxiliary Transport Activities, Activities of Travel Agencies	87.58	12.42
Post and Telecommunications	99.47	0.53
Financial Institutions, Except Insurance and Pension Funding	100.00	0.00
Activities Auxiliary to Financial Intermediation	100.00	0.00
Real Estate Activities	91.76	8.24
Renting of Machinery and Equipment with Operator and of Personal and Household Goods Computer and Related Activities	73.18	26.82
Research and Development	100.00	0.00
Professional, Science, and Technology Service	98.24	1.76
Business Support Services	100.00	0.00
Public Administration and Defense; Compulsory Social Security	100.00	0.00
Education	94.63	5.37
Human Health and Veterinary Activities	100.00	0.00
Social Work Activities	99.25	0.75
Other Recreational, Cultural and Sporting Activities	97.33	2.67
Sewage and Refuse Disposal, Sanitation and Similar Activities	83.18	16.82
Membership Organizations n.e.c.	100.00	0.00
Other Services Activities	90.49	9.51

Note: The shaded industries denote the ones in which bankrupt firms are clustered.
Source: Author's own calculation for all the firms in the NICE data.

If this is the case, then the rehabilitation mechanisms applied to such firms are most likely doomed to failure from the start. Ailing firms in structurally depressed industries do not have the potential for recovery. Other policies that help firms reallocate resources would be more appropriate. For example, instead of giving such firms a second chance, policies are needed for removing exit barriers and inducing the reallocation of capital and labor to growing sectors. Theoretically, this consideration should be captured by the economic efficiency test for rehabilitation programs. However, it is not easy to make this stipulation operational. The economic efficiency test inevitably compares the liquidation value with the going-concern value in a myopic way. Therefore, the administration should cooperate closely with the court in designing better mechanisms for dealing with this class of ailing firms.

The 1998–99 reforms and the relative performance of different bankruptcy procedures

Figures 9.4–9.6 show the productivity distribution of newly insolvent firms by bankruptcy procedure for each year from 1997 to 1999; again the insolvent firms in a given year include only the ones that go bankrupt in that year for the first time. In the figures, we put together the productivity distribution of solvent firms as a reference point.

Ailing firms have the freedom to choose between the two court procedures. Changes in the provisions governing them thus have an effect on firms' choice; changes in laws and procedures lead to changes in the incentives facing newly insolvent firms.

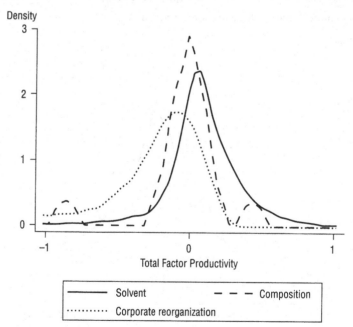

Figure 9.4   Productivity of the 1997 bankruptcy cohort, 1997

Source: Author's calculation for all the firms in the NICE data.

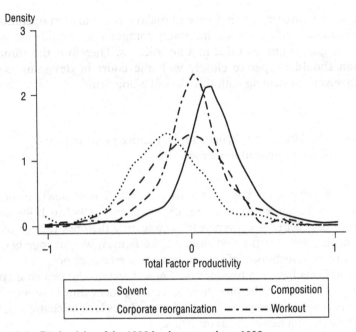

Figure 9.5   Productivity of the 1998 bankruptcy cohort, 1998

Source: Author's calculation for all the firms in the NICE data.

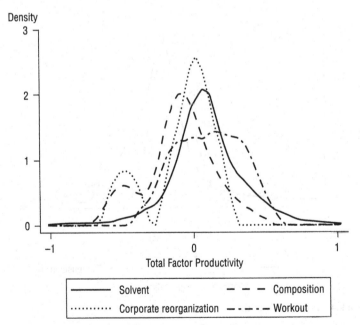

Figure 9.6   Productivity of the 1999 bankruptcy cohort, 1999

Source: Author's calculation for all the firms in the NICE data.

With the changes of the laws and procedures in 1998 and 1999, some restrictions were put on the composition procedure to prevent its abuse, including limits on firm size: as mentioned, large firms with complicated capital structures were not allowed to enter composition. These changes, together with the ones in corporate reorganization procedure, have a significant effect on the outcome of the two court procedures. In 1997 and 1998, the productivity of the firms in composition was higher than those in corporate reorganization, whereas in 1999 the opposite was the case.

The bankruptcy procedures are basically a structured bargaining game among interested parties; the court mainly oversees the process according to predetermined rules. The outcome of this bargaining game sometimes depends on these rules in very subtle ways. This is particularly so when the legal infrastructure in the area of corporate governance is lacking. Under these circumstances, giving ailing firms the freedom to choose between bankruptcy procedures often leads to unexpected outcomes; each procedure does not select the right firms in equilibrium. In other words, the bargaining game produces an unwanted pooling equilibrium instead of the separating equilibrium that is sought. Some restrictions are needed on the ailing firm's freedom to choose between bankruptcy procedures even if it does not produce a first-best outcome.

The 1999 workout cohort needs special mention, because productivity was distributed in a quite dispersed manner. We could interpret this observation as meaning that some portion of these firms were financially distressed because of temporary bad luck. Unlike other bankruptcy cohorts, they might have suffered from the crisis but not from persistent difficulties. More importantly, it also tells us that the 1999 workout cohort was selected not purely on the basis of economic efficiency. Other political or social factors were possibly at work; in fact, this is one of the most important criticisms of the workout program (see Chapter 8).

The performance of insolvent firms before and after bankruptcy

Figures 9.7 and 9.8 show that the 1997 and 1998 bankruptcy cohorts suffered not simply from the crisis but from persistent difficulties. Several years before they went bankrupt and were accepted into one of the rehabilitation programs, their productivity was lower than solvent firms. As with the depressed industry cases, rehabilitation mechanisms applied to such firms are most likely doomed to failure. Again, rehabilitation must target firms that have high potential for recovery.

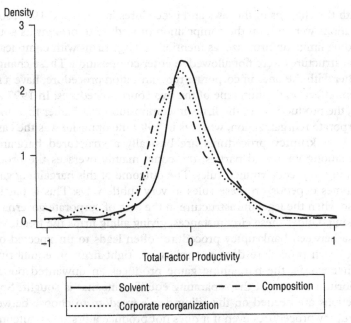

Figure 9.7   Pre-exit productivity of the 1997 bankruptcy cohort, 1994

Source: Author's calculation for all the firms in the NICE data.

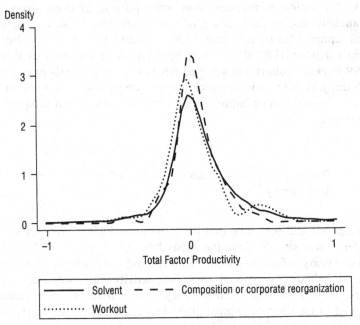

Figure 9.8   Pre-exit productivity of the 1998 bankruptcy cohort, 1995

Source: Author's calculation for all the firms in the NICE data.

Having said this, the reforms in 1998 appear to have affected the choices of target firms. Remember that one of the important changes in the 1998 revision was the introduction of the economic efficiency criterion. Now, the court compares the going-concern value of the firm with its liquidation value for the initiation of judicial bankruptcy proceedings. Figures 9.7 and 9.8 show that the 1998 bankruptcy cohorts suffered less from persistent difficulties than the 1997 cohort. Figures 9.9 and 9.10 show that the productivity of these insolvent firms was lower than that of solvent firms several years after the start of the rehabilitation program. Moreover, the gap continues to widen.

There are two possible ways of interpreting this observation. One interpretation is that the 1997 and 1998 bankruptcy cohorts suffered from persistent and firm-specific shocks. This would imply that the rehabilitation mechanisms put in place after the economic crisis targeted firms that did not have the potential for recovery. The other interpretation is that the rehabilitation programs were not well designed, regardless of whether the rehabilitation mechanisms targeted the right firms. For instance, the court-administered procedure was biased against the controlling shareholders of ailing firms because of their exploitation of the bankruptcy system in the past. In many cases,

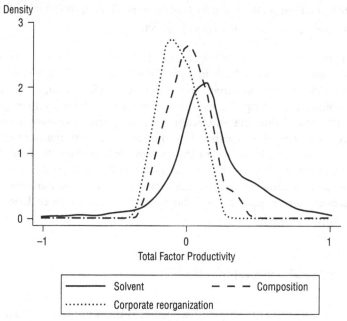

Figure 9.9   Post-exit productivity of the 1997 bankruptcy cohort, 2000

Source: Author's calculation for all the firms in the NICE data.

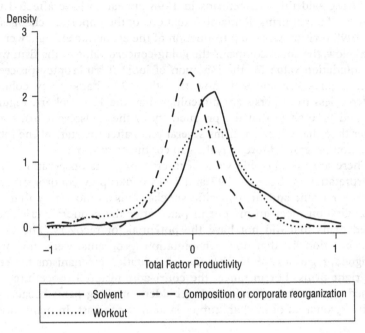

Figure 9.10   Post-exit productivity of the 1998 bankruptcy cohort, 2000

Source: Author's calculation for all the firms in the NICE data.

however, the owners-cum-management are best suited to the task of rehabilitating ailing firms, both in terms of incentives and information. If retaining previous owner-managers seems to be a bad idea, the court should consider aligning the incentives of post-bankruptcy management with firm value maximization by giving the court-appointed manager a stock option or expediting the sale of the company to new private management. If we accept the hypothesis that the 1998 revision had some positive effect on the choices of target firms, then the second interpretation is also somewhat persuasive for the 1998 bankruptcy cohorts; and there is still much to be desired in the design of Korea's rehabilitation programs.

A formal statistical test

The discussion so far has shown that insolvent firms are less productive than solvent firms not just at the time of entering into the bankruptcy procedures, but both before and after bankruptcy as well. This hypothesis can be tested statistically. Tables 9.5–9.7 show regressions of productivity on a set of year dummies (not reported) and a dummy variable denoting the 1997 or 1998 bankruptcy cohort interacted with year dummies. Only the particular cohort and the group of solvent firms are included in the sample of each regression. The reported coefficients thus indicate the average productivity differential between the 1997 or 1998 cohort and the group of solvent firms.

Table 9.5 shows that for the 1997 (corporate reorganization or composition) cohort, the coefficients reported are negative from 1993 to 2000, and significant from 1995 to 2000. Table 9.6 shows a similar result for the 1998 (corporate reorganization or composition) cohort:

Table 9.5   Productivity performance of the 1997 bankruptcy cohort (firms undergoing corporate reorganization or composition)

Independent variables Dummy variable denoting a specific cohort interacted with year dummies	Dependent variables Productivity
1993	–0.07916 (–1.35)
1994	–0.08544 (–1.44)
1995	–0.13336** (–2.31)
1996	–0.12595** (–2.16)
1997	–0.27941** (–4.50)
1998	–0.25702** (–4.03)
1999	–0.14458** (–2.10)
2000	–0.14458** (–2.10)
Year dummies included	Yes
Number of observations	37,673

Notes:
Numbers in brackets are t–values.
* significant at the 10% significance level
** significant at the 5% significance level

Table 9.6 Productivity performance of the 1998 bankruptcy cohort
(firms undergoing corporate reorganization or composition)

Independent variables Dummy variable denoting a specific cohort interacted with year dummies	Dependent variable Productivity
1993	-0.17715 (-0.50)
1994	-0.04894 (-1.44)
1995	-0.05300 (-1.59)
1996	-0.00327 (-0.10)
1997	-0.07709** (-2.21)
1998	-0.34197** (-7.79)
1999	-0.17034** (-3.72)
2000	-0.19210** (-4.01)
Year dummies included	Yes
Number of observations	38,222

Notes:
Numbers in brackets are t–values.
* significant at the 10% significance level
** significant at the 5% significance level

the coefficients reported are negative from 1993 to 2000, and significant from 1997 to 2000. Table 9.7 shows the result of a similar
statistical test for the 1998 workout cohort. The coefficients reported
are negative from 1993 to 2000 but significant only for 1998 and 2000.

These statistical results are compatible with the observations based on
the productivity distributions. First, the 1997 and 1998 bankruptcy
cohorts suffered not simply from the crisis but from persistent difficulties. Several years before they went bankrupt and were accepted into one
of the rehabilitation programs, their productivity was lower than solvent
firms. Second, the 1998 bankruptcy cohorts suffered less from persistent
difficulties compared to the case of the 1997 bankruptcy cohorts.

Table 9.7   Productivity performance of the 1998 bankruptcy cohort (firms undergoing workout)

Independent variables Dummy variable denoting a specific cohort interacted with year dummies	Dependent variable Productivity
1993	−0.02323 (−0.43)
1994	−0.02563 (−0.49)
1995	−0.01923 (−0.37)
1996	−0.01489 (−0.29)
1997	−0.02359 (−0.45)
1998	−0.16130** (−3.13)
1999	−0.03336 (−0.60)
2000	−0.01215* (−1.91)
Year dummies included	Yes
Number of observations	37,774

Notes:
Numbers in brackets are t–values.
* significant at the 10% significance level
** significant at the 5% significance level

Remember we interpreted this result as implying that the 1998 revision had a positive effect on the choice of the target firms for rehabilitation procedures. Third, several years after the start of the rehabilitation program, the productivity of these insolvent firms is still lower than that of solvent firms.

Tables 9.8 and 9.9 report the regression results using the pooled 1993–2000 data. In Table 9.8, the measured firm productivity is regressed on a set of dummy variables indicating whether the firm is a member of the composition, corporate reorganization, or workout group, as well as year dummies (not reported). The estimated coefficients can be interpreted as the average productivity differential

Table 9.8 The productivity performance of bankruptcy procedures

Independent variables Dummy variable denoting specific categories of bankruptcy proceedings	Dependent variable Productivity
Corporate reorganization	-0.08008** (-6.95)
Composition	-0.11024** (-8.17)
Workout	-0.03565** (-2.10)
Year dummies included	Yes
Number of observations	39,787

Notes:
Numbers in brackets are t–values.
* significant at the 10% significance level
** significant at the 5% significance level

Table 9.9 Comparing the productivity performance of bankruptcy procedures

Null hypotheses	F–statistics
Corporate reorganization = Composition	2.96*
Composition reorganization = Workout	4.77**
Composition = Workout	12.00**
Year dummies included	Yes
Number of observations	39,787

Notes:
* significant at the 10% significance level
** significant at the 5% significance level

between each group of firms and the solvent firms that are assumed to be common across years.[15] The table shows that the productivity differential between each group of firms and the solvent firms is statistically significant.

Table 9.9 tests the null hypothesis that there is no productivity difference between the composition, corporate reorganization, and workout groups. The productivity of the workout group is higher than that of the composition or corporate reorganization groups. The comparison between the composition and corporate reorganization groups produces a less statistically significant result. Using the pooled 1993–2000 data, the productivity of the composition group is slightly higher than that of the corporate reorganization group.

The statistical results in Table 9.8 and Table 9.9 are again compatible with the observations based on the productivity distributions. Several years before and after they went bankrupt and were accepted into one of the rehabilitation programs, the productivity of these firms was lower than solvent firms. This is more so for the case of corporate reorganization or composition than for the case of workout.

4 Concluding Remarks: Evaluation of the 1998–99 Reforms and the Agenda for Future Reforms

This paper uses firm-level data to show that a significant portion of ailing firms suffered not simply from the crisis but from persistent difficulties. Several years before they went bankrupt and were accepted into one of the rehabilitation programs, the productivity of these firms was already lower than solvent firms'. Additional evidence that ailing firms suffered not simply from the crisis but from persistent, industry-specific shocks is the fact that corporate bankruptcy was not evenly distributed across industries. Instead, it was clustered in some structurally depressed industries such as textiles, construction and wholesale trade. Rehabilitation procedures applied to such firms are most likely doomed to failure. Indeed, we provide evidence that the productivity of these firms remained lower than that of solvent firms for several years after the start of the program, and that the gap continues to widen. In general, rehabilitation procedures in place after the crisis did not target the right firms.

The analysis also shows that the 1998–99 reforms in the corporate bankruptcy system governing in-court settlements had some positive effects on the way the government dealt with ailing firms. One of the most important changes was the shift in criteria for target firms of rehabilitation programs from high social value to economic efficiency. The court now compares the value of firms as going concerns with their liquidation value for the initiation of judicial bankruptcy proceedings. The statistical analysis shows that this reform had some positive effect on the court's choosing the right target firms for rehabilitation programs. We then discuss evidence that the productivity of the bankruptcy cohorts even after this reform remained lower than that of solvent firms for several years after the start of the program. We interpret this as implying that the rehabilitation programs were not well designed to induce the recovery of target firms.

This chapter also documents that the workout program was used as an out-of-court bankruptcy mechanism for large *chaebol* after the crisis, and provides indirect evidence that the workout program did not select target firms purely on the basis of an economic efficiency test. Other political or social factors were possibly at work, which was one of the criticisms for the workout program.

While the corporate bankruptcy system in Korea made progress through the reforms of 1998–99, there is still much to be desired. First, for the case of ailing firms in structurally depressed industries, other policies are needed to help firms reallocate resources. Instead of giving a second chance to such ailing firms, some policy is needed for removing exit barriers in these industries. The administration should cooperate closely with the courts in designing better mechanisms for dealing with ailing firms.

Second, a consolidation among different bankruptcy procedures is needed. The 1999 revision achieved some improvement in the transition between corporate reorganization and liquidation. This should be pushed further to link all the different bankruptcy procedures. The unified code of corporate bankruptcy is one form of consolidation, although others may also be appropriate. Our analysis implies that we need some restrictions on ailing firms' freedom to choose between different bankruptcy procedures. With a weak legal infrastructure, the freedom to choose has led to sub-optimal results.

Third, the relationship between the in-court and out-of-court bankruptcy procedures must be improved. The optimal weight of in-court and out-of-court procedures necessarily varies, depending on the underlying economic situation and particularly the threat of systemic risk. But the in-court process works better if the out-of-court process works efficiently, and *vice versa*, and reform efforts must develop in tandem.

Lastly, rehabilitation programs must target the ailing firms with good prospects for recovery in a timely fashion. The Illegal Check Control Act makes the management or owners of ailing firms criminally liable for bad checks; note that this system was a mechanism to get around the severe informational asymmetry between debtor and creditors. Under these circumstances, the management of an ailing firm has strong incentives to file for bankruptcy procedures as late as possible, which ruins prospects for recovery. However, to induce ailing firms to file for rehabilitation programs in a timely way is critical for successful rehabilitation programs.

Notes

1   When the financial crisis broke in 1997, Korea had a better system of corporate bankruptcy than Thailand or Indonesia did. However, the inefficient corporate bankruptcy system of Korea was regarded as one factor for the crisis, or at least making systemic risks larger than otherwise.

2   The Act on the External Audit of Stock Companies requires a firm with assets of 7 billion *won* or more to issue audited financial statements. Firm productivity is estimated using the chained-multilateral index approach. For details on this methodology, see Chapter 5 and Good, Nadiri and Sickles (1996).

3   Neither the Federation of Korean Industries nor other industry groups expressed opinions against the government's reform proposals. The federation usually presents strong opinions about issues that have negative effects on the business operation of firms, such as class action suits.

4   The 1998 revision mainly focused on corporate reorganization. In 1998, the revision of the Composition Act was made for the first time since 1962.

5   Table 9.1 also shows that the number of corporate reorganization filings decreased from 1998 to 1999. The use of the out-of-court workout program for large ailing firms could explain this.

6   The revisions in the Composition Act and the Liquidation Act were made in early 2000.

7   The legal profession expressed some concerns about the instability that is caused by frequent revisions in the bankruptcy laws.

8   Some people in the legal profession were against this change. They pointed out that it only changed the order of the economic efficiency test and the initiation decision, and that what follows after the initiation decision could be meaningless and unstable due to the possibility of liquidation.

9   The Liquidation Act was never applied to large firms after 1962.

10   According to the revised corporate reorganization procedure, the comparison of the liquidation value and the going-concern value is made after the initiation decision, whereas the opposite was the case in the law revised in 1998.

11   The *chaebol* are ranked by relative asset size in 2001.

12   The 31st–60th largest *chaebol* show their highest incidence of bankruptcy in 1998.

13   Small business groups also belong to this category.

14   The figures show the relative share of solvent and insolvent firms, weighted by the size of assets. Bankrupt firms in a given year include only those that go bankrupt in that year for the first time. Hence, the figures tell us the incidence of new bankruptcies. We define solvent firms as the ones that have not gone bankrupt in any year from 1997 to 1999.

15   Here, the group of the bankrupt firms under no rehabilitation procedures is excluded from the sample in the regression.

References

Aw, B. Y., Chen, X., and Roberts, M. J. 1997. "Firm-level Evidence on Productivity Differentials, Turnover, and Exports in Taiwanese Manufacturing." National Bureau for Economic Research Working Paper No. 6235.

Good, David H., Nadiri, M. Ishaq, and Sickles, Robin. 1996. "Index Number and Factor Demand Approaches to the Estimation of Productivity." National Bureau for Economic Research Working Paper No. 5790.

Hahn, Chin-Hee. 2000. "Entry, Exit, and Aggregate Productivity Growth: Micro Evidence on Korean Manufacturing." Seoul: Korea Development Institute Policy Study No. 2000–04.

Kim, Beom Sik. 1999. *The Revision of Corporate Bankruptcy Laws and the Implications* (in Korean). Seoul: Samsung Economic Research Institute.

Kim, Jae Hyung. 2001. *Policy Proposals for Corporate Rehabilitation* (in Korean). Seoul: Korean Chamber of Commerce and Industry.

Koo, Bon Cheon. 1998. *The Economic Analysis of Corporate Exit and the Reform Proposals* (in Korean). Seoul: Korea Development Institute.

Lim, Youngjae. 2001. "Sources of Corporate Financing and Economic Crisis in Korea: Micro-evidence." Paper presented at the Twelfth Annual East Asian Seminar on Economics, National Bureau for Economic Research.

Nam, Il Chong, Oh, Soogeun, and Kim, Joon-Kyung. 1999. "Insolvency Mechanisms in Korea." Korea. Development Institute Working Paper No. 9918. Seoul: KDI.

Yoo, S. M., Lim, Y. J., Koo, B. C., Lee, S. W., and Lee, J. H. 1997. *Corporate Exit: Proposals for Reform* (in Korean). Seoul: Korea Development Institute.

Yun, Mikyung. 1998. "Bankruptcy Procedure in Korea: A Perspective," Korea Institute for International Economic Policy Working Paper No. 98–02.

10 Foreign Direct Investment and Corporate Restructuring after the Crisis

Mikyung Yun

Korea has seen tremendous changes in its foreign economic relations since the outbreak of the currency-cum-financial crisis in 1997. One notable result is a significant increase in foreign direct investment (FDI), following dramatic liberalization measures and active solicitation of foreign investors. Ceilings on foreign equity ownership in the stock market have been eliminated, cross-border mergers and acquisitions are now allowed, and foreign land ownership has been fully liberalized. Indeed, the Korean economy has become more "internationally contestable" than it ever was before.[1]

This chapter focuses on the role of FDI in corporate restructuring and its general impact on the competitive environment. Of course, the effect of FDI takes place over the long term, and it may be too early to evaluate the impact of these policy changes. However, because these changes have been so dramatic and significant, it is worthwhile to explore some of their effects on economic restructuring. This is especially true because many in Korea feel threatened by massive inflows of FDI, and the potentially anti-competitive effects of large multinationals. The first section surveys the literature. The second section examines policy changes regarding FDI and the general pattern of inflows. The third section looks at changing modalities of FDI and the increasing role of subnational governments in attracting it. The fourth section provides some brief case studies.

1 Foreign Direct Investment, Corporate Restructuring and Competition

The benefits of FDI are well established in the literature. FDI induces stable, long-term capital and spillovers in technology and managerial know-how, employment creation and regional development.[2] The World

Bank (1998) shows that FDI into the Asian nations affected by financial crisis in 1997 was more stable than other forms of international financial flows. Recent studies of Korea by J. D. Kim (1997, 1999) show that FDI played an important role in transferring technology and know-how, especially in industries such as semiconductors, pharmaceuticals and retailing.

Foreign investment has an added significance for post-crisis Korea: it can be a source of funds for restructuring firms that cannot find qualified domestic investors. Even if not directly involved in the restructuring of distressed firms, the presence of foreign firms in the Korean economy can encourage the adoption of international best practice and promote better corporate governance.

FDI is seen by some as providing the only viable competition for dominant domestic *chaebol*, both in managerial and product markets. In fact, the domination by *chaebol* is seen by some to have inhibited foreign investors in the past.[3] There may be some truth to this claim, as *chaebol* firms have been extremely reluctant to sell to foreign investors in their restructuring efforts. However, Samsung Heavy Industry's sale of its construction equipment operation to Volvo, Philip's acquisition of LG's liquid crystal display division, and Renault's investment in Samsung Motors show that sectors previously dominated by top *chaebol* firms are increasingly open to foreign investment.

The lagging financial sector has also seen increasing foreign investment, evident in the difficult sale of the Korea First Bank, discussed in more detail below. FDI in the financial sector is expected to improve how financial institutions evaluate risk, reduce moral hazard, and change the environment under which *chaebol* and financial institutions compete in the domestic market.

Serious concerns remain, however, with respect to the concentrating effects of multinationals, especially because recent FDI has entered through mergers and acquisitions (M&As) rather than greenfield investment. Critics suspect that foreign monopolies may simply substitute for domestic ones. FDI may induce greater competition initially. But because of their financial and technological advantages, foreign firms may quickly take dominant positions in the domestic market, with adverse welfare consequences for the economy as a whole (higher prices, profit transfers out of the country, etc.).[4]

Most empirical studies of developed countries show a negative correlation between FDI and concentration, indicating that FDI entry has pro-competitive effect in these economies (see Gorecki 1976; Frischtak and Newfarmer 1994). But similar studies for developing countries show opposite results.[5] These studies are not entirely conclusive. For one, they do not take simultaneity effects into consideration. FDI can cause greater concentration, but it can also be attracted to more profitable, concentrated markets.[6] However a preliminary study applying an instrumental variables estimation to pre-crisis Korean data shows FDI to be *negatively* correlated with concentration, suggesting that FDI may have been a pro-competitive force (Yun 1999).

The empirical studies in the foregoing discussion are mainly based on the structure-conduct-performance paradigm. That paradigm does not provide a good theoretical basis on which to distinguish concentration based on market power from that based on superior efficiency. Demsetz (1973) argues that firms in concentrated industries earn higher profits not because they abuse their monopolistic power to set prices above marginal cost, but because they are more efficient.[7] In this case, higher concentration would not necessarily imply lack of competition and could be accompanied by lower prices.

Modern industrial organization theory highlights the types of competitive weapons that firms use, rather than market structure *per se*. Where goods are differentiated and/or technologically sophisticated, competition encourages heavy and escalating outlays on advertising and R&D as incumbent firms strive to enhance the quality of their product and new innovative firms enter the market (Davies, Lyons et al. 1996; UNCTAD 1997). This type of competition has a welfare-enhancing effect because consumer welfare depends on quality as well as on price. At the same time, these types of expenditures are invariably sunk costs, making the market less amenable to new entry.[8]

Showing the relationship between FDI and concentration or profit levels does not necessarily throw light upon how FDI affects the competitive process, however. The more relevant questions are whether entry through FDI leads to lower prices and/or greater innovation, and whether foreign firms earn super-normal profits due to superior managerial performance or other reasons such as predatory pricing followed by mark-ups. Persistence of super-normal profits, accompanied by high prices, would also indicate absence of entry and effective competition and may suggest strategic entry deterrence behavior by incumbent firms.

The initial level of concentration before FDI enters and the mode of FDI (for instance, merger as opposed to greenfield investment) are two other important factors for analyzing the effect of FDI on competition. If concentration is initially high, as it has been in Korea, new entry by a foreign investor may enhance competition at entry. However, there is also the possibility that the multinational has financial and technological advantages and quickly displaces local firms, leading to even greater concentration over time. If the initial concentration level is not very high, entry by a large multinational may induce greater concentration and inhibit new entry.

The effect of mergers is also not always straightforward. Mergers among firms within a market usually increase concentration, but if there is sufficient potential entry within a reasonable amount of time, higher post-merger profits can have an entry-inducing effect. When the acquiring firm is a foreign one entering the market for the first time, the effect on concentration should be neutral, especially if it is a small multinational corporation that is not dominant in the international market. Moreover, in times of restructuring, acquisition of firms or mergers between firms that would otherwise exit the market has a competition-enhancing effect, as the acquisition of Samsung Motors by Renault demonstrates.

At the same time, such acquisitions would be an easy way to acquire large market share in a short period of time. The successive acquisitions of Seminis Vegetable Seeds Inc., through which the firm came to control about 45 percent of the Korean market within two years, is an example.

Concentration may merely be the end result of a competitive process, and whether FDI entry is desirable or not should also be based on other considerations such as opportunities for technology transfer, employment and development of related industries. Even if FDI is initially anti-competitive, it may stimulate related local industries, attract new domestic as well as foreign entry, and contribute to corporate restructuring. Case studies of Hansol PCS, Volvo Construction Equipment Korea and the Korea First Bank suggest this is the case. Before considering those cases in detail, we examine recent trends and policy changes regarding FDI in Korea.

2   From a Closed to an Open Economy: Trends in Policy and FDI

It is well known that FDI has traditionally played only a minor role in the Korean economy. Korea has preferred loans, technology licensing and joint-venture investments to wholly owned FDI, which was first allowed only in 1982.

In the mid-1980s, Korea began to liberalize its FDI regime. The most important reason for this change is probably foreign, particularly American, pressure to liberalize. The most significant breakthrough came in 1989, when the United States threatened to designate Korea a Priority Foreign Country for negotiations and possible sanctions under its "Super 301" trade laws. Korea was ultimately not designated a Priority Foreign Country, but it ceded to significant liberalization demands from the United States. Korea agreed to expand the number of sectors open to FDI; abolish performance requirements such as local content, export levels and mandatory technology transfer; switch to a notification system from 1991; shorten the approval period; and streamline regulations regarding technology imports. The bilateral pressure to liberalize continued under the President's Economic Initiative of 1992, and the Dialogue for Economic Cooperation, which started in 1993. The two channels of dialogue covered a variety of economic topics, but investment-related matters received high priority. Until Korea joined the OECD in 1996, most liberalization measures implemented during the 1990s were the result of bilateral negotiations under the framework of these dialogues (Joo and Kim 1995: 52; K. H. Kim 1998: 68).

The second reason for the opening is that as certain sub-sectors of Korean industry moved close to the technology frontier, barriers to accessing new technology rose and knowledge acquisition through licensing and joint ventures became limited. Consequently, Korea had its own reasons to embark on a gradual process of liberalization, which gained momentum with bilateral negotiations with the United States and membership of the OECD in 1996.

In response to these liberalization measures, FDI flows as a share of GDP started to increase rapidly from 1984 until peaking in 1988, as shown in Figure 10.1. Table 10.1 shows that FDI totaled an annual average of more than $230 million during 1982–86 and almost $760 million during 1987 and 1988 on an arrival basis.[9] Although FDI declined in the early 1990s, it started to increase substantially from 1994. FDI increased throughout the slower growth years of 1995 and 1996, expanding at more than 30 percent per year.

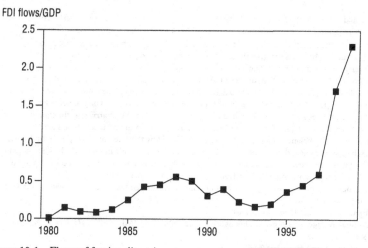

Figure 10.1   Flows of foreign direct investment as share of GDP, 1980–99

Source: FDI data from Ministry of Industry, Commerce and Energy; GDP figures from Bank of Korea.

Table 10.1   Flows of foreign direct investment into Korea, 1962–2000 ($million, %)

Year	FDI inflows[1]			Withdrawn
	Notification basis	Arrival basis	Balance of payment basis[2]	
1962–1981[3]	93.31	73.89	67.8[4]	10.21
1982–1986	353.55	231.56	188.2	38.28
1987–1988	1,173.54	759.83	815.2	34.89
1989	1,090.28	812.32	1,117.8	75.05
1990	802.64	895.40 (10.23)	788.5 (–29.46)	136.20 (81.47)
1991	1,396.00	1,177.25 (31.48)	1,179.8 (49.63)	47.29 (–65.29)
1992	894.48	803.31 (–31.76)	728.3 (–38.27)	240.16 (407.832)
1993	1,044.27	728.15 (–9.36)	588.1 (–19.25)	193.09 (–19.60)
1994	1,316.51	991.57 (36.18)	809.0 (37.56)	205.03 (6.18)
1995	1,947.23	1,361.93 (37.35)	1,775.8 (119.51)	114.22 (–44.29)
1996	3,202.58	2,309.98 (69.61)	2,325.4 (30.95)	308.46 (170.07)
1997	6,970.92	3,087.86 (33.67)	2,844.2 (22.31)	449.91 (45.85)
1998	8,852.32	5,219.58 (69.04)	5,412.3 (90.29)	250.27 (–44.37)
1999	15,541.37	10,598.46 (103.05)	9333.4 (72.45)	1,370.61 (447.65)
2000, 1 Oct.	12,171.03	7,213.80[5]		658.30[6]
Cumulated 1962–Oct. 2000	61,210.52	39,355.21[5]		4,515.10[6]

Notes: Figures in brackets are growth from the previous year in percentage terms.
1. Equity investment of more than 10% of equity capital by a single person or firm, and intra–company loans with maturities of five years or more are considered foreign direct investment. Notification and arrival basis measures (composed of equity purchased and long–term, intra–company loans) are from administrative records of the MCIE. The notified amount of investment does not necessarily coincide with the actual capital that arrives at the time the notification is made, resulting in the large difference between the notification and arrival-based measures. The balance of payments measure is collated by the Bank of Korea, using both foreign exchange receipts and payments statistics maintained by the bank and the MCIE. This measure combines three elements (purchase of equity, retained earnings, and net lending from parents to subsidiaries) and is close to the arrival–based measure for most years.
2. Balance of payment basis figures are from Bank of Korea (2000), *Balance of Payment Statistics* (http://www.nso.go.kr).
3. Figures for 1962–81 are annual averages.
4. Annual average for 1976–81. This figure is calculated from IMF (1999), *Balance of Payments Statistics Yearbook*.
5. Includes up to September 2000.
6. Includes up to July 2000.

Source: Ministry of Commerce, Industry and Energy, *Trends in Foreign Direct Investment*, October 2000.

Sectoral liberalization began in 1984, when the government replaced the positive list system with a negative list system, in which all industries not listed were open for FDI approval. Restricted business categories have been liberalized annually since 1994, and multilateral negotiations, such as the GATT and government policy to introduce greater competition, fostered a gradual opening of the service sector.

The effect of these liberalization measures can be seen in Table 10.2. The manufacturing sector was the largest recipient of FDI, constituting more than 60 percent of total FDI until 1994. Since then, the service sector has gained greater importance, consistently receiving about 40 percent of total FDI. Among manufacturing industries, electric and electronics, chemicals, and machinery consistently attracted a high proportion of total FDI.

Even so, FDI formed a relatively low proportion of total gross capital formation compared to other newly industrializing Asian economies such as Taiwan or Singapore. During 1986–91, FDI's contribution to total gross capital formation in Korea was 1.1 percent, compared to 29.4 percent in Singapore, 9.7 percent in Malaysia and 3.5 percent in Taiwan for the same period (Joo and Kim 1995: 21). In 1996, the ratio of FDI inflows to total fixed capital was 1.3 percent, and the ratio of the stock of FDI to GDP only 2.6 percent. These figures are quite low in comparison with the average of 7.4 percent and 14.6 percent for Southeast Asian countries respectively, and the world averages of 5.6 percent and 10.6 percent (J. D. Kim 1999: 13).

Liberalization policies significantly changed the Korean FDI regime. But the major sources of foreign investor discomfort came from the heavily regulated business environment and business practices that were often not transparent. These issues were not seriously addressed until after the crisis of 1997–98. Nor did the government actively solicit FDI until that time.

Since then, the government has actively encouraged FDI, at first for balance of payments reasons but later to assist with corporate restructuring. Various measures supported this change in policy. Changes in the Securities Exchange Law eliminated ceilings on foreign equity ownership in the stock market as of May 1998. Cross-border M&As were allowed beginning in April 1997, but were still restricted in many ways; these restrictions were removed in May 1998.[10] The mandatory tender offer rule was abolished and merger procedures streamlined in February 1998 to promote M&As of restructuring firms. The Foreigner's Land Acquisition Act was also amended in 1998, under which foreign land ownership was fully liberalized. The Foreign Exchange Transaction Act was enacted in April 1999 to liberalize foreign exchange controls (J. D. Kim 1999: 22–39).

Table 10.2 Inflows of foreign direct investment by sector and home country, 1962–2000 (arrival basis: $ million, %)

	1962–68	1982–94	1995	1996	1997	1998	1999	Jan.–Sept. 2000	Cumulated 1962–Sept. 2000
Total	73.9	621.9	1,357.1	2,308.3	3,085.9	5,155.6	10,335.5	7,213.8	39,355.2
Manufacturing	52.6 (71.2)	396.6 (63.8)	585.6 (43.2)	1,296.8 (56.2)	1,832.6 (59.4)	2,831.6 (54.9)	6,091.3 (58.9)	4,558.8 (63.2)	23,497.9 (60.0)
Food	1.9 (2.6)	26.1 (4.2)	15.5 (1.1)	42.2 (1.8)	463.9 (15.0)	629.8 (12.2)	291.2 (2.8)	78.4 (1.1)	1,897.7 (4.9)
Chemicals	14.7 (19.9)	95.9 (15.4)	136.0 (10.0)	233.9 (10.1)	255.8 (8.3)	429.1 (8.3)	752.5 (7.3)	158.4 (2.2)	3,509.0 (9.0)
Electric and electronics	110.1 (13.2)	76.7 (12.3)	137.8 (10.2)	281.2 (12.2)	219.3 (7.1)	231.7 (4.5)	2,515.2 (24.3)	1,609.6 (22.3)	6,224.3 (15.9)
Transport equipment	104.5 (3.9)	56.4 (9.1)	45.8 (3.4)	250.0 (11.2)	358.4 (11.6)	154.0 (3.0)	425.7 (4.1)	762.7 (10.6)	2,806.7 (7.2)
Service	305.3 (27.9)	223.7 (36.0)	770.3 (56.8)	1,010.7 (43.8)	1,202.4 (39.0)	2,139.8 (41.5)	4,190.0 (40.5)	2,652.7 (36.8)	15,529.8 (39.2)
Hotel	176.6 (13.9)	97.0 (15.6)	58.7 (4.3)	115.8 (5.0)	95.6 (3.1)	0.0 (0.0)	64.5 (0.6)	4.4 (0.1)	1,805.7 (4.6)
Wholesale and retail	1.2 (0.0)	5.0 (0.8)	58.1 (4.3)	330.4 (14.3)	256.2 (8.3)	519.6 (10.1)	437.1 (4.2)	226.1 (3.1)	1,980.6 (4.9)
Trading	20.7 (0.0)	26.3 (4.2)	108.3 (8.0)	111.5 (4.8)	195.0 (6.3)	243.0 (4.7)	93.0 (0.9)	146.6 (2.0)	1,349.6 (3.2)
Financing and insurance	100.0 (7.6)	70.7 (11.3)	410.2 (30.3)	194.3 (8.4)	309.6 (10.0)	544.4 (10.5)	1,156.4 (20.8)	949.8 (13.1)	5,604.3 (14.3)

Home country								
Japan	813.6 (55.1)	226.5 (36.4)	337.5 (24.9)	279.4 (12.1)	197.2 (6.4)	413.6 (8.0)	805.6 (7.8)	643.91 (8.9)	6,474.9 (16.6)
Malaysia	0.0 (0.0)	0.4 (0.1)	119.7 (8.8)	666.1 (28.9)	431.4 (14.0)	263.4 (5.1)	1,337.8 (12.9)	640.5 (8.9)	3,465.1 (8.9)
USA	377.6 (25.6)	182.0 (29.3)	342.0 (25.2)	393.5 (17.0)	390.6 (12.7)	1,450.5 (28.1)	1,882.3 (18.2)	1,160.2 (16.1)	8,380.1 (21.4)
Europe	6.4 (8.7)	176.1 (28.3)	437.8 (32.3)	861.5 (37.3)	1,734.6 (56.2)	2,676.4 (51.9)	5,054.3 (48.9)	1,934.9 (26.8)	15,117.0 (38.4)
UK	1.5 (2.0)	20.0 (3.2)	50.1 (3.7)	48.0 (2.1)	94.3 (3.1)	47.7 (0.9)	476.0 (4.6)	13.1 (0.2)	1,048.4 (2.7)
France	16.6 (1.1)	20.0 (3.2)	33.2 (2.4)	90.0 (3.9)	501.2 (16.2)	2,676.4 (51.31)	348.6 (3.4)	333.7 (4.6)	1,962.1 (5.0)
Netherlands	28.6 (1.9)	58.6 (9.4)	123.9 (9.1)	252.1 (10.9)	316.1 (10.2)	1,218.1 (23.6)	3,062.7 (29.6)	453.6 (6.3)	6,229.9 (15.9)
Germany	29.4 (2.0)	35.0 (5.6)	45.6 (3.4)	47.0 (2.0)	396.8 (12.9)	643.9 (12.5)	763.8 (7.4)	1,017.8 (14.1)	3,404.9 (8.7)
Ireland	0.0 (0.0)	9.5 (1.5)	115.5 (8.5)	358.7 (15.5)	331.1 (10.7)	90.1 (1.7)	21.4 (0.2)	13.1 (0.2)	1,025.1 (2.6)

Notes:
1. 1962–94 figures are annual averages.
2. Figures in brackets are percentage share of the sector or the source country in total FDI inflows.
Source: Ministry of Commerce, Industry and Energy, *Trends in Foreign Direct Investment*, October 2000.

Table 10.3   Sectoral liberalization of foreign direct investment (at the 5–digit level, Korea Standard Industrial Classification)

Classification	Number of sectors liberalized (partial and full)					Sectors remaining fully or partially restricted, April 1999
	1993	1996	1997	1998	1999	
Manufacturing	2	6	1	2	–	2
Services	9	39	16	20	1	16
Agriculture, fisheries, mining	5	4	10	–	–	4
Total	16	49	27	22	1	22

Note: Wholly restricted sectors included cattle husbandry, inshore and coastal fishing, wholesale trade in meat, radio and television broadcasting, and news agency activities. Of these, cattle husbandry and news agency activities were partially liberalized in January 2000, and wholesale trade in meat was partially liberalized in January 2001. Partially restricted sectors included cereal grains production, publishing (newspapers, periodicals), coastal water transport, air transport, telecommunications, domestic banking, trust and trust companies, broadcasting, electric power generation, and gambling. Of these, gambling was completely liberalized by May 1999.
Source: World Bank (1999: 73); J. D. Kim (1999: 24–5).

Thanks to these measures, coupled with the depreciation of the won and asset values, FDI hit record levels after 1997. The phenomenal rise in FDI flows as a share of GDP is represented by the steep slope of the curves between 1997 and 1999 in Figure 10.1.[11] FDI increased by 69 percent from 1997 to 1998, and then by more than 100 percent from 1998 to 1999, reaching more than $10 billion. Although there was a substantial increase of FDI withdrawn in 1999, the increase in FDI inflows more than compensated. The increasing trend of FDI inflow continued into the year 2000, reaching more than $7 billion during the first ten months of 2000 compared to the same period in 1999. By 1999, cumulative FDI relative to GDP surged to 7.8 percent, bringing the ratio close to the world average. Similarly, FDI flows as a share of GDP reached 1.7 percent and 2.3 percent in 1998 and 1999, respectively (see Figure 10.1). These trends show the tremendous impact of the crisis and consequent liberalization of the FDI regime on expansion of foreign investment in Korea.

Traditionally, Japan and the United States had been the main source of FDI for Korea, but investment from these two countries declined substantially around the time of the crisis. FDI from European countries increased substantially. Europe as a whole accounted for more than half of total FDI in 1997 and 1998. FDI from Malaysia, the Netherlands and Ireland is mostly investments from holding companies seeking low taxes and may include Korean funds invested indirectly from abroad (see Table 10.2).[12]

Sectoral liberalization also accelerated greatly after the crisis, with more than thirty sectors liberalized in 1998 and 1999. Ten business categories including real estate rental and sales, securities dealings, the operation of golf courses, grain processing, and insurance-related businesses were fully opened to FDI in April 1998. In August of the same year, twelve more business categories – including the operation of gas stations, land development, commodity exchanges, investment companies and trusts, and waterworks – were opened. Notably, manufacturing of refined petroleum products was liberalized to facilitate restructuring after business swaps took place among domestic firms. Foreign investment into private electric power generation was fully opened, and ceilings on foreign equity ratios were raised in five business categories (including the public sector) by January 1999 (J. D. Kim 1999; 24).[13] As a result, only twenty-two sectors remained restricted or partially restricted by April 1999 (see Table 10.3). These sectors remain closed mainly for reasons of national security, cultural protection, and protection of the agricultural sector, all restrictions found in many developed countries.

Table 10.2 shows that FDI in services rose after 1997, especially in finance and insurance as restructuring progressed. Finance and insurance accounted for more than 10 percent and 20 percent of total FDI in 1998 and 1999 respectively. Services also include the newly liberalized sectors such as telecommunications and electricity, which received high proportions of FDI. In the manufacturing sector, which still receives more than half of total FDI, metal and food have been attractive sectors for foreign investors in recent years. Electricity and electronics continue to attract a high proportion of FDI (24.3 percent in 1999), as the expanding information and telecommunication industry remains vibrant.

3   Changing Modes of FDI

Of particular importance in the changed landscape is the emergence of altogether new modes of FDI. Cross-border mergers, privatization, and activities by regional governments have become significant new channels for FDI.

M&As have become an increasingly popular means of investing

abroad worldwide. The world's total value of completed cross-border M&As rose from less than $100 billion in 1987 to $720 billion in 1999. Although it is not possible to precisely measure the share of M&As in total FDI, UNCTAD estimates that this ratio increased from 52 percent in 1987 to 83 percent in 1999 (UNCTAD 2000: 14).

In Korea, cross-border mergers increased significantly after they were allowed in 1997. M&As by foreign firms increased after the Asian crisis in response to deregulation of laws restricting M&As,[14] lower asset prices, and depreciation of the won. A plethora of acquisition opportunities emerged as distressed firms sold off parts of their business operations in the process of restructuring. In many cases, rescue funds flowed in from existing foreign partners to ease liquidity constraints. Common forms of M&A have included buying out joint venture partners, existing investors expanding through acquisition and the creation of new establishments in collaboration with Korean partners to acquire existing business units.

In 1997, foreign acquisition of outstanding shares amounted to about $699 million, accounting for 10 percent of total FDI (on a notification basis). This figure increased to $1244 million or 14 percent of total FDI in 1998 and $2333 million or 15 percent of total FDI in 1999 (see Table 10.4). However, during the first ten months of 2000, the share of acquisitions abated, accounting for 5.6 percent of total FDI, presumably because there are fewer restructuring firms.

Table 10.4 Flows of foreign direct investment by mode of entry, 1997–2000 (notification basis; number of cases, $million)

Mode of entry	1997	1998	1999	Jan.–Oct. 2000
Acquisition of newly issued shares				
Cases	944	1,106	1,834	3,197
Amount	6,207.5	6,524.8	12,570.6	11,204.0
Acquisition of outstanding shares				
Cases	92	236	240	241
Amount	699.6	1,244.1	2,333.3	687.0
Long–term intra–firm loans				
Cases	19	57	28	21
Amount	63.6	1,083.3	637.3	279.9
Total FDI				
Cases	1,055	1,399	2,102	3,459
Amount	6,970.9	8,852.3	15,541.3	12,171.0

Source: Ministry of Commerce, Industry and Energy, October 2000.

Official statistics considerably underestimate the extent of cross-border M&As because acquisition of assets and business units is counted as acquisition of new shares. If properly counted, the proportion of cross-border M&As would increase substantially. According to the Ministry of Commerce, Industry and Energy, the combined figure is estimated to be 53 percent of total FDI in 1998 (J. D. Kim 1999: 16). According to Rhee (1999), roughly 37 percent of investments exceeding $10 million came in through asset acquisition, while another 11 percent came through acquisition of outstanding stocks. Thus the two types of M&A together formed slightly less than half of total incoming FDI (see Table 10.5).

Large M&As have to be notified and cleared by the Korea Fair Trade Commission (KFTC). Because KFTC statistics include all types of M&As, they give a better picture of the nature of recent cross-border M&As.[15] In 1997, only 4.5 percent (19 cases) of total M&As were cross-border. This increased rapidly to 27.2 percent (132 cases) and 30.2 percent (168 cases) in 1998 and 1999 respectively. Asset and business acquisitions formed 10.5 percent of each in 1997. This increased significantly, to 29.5 percent and 22 percent respectively in 1998 and 36.3 percent and 29.2 percent respectively in 1999. On the other hand, establishment of new firms through mergers decreased from 68.4 percent in 1997 to 39.4 percent and 22 percent in 1998 and 1999 respectively (see Table 10.6).

According to KFTC statistics, most of the cross-border M&As in 1997 (92.9 percent) were vertical mergers, indicating that the merging

Table 10.5 Patterns of foreign direct investment into Korea, 1998 ($million, %)

Investment	Invested amount ($million)	(%)	Investment size per case
Acquisition of newly issued stocks			
New	1,020	(13.0)	46.4
Added	2,049	(26.1)	42.7
Sub–total	3,069	(39.2)	43.8
Mergers and acquisitions			
Acquisition of outstanding shares	820	(10.5)	27.3
Acquisition of assets	2,930	(37.4)	154.2
Sub–total	3,750	(47.8)	76.5
Long–term loan	1,019	(13.0)	113.2
Total	7,838	(100)	61.2

Note: Investments exceeding $10 million, notification basis.
Source: Rhee (1999: 32).

Table 10.6   Trends in cross-border mergers and acquisitions by type, 1997–99

Year	Total cases	Stock acquisition	Mergers	Business acquisition	Interlocking directorate	New establishment
1997						
Total	418	130	75	23	27	163
Cross–border	19	2	1	2	1	13
		(10.5)	(5.3)	(10.5)	(5.3)	(68.4)
1998						
Total	486	92	151	81	32	130
Cross–border	132	39	9	29	3	52
		(29.5)	(6.8)	(22.0)	(2.3)	(39.4)
1999						
Total	557	146	145	111	42	113
Cross–border	168	61	11	49	10	37
		(36.3)	(6.5)	(29.2)	(6.0)	(22.0)

Note: Figures in brackets are percentage shares of cross–border mergers and acquisitions.
Source: Korea Fair Trade Commission.

firms were trying to expand their sales operations in the Korean market. Table 10.6 shows that the trend reversed in 1998 and 1999, with horizontal mergers (44.7 percent in 1998 and 26.2 percent in 1999) and combination mergers (40.2 percent in 1998 and 67.9 percent in 1999) constituting the bulk of total cross-border M&As. Since horizontal mergers tend to have greater anti-competitive effects than vertical mergers, this reverse in trend suggests that mergers involving foreign firms may have concentrating effects.

Interestingly, the three orders for corrective measures by the KFTC in 1998 all involved M&As by foreign parties (KFTC 1999). In the case of P&G's acquisition of Ssangyong Paper Ltd, the KFTC ruled that the merger would affect competition in the sanitary napkins market, and ordered the sales of manufacturing facilities and industrial property rights to a third party. When Hansol's paper manufacturing business was acquired by a joint venture of three companies, Hansol Pulp and Paper, Abitibi Consolidated (Canada) and Norske Skog (Norway), the KFTC ruled that the acquisition would limit competition and ordered the market share of the joint venture be maintained under 50 percent until 2003 when import tariffs on newsprint would be lifted. For Gillette Company's acquisition of Rocket Korea Ltd, the KFTC ruled that it would limit competition in certain segments of the battery market and ordered that the product price of the acquired firm should not rise above a certain level for the next five years.

Three cases out of 132 cases does not warrant excessive concern about economic concentration increasing through cross-border M&As. Foreign invested firms usually aim to maximize profits and do not typically go out of their way to increase market share. Further, the *quality* of competition (that is, competition from firms with better technology or managerial practices) is as important as the *degree* of competition. Nevertheless, it is clear that, in particular sectors, the presence of an individual multinational can be large. In the long run, increased concentration levels may allow dominant multinationals in a given industry to raise prices, and continued vigilance through competition policy is necessary (see Chapter 11).

A second new channel for FDI is privatization. Most foreign investment into the public sector, however, has been in the form of portfolio investment; the government has preferred public offerings in capital markets to strategic sales. For example, both Pohang Iron and Steel Co. Ltd (POSCO) and Korea Electric Power Corporation (KEPCO) have issued depository receipts in international capital markets on several occasions, and foreign ownership accounts for around 30 percent of both firms (Yun and Park 1999). Korea Telecom has also issued depository receipts internationally, lowering the government's share to 59 percent of the company as of January 2001 (see Table 10.7). The sale of KEPCO's two generation plants is a notable exception to this. In 2000, the two plants were sold to LG Power, an international consortium, for 771 billion won.[16]

Subnational governments have also become a new channel for inducing FDI. In November 1998, the Foreign Investment Promotion Act was enacted to replace the Act on Foreign Direct Investment and Foreign Capital Inducement. The new legislation created a more investor-oriented policy environment by streamlining procedures, strengthening incentives and establishing a one-stop service for investors.

One notable feature of the law is its provisions to encourage local governments in attracting foreign investment (Korea Investment Service Center). Local governments are given more freedom to attract foreign investors through local tax exemption, land leases, or development and management of foreign investment zones. Under the new law, the central government can give financial support to local governments in accordance with their efforts and achievements in attracting greenfield FDI. This policy creates an environment in which local governments compete with each other to induce foreign capital.

At the beginning of 2000, the Ministry of Commerce, Industry and Energy allocated 50 billion *won* to assist local governments in FDI-related projects, with the rule that the central ministry and local governments would share project costs on a fifty-fifty basis. Rules later changed to strengthen support from the central government by

Table 10.7 Foreign investment in major state-owned enterprises (million *won*, %)

	Korea Electric Power Corporation	Pohang Iron and Steel Co., Ltd.	Korea Telecom
Form of privatization	–DR Issue –Sale of generation plants	–DR Issue –Sale of KDB shares (20.84%) by Sept. 2000	–DR Issue –Strategic tie–ins with foreign telecommuni- cations firms
Total assets	64,149,428 (Dec. 1999)	17,766,700 (Dec. 2000)	17,015,197 (Sept. 2000)
Government share (Jan. 2001)	Govt (52.2%) KDB (1.8%)	IBK (4.0%)	Govt (59.0%)
Foreign share (June 1999)	25.8%	51.0%	19.4%
Notes	Foreign ownership ceiling 40% Must maintain 51% of govern- ment ownership due to terms signed for foreign loans	No ceiling on foreign ownership Effectively fully privatized Govt ownership is only indirectly held by the IBK	Foreign ownership ceiling 49% Single–person ceiling 15%

Note: Govt: Central Government; KDB: Korea Development Bank; IBK: Industrial Bank of Korea.
Source: Yun and Park (1999: 34); Telephone interviews, January 2001.

enabling it to vary the proportion of its contributions depending upon the type of FDI project and the financial state of the regional government in question (MCIE press release, September 8, 2000).[17]

There have been both successes and failures on the part of local governments. The decision of a Japanese firm to invest in South Kyungsang Province to manufacture multi-layer chip condensers in 1999 is widely regarded as a success, and the location of its investment will be developed as a foreign investment zone. The investing firm is therefore entitled to all the incentives accorded to foreign investment industrial complexes, including tax exemptions for ten years and free lease of land for fifty years. The $209 million investment is expected to create employment for more than 2000 workers in this region, which has relatively low income levels. The investing firm plans to export 80 percent of its production back to Japan, and the rest will replace its imports into Korea. At the same time, significant technology spillovers are also expected (MCIE press release, October 8, 1999).

Another example is a $453,000 investment by an Italian consortium, Ultratec, in North Cholla Province to produce printed circuit boards. The consortium plans to build production facilities both for the boards themselves and for equipment to manufacture them by March 2004, creating 460 jobs in the region. While Korea is strong in manufacturing the boards, it depends on imports for more than 80 percent of its manufacturing equipment; this investment is expected to have an import-substitution effect of around 21 billion *won*. This region will be declared a foreign investment zone and the consortium will benefit from tax exemption. When the exemption period expires in 2012, it is expected to provide a significant tax base (MCIE press release, September 8, 2000).

Failures are less publicized, for obvious reasons. Interviews and press reports suggest that local government's inexperience in dealing with foreign businesses and politically motivated investments has sometimes resulted in FDI projects with dubious economic impact. More case studies are warranted to give a clearer picture of the recent FDI landscape in Korea at the regional level.

While the power to provide tax exemptions, develop regional foreign investment zones, and select foreign investors has become decentralized, regulatory powers remain with the central government. The financing of FDI inducement also remains heavily dependent on the central government. In sum, the new policy does not imply a significant decentralization of power where major economic policies are concerned. Nor does it seem a reasonable way of attracting and selecting quality foreign investment, given the present capability of most local governments. In addition, although competition among jurisdictions undoubtedly has a positive impact on upgrading infrastructure provision and administrative efficiency, competition in giving away incentives may give too much bargaining power to foreign investors.

4   The Role of FDI in Corporate Restructuring: Case Studies[18]

As other chapters in this volume have shown, many recent problems encountered by Korea are related to the system of corporate governance: lack of transparency, unwillingness to relinquish managerial control, and autocratic decision-making by owner-managers. The experience of at least one firm, Hansol PCS, shows that foreign investment can have a significant effect on how corporations organize their governance systems, especially with respect to sharing control and power.

The failure of the financial sector to monitor borrowers is also seen as one of the key governance problems in pre-crisis Korea (see Chapter 4). Due to ownership restrictions, the share ownership of banks is diffused, and the government has been able to direct much of their lending activities, sometimes without proper risk evaluation. At the same time, the control rights attached to a large portion of the shares of the conglomerates are exercised by securities houses attached to the *chaebol*. Institutional shareholding in listed firms is relatively low from an international perspective and their shareholder rights severely limited by regulation (World Bank 1999: 69–79). The Korea First Bank, which was laden with non-performing corporate debt, provides insight into the influence of FDI in addressing these weaknesses.

One of the most important benefits of FDI is the transfer of new technology. However, restructuring requires not just product or production technology, but organizational skills, financial techniques and managerial know-how that improve the efficiency of investment. Volvo's acquisition of Samsung Heavy Industry's construction equipment operation resulted in a new managerial paradigm, and is widely cited as a successful case of FDI-assisted restructuring.

Bell Canada's investment in Hansol PCS[19]

After three months of negotiations in early 1998, Bell Canada International and AIG, an American investment fund, invested a total of 350 billion *won* ($291.7 million)[20] in Hansol PCS. Of this Bell Canada invested 60 percent and AIG 40 percent, giving Bell Canada 23 percent and AIG 15 percent of total outstanding shares of Hansol PCS at the time of the investment. The investment took the form of purchase of common shares, preferred shares and convertible bonds, which were due to mature in 2001.[21]

The greatest difficulty at the time of negotiations was about how to share managerial control. The problem was ultimately solved by carefully designing the structure of the board and adopting what is known as "super-majority voting rights," which give minority shareholders a great deal of power. Bell Canada was negotiating at the depths of the crisis, and this probably had an effect on Hansol's negotiating position. However, the super-majority voting rights would continue to prevail if and when major shareholders change, which may well happen when the foreign ownership ceiling in the sector is lifted.

The corporate governance issue was resolved by establishing a board of sixteen people with specific shareholder rights. Currently, Hansol has managerial control as the majority shareholder, but Bell Canada can elect four representatives to the board, which represents about 33–49 percent of voting rights. To pass ordinary operational decisions, only a simple majority is needed, but for major corporate decisions, super-majority voting rights are triggered and thirteen votes are necessary.

Major corporate decisions include those relating to the CEO's conduct, and the appointment of an auditor or external financial adviser. They also include fundamental changes to the firm (liquidation, M&As, corporate sales, recapitalization, restructuring), changes in the articles of association, changes in the corporate name and address, and establishing or liquidating a subsidiary. Transactions involving more than 10 percent (or one billion *won*) of corporate shares, transactions with related parties, changes in debt structure or other financial policies, business plans and budgets are also corporate decisions.

The super-majority voting rights also provide a way of solving a situation when there is an impasse. The formula includes a pre-calculated pricing mechanism to buy out the other's shares as a last resort when involved parties cannot reach an agreement over an important issue. However, only specific items trigger the mechanism and therefore it is not easy to initiate a takeover. For example, the parties are first encouraged to sort things out at the executive level (that is, a meeting between the chairmen of Hansol and Bell Canada), and if this fails, to refer to an arbitration panel. If arbitration fails, the mechanism to buy out the other party is triggered. The party which wishes to sell makes a "take it or leave it" offer. If the offer is refused, the party which made the offer is forced to buy at the price it itself has made. The scheme is designed so that the parties are forced to make a reasonable calculation of corporate value and to be cautious about selling to or buying out the other party.

The Hansol case is a good example of FDI introducing an innovative governance system. The investment enabled reasonable power sharing between the majority shareholder and the minority shareholders and provided an effective check against the CEO or the founder-owner from acting in a discretionary fashion.

Korea First Bank[22]

The Korea First Bank had the most assets and largest profits among the Korean banks in the early 1990s. It went insolvent in 1998, with non-performing loans of $3.2 billion as of December of that year.[23] Korea First was the largest creditor to the bankrupt Hanbo Iron and Steel, Kia Motors, and the Daewoo Group. It was also involved in the Hanbo scandal, and its top officials were indicted for fraud and bribery. Korea First was the embodiment of the worst of Korea's pre-crisis banking system. Turning this bank around therefore became a symbol for successful economic restructuring.

The bank was nationalized in 1998 through recapitalization using public funds, with a plan to sell to a foreign investor in line with IMF recommendations. After a year of tortuous negotiations, Newbridge Capital acquired 50.99 percent of the outstanding common stock from the Korea Deposit Insurance Corporation (KDIC) for cash proceeds of 500 billion *won* ($417 million) in December 1999. An Assistance Agreement, including a put-back option, accompanied the acquisition. The government will buy back defaulted loans over the next two years (three years for Daewoo and workout corporate loans) after the acquisition. The government also agreed to build up relevant loan loss reserves against newly classified nonperforming loans for the next two years after the acquisition.[24] While a controlling stake was transferred to Newbridge, with full managerial rights, the government maintained a 49 percent share (KDIC, 45.92 percent; Ministry of Finance and Economy, 3.09 percent), with the hope of recovering the large sum of public funds sunk into saving the bank.

In January 2000, Wilfred Y. Horie, an American of Japanese descent, was elected president and CEO of the bank; by April, a new executive management team was installed. The bank achieved a capital adequacy ratio of 13.7 percent, exceeding the standards of the Bank for International Settlements, in the first half of 2000. During the same period, return on equity and asset ratios turned positive to 57 percent and 4.6 percent respectively. The nonperforming loan ratio was reduced to 10 percent from 18.5 percent in 1999.

No doubt, most of this achievement cannot be attributed to the new management. The Korea First Bank has received the greatest amount of government assistance of all Korean banks. From the time it was nationalized until September 2000, about 23 percent of the initial public funds allocated to restructure the financial sector (64 trillion *won*) was used for Korea First (*Maeil Business Paper*, September 23, 2000; *Korea Economic Daily*, September 8, 2000). As part of the acquisition deal, the government contributed 209.8 billion *won* to increase the total net assets of the bank. Before the acquisition, the bank sold 4503.9 billion *won* worth of nonperforming loans to Korea Asset Management Corporation (KAMCO) in July, and transferred nonperforming assets to KDIC in return for 5856 billion *won* worth of KDIC-issued cashable bonds. In December, the bank further transferred nonperforming assets of 3094.7 billion *won* in banking accounts and 524.7 billion *won* in trust accounts to KDIC. This effectively gave the bank a clean balance sheet before the acquisition (KFB, *Annual Report 1999*: 21–665).

More than the spectacular improvements in these numbers, probably the most important change that took place in the Korea First Bank was the general reorganization of the bank. This involved changes in the organizational structure, an employee-reward mechanism, and new business strategy.

The bank's organizational structure was redesigned after the Western-style division system headed by chief officers. Layers between managerial levels have been minimized to enable direct reports to top management, and major job roles have been defined with clear accountability. The new management has also instituted stronger financial discipline in terms of pricing and balance-sheet management and more rigorous accounting and information systems to enhance accountability.

However, by far the greatest emphasis is put on credit analysis. The responsibility of the chief credit officer, who controls all the bank's credit-related operations and reports directly to the CEO, has been vastly strengthened. The number of risk analysts has been doubled to about 100. Cross-checking procedures have been strengthened.[25] At the same time, the credit approval procedure was centralized, and loan compliance officers assigned to each branch to ensure transparency in the lending process. With lending and other back-office functions consolidated at either the head office or regional centers, the branches now focus on sales.[26]

The new credit evaluation methodology is exemplary of international best practice. Lending policy based on collateral and corporate name recognition has been replaced with a strong emphasis on cash flow. For closer monitoring of loans, existing loans have been classified into eight categories, on top of the five-class system of the Financial Supervisory Service. The bank is also developing an advanced credit scoring system modeled on those used by its overseas affiliates, since an efficient and accurate credit evaluation process is necessary for faster turnaround of loan applications, particularly in the area of finance for consumers and small and medium-sized firms.

In an effort to enhance the staff's profit orientation, Western-style performance-based pay and promotion are being instituted to replace the traditional practice of payment and promotion based on seniority. Pay can differ as much as 50 million *won* among the same rank, and more profitable marketing segments will receive greater payment, even within the same branch. Reward is also differentiated by function, rather than simply based on vertical hierarchy. Direct superiors, rather than the personnel office, now evaluate employee performance.

The new management has moved away from the past emphasis on

large corporate financing to retail lending and SME financing, recognizing the growth potential and returns in these markets. Competition is already intense in consumer retailing, and the Korea First Bank is emphasizing rapid development of products and services that are new to the Korean market. The bank has aggressively pursued business alliances and strategic partnerships to sell diverse new products and services. Such cross-selling and bundling sales strategies are fairly new to the Korean banking industry. For example, the bank has introduced the First Mortgage Loan, the first Korean product to have a 30-year maturity. It has also developed new services and flexible, high-yield investment products in cooperation with securities and insurance firms. Korea First is also targeting the growing and lucrative credit card market by introducing revolving and corporate purchasing cards (especially for small businesses), while raising credit ceilings on bank credit cards.

Of all these changes, the most notable is the ability of the Korea First Bank to resist government intervention. Although financial markets have been deregulated in many ways, government intervention continues through informal meetings with financial leaders to stabilize financial markets, curb high interest rates, influence lending policies, and pursue other political or public policy objectives. Unlike other Korean banks, which are accustomed to slavish compliance with government directives, Korea First is less constrained. First of all, it has a foreign CEO who has more latitude with government authorities. Newbridge has also openly declared its intention to turn the bank around and then exit with a profit, either by selling or listing it. Therefore, the authorities find it difficult to impose sanctions without jeopardizing the future prospects of the bank itself.

Several incidents point to the changed relationship. The Korea First Bank turned down a government request that it purchase a proportion of corporate bonds maturing in 2000 to help stabilize the local bond market. It also refused to keep credit lines to Hyundai Construction and Engineering Co., quoting its general policy that it no longer lends on an unsecured basis to general contractors. It has also vetoed new credit flows to some workout firms, and is contributing only a minimal amount to other major workout firms such as Daewoo Electronics and Ssangyong Motors.

While other competing banks have complained that Korea First is receiving special treatment, jeopardizing the government's overall restructuring policies and undermining the competitiveness of Korean-owned banks, most analysts regard its ability to oppose government intervention as a pace-setting example which other banks should follow.

It is difficult to assess accurately to what extent these changes have had spillover effects in the financial market in general. However, the renewed operation of the Korea First Bank appears to have intensified competition in the finance industry (especially in the retail sector). Most Korean banks have undertaken reforms to improve credit analysis capabilities and introduced new products in anticipation of competition from Korea First. Public opinion against government intervention in ordinary banking operations is also mounting. This fact undermines Korean-owned financial institutions that have less leverage with authorities and also face higher interest rates in the international capital markets compared to foreign-owned banks. In addition, non-strategic foreign investors (such as Goldman Sachs in Kookmin Bank) are showing an interest in having a greater voice in management. This will further strengthen resistance against direct government intervention.

Volvo Construction Equipment Korea[27]

In July 1998, Volvo acquired the construction equipment unit of Samsung Heavy Industry for $572 million and set up Volvo Construction Equipment Korea (VCEK). The contract includes transfer of Samsung's technology, and marketing and procurement network. Further, VCEK will pay a royalty to Samsung for continuing to use its brand for three years. The acquired firm had been making losses for some time, and VCEK is expected to inject capital to restructure the firm. VCEK announced intentions to invest $200 million in the excavator business by 1999, including the establishment of an R&D center for product development. Volvo foresaw a close cooperative relationship with Samsung, with about 13 percent of Samsung Heavy Industry's share remaining in the new firm. There were neither layoffs nor pay cuts at the time of the acquisition.

Volvo's main motivation for investing in Korea is to upgrade its excavator business. While Volvo is a significant producer of construction equipment (loaders, excavators, haulers, graders) it holds only 1 percent of the world market for excavators, which in turn constitutes about 40 percent of the construction equipment market. Samsung's high-quality products and high market share, both in Korea (the world's fourth-largest in the excavator market) and in Southeast Asia, were top considerations when making the acquisition decision. Caterpillar and Japanese firms dominate the Southeast Asian market but Korean manufacturers, including Samsung, have 20 percent of the market. In Southeast Asia, there were no established plants that it could acquire and it would have been too expensive and time-consuming to make a greenfield investment in this region. Volvo has been planning to establish production facilities in the Asian region for the past few years, and its strategic interests thus coincided well with Samsung's need for foreign capital. Another motive in investing in Korea was to lower production cost. For the first few years, Volvo will therefore be producing Samsung's products, continuing to use its label on license, until it can develop indigenized Volvo models to be sold under its own brand name.

At the level of operations, Volvo found no particular difficulty with Samsung's production facilities, which were transferred along with suppliers, procurement and marketing as a going concern. The changes will be more internal, as the firm moves from "Samsung culture" to "Volvo culture." Volvo has shown considerable respect for Korean culture and its system of business and therefore the process of restructuring (and downsizing due to a drastic fall in demand) will progress gradually, especially as the new company tries to soothe a sense of insecurity on the part of the employees.

The most significant contribution Volvo can make, therefore, is not in the area of product technology but in managerial techniques, organization, and quality control. Volvo's approach to internal organization is to make it "flat" and to network with other Volvo companies globally in a matrix organization. "Flat management" allows minimization of direct and indirect transaction costs by eliminating steps in decision-making.[28] The flat system has four fewer steps in the decision hierarchy than the old system (see Figure 10.2). In a flat hierarchy, the responsibilities of middle managers are increased while their numbers are reduced. The staff works as a team, and the middle manager becomes the team leader. This kind of team differs from Korean teams, in which most of the responsibility accrues to the team leader while other members are marginalized.

The essence of "matrix management" is combining functional and product or sales department in the same organizational structure. Under a traditional system that organizes the firm only into sales departments, or only into functional departments, there may be waste of company resources. In a multi-product or multi-divisional company, technology and economics dictate that the company will not have separate manufacturing facilities or sales forces for each product, division or geographic area, but utilize functional expertise across products, divisions or geographic areas. One difficulty with such a system is that it may not be possible to trace fault when something goes wrong. Clear specification of authority, which seems to be important in Volvo's flat management system, is therefore the key to the successful operation of a matrix organization. The Volvo case demonstrates that the potential benefits of FDI are not limited to capital and technology in the traditional sense; they extend to innovations in organizational management that increase efficiency.

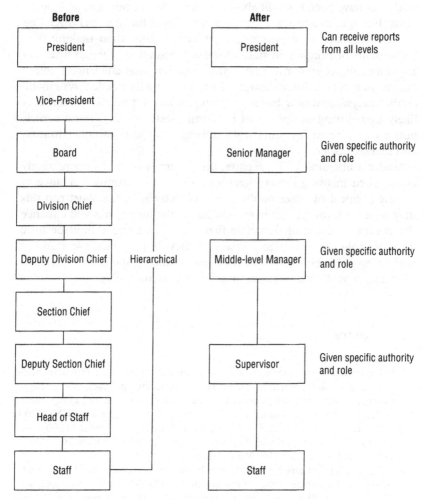

Figure 10.2 Comparison of organizational structure before and after acquisition

Source: Adopted from Employee Training Material, VCEK 1998.

5 Conclusions

The financial crisis marked a watershed in the evolution of the FDI regime in Korea, fully opening the domestic market to foreign competition. Despite the possibility that FDI may eventually increase concentration, the greater presence of foreign players in the domestic market appeared to change the nature of competition in a way that could not have been brought about through competition among Korean firms. Foreign investors are setting a role model for financial discipline and for improving corporate governance. Rather than making new investments or bringing in state-of-the-art technology, foreign investors are enhancing overall investment and organizational efficiencies, introducing managerial know-how, and initiating badly needed systematic credit analysis and new business strategies in the financial sector. It is likely that during the phase of economic restructuring, these contributions by foreign investors will outweigh problems of concentration and market power.

Under a liberalized FDI regime, the government is also increasingly constrained in using direct intervention or administrative guidance to pursue political or other public policy objectives. In the short run this may seem to favor foreign investors, but in the long run it will enhance the competitiveness of domestic firms. In fact, there should be little objectionable about foreign investors if they do not engage in fraud or anti-competitive behavior, and for these problems, the government has recourse to prudential regulation and competition policy.

Notes

1 International contestability refers to genuinely open markets where non-border measures, such as trade and investment policies, government procurement, corporate governance, standard setting, tax and competition policies do not constitute artificial barriers against foreign entry (UNCTAD 1997: 127). Also see OECD (1996) and Graham and Lawrence (1996). See Martin (1993) for a critical discussion of the concept; see Bunte and Maks (1997) and Stefanadis (1999) for defenses.
2 Although foreign direct investors can be expected to withdraw liquid funds in times of financial crisis (Graham and Wada 2000). For example, see Blomstrom (1986) on innovative capacity, and Dunning (1993) and Driffield and Munday (1998, 2000) on labor productivity.
3 Lawrence (1993) argues that domestic concentration effectively deters foreign entry, citing Japan as the relevant case. However, Noland (1999) tests this hypothesis and finds that policy variables, rather than market structure (i.e., concentration) as such, are more important in deterring FDI.
4 These concerns mostly stem from early theories of FDI based on oligopolistic competition theory. In a seminal study, Kindleberger (1969) argued that foreign direct investment resulted from oligopolistic competition in home countries, and would not exist in a world of perfect competition (see Caves 1971). Going further, Hymer (1970), Vernon (1970) and Newfarmer (1979) took the position that FDI was a device for restraining competition (Nelson and Silvia 1985: 97).

5 Lall (1979) finds a positive correlation between FDI and concentration in Malaysia, after controlling for other determinants of concentration such as capital intensity, advertising, market size, economies of scale and R&D. Blomstrom (1986) finds that the presence of multinational corporations is an independent source of concentration in Mexico, and Willmore (1989) offers similar results for Brazil.

6 When simultaneity is taken into account, Gupta (1983) shows that some of the significant results found in previous studies disappear, and that even in developed countries FDI can lead to higher concentration. For example, in Canada, positive effects of R&D on concentration disappear when simultaneity is taken into account. Similarly, the positive effect of concentration on price-cost margins becomes insignificant, refuting the traditional concentration-profitability hypothesis. At the same time, FDI is shown to exert a direct downward impact on price-cost margin, but this is countered by an indirect upward effect through FDI's upward influence on advertising, which is positively related to concentration.

7 Competition leads to lower prices, ultimately forcing out marginal producers, while offering less favorable prospects for new potential entrants (Hay and Morris 1993; Davies, Lyons et al. 1996).

8 Davies, Lyons et al. (1996) show that in Europe, some concentrated industries are highly multinational, but it is not always the case. Unlike the results of Gupta (1983), concentration accompanies multinationality only if endogenous sunk costs are due to R&D and if there is trade integration. R&D still acts as an effective entry barrier, even in expanding markets.

9 The three measures of FDI are explained in the note to Table 10.1. Notification figures tend to exaggerate FDI flows; balance of payment measures generally underestimate FDI by not including foreign investment financed by selling debt or equity to unrelated parties, and not allowing for the increase in the value of foreign-controlled assets (Graham and Krugman 1995: 11). The arrivals-based measure is close to the balance of payment measure for most years. The discussion will be based on the arrivals measure for consistency, except for the analysis of mode of entry for which only the notification-based measure is available.

10 For example, the requirement for foreigners to obtain board approval for ownership of more than one-third of the outstanding shares was removed, allowing hostile, cross-border M&As.

11 High FDI flow to GDP also reflects the contraction of GDP in 1998.

12 Although not shown in Table 10.2, FDI from tax havens such as the Cayman Islands, Virgin Islands and Bermuda has increased substantially in 2000, particularly from American firms (MOFE and MCIE 2000a).

13 Also see Consolidated Public Notice for Foreign Investment (2000) published by MCIE for the most recent information on sectoral restrictions and other regulations.

14 Non-regulatory barriers to successful M&As also exist. Some of the primary problems are differences in valuation methods and the unwillingness of Korean owners to relinquish managerial control. Koreans tend to use book values, while the Western approach centers on discounted cash flows. Different accounting methods and different approaches to assessing

future contingencies (including assessment of receivables and inventory, tax exemptions that give different incentives to sellers and buyers) also increase the transaction costs of an M&A deal. See Telepak (1999).

15 Acquiring firms with total assets or sales of 100 billion *won* or with special relations with the target firms (under certain situations), have to notify the KFTC (MRFTA, Article 12).

16 The consortium, with a paid-in capital of 78.24 billion *won*, consists of LG–Caltex Oil (26 percent), LG–Caltex Gas (24.5 percent), Texaco (25 percent) and Geug-Dong City Gas (24.5 percent).

17 By May 2000, only 13 percent of this budget had been used (*Korea Economic Daily*, June 6, 2000). The reason for the sluggish performance seems to be that local governments are short of funds, even with central government assistance. However, there is, to date, very little public information concerning the use of this fund, making any assessment of the policy difficult.

18 The Hansol PCS and Volvo Construction Equipment Korea cases draw on Yun (1999) and interviews. The Korea First Bank case relies largely on published materials.

19 This section relies on interviews with Jim Wilkinson, Executive Vice-President, Hansol PCS (11 June 1999) and Han Hoon, Director of Corporate Planning Division, Hansol PCS (28 July 1999). Hansol PCS has since been acquired by KT Freetel.

20 This would be $233.33 million if the exchange rate of 1500 *won* to the dollar were applied.

21 The complex structure of the investment arose due to delays in raising the foreign ownership ceiling in the telecommunications sector from 33 percent to 49 percent.

22 The case study mainly relies on KFB's *Annual Report 1998*; *Far Eastern Economic Review*, various issues; *Business Korea*, February 2000; press releases from FSC, 1999–2000; *New York Times*, various issues; *Korea Economic Daily*, *Maeil Business Paper*, and other daily newspapers 1999–2001, various issues.

23 The nonperforming loans (pre-1998 loan classification basis) accounted for 26.8 percent of the bank's total loans (KFB, *Annual Report 1999*: 20; Financial Supervisory Commission). Its capital ratio (BIS basis) was −2.7 percent and −1.5 percent at the end of 1997 and 1998 respectively.

24 Newbridge was obligated to hold its stake for at least two years, and has a contingency plan to invest an additional 200 billion won in the next two years to keep the bank financially sound. It is also required to maintain the BIS capital ratio above 10 percent at all times (KFB, *Annual Report 1998*: 10–11).

25 The same person previously did loan recommendation and approval, but now two different people do it and a third person checks it.

26 The bank acknowledges that this will be a challenging process because passive sales have been the entrenched norm in traditional Korean banking industry.

27 This section relies on an interview with T. I. Lee, Volvo Construction Equipment Korea, December 1998.

28 Examples of reduced indirect costs are elimination of excessive documenta-
tion, reduction in meeting and administration time, speedy decision-
making, prevention of power struggle between managers, and reduction in
superfluous support staff. Examples of reduction in direct costs are
increased transparency in administration, allowing ready identification of
inefficient areas, and allowing managers to concentrate on their work rather
than on administration.

References

Blomstrom, M. 1986. "Multinationals and Market Structure in Mexico," *World
Development*, 14: 523–30.
Bunte, F., and Maks, H. 1997. "Contestability and Sunk Costs: An Analysis of
Product and R&D Competition." *Research Memoranda No. 15*. Maastricht:
Maastricht Research School of Economics of Technology and Organization.
Business Korea. 2000. "Daewoo Losses Eat into Bank Profits," *Business Korea*,
17 (2): 36–7.
Caves, R. E. 1971. "International Corporations: The Industrial Economics of
Foreign Investment," *Economica*, 38 (149), February: 1–27.
Davies, S., Lyons, B., et al. 1996. *Industrial Organization in the European Union:
Structure, Strategy, and the Competitive Mechanism*. Oxford: Clarendon Press.
Demsetz, Harold. 1973. "Industry Structure, Market Rivalry, and Public
Policy," *Journal of Law and Economics*, 16: 1–10.
Driffield, N., and Munday, M. 1998. "The Impact of Foreign Direct Investment
on UK Manufacturing: Is There a Profit Squeeze in Domestic Firms?"
Applied Economics, 30 (5): 705–9.
——. 2000. "Industrial Performance, Agglomeration, and Foreign Manufactur-
ing Investment in the UK," *Journal of International Business Studies*, 31 (1):
21–37.
Dunning, John H. 1993. *Multinational Enterprises and the Global Economy*.
Wokingham: Addison Wesley.
Frischtak, C. R., and Newfarmer, R. S., eds. 1994. *Market Structure and Indus-
trial Performance*. United Nations Library on Transnational Corporations,
Volume 15. London and New York: Routledge.
Gorecki, P. K. 1976. "The Determinants of Entry by Domestic and Foreign
Enterprises in Canadian Manufacturing Industries: Some Comments and
Empirical Results," *Review of Statistics*, November, 58 (4): 485–8.
Graham, E. M., and P. R. Krugman. 1995. *Foreign Direct Investment in the United
States*. Washington, DC: Institute for International Economics.
Graham, E. M., and Lawrence, R. Z. 1996. "Measuring the International
Contestability of Markets," Off-prints of *Journal of World Trade*, 30 (5): 1–20.
Graham, E. M., and Wada, E. 2000. "Domestic Reform, Trade and Investment
Liberalisation, Financial Crisis, and Foreign Direct Investment into Mexico,"
in K. Maskus, ed., *The World Economy*, 23 (5): 777–97. Washington, DC:
Institute for International Economics.

Gupta, V. K. 1983. "A Simultaneous Determination of Structure, Conduct and Performance in Canadian Manufacturing," *Oxford Economic Papers*, 35 (2): 281–301.

Hay, D. A., and Morris, D. J. 1993. *Industrial Economics and Organization: Theory and Evidence*, 2nd edn. Oxford: Oxford University Press.

Hymer, Stephen. 1976. *The International Operations of National Firms: A Study of Direct Foreign Investment*. Cambridge: MIT Press.

International Monetary Fund. 1999. *Balance of Payments Statistics Yearbook*. Washington, DC: International Monetary Fund.

Joo, H. K., and Kim, S. J. 1995. *Trends in FDI and Policy Measures* (in Korean). Seoul: Institute for Global Economics.

Kim, J. D. 1997. "Impact of Foreign Direct Investment Liberalization: The Case of Korea." Korea Institute for International Economic Policy Working Paper No. 97–01, Seoul: KIEP.

———. 1999. "Inward Foreign Direct Investment Regime and Some Evidences of Spillover Effects in Korea." Korea Institute for International Economic Policy Working Paper No. 99–09, Seoul: KIEP.

Kim, J. D., and Hwang, S. I. 1998. "The Role of Foreign Direct Investment in Korea's Economic Development: Productivity Effects and Implications for the Currency Crisis." Korea Institute for International Economic Policy Working Paper No. 98–04, Seoul: KIEP.

Kim, K. H. 1998. "Prospects for Bilateral Investment Treaty between Korea and the US" (in Korean). Korea Institute for International Economic Policy, Policy Analysis No. 98–03, Seoul: KIEP.

Kim, S. 1999. "Host Country Effects of FDI: The Case of Korea." Paper presented at the International Seminar: The Entry of Foreign MNCs and The Globalization of the Korean Economy, Korea Institute for International Economic Policy, Seoul, November.

Kindleberger, Charles. 1969. *American Business Abroad: Six Lectures on Direct Investment*. New Haven: Yale University Press.

Korea Economic Daily, various issues.

Korea Fair Trade Commission (KFTC). 1998. *White Paper on Fair Trade*. Seoul: KFTC.

———. 1999. *White Paper on Fair Trade*. Seoul: KFTC.

———. 2000. Unpublished Data on Cross-border Mergers. Seoul: KFTC.

Korea First Bank. 1998, 1999. *Annual Reports*.

Korea Investment Service Center. http://www.kisc.org

Lall, S. 1979. "Multinational and Market Structure in an Open Developing Economy: the Case of Malaysia," *Weltwirtsch. Arch.* 115 (2): 325–50.

Lawrence, R. Z. 1993. "Japan's Different Trade Regime: An Analysis with Particular Reference to *Keiretsu*," *Journal of Economic Perspectives*, 7 (3): 3–19.

Lee, C. S. 2000. "Makeover at the Bank," *Far Eastern Economic Review*, 163 (9): 42–3.

Lee, S. B., and Lee, H. G. 1998. *Attracting Foreign Direct Investment: International Success Cases and their Implications* (in Korean). Korea Institute for International Economic Policy, Policy Analysis No. 98–09. Seoul: KIEP.

Maeil Business Paper, various issues.

Martin, Stephen. 1993. *Advanced Industrial Economics*. Oxford and Cambridge: Blackwell.

Ministry of Commerce, Industry and Energy (MCIE). 2000a. *Trends in Foreign Direct Investment.* Seoul: MCIE.

——. 2000b. *Consolidated Public Notice for Foreign Investment.* Seoul: MCIE.

Nelson, P., and Silvia, L. 1985. "Antitrust Policy and Intra-industry Direct Foreign Investment: Cause and Effect," in E. Asim, ed., *Multinationals as Mutual Invaders: Intra-Industry Direct Foreign Investment,* pp. 97–123. New York: St Martin's Press.

Newfarmer, Richard. 1979. "TNC Takeovers in Brazil: the Uneven Distribution of Benefits in the Market for Firms," *World Development,* 7 (1), January: 25–43.

Newfarmer, R., and Marsh, L. 1994. "Industrial Structure, Market Power and Profitability," in C. R. Frischtak and R. S. Newfarmer, eds, *Market Structure and Industrial Performance.* United Nations Library on Transnational Corporations, Volume 15, pp. 213–33. London and New York: Routledge.

Noland, M. 1999. "Competition Policy and FDI: A Solution in Search of a Problem?" Institute for International Economics, Working Paper No. 99–3, Washington, DC.

Organization for Economic Cooperation and Development (OECD). 1996. "The International Contestability of Markets – Economic Perspectives." Issue Paper, TD/TC (96) 5. Paris: OECD.

Rhee, D. K. 1999. "The Entry of Foreign Multinationals and Its Impact on the Korean Market." Paper presented at the International Seminar: The Entry of Foreign MNCs and The Globalization of the Korean Economy, Institute for International Economic Policy, November. Seoul: Korea.

Sender, H. 2000. "The Price of Freedom," *Far Eastern Economic Review,* 163 (39): 67–74.

Stefanadis, C. 1999. "Sunk Costs, Contestability, and the Latent Contract Market," *Staff Reports No. 75,* Federal Reserve Bank of New York. <http://netec.mcc.accu.uk/doc/paperfaq.html>

Telepak, D. 1999. "Acquisition Due Diligence." Paper presented at American Chamber of Commerce, Investment Committee Meeting, Seoul, April 28.

United Nations Conference on Trade and Development (UNCTAD). 1997, 1998, 2000. *World Investment Report.* Geneva: UNCTAD.

Vernon, Raymond. 1970. "Foreign Enterprises and Developing Nations in the Raw Materials Industries," *American Economic Review,* 60 (2), May: 122–6.

Willmore, L. 1989. "Determinants of Industrial Structure: A Brazilian Case Study," *World Development,* 17 (10): 1601–17.

World Bank. 1998. *Global Development Finance.* Washington, DC: World Bank.

——. 1999. "Republic of Korea: Establishing a New Foundation for Sustained Growth." Poverty Reduction and Economic Management Unit, East Asia and Pacific Region, Report No. 19595 KO. Washington, DC: The World Bank.

Yun, M. 1999. "Foreign Direct Investment: A Catalyst for Change?" Paper presented at the symposium The Korean Economy in an Era of Global Competition. Joint US–Korea Academic Studies, Washington, DC, September.

——. 2000. "Impact of FDI on Competition in Korea." Unpublished MS. Seoul: Institute for International Economic Policy.

Yun, M., and Park, Y. H. 1999. "The Role of Foreign Investment in Korean Privatization," *Journal of International Economic Policy Studies*, Summer, 3 (2): 29–70. Seoul: Korea Institute for International Economic Policy.

11   Competition Law and Policy

Kwangshik Shin

Korea is one of the few newly industrialized countries that have successfully institutionalized its own competition law and policy. In December 1980, the general competition law, the Monopoly Regulation and Fair Trade Act (MRFTA), was enacted. Competition policy and institutions began to emerge in a country with a strong tradition of extensive economic management by the state.

The MRFTA was modeled on competition laws in Germany and Japan and covers all of the principal competition policy problems: monopoly, monopolistic behavior, collusion and unfair practices. But the Act is more than a conventional competition law. Since amendments in 1986, the MRFTA and its instruments have become a means for directly controlling *chaebol's* expansion and exercise of economic power. As a result, the law has many distinctive features in terms of its goals, basic concepts, legal rules and standards, and enforcement.

Chaebol regulation under the MRFTA has been strengthened in the wake of the 1997 economic crisis. *Chaebol* became the target of major reforms, and the Korea Fair Trade Commission (KFTC), the administrative agency responsible for enforcing the MRFTA and related statutes, has played a central role in those reforms. This chapter examines these policy efforts by the KFTC and their effect on *chaebol* restructuring. The first section discusses some common perceptions of the *chaebol* problem that serve as the intellectual foundation of the MRFTA and some of the historical factors that motivated its legislation and subsequent amendments and enforcement. The *chaebol* problem was generally conceived to lie in the special power stemming from conglomerate bigness and distorted corporate governance. This has led Korea's competition law and policy to direct controls on *chaebol's* corporate structure and efforts to ensure "fair" trade based on a very broad concept of economic power and dominance.

The second section assesses competition policy regulation and enforcement in terms of *chaebol* reform. It suggests that the approach of the MRFTA has been rather ineffective because of insufficient attention to conventional competition concerns as well as exemptions reflecting industrial policy considerations.

The chapter concludes by drawing policy suggestions for improving *chaebol's* structure and behavior from a competition policy perspective. For a rational, consistent and effective competition policy, the MRFTA needs to be based on the concept of market power rather than conglomerate bigness. Administrative controls on the behavior of *chaebol* should be phased out as Korea makes a transition toward a more market-oriented economy.

1   Korea's Competition Law: History and Analysis

Given their large size, diversification, and enormous aggregation of economic resources under family ownership and control, it is not surprising that "the *chaebol* problem" was generally conceived in terms of the concentration of economic power. *Chaebol* were presumed to possess and exercise special power associated with conglomerate bigness, posing a unique threat to the free market system and democratic values.

It was further thought that conventional competition policy would not be enough to address the problem of concentrated economic power, and many argued for direct and decisive government control of the *chaebol's* structure and behavior.[1] This view was based on a belief that *chaebol* had substantial advantages over small, independent enterprises in almost all aspects of business. They could thus jeopardize the interests of suppliers, competitors and customers, ensure their survival and growth irrespective of efficiency, and ultimately dominate the whole economy.

Chaebol were also seen to engage in "unfair competition." Hence, it seemed necessary that government establish an environment in which *chaebol* compete on equal terms with other economic agents. Moreover, to the extent that *chaebol's* advantages stemmed from bigness and diversity rather than market power, conventional competition policy efforts would not be sufficient to ensure fair competitive conditions. If *chaebol's* power inhered in conglomerate bigness, then government should limit their expansion and diversification. This perception led to the adoption of various regulations on *chaebol's* entry and investment decisions and bank borrowing, as well as a variety of programs to support small and medium-sized enterprises (SMEs). A more sophisticated view justified these measures by pointing to distortions in the financial sector that granted preferential access to *chaebol*.

These perceptions have had a profound impact on many aspects of Korea's competition law and policy. Concern about large aggregations of private power was one of the primary factors underlying the enactment of the MRFTA, which proclaims that its objective is "to encourage fair and free competition by preventing the abuse of market dominating position and excessive concentration of economic power and by regulating undue collaborative acts and unfair business practices, thereby stimulating creative business activities, protecting consumers and promoting the balanced development of the national economy."

The law is thus aimed at the dual goals of promoting competition *and* promoting fairness and balanced development. To serve these latter objectives, the MRFTA was amended to limit the concentration of economic power by directly regulating *chaebol's* corporate structure and investment decisions. The Act's stated purposes are broad enough to justify attacks on aggregate concentration and to support rules about competitive fairness and equity in bargaining relationships.

The enactment of the MRFTA

Before 1981 Korea did not have a competition policy as normally conceived; the government relied on administrative fiat and direct controls. The MRFTA, Korea's first competition law, was enacted on the last day of 1980.[2] To better understand the major features of the Act, we need to look at the economic and political context of its legislation.

The MRFTA was passed by the Emergency Committee for National Security, the organization set up by General Chun Doo Hwan's new military regime after it declared martial law, disbanded the National Assembly, and banned all political activities. The enactment of the MRFTA was a response to the serious difficulties the Korean economy faced in 1980. The government's ambitious heavy and chemical industry drive and excessive intervention in the 1970s had produced serious moral hazard and driven the economy to the verge of a debt crisis. Extensive and prolonged price controls severely hampered the price mechanism and created substantial distortions.[3] This experience prompted a reappraisal of the way the economy was run and led to a consensus that a fundamental shift in policy orientation was necessary. The government under General Chun's rule began to take liberalization measures, abolishing direct price controls and opening trade and investment.

Another significant factor in the legislation, however, was Chun's political need to initiate reforms in accordance with his slogan of "social justice." There already was a growing concern about *chaebol's* dominance of the economy and its negative consequences, which included increasing concentration of economic power, widening imbalances among businesses and income classes, and the declining position of SMEs. Chun's regime sided with this popular sentiment and incorporated sociopolitical goals into the MRFTA, such as protecting small businesses, balanced development, and restraining *chaebol's* economic power. The MRFTA was thus envisioned as a symbol of political commitment to ensuring fairness, and generally conceived by the public as a law to protect the weak from the abuse of economic strength.

Despite its multiplicity of goals, the MRFTA as enacted in 1980 was limited and weak in substance. It was only with a series of amendments in subsequent decades that it became a substantive tool for the promotion of competition and regulation of the *chaebol*. The original MRFTA also established the KFTC within the Economic Planning Board, the dominant ministry in charge of overall economic policy at the time. The KFTC became an independent agency under the prime minister in December 1994, however, and the status of its chairman was elevated from the deputy minister to the ministerial level in March 1996.[4] The commission now consists of nine commissioners (including the chairman) and about 410 staff members, and has jurisdiction to enforce six statutes including the MRFTA.

Korea's approach to competition law and policy

The Korean approach is characterized by three factors: a preoccupation with market dominance and fairness; a preference for behavioral restrictions rather than structural remedies; and considerations of industrial policy. We will look at them in turn.

The MRFTA declares the goal of enhancing competition and efficiency. At the same time, it strives for the objective of "fair" trading conditions and balanced development. To support these dual goals, Korea's competition law and policy are based on a broad concept of dominance. The concept sometimes encompasses the exercise of market power and to that extent its application tends to emphasize economic efficiency and consumer welfare. But most often dominance is taken simply to refer to a position of economic strength held by a firm *vis-à-vis* its trading partners and competitors. Firm size, although by itself not indicative of the ability to exercise market power, is important. Applications of such a concept concern primarily the welfare of trading partners and competitors rather than that of final consumers.

This tendency is most apparent in addressing *unfair trade practices* as defined by Article 23 of the Act. Article 23 lists categories of conduct such as refusal to deal, discrimination, non-price vertical restraints, and in-group inter-subsidiary transactions, and forbids those practices that are likely to harm fair trade.[5] Practices that constitute unreasonable exploitation of bargaining position in subcontract relationships and adhesion contracts are regulated under separate statutes, and the KFTC has jurisdiction to enforce these laws.[6]

The notion of "unfair trade" contains two elements: a position of economic strength in relation to one's trading partners or competitors; and taking advantage of such a position to the detriment of their welfare or viability. This notion leads competition law enforcement to protect incumbents and small businesses rather than consumers, for what matters is not the anti-competitive potential or efficiency consequences of the practice in question but its possible harm to trading partners or competitors. For example, the KFTC can limit premium offers, discount sales, and other means of sales promotion on the grounds that they may constitute unreasonable inducement to competitors' customers; such action could not be understood without the notion of "fair trade." Condemning vertical restraints on the grounds that they cripple the freedom of dealers and restrain their ability to sell in accordance with their own judgment could also not be understood without this notion.

To address competition policy problems, the KFTC has tended to rely on behavioral restrictions rather than structural remedies. This tendency to control the result rather than attack the cause is particularly pronounced in dealing with *abuse of a market dominant position* under Article 3.2 of the MRFTA.

In general, abuse of dominance or monopolization under competition laws requires, first, the possession of a dominant position or monopoly power in the relevant market and, second, the presence of abusive or exclusionary conduct. The Korean approach has been unique with respect to both requirements. Before the February 1999 amendment, the Act required the KFTC to designate "market-dominating enterprises" each year in accordance with two market share criteria: a single firm with a market share of over 50 percent and two or three firms with a combined market share of more than 75 percent (as long as each individual share exceeds 10 percent)[7] in a market with total domestic sales of more than a certain amount. The designation of market-dominating firms amounted to making an irrefutable inference of dominance if a firm satisfies one of the criteria, while ruling out a finding of dominance for all other companies. The February 1999 amendment changed this framework and required the KFTC to determine the presence of dominance when a case is brought to its attention, considering such factors as market share, barriers to entry, and the relative size of competitors.[8]

Another peculiar feature of the MRFTA is that it prohibits not only exclusionary conduct but also "unreasonable" monopolistic pricing and output restriction, and authorizes the KFTC to impose price and output directives as remedial measures. Until 1998, under Article 3.2 of the Act, pricing by a market-dominating firm was regarded as "unreasonable" if its price changes were out of proportion with changes in market demand and supply or costs of supply, or if its sales expenses and general overhead expenses were excessive compared to the "normal level" in the relevant or comparable market.[9] Intervention to limit excess price increases reflects the perceived need for price controls in concentrated markets. But the application of the law involves the difficulty of determining the "proper" level of prices and output and is incompatible with the belief that markets do better than administrators in determining prices and outputs. Instead of attempting to place restrictions on the profit-maximizing behavior of the firm, it would be far more effective to address the problem of monopolization by using structural remedies such as divestiture.

Industrial policy considerations also tended to weigh heavily on Korea's competition law and policy, but in recent years, the KFTC has increasingly embraced its competition advocacy role. Changes in provisions dealing with combinations and agreements among enterprises reflect this trend.

Article 7 of the MRFTA prohibits mergers that would substantially restrain competition in any line of business. Any merger involving a company with assets or sales volume (including those of its subsidiaries) of over 100 billion won must be notified to the KFTC within thirty days of the transaction. The law, though, provides for statutory exemptions for anti-competitive mergers, and gives the KFTC substantial discretion in allowing a merger otherwise subject to challenge.[10] Prior to the economic crisis, Article 7 included a proviso that a merger may be exempt from the ban if the KFTC finds it necessary to rationalize an industry or strengthen international competitiveness. This provision was criticized for its preoccupation with industrial policy considerations, and was replaced in February 1999 by an exemption clause more in line with the objective of competition policy. Under the revised provision, anti-competitive mergers will not violate Article 7 if the KFTC finds that merger-specific efficiencies outweigh the harmful effects of reduced competition; or if the merger involves a failing company whose assets would go under-utilized absent the merger, and less anti-competitive mergers are unlikely to occur.

Although this revision marked a major improvement over the previous language, the KFTC has applied the two exceptions in a rather permissive manner. For example, the 1999 Guidelines for Evaluating Mergers state that merger-specific efficiencies under Article 7 cover not only firm-level efficiencies in production, sales and R&D but also efficiencies in the entire economy, including contributions to employment, the local economy, related industries, and environmental protection. Evaluating efficiencies in this way can save almost any anti-competitive merger.

With respect to undue collaborative acts, Article 19 forbids concerted activities by "contract, agreement, resolution, or any other means" that would unreasonably restrain competition and specifies eight types of conduct that are subject to the prohibition. Two elements must be established to prove a violation: the existence of an agreement to engage in concerted action and unreasonable restraint of competition.[11] Article 26 extends the prohibition of undue collaborative activities and unfair trade practices to trade associations and their members. In addition, it prohibits trade associations from limiting the number of firms and unreasonably restricting business activities of member firms.

As originally enacted, the MRFTA required parties to a restrictive agreement to register it with the competition authorities for prior approval. Through subsequent amendments, legal rules and sanctions against restrictive agreements strengthened substantially. The Act as amended in 1986 generally prohibited collaborative activities that would substantially restrain competition. But industrial policy considerations also limited progress on this front. In fact, from 1987, the KFTC was empowered to permit cartels for the purposes of rationalizing an industry, overcoming depression, facilitating industrial restructuring, rationalizing terms of trade, or enhancing the competitiveness of SMEs. Nine such cartels were exempted in 1987. A 1991 survey by the KFTC revealed that there were forty-four cartel-authorizing provisions in thirty-five statutes.

In recent years, however, the KFTC has toughened its stance on cartels, and by 1997, all KFTC-approved cartels had been revoked. The Omnibus Cartel Repeal Act enacted in January 1999 removed legal exemptions for twenty cartels under eighteen statutes. In 1999, the legal standard changed from "substantial restraint of competition" to "unreasonable restraint of competition," which means that it is no longer possible to defend a restrictive agreement on the grounds that it has insignificant actual effect. The new standard reflects the KFTC's intention to apply a per se rule to naked agreements to fix prices, limit output, rig bids, or allocate markets.[12]

Article 63 of the MRFTA requires government authorities to consult with the KFTC before they take any legislative or administrative measure that is likely to restrain competition. This provision enables the

KFTC to prevent the promulgation of new regulations that unreasonably suppress competition and to advocate competition principles in
the government rule-making process. The decision to grant ministerial
status to the chairman of the KFTC in 1996 has enhanced the commission's competition advocacy role within the government. Since gaining
ministerial status, the KFTC has issued more opinions, and other
ministries have accepted a larger proportion of them.

Chaebol regulation under the MRFTA

Although the original MRFTA explicitly identified the prevention of the
"excessive concentration of economic power" as one of its purposes,
it did not include measures to directly tackle the problem of concentration. It was not until 1986 that new amendments were added to
contain *chaebol's* expansion and thereby to mitigate the concentration of
economic power.

The 1986 amendments to the MRFTA prohibited holding companies.
They also required the KFTC to designate "large business groups"[13]
each year and subject them to special regulations to contain their
economic power. In order to eliminate the problem of "fictitious
capital," the amendment banned direct cross-shareholdings between the
subsidiaries of the same business group. It also prevented financial
subsidiaries from exercising their voting rights with shares in other
subsidiaries of the same business group. The rationale was to restrain the
controlling family of the business group from using financial subsidiaries
entrusted with customers' money to expand its business empire.

The amendment further limited total equity investments by a non-
financial affiliate of a large business group in other domestic companies to
40 percent of its net assets; the ceiling was lowered to 25 percent in 1995.
But several discretionary exemptions were provided to accommodate
other policy goals, including rationalizing an industry, encouraging
technical cooperation with SMEs, strengthening the international
competitiveness of an industry, and promoting private investment in
social overhead capital. One of the exceptions for enhancing industrial
competitiveness was the exemption of "core companies" as part of the
so-called "specialization policy." Based on the judgment that *chaebol* were
too widely diversified to be internationally competitive, the government
tried to induce specialization in the early 1990s. They did this by offering
preferential treatment to the "core companies" chosen by each of the top
thirty *chaebol* with respect to regulations such as credit controls and
restrictions on equity investment (see Chapter 3).

To reduce the *chaebol's* advantage in obtaining financing and to prevent bankruptcy from spreading among affiliates, the total amount of loan guarantees that a company could provide for its affiliated companies was limited to a maximum of 200 percent of its own equity capital in April 1993; the ceiling was lowered to 100 percent in 1997. Again, several exemptions were granted for loan guarantees necessary for other policy goals, compromising the effectiveness of this measure.

From 1993, inter-subsidiary transactions in goods and services began to be regulated under Article 23 of the MRFTA (proscribing unfair trade practices) if these transactions contained preferential terms that discriminated against their competitors. This regulation was expanded to include financial transactions by 1996 amendments to Article 23, although enforcement actions by the KFTC were confined to non-financial transactions before the economic crisis.

Some commentators emphasized that the key aspect of the *chaebol* problem was not high aggregate concentration and large size, but rather pyramid ownership structures leading to control by an individual or family. These critics urged the government to shift its policies to the goal of dispersing ownership and decision-making power. As a result, from April 1995, business groups whose ownership and financial structures met certain requirements ("business groups with sound ownership structures") were excluded from the KFTC designation of "large business groups." Likewise, companies whose ownership and financial structures met certain requirements ("companies with sound ownership structures") were exempt from the restriction on total equity investments.[14]

The crisis of 1997 deepened the negative perception of the *chaebol*. Prior to the crisis, the power associated with conglomerate bigness was identified as a major problem but there was a general recognition of the possible efficiency gains from the conglomerate form of organization (see Chapter 1). The crisis led some to believe that the business group *itself* was an inefficient organizational form that had to be dismantled. Others emphasized corporate governance problems, and argued that each subsidiary of a business group, each with a different set of shareholders, should strive to maximize value for its shareholders. Discussions linking the *chaebol* to the crisis pointed to their lack of transparency and excessive diversification, allegedly resulting in reduced efficiency and the "too big to fail" problem. The *chaebol's* extensive ownership links, complex financial relationships and inter-subsidiary transactions were said to facilitate highly leveraged expansion, to insulate subsidiaries from market forces, to cause the risk of chain bankruptcies, and to prevent inefficient companies from exiting the market.

Hit by the crisis, the government set *chaebol* reform as one of its top priorities with two principal objectives. One was to develop a better framework for corporate governance and to strengthen the accountability of controlling shareholders and management (see Chapter 12). The other was to enhance independent management by loosening ownership, management, financial, and other business ties among *chaebol* companies. The government relied primarily on the instruments of the MRFTA for the latter purpose. It revised the Act three times to strengthen *chaebol* regulation, and the KFTC actively took enforcement actions to break up or loosen internal links among *chaebol* subsidiaries.

In 1996, Article 23 proscribing unfair business practices had been revised to prohibit unreasonable assistance of "specially related persons" (that is, members of the controlling family and their relatives) or other companies through loans, assets, and manpower on preferential terms or for free. From March 1999, the KFTC gained special powers for two years to investigate the bank accounts of the top thirty *chaebol* affiliates. In addition, from April 2000, the top ten *chaebol* were legally obliged to obtain prior approval of the board of directors and to issue a public notice before engaging in "large scale" in-group transactions. One year later the requirement was expanded to include the top thirty *chaebol*.

A 1998 amendment to the MRFTA prohibited new inter-subsidiary loan guarantees, and required clearing all outstanding guarantees by March 2000. But, at the same time, equity investment caps were eliminated to facilitate *chaebol* restructuring and to protect the *chaebol* from the increased threat of hostile takeovers following the crisis. As a result, the total equity investments of the top thirty *chaebol* in other companies increased substantially both in absolute terms and in percentage of net assets, which in turn caused a significant rise of the "in-group" share. This was mainly attributable to inter-subsidiary acquisitions of new stock issues (see Chapter 13).

Enforcement before and after the economic crisis

During 1981–2000, unfair business practices were the most common type of conduct handled by the KFTC (Table 11.1). It took as many as 3913 corrective measures (2731 corrective orders and 1182 recommendations of correction) against violations of the MRFTA, of which about 76 percent (2971 corrective measures) were against unfair business practices. Unfair luring of customers, exploitation of a superior bargaining position, and unfair labeling and advertising account for the

Table 11.1   KFTC actions by type of violation of the MRFTA, 1981–2000

Violation	Corrective orders		Sub-total (A)	Recommendation of correction (B)	Grand total A + B
	Request for indictment	Surcharge			
Chaebol regulation	4	33	76	8	84
Abuse of dominance	3	5	18	5	23
Merger	1	–	11	–	11
Collusion	7	76	175	44	219
Trade association activity	27	29	429	94	523
Unfair business practice	66	253	2022	949	2971
Unfair inter- national contract	–	–	–	82	82
Total	108	396	2731	1182	3913

Source: Korea Fair Trade Commission (2001: 485).

bulk of the actions against unfair practices. Article 23 has clearly thrust a heavy enforcement burden upon the agency.

The most notable development in post-crisis enforcement is that "undue" transactions in shares, real estate, and particularly loans among *chaebol* affiliates have become a major KFTC priority. Between 1998 and 2000, it launched nine rounds of dragnet investigations (of which four were targeted at the top five *chaebol*), and imposed surcharges of about 218 billion *won* on 244 companies (Table 11.2). This amount is more than 40 percent of the total surcharges imposed by the KFTC.

Inter-subsidiary transactions of *chaebol* may also give rise to conventional competition policy problems such as exclusion, domination, and discrimination. The 1999 Guidelines for Evaluating Unreasonable Assistance mention some of these concerns, and outline a number of factors affecting the likelihood of competitive harm that must be considered. But, in actual enforcement, competitive harm is not an issue and the legal standard applied is simple and straightforward. If an in-group transaction is different from what would be expected in an arms'-length relationship, it is unreasonable and therefore illegal, because it gives the *chaebol* subsidiary "unfair" financial and commercial advantages over its independent competitors. In effect, the law requires that

Table 11.2   Surcharges imposed, by type of violation of the MRFTA, 1981–2000

Violation	No. of cases	No. of firms	Amount (million *won*) Total	Average per case
Chaebol regulation	33	48	13,672	414
Abuse of dominance	5	6	3,463	693
Collusion	76	372	287,692	3,785
Unfair business practice				
Discrimination	50	54	920	18
Undue in–group transaction	47	244	217,592	4,630
Others	194	246	14,667	76
Sub–total	291	544	233,179	801
Total	405	970	538,006	1,328

Note: The category of unfair business practice includes not only 282 MRFTA cases (253 unfair practice cases and 29 trade association cases) but also nine cases of unfair subcontracts.
Source: Korea Fair Trade Commission (2001: p. 484).

transactions between subsidiaries of a business group be on the same terms as those between unaffiliated companies. This prohibition of "undue" in-group transactions appears to be motivated by the objective of post-crisis *chaebol* policy of enhancing independent management. More fundamentally, it flows from the goal of ensuring fair trading conditions.

Enforcement of the rule against undue collaborative acts has steadily been strengthened (Table 11.3). From 1995, corrective orders together with the imposition of surcharges on colluding firms became frequent. More significant are the sharp increase in the number of corrective orders and the amount of surcharges imposed after the 1997 crisis. Surcharges imposed during the three years after the crisis account for about 93 percent of the total amount.

Active enforcement of the MRFTA coupled with the frequent imposition of heavy surcharges, especially against undue inter-subsidiary transactions and collusive acts, has triggered an unprecedented number of legal suits against the KFTC. The number of legal actions brought by businesses and individuals has increased dramatically, from less than ten a year before 1996 to thirty-one in 1998 and sixty-four in 1999.

By contrast, enforcement against abuse of dominance and potentially anti-competitive mergers has been weak. From 1981 to 2000, only twenty-three corrective measures (less than 1 percent of the total) were

Table 11.3   KFTC measures against undue collaborative acts, 1981–2000

	Request for indictment	No. of cases	Amount (million won)	Total corrective order (A)	Recommendation of correction (B)	Total (A+B)
		Surcharges				
1981–86	–	–	–	–	15	15
1987–92	1	2	2,367	24	12	36
1993	–	1	650	4	–	4
1994	2	2	398	5	1	6
1995	–	6	1,031	13	–	13
1996	–	13	14,513	19	6	25
1997	1	6	1,092	11	8	19
1998	–	19	32,058	32	2	34
1999	–	15	38,835	34	–	34
2000	–	12	196,748	33	–	33
Total	4	76	287,692	175	44	219

Source: Korea Fair Trade Commission, Annual Reports.

taken against abuse of dominance. The KFTC reviewed 5506 mergers and blocked only three (two horizontal mergers in 1982 and one vertical merger in 1996). In the 1990s, all sixteen mergers that were legally presumed to be anti-competitive were allowed.

Although allowing several large-scale acquisitions after the crisis, the KFTC has made extensive use of its authority to impose restrictions to eliminate mergers' potential anti-competitive effects. In two cases, it ordered the sale of part of the acquisition, raising competitive concerns. But its actions in other cases revealed a continuing tendency to regulate. A price restraint was imposed as a relief measure in five cases, and a market share ceiling in two cases.

2   Competition Policy and Corporate Restructuring

With the first amendments to the MRFTA in 1986, the government actively launched its so-called "*chaebol* policy." This policy pursued the goals of containing *chaebol's* economic power and promoting fairness, relying primarily on various direct regulations on financing, investment and loan guarantees. The 1997 crisis led the government to embark on a comprehensive *chaebol* reform, and the KFTC stepped up its application of existing *chaebol* regulations. The budget of the KFTC more than doubled between 1994 and 1999 and the number of personnel increased 47 percent to more than 400. Increased resources have helped the KFTC to become more active in enforcing laws under its jurisdiction.

As other chapters have shown, the economic crisis is generally taken as a manifestation of weaknesses in the *chaebol's* structures. The crisis also raises the question of whether Korea's competition policy has been effective in addressing *chaebol*-related problems. The crisis suggests that the extension of the competition law to impose special limits on corporate investment and financial structures was in fact not effective.

What the *chaebol* policy has achieved in terms of limiting *chaebol* influence is not impressive. The share of the top thirty *chaebol* in the mining and manufacturing sectors has remained stable. Due to restrictions imposed by the MRFTA, both the ratio of equity investments to net assets and the share of debt guarantees to total assets have dropped substantially. But the *chaebol's* high leverage and "reckless" expansion have continued as shown in the increased total assets and number of subsidiaries, several of which failed. Only after the crisis has the total number of companies affiliated with the top thirty groups fallen, from 804 in April 1998 to 544 in April 2000, and their total debt decreased.

The degree of overall concentration remained fairly stable from the mid-1980s when *chaebol* regulations under the MRFTA were introduced (Table 11.4). The level of industrial concentration, despite a significant fall during 1981–96, remained high (Table 11.5). In 1981, about 27 percent of total shipments in the manufacturing sector were in structurally competitive industries ($CR_3 < 40\%$). This share rose to as high as 43.6 percent by 1996, then dropped to 37.2 percent in 1998. The economic crisis appears to be responsible for this increased concentration. In 1998, almost two-thirds of total shipments came from highly concentrated industries.

The degree of competition is a key factor determining the growth of productivity and output in an economy. But competitive forces have been relatively weak in Korea. Through industrial policies and other government interventions, large enterprises with considerable political power were shielded from domestic competitive pressures in various ways. Companies were encouraged to expand horizontally and occasionally forced to merge. Import regulations and barriers to foreign direct investment often blunted foreign competition (see Chapter 10). Many *chaebol* subsidiaries secured entrenched monopolistic positions,

Table 11.4   Overall concentration in manufacturing, 1970–98 (%)

Year	Shipments		Employment	
	50 largest	100 largest	50 largest	100 largest
1970	17.8	28.7	15.4	22.8
1977	35.0	44.9	16.9	23.9
1982	36.9	46.2	16.4	22.2
1987	30.0	38.1	13.3	19.1
1992	31.9	39.2	13.8	18.3
1997	32.6	39.6	13.7	17.5
1998	40.2	47.8	17.4	21.0

Source: Korea Development Institute (1999: 101).

Table 11.5   Classification of manufacturing industries by level of concentration, 1981–98

Industries with a high level of concentration	1981	1986	1991	1995	1996	1997	1998
$CR_3 < 40$							
No. of industries	99	150	226	273	289	269	260
Share of shipments (%)	27.23	32.76	35.79	42.85	43.55	41.05	37.18
$40 \leq CR_3$, $CR_1 < 50$							
No. of industries	210	270	266	227	221	237	230
Share of shipments (%)	58.09	49.92	50.26	45.72	42.81	42.37	45.14
$50 \leq CR_1 < 90$							
No. of industries	83	84	87	79	69	71	77
Share of shipments (%)	11.51	13.99	13.30	10.19	12.53	15.17	15.66
$90 \leq CR_1$							
No. of industries	25	29	17	19	18	22	25
Share of shipments (%)	3.18	3.33	0.66	1.24	1.11	0.41	2.02
Total number of industries	417	533	596	598	597	599	592

Note: CR is concentration ratio, the share of sales accounted for by the specified number of the largest firms in the industry.
Source: Database of the Korea Development Institute.

sheltered from competition in product markets, monitoring in financial markets, and takeover threats.[15] As the OECD observed, higher price mark-ups over costs in Korea compared to other OECD countries suggest relatively weak competitive forces in the economy.[16]

The monopoly power of *chaebol* and their expansion strategies resulted in vertical and conglomerate structures that contributed to the exercise of market power, further enhancing dominant positions and aggravating the concentration of economic power. The *chaebol* structure created competition problems not because of the nature of conglomerates *per se*, but because extensive non-horizontal linkages provided *chaebol* companies with a wider range of opportunities to exert market power and engage in anti-competitive practices. These structures demand an even larger role for competition policy, transparent implementation, and a more integrated approach to the problems of market power.

If strictly enforced, the MRFTA should have been able to address these problems. However, the government used direct regulation rather than competition policy instruments to shape market structure and to limit the *chaebol's* economic power. In addition to distortions in the financial sector and corporate governance, insufficient attention to market competition was, to an appreciable degree, responsible for Korea's failure to address *chaebol*-related problems in the period before the crisis.

Such a policy approach has had several negative consequences. First, the enforcement activities of the KFTC have focused on *chaebol* regulation and unfair trade practices rather than attacking the *chaebol's* monopoly positions and problems of market power. Second, the approach implied considerable government intervention in the private sector's decision-making, thus limiting the role of market forces. These problems were compounded by the lack of an effective corporate governance framework to guide management decision-making (see Chapter 12). Third, measures that sought to restrain diversification ran counter to the competition policy objective of limiting monopoly power and market concentration. Diversification, if pursued and maintained by all the *chaebol*, should lead to lower, rather than higher, industrial concentration. The efforts to force groups to consolidate and concentrate on core businesses would also tend to increase, rather than decrease, market concentration. Fourth, the mixing of competition policy goals with an emphasis on controlling *chaebol* may reduce the resources available for genuine competition policy concerns. Fifth, the law contains elements of industrial policy by allowing the KFTC wide discretion and permitting many exemptions.

3   Policy Implications

One can blame debt-ridden business groups and weak financial institutions for the economic crisis in Korea. But the root causes of the crisis lie in government controls, which have led to poor incentives, a distorted financial sector, and an inadequate legal framework.

Structural adjustments and policy reforms are required to stimulate a sound economic recovery and growth based on market forces. Competition law and policy have a significant role to play in these efforts. They can facilitate restructuring by supporting and strengthening competitive processes and influence the political fate of the competitive, free-market ideal. For competition law and policy to perform these functions, they should be based on the concept of market power and strive to promote economic efficiency by protecting competitive processes.

Based on the wider concepts of economic power and fair trade, competition law and policy in Korea have placed a strong emphasis on mitigating concentration in the economy and preventing its abuse. However, the concepts of economic power and fairness are too broad and subjective to provide a useful conceptual foundation for a rational, internally consistent competition policy. The usual definition of economic power encompasses three, potentially conflicting, dimensions: the overall concentration in the economy; the extent of diversification; and the concentration of ownership and control. The goal of limiting economic power in these senses can contradict the pursuit of economic efficiency. Promoting fairness by protecting small economic entities against large ones often attenuates the degree to which competition policy promotes economic efficiency.

A competition policy with multiple goals that includes diffusion of economic power and fairness may appear attractive. But multiple objectives lead to inconsistent application of the law as regulators try to reconcile a wide range of often conflicting social, political and economic values on a case-by-case basis. This approach also invites lobbying by different stakeholders. As a result, competition policy loses much in both effectiveness and ease of administration, often protecting competitors at the expense of competition. Making economic efficiency the principal objective of competition law supports consistent application of policy and is thus more likely to limit lobbying by vested interests.

Korea still requires a transition to a free-market economy in which the pressure of competition and the threat of bankruptcy discipline *chaebol* behavior. Direct regulation of *chaebol's* structure and behavior does not necessarily ensure competitive market behavior and efficient outcomes. Establishing a more market-oriented economy and strengthening competition therefore require changing the role of the state in the economy, and shifting the emphasis of the KFTC to the problems of monopoly and away from direct intervention.

In the context of corporate restructuring, competition policy should focus its efforts on countering policies and regulations that retard or delay market reforms, create or enhance market power, and prevent market access. Competition authorities should actively work to eliminate artificial barriers to entry. In economies characterized by highly concentrated industries, removing barriers to foreign trade and investment and lifting regulatory barriers to entry best curb market power. The competition authority should also spell out the implications of restructuring measures and market reforms for competition and efficiency so that government decision-making takes these considerations into account and does not work at cross-purposes with them.

The KFTC needs to intervene in sectors where the market is highly concentrated and organized in a way that effectively suppresses competition. So far, it has not been active in addressing monopolistic market structures and investigating industries where the KFTC itself has identified structural barriers. As the *chaebol* restructure and foreign investment increases, the number of mergers is likely to rise and the KFTC will have an important role to play in preventing combinations that reduce competition. The simple structural standard for merger control needs reconsideration. In addition, the KFTC should give priority to enforcing a rule-of-reason approach to dealing with vertical restraints, and gaining the high level of requisite knowledge and expertise required for effective implementation.

Notes

1 See, for example, Lee and Lee (1990), Kang et al. (1991), Choi (1993), and Lee (1998).
2 Several previous attempts to legislate a competition law had been blocked by persistent resistance from the business community and concern that a competition law would be a hindrance to economic growth.
3 In the aftermath of the first oil crisis, the government adopted widespread price controls under the Price Stabilization and Fair Trade Act of 1975. Extensive price regulation of about 150 monopolistic and oligopolistic products continued until 1979.
4 The KFTC has almost exclusive jurisdiction to enforce the MRFTA. While the Attorney-General may prosecute violations of the Act, such an action is contingent on the KFTC's filing of a complaint. When the KFTC finds a violation, it may recommend a voluntary correction. For major violations, it issues a corrective order, which most commonly consists of a cease-and-desist order and public acknowledgement of the violation. It may also decide to impose a surcharge (an administrative fine). Complaints are usually filed with the Attorney-General for prosecution when the corrective order is not complied with, or the violation is deemed serious, or the same offense is repeated. Final decisions of the KFTC can be appealed to the Seoul High Court and ultimately to the Supreme Court.

5 Unfair practices in labeling and advertising had been proscribed under Article 23 before the enactment of the Fair Labeling and Advertising Act in July of 1997.

6 The Fair Subcontract Transactions Act of 1984 calls for "a fair order for subcontracting so that contractors and subcontractors may enjoy balanced development on an equal footing in a mutually complementary manner." The Regulation of Adhesion Contracts Act of 1986 is designed to protect consumers by preventing adhesion contracts containing unfair terms.

7 Under the MRFTA as originally passed, the criterion for the combined share of two or three firms was 70 percent and the requirement of individual share was 5 percent. These figures were raised to 75 percent and 10 percent from 1987. In 1998, 311 companies in 128 product or service markets were designated as market-dominating enterprises, of which 172 were affiliates of the top thirty *chaebol*. From 1997, a blanket exemption was provided for financial and insurance companies, and the KFTC was authorized to grant exemptions if a firm satisfies certain conditions and if the KFTC finds the firm unlikely to engage in abusive conduct. About twenty companies applied for exclusion from the designation, but no firms were actually dropped from the list.

8 The previous market share thresholds for designating market-dominating enterprises were changed into those for presumption of dominance.

9 The second definition was dropped in the February 1999 amendment. Until 1992, parallel price increases were also regarded as abusive pricing.

10 Under Article 7 a merger is presumed to substantially restrain competition in the relevant market if the combined market share of the merging companies meets either of the definitions of a market-dominating enterprise, in addition to being the largest and significantly greater than that of the second-largest firm in the market; or if the merger involves a "large-size company" with assets or sales volume (including those of its subsidiaries) of over 2 trillion won, creating a firm with a market share of over 5 percent in a market where the combined share of the SMEs exceeds two-thirds.

11 Evidence of an express agreement can establish concerted action, but it is not necessary. An agreement can be inferred based on a pattern of uniform conduct, often referred to as "conscious parallelism."

12 The offense of undue collaborative acts has been subject to discretionary surcharges from 1987. The maximum amount of the surcharge was initially 1 percent of sales revenue of the product involved during the period of collusion. It was raised to 5 percent from 1995. In 1997, the KFTC adopted a policy of according lenient treatment to corporations or individuals which voluntarily disclosed violations.

13 From 1993, the KFTC has been designating the thirty largest conglomerates in terms of total assets as "large business groups." The original criterion for designation was total assets of over 400 billion *won*.

14 These exemptions were repealed in February 1998.

15 According to Kim (1994), 533 out of 1195 (5-digit) industries were subject to some kind of entry regulation in 1992. Special restrictions on imports from Japan were in place from 1978; corporate takeovers by foreigners were banned until 1996. Only after the 1997 crisis were foreign direct investment

and corporate takeovers fully liberalized, and discriminatory restrictions on imports from Japan removed.

16 OECD (2000a: 72). World Bank (1999) found that the overall mark-up for manufactured goods was 36 percent in Korea, while Oliveira Martins et al. (1996) estimated the ratio to be 15 percent for the United States, 18 percent for the United Kingdom, 20 percent for Germany and 25 percent for Japan.

References

Amsden, A. 1997. "South Korea: Enterprising Groups and Entrepreneurial Government," in A. D. Chandler, F. Amatori, and T. Hikino, eds, *Big Business and the Wealth of Nations*, pp. 336–67. Cambridge: Cambridge University Press.

Boner, R. A., and Krueger, R. 1991. *The Basics of Antitrust Policy*. World Bank Technical Paper No.160, Washington, DC: World Bank.

Chang, Sea Jin, and Choi, Unghwan. 1988. "Strategy, Structure and Performance of Korean Business Groups: A Transactions Cost Approach," *Journal of Industrial Economics*, 37 (2): 141–58.

Choi, Jung Pyo. 1993. *Dissolving Chaebol* (in Korean). Seoul: Bebong Publishing Co.

Edwards, C. 1957. "Conglomerate Bigness as a Source of Power," in *Business Concentration and Price Policy*. National Bureau for Economic Research, Conference Report, pp. 331–52. Princeton: Princeton University Press.

Hwang, In Hak. 1997. *Problems in Assessing the Concentration of Economic Power in Korea* (in Korean). Seoul: Korea Economic Research Institute.

Kang, Chul Gyu, Choi, Jung Pyo, and Jang, Ji Sang. 1991. *Chaebol* (in Korean). Seoul: Bebong Publishing Co.

Khanna, T., and Palepu, K. 1997. "Why Focused Strategies May Be Wrong for Emerging Markets," *Harvard Business Review*, 75 (July–August): 41–51.

Khemani, R. S. 1997. "Competition Policy and Economic Development," *Policy Options*, 48 (8): 23–7.

Kim, Jae Hong. 1994. *Entry Regulation in Korea* (in Korean). Seoul: Korea Economic Research Institute.

Korea Development Institute. 1999. *Analysis of Market Structures in Korea* (in Korean). Seoul: Korea Development Institute.

Korea Fair Trade Commission (KFTC). 2001. *2001 Annual Report* (in Korean). Seoul: KFTC.

Lee, Kyu Uck. 1998. *Competition Policy, Deregulation and Economic Development – The Korean Experience*. Seoul: Korea Institute for Industrial Economics and Trade.

Lee, Kyu Uck, and Lee, Jae Hyung. 1990. *Business Groups and the Concentration of Economic Power* (in Korean). Seoul: Korea Development Institute.

Leff, N. 1978. "Industrial Organization and Entrepreneurship in the Developing Countries: The Economic Groups," *Economic Development and Cultural Change*, 26: 661–675.

Oliveira Martins, J., Scarpetta, S., and Pilat, D. 1996. *Mark-up Ratios in Manufacturing Industries: Estimates for 14 Countries*. OECD Economics Department Working Paper No. 162.

Organization for Economic Cooperation and Development (OECD). 2000a. *OECD Economic Surveys: 1999–2000 Korea*.

———. 2000b. *Review of Regulatory Reform in Korea*.

Shin, Kwangshik. 1992. *Regulation of Unfair Trade Practices and Competition Policy* (in Korean). Seoul: Korea Development Institute.

———. 1998. "Economic Crisis and Competition Policy" (in Korean), *Korean Development Institute Policy Studies*, 20(1): 3–69.

———. 2000. *Policy Issues and Directions of Chaebol Reform* (in Korean). Seoul: Korea Development Institute.

World Bank. 1999. *Republic of Korea: Establishing a New Foundation for Sustained Growth*. Washington, DC: World Bank.

Yoo, Seong Min, and Lim, Youngjae. 1999. "Big Business in Korea: New Learning and Policy Issues." Korea Development Institute, Working Paper No. 9901. Seoul: KDI.

12 Reform of Corporate Governance

Myeong-Hyeon Cho

In Korea, the term *corporate governance* was rarely mentioned until the economic crisis in 1997, despite a long-standing controversy over the way Korean *chaebol* are managed and governed. When the economic crisis hit, however, a consensus emerged that the high leverage, over-diversification, and the resulting weak competitiveness of Korean corporations could be traced to poor corporate governance. The discretionary power of the chairman and his control over resource allocation decisions lie at the center of this line of criticism.[1] The chairman could exercise such discretionary power and control because of the ownership structure of the *chaebol* and the lack of checks and balances.

Ownership structure has been an important subject in modern economics. The literature has focused on the potential conflicts of interest between owners (shareholders) and managers, or the principal-agent problem. Jensen and Meckling (1976) show that as managerial ownership increases, the interests of management become more closely aligned with those of shareholders. The "convergence-of-interest" hypothesis suggests that a firm's performance and value increase as the managers' stake in the firm's future cash flows increases.

On the other hand, the entrenchment hypothesis predicts the opposite. When managerial ownership is low, firm performance is maximized because of the threats from various markets such as the capital market, the managerial labor market (Fama 1980), and the market for corporate control (Shleifer and Vishny 1986). However, when managerial ownership is high enough to provide effective control and to guarantee their jobs, managers will indulge their preference for non-value-maximizing behavior. The entrenchment hypothesis suggests that corporate performance worsens as the managers' ownership, and resulting control rights, increase.

Morck et al. (1988) and McConnell and Servaes (1990) empirically explore the relationship between ownership structure and corporate performance measured by Tobin's Q, the ratio of the market value of assets to the current replacement cost of assets. They find that the relationship is non-monotonic. Firm performance improves as managerial ownership increases at "low" levels of managerial ownership. But as managerial ownership increases to "high" levels, firm performance decreases. The findings of Morck et al. suggest that at "low" levels of managerial ownership, an increase in managerial ownership aligns managerial interests with the interests of shareholders, which results in improved corporate performance. However, at "high" levels of managerial ownership, management becomes more entrenched and less subject to market discipline, thereby reducing corporate performance and value.

The ownership structure of Korean *chaebol* has a unique feature: an exaggerated separation of ownership rights (cash-flow rights) from control rights. Ownership is concentrated in the founding family and affiliated firms in the same *chaebol* group. On average, the founding family owns less than 10 percent of company shares but affiliated firms own more than 30 percent. This in-group inter-subsidiary ownership of affiliated firms has enabled the manager (the chairman) to retain full control over all affiliated firms.[2] The chairman exerts a strong influence on resource allocation decisions through the Chairman's Office and a centralized planning and coordination office.

The extreme separation of ownership rights from control rights observed in the Korean *chaebol* creates severe conflicts of interest between shareholders and management, serious agency problems, and managerial entrenchment. In theory, a high concentration of ownership and the existence of coordination mechanisms can reduce such conflicts of interest. In the *chaebol*, however, control rights are concentrated around the manager (chairman), while ownership rights are not. The resulting agency problem is heightened due to the virtual absence of monitoring and of checks and balances, resulting in managerial entrenchment. The entrenchment problem prevails primarily because the chairman maintains effective control through inter-subsidiary shareholdings of affiliated firms (Shleifer and Vishny 1997). With effective control, the chairman can indulge his or her preference for non-value-maximizing behavior at the expense of shareholders of the affiliated firms. Furthermore, boards of directors have been ineffective while minority shareholders and institutional investors have been passive. Nor do the market for corporate control and the executive labor market function to check the chairman.

In the wake of the crisis, the issues of entrenched chairmen, the power and responsibilities of boards of directors, outside directorship, the role and influence of institutional investors, and the rights of minority shareholders gained public attention and dominated the business press. Both the government and shareholders' rights activists pushed for reform of the corporate governance system, and several major steps were made in 1998–2000. The Corporate Governance Amendment Improvement Committee published Model Corporate Governance Rules after a year of study and benchmarking, providing tools to monitor entrenched management. Measures to strengthen the role of boards of directors and minority shareholders' rights have been proposed and efforts made to boost takeover activities.

Despite this progress the reform is by no means complete. Many areas in Korean corporate governance still need improvement, and problems have arisen in the implementation of the reforms. The first section discusses the important characteristics of the *chaebol* from a corporate governance perspective, and analyzes corporate governance in Korea prior to the crisis. The second section provides a progress report on corporate governance reform through 2000. The third section discusses the future direction of Korean corporate governance and whether the Anglo-Saxon model is the appropriate one for Korea to follow.

1   Corporate Governance Prior to the Economic Crisis

Ownership and management structure of the *chaebol*

As outlined in Chapter 1, *chaebol* are conglomerates operating in various industries under common entrepreneurial and financial control.[3] While Korean law does not permit holding companies, member firms in the group are in fact linked through inter-subsidiary shareholdings, debt payment guarantees, and centralized planning and coordination. Ownership is concentrated around the founding family and its affiliated firms. Typical group structures also include frequent business transactions, ineffective corporate boards, and structured interactions among affiliated member firms through management council meetings.

The founding family tightly controls most of the Korean *chaebol*. As Table 1.1 shows, at the end of 1995, about 10.3 percent of the total shares of the thirty largest *chaebol* was held by a majority individual shareholder such as the chairman and his family. In addition, a significant portion of any firm's stock is held by other firms affiliated with the same *chaebol*. At the end of 1995, firms affiliated with *chaebol* owned 33.8 percent of the total shares of the thirty largest *chaebol*. Prior to the crisis, the sum of ownership by the family and member firms amounted to approximately 40 percent of total group equity, enabling the chairman to retain effective control.

There are several patterns of shareholding among member firms affiliated with the same *chaebol* group. A typical pattern is the so-called "pyramid." One or several major parent firms in the group own large equity stakes in various other member firms belonging to the same group. The major parent firm thus plays the role of an equity-holding company. Although most parent firms in the *chaebol* are manufacturing companies, financial intermediaries sometimes own a large portion of member firm equity. For example, Samsung Life Insurance and Samsung Electronics play the role of holding company for the group. The member firms in which a major parent company has large stakes are used to "pyramid" their equity holdings.

Another typical pattern of shareholdings is the "circular" structure. Figure 12.1 shows such a structure for the Hyundai Group. Firm A owns equity stakes in member firm B; firm B owns equity stakes in member firm C; firm C, in turn, owns equity in firm A. This circular ownership may result from the efforts of Korean firms to appear large enough to borrow from banks. However, it is also true that many Korean firms have used this circular structure to overcome legal restrictions on equity cross-holdings. Korean law prohibits direct cross-holdings to prevent the problem of fake or fictitious capital. For example, if firm A invests $100 in firm B and firm B, in turn, invests $50 in firm A, then equity capital increases by $50 for firm A and by $100 for firm B

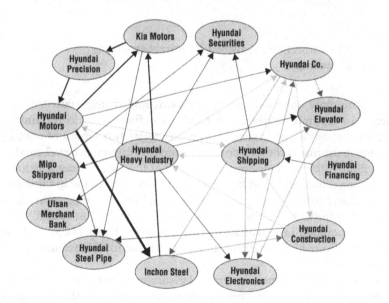

Figure 12.1   Circular shareholding structure of Hyundai

Note: The larger the equity stake a company has in another, the darker the arrow.
Source: Jang (2000).

according to their balance sheets. However, the increases are illusory, as there is no capital injection from outside investors.

It is interesting to note that parent firms have a relatively higher portion of equity in firms engaged in closely related businesses, suggesting vertical integration (see Chapter 2). Hyundai Motor Co., for example, holds about 10 percent of the stock in Hyundai Corporation, which exports Hyundai Motor Co.'s vehicles to foreign countries. Samsung Electronics holds approximately 17 percent of Samsung Electric Device, an electric component production company.

There is also structured interaction among member firms. The "management council" enables this interaction, and important financial and strategic decisions are made through this body. Although there is a formal CEO in charge of each firm in the group, the chairman of the group handles the major investment and financial decisions for all firms through the management council. Furthermore, the chairman of the group is solely responsible for the appointment of management and directors of all the affiliated firms. Consequently, internal checks and balances have been virtually absent.

Table 12.1 briefly describes the important features of the Korean corporate governance system prior to the economic crisis and compares them with those of the US and Japanese governance systems.

Monitoring mechanisms I: Internal corporate governance

The commonly observed agency problems and managerial entrenchment in corporate Korea are a result of deficiencies in monitoring. Recent corporate governance literature suggests two types of monitoring mechanisms: internal corporate monitoring and external market discipline. Internal monitoring is carried out by shareholders, including institutional investors, and by the board of directors acting in the interest of shareholders. External monitoring and disciplining mechanisms are driven from the capital market (Easterbrook 1984; Rozeff 1982), forces operating in the managerial labor market (Fama 1980), and the takeover threats in the market for corporate control (Shleifer and Vishny 1986).

The board of directors is a critical institution in corporate governance as it serves as the link between the suppliers of capital – shareholders – and managers. In Korea, however, the board of directors has been ineffective in monitoring and disciplining management. Since directors were exclusively internal and therefore loyal to the chairman, the boards

Table 12.1   Corporate governance in the United States, Japan and Korea

Firm	Equity–holding patterns and regulations	Composition and role of the corporate board
United States	• The Glass–Stegall Act prohibits banks from holding stock in industrial firms.	• Boards of publicly held firms are usually made up of outside directors.
	• The Bank Holding Company Act prohibits banks from affiliating with non–banks, except passive ownership of 5 percent of a non–bank's stock.	• The CEO controls the firm with little oversight.
	Example: Five financial inter- mediaries hold 5.7 percent of the outstanding stock in General Motors.	
Japanese *keiretsu*	• A main bank holds stock in *keiretsu* firms, which, in turn, hold stock in the main bank.	• Boards of Japanese firms are made up of insiders formally elected by stockholders, but usually by the CEO.
	• Institutional investors hold significant portions of an industrial firm's stock.	• Financial intermediaries' managers interact with the managers of firms.
	Example: Five intermediaries hold 22 percent of outstanding stock in Toyota Motors.	
Korean *chaebol*	• A large portion of the stock in a group firm is held by other members of the group.	• Corporate boards are staffed with insiders.
	• The Banking Act prohibits banks from holding mor than– 10 per cent of stock in industrial firms.	• Managers of financial inter- mediaries do not appear in Managers' Council meetings, where important business decisions are made.
	Example: Two member firms hold 19.2 percent of stock in Hyundai Motors.	

of directors in Korean *chaebol* represented the interests of the chairman and his family, playing a rubber-stamp role.

Outside shareholders consist of minority shareholders and institu- tional investors. For most corporations, minority shareholders were typically individual investors, but as a group they own a large fraction of total shares. Shares owned by minority shareholders of less than 1 percent accounted for more than 60 percent of the total company stake. Despite large outside shareholding, the widely dispersed ownership structure has made it difficult for the minority shareholders, who lacked the necessary information and incentives, to actively monitor management.

Although institutional investors owned blocks of shares in many corporations listed on the Korea Stock Exchange, they were not active monitors. They were required to comply with a system of shadow voting under which they cast their votes proportionate to other votes. Under this system, the institutional investors could not effectively raise their voice to preserve shareholder value. In many cases, the management of the investment funds was affiliated with the *chaebol*, further reducing their incentives to monitor the management of the company in which they invested.

Monitoring mechanisms II: External corporate governance

In Korea, the external corporate governance mechanism was also poorly developed. In fact, a market for corporate control did not exist. Although over 200 mergers and acquisitions (M&As) were recorded annually since the early 1980s, they were primarily friendly in nature with the purpose of streamlining a line of business or restructuring a failing firm. Hostile takeovers were rarely observed in Korea and it was only in 1993 that the first tender offer was recorded in Korean history. Takeover threats, important forces in disciplining managers, were very rare and did not properly function as a monitoring mechanism.

There were several reasons why M&As did not work as a disciplinary device on mismanagement. First, incumbent management usually maintained a high level of control through friendly shareholders such as relatives or affiliates, making takeovers very burdensome for an attacking party. Second, since incumbent management enjoyed very large private benefits of control due to opaque management practices, an extremely high control premium persisted. Incumbent management in effect set up a number of barriers to deter M&As and retained their high premium. The lack of accounting transparency was one of the major impediments. Third, regulations on M&As were restrictive, especially for hostile takeovers, as will be explained below.

According to the Korean Commercial Code, a merger requires a special quorum in the shareholders' meeting, and shareholders are given appraisal rights in the case that they are not satisfied with the conditions of a merger. A two-week period of prior notice and a disclosure of financial statements are also required before the resolution of a merger so that creditors can file their opinions.

According to the Securities Exchange Act, if an individual (including his relatives) owns more than 5 percent of a firm or increases ownership by more than 1 percent thereafter, he must inform the Securities Exchange Commission (SEC) as well as the Korea Stock Exchange within five days of the event (Article 200.2). If a firm acquires more than 10 percent of the target firm, the former should inform the latter of the fact immediately. A firm cannot exercise shareholder rights for the shares of a firm that owns more than 10 percent of the former.[4] In the case of a tender offer, the acquiring firm should notify the SEC and file a report on the detailed contents of the tender offer. Furthermore, the acquirer cannot purchase the shares of the target firm in ways other than through a tender offer (SEA Articles 21–27).

The SEA also requires shareholders who want to pursue a proxy fight to report their intentions to the SEC two days prior to the offer (Article 199).[5] The most binding rule that thwarted M&As in Korea was Article 200.2 of the SEA, which prohibited any shareholders other than the founder or dominant shareholders from purchasing more than 10 percent of the shares in the exchange. This rule made it impossible for any outsider to collect a major portion of the target shares, which protected existing management.[6] This rule was abolished in April 1999.

Another rule that limited takeover activities in Korea was a restrictive requirement of tender offers. Until 1999, the SEA required the acquiring party to purchase more than 50 percent of the target firm if it planned to acquire more than 25 percent of it. This rule was intended to prevent the transfer of control of firms at a premium that did not properly reflect the value of the target firm. However, where existing management enjoyed control, such a rule effectively pre-empted hostile takeover attempts. This rule was abolished in 1999. On the other hand, the revised SEA also abolished restrictions on target firms' ability to repurchase their own stock and thus gave them more flexibility in implementing a defensive strategy.

The market for managerial talent also failed to serve as a disciplining mechanism. Before the crisis, lifetime employment was a widely accepted practice. Workers, including managers in long-term employment relationships, expected to make a career with the firm and hoped to rise through the ranks via promotions. This led to the development of an internal labor market and hindered the development of an external labor market, including a managerial labor market where professional managers' reputations are important. The underdevelopment of the managerial labor market weakened managers' incentives to increase shareholder value.

In principle, creditors can practice sound corporate monitoring by exercising contractual rights in debt instruments, by enforcing collateral, or by reorganizing the firm in financial stress. Credit agreements also entitle creditors access to periodic corporate reports that provide information on the borrowing firm's financial status.

In the Korean capital market, banks served as the main creditors, enabling them to monitor the borrowing firms' management if they wanted.[7] However, shortcomings in corporate governance within the banks themselves compounded poor corporate governance within firms (see Chapter 4). Because the government encouraged banks to lend to the *chaebol*, the board of directors in the banks did not maintain a sound credit review system based on the borrowing firms' repayment capacity.

Non-bank financial institutions, such as merchant banks and insurance companies, also accounted for a significant proportion of credit to corporations. These institutions also failed to play an adequate monitoring role (see Chapter 4). This was because a large number of these insurance companies and merchant banks were affiliated with *chaebol*.

2   Improving Corporate Governance: A Work-in-Progress

Since the crisis, corporate governance reform has been a key issue on the policy agenda. A wide range of significant legal reforms were undertaken by 2001, but due partly to the resistance of the *chaebol*, these reforms are not yet complete.

Ownership structure of *chaebol*

In the wake of the economic crisis, the government came to have a better understanding of the agency problems and managerial entrenchment resulting from the *chaebol's* ownership structure, and it made efforts to reduce the gap between ownership and control rights and to loosen equity ties among affiliated firms. However, the data presented in Table 1.1 suggest that this government drive was not effective. Since the crisis, ownership has become more concentrated around the chairman through higher ownership among affiliated firms. Table 1.1 shows that total inside ownership has increased among the *chaebol*. The inside ownership level was 43.3 percent in 1996, the year prior to the crisis, and reached 50.5 percent in 1999. Inside ownership decreased to 43.4 percent in 2000 because Daewoo was excluded from the statistics.

A close look at changes in ownership structure indicates that, while the founding families' stake has decreased, the stake controlled by affiliated firms has *increased*. It is important to note that this structural change worsens agency and entrenchment problems; the gap between rights to cash flow and rights to control has become *larger*. Indeed, the chairman has strengthened his control at the expense of minority shareholders in affiliated firms (see Chapter 13).

A possible reason for such increases in inside ownership of affiliated firms is that the government lifted a ceiling on investment in affiliated firms in 1998. This change in policy enabled the *chaebol* to increase their investment in affiliated firms using circular inter-subsidiary shareholdings even if *direct* cross-holdings were not allowed. The ratio of total investment in affiliated firms to total investment reached 32.5 percent in 1999 and 32.9 percent in 2000.

Code of corporate governance

A critical institutional step toward sound corporate governance practices was the formation of the Corporate Governance Improvement Committee to devise a code of best practice. The code introduces and stresses independent outside directorship as well as an audit committee. It also recommends that firms listed on the Korea Stock Exchange set up nomination and compensation committees and introduce cumulative voting for the appointment of boards of directors. Although the code is not mandatory, some important clauses have become legally binding. The code also requires listed companies to disclose the extent of their compliance to the market.

Two important recommendations dealt directly with monitoring mechanisms. To strengthen boards of directors, the code proposed to: compose boards of more than eight directors for large listed firms; require more than half of the directors to be independent outsiders; hold a board meeting at least once a quarter; establish a nomination committee; and set up an audit committee consisting mainly of outside directors. To strengthen shareholders' rights, the code would: allow cumulative voting for the election of the board of directors; lower the threshold of shares required to inspect financial information (from 3 percent to 1 percent); and hold owner-managers more responsible for their decisions.

In addition, enormous efforts have been made to establish transparent procedures involving accounting, auditing and reporting. Improved accounting standards have been issued for debt restructuring and the disclosure of financial statements. Rules for combined financial statements have also been issued and implemented for large firms that are stricter than those employed in other developed countries.

Legal reforms of internal corporate governance

Reforms are useful only if a credible threat of sanctions is made by the courts. Major laws now support these changes, including the Korean Commercial Code, the Securities Exchange Act, Monopoly Regulation and Fair Trade Act, the Independent Audit Act, the Regulations on Securities Listing (RSL), and the Securities Investment Trust Acts.

The Korean Commercial Code defines the roles of the shareholders, management and directors of firms, and institutions such as the board of directors, shareholders' meetings and auditors. It also defines shareholder rights, transfer of businesses, mergers and acquisitions, and other issues that relate to the governance of firms. Enacted in 1962, the code was amended in 1995, 1998 and 1999. Recent amendments, including those that were drafted during the aftermath of the economic crisis, were unprecedented in terms of changes made with respect to shareholder rights and boards of directors.

Since 1998, shareholders' rights have been strengthened to counterbalance owner-managers' power. The Securities Exchange Act has also lowered the minimum shareholding requirements for these rights. For example, shareholder derivative actions can be taken with 0.01 percent of the total shares issued, injunctive action against illegal acts can be sought with 0.5 percent of shares, termination of directors or auditors can be requested with 0.5 percent, and so on (see Table 12.2).[8] Under the new codes, shareholders with more than 1 percent of total shares also have the right to propose agenda items at the shareholders' meeting. A new "cumulative voting rule" gives minority shareholders the opportunity to elect outside directors by allowing them to cumulate their votes for one candidate when more than two directors are elected. However, the rule is not compulsory.

Stronger expectations regarding the role of institutional investors are also developing. In 1998, the shadow-voting rule for institutional investors was abolished. The new Securities Investment Trust Act revived the voting rights of investment trust company funds and the trust accounts of commercial banks, allowing them to play the role of active

Table 12.2   Minimum requirement for minority shareholder rights (%)

Type of shareholder rights	Korean Commercial Code	Securities Exchange Act
Request for termination of directors and auditors	3	0.25 (0.125)
Injunctive action against illegal acts of management	1	0.25 (0.125)
Shareholder derivative action	1	0.005
Request for convening a special shareholders' meeting	3	1.5 (0.75)
Inspection of financial records	3	0.5 (0.25)
Appointment of an inspector to examine corporate affairs, records, and financial statements	3	1.5 (0.75)
Termination of a liquidator	3	0.25 (0.125)
Request for cumulative voting	3	–
A shareholder proposal	3	0.5 (0.25)
Request for dissolution of the firm	10	–

Note: The requirements of the Securities Exchange Act are applied to listed or registered companies, while the numbers in brackets are applied to those firms with the paid–in capital of 100 billion won or more.
Source: Park (2000).

shareholders. However, it still prohibits those institutional investors from exercising voting rights for the purpose of controlling a firm.

Despite these improvements, the reforms for stronger shareholders' rights are not yet complete. To further strengthen outside shareholders' rights additional information on corporate decisions affecting shareholder value should be disclosed. For example, information about corporate decisions on the disposal of major assets should be provided to shareholders. Currently, such information is not provided outside the boardroom, and outside shareholders' rights are limited accordingly. Only the subsidiaries of the top thirty business groups are required to disclose major inter-subsidiary transactions.

More importantly, amendments for cumulative voting for the election of board of directors should be made. Most firms do not adopt cumulative voting because ownership is concentrated among inside majority shareholders and a simple majority vote can override a cumulative voting system. Also, the law contains a loophole, allowing firms to preclude cumulative voting through their articles of association. Thus, in spite of the introduction of cumulative voting to strengthen outside shareholders' rights, the system is not well implemented in practice.

Another key issue lies in the role of institutional investors. A global trend in corporate governance is a stronger role for institutional investors with sufficient economic incentives to efficiently monitor management. Direct involvement such as proposing business strategies is not necessary or appropriate, but indirect involvement through the appointment of officers and directors and the determination of managerial compensation would be desirable. For example, institutional investors with a large stake could have a right to recommend an outside director.

To achieve a stronger oversight role for institutional investors, some institutional and legal changes are required. Restrictions on the maximum share ownership of institutional investors should be lifted. For those who are not affiliated with *chaebol*, the voting rights of these investors should also be guaranteed. But the governance of institutional investors should also be improved, particularly for non-bank financial institutions affiliated with *chaebol* as well as for banks and pension funds.

Boards of directors have become more accountable. Previously, directors only had the "duty of diligence as a good custodian," which was based on a provision in Article 382.2 of the Commercial Code, which in turn was based on Article 681 of the Civil Code. A new article in the Commercial Code (382.3) now explicitly defines the "fiduciary duty of directors," which enables the courts to treat the arguments of shareholders more favorably. New amendments also require directors to immediately report to the company's statutory auditor any "significant injury" to their firms.

The large shareholders who had maintained nominal positions but exercised significant influence on the management of their firms are now equally responsible and liable for any results of their conduct as directors.[9] The amendment prevents principal shareholders without official positions from exercising undue influence on the management of firms, thus making them assume appropriate legal obligations.

Another major change in the boardroom is the establishment of subcommittees for areas such as selection, audit, evaluation and operations, which can assume the delegated functions of the board. The audit committee, in particular, is designed to help the board focus on its responsibility for financial oversight of management performance. The audit committee would be filled with outside directors and the auditor only, and the latter is now being protected from any unjust termination during incumbency.

The revised Regulations on Securities Listing mandate that the boards of listed firms have at least one outside director. As of 2001 more than 50 percent of the total board members were to be outside members who are not related to the management or principal shareholders. Table 12.3 shows the trend in the number of outside directors of firms listed on the Korea Stock Exchange. The absolute number of outside directors almost doubled in 1999 and the ratio of outside directors to insiders has also increased by more than 200 percent. Considering that the boardrooms had previously been filled with executive officers who are subservient to CEOs and dominant shareholders, the new requirements are expected to bring about a major change in the management of firms by enabling boards to monitor management more effectively.

However, despite these institutional and legal changes, further efforts are required to strengthen the role of the corporate board. In particular, special efforts are required to achieve the independence of outside directors. Without independence from the management and dominant shareholders, outside directorship is an ineffective means of monitoring managers, a corporate ornament. Table 12.4 shows the composition of outside directors by occupation and compares Korea with the United States. The higher ratio of lawyers and accountants in Korea may suggest that Korean firms consider the outside directors' job to be providing professional advice to the management, not monitoring and evaluating the management nor actively participating in the decision-making process.

The high ratio of professors may be a reflection of the fact that professors are considered relatively independent in Korean society. However, a recent case concerning a former Minister for Education shows that even professors are not independent, revealing problems embedded in the outside directorship system in Korea. During his directorship at Samsung Electronics Co., Professor Song Ja earned more than $2 million through the purchase of company stock at a deep discount using company loans. A number of similar cases have been reported in other firms. Members of the Korean Financial Supervisory Commission have also held seats on the boards of several *chaebol*-affiliated firms. Media reports reveal that many former government officials are board members of listed companies, suggesting that outside directors may play the role of lobbyists. These incidents cast doubt on the theory that outside directors are sufficiently independent to monitor management and protect outside shareholders.

A survey on the director selection process conducted by the Korea Stock Exchange reveals the source of the problem. As we can see in Table 12.5, about 80 percent of outside directors are chosen by the

Table 12.3 Outside directors in firms listed on the Korea Stock Exchange, 1998–2000

	1998	1999	2000
Number of firms	736	701	704
Number of directors	5,853	4,850	4,625
Number of outside directors	669	1,204	1,495
Proportion of outside directors	11.4%	24.8%	32.3%
Average number of outside directors per firm	0.91	1.72	2.12

Source: Korea Stock Exchange.

Table 12.4 The professions of outside directors of Korean and US companies, 2000 (%)

Profession	Korea	United States
Present or former professional managers	30.2	81.1
College professors	19.3	9.8
Lawyers	11.0	1.3
Accountants	8.7	2.3
Former government officials	3.3	1.9
Others	26.5	1.0

Source: The Association for Listed Companies, "Listing" (May 2000).

dominant shareholders or the management. Another survey conducted by the exchange shows that the attendance rate at outside directors' board meetings was only about 50 percent in 1999 and 2000. The survey also shows that outside directors approve 99.3 percent of the issues discussed in board meetings. These facts suggest that it is unrealistic to expect outside directors to actively monitor management and dominant shareholders (see Jang 2000).

To solve these "independence" problems, a nomination committee, comprised of outside directors, should recommend outside director candidates. Hiring foreign directors representing foreign shareholders could play an important role in achieving greater board independence. At the same time, it is important to provide directors with sufficient incentives to maximize the firm's value by monitoring management. The current fixed payment compensation scheme does not motivate

Table 12.5 Selection of outside directors in firms listed on the
Korea Stock Exchange, 2000

Recommended by:	No.
Dominant shareholder and management	343
Institutional investors	3
Employees	20
Creditors (main banks)	25
Others	74
Total	465

Source: Korea Stock Exchange (2000).

outside directors to exert significant effort and time on the board. Compensation by stock grants or stock options might provide greater incentives.

Legal reforms of external corporate governance

Steps to improve external corporate governance mechanisms have also been implemented. The Korean corporate governance system lacked an active market for corporate control. The new Commercial Code streamlined merger procedures and enhanced the rights of shareholders in takeovers while providing commensurate protective measures to existing managers. First, a new voting quorum requires that a merger be approved by two-thirds of the shareholders attending the shareholders' meeting. Previously, it required the presence of shareholders with at least one-half of all the shares to vote, making it difficult for a company of concern to proceed with a merger. Second, a "simplified-form merger" can be implemented when the acquiring firm purchases more than 90 percent of the target company's shares. In this case, the approval of the target company's board of directors substitutes for that of the shareholders.[10] Third, the new code requires that various documents be available for shareholder inspection in the takeover processes. The board of directors must also provide post-merger information. These procedures protect the property rights of shareholders, who can claim appraisal rights if not satisfied with ongoing mergers. The price of repurchased shares in exercising appraisal rights will be determined by negotiation between the shareholder and the company. If agreement is not reached, a third party, such as a public accountant or a court, is invited to determine the appraisal price.

The new SEA abolished the minimum proportion of shares that must be bought in a tender offer to ease the burden on the acquiring companies. The Ministry of Finance and Economy also recently alleviated the restrictions on the asset portfolios of private M&A funds.[11] The government has also lifted most regulations restricting share purchases by foreigners, who can now buy up to 100 percent of the shares of most Korean companies.

A second area of external corporate governance reform is creditor rights. In the period before the crisis, one of the important characteristics of Korean conglomerates was their high leverage and heavy reliance on external funding. Korean banks and non-bank financial institutions should have closely monitored the management of borrowing firms, especially main creditor banks. However, we have seen in Chapter 4 that financial institutions failed to play this role because of their own poor governance structure.

Banks themselves are now undergoing reform of their governance structure. The government recently declared that there would be no more intervention into the management of banks, restoring incentives to monitor and evaluate borrowing firms. Since the main creditor bank has a long-term relationship with borrowing firms, the bank can easily access management information. In addition, the bank can pose a credible threat to poorly managed firms by simply calling in loans. Establishment of a bank-led monitoring mechanism would thus be a very important step towards corporate governance reform (see Chapter 8). Changes in insolvency laws also strengthen creditor rights by requiring that a committee of creditors be formed and that court-appointed administrators consult the committee on major decisions affecting the administration of the company (see Chapter 9).

Although not well institutionalized, a managerial labor market has slowly evolved in Korea and constitutes a final element in external corporate governance. Through the restructuring process, the practice of lifetime employment has been more or less abolished. Employees no longer expect to rise up the internal corporate ladder; rather, they try to increase their own market value and constantly seek better outside employment opportunities. For example, a senior executive of DACOM recently took a job as the head of HITEL Co., which is an affiliate of Korea Telecom. This type of job change was unimaginable before the crisis.

Table 12.6 summarizes these institutional and legal reforms of corporate governance.

Table 12.6   Summary of recent changes in Korean corporate governance

Issues	Major reforms	Related regulations
Board of directors	• A listed firm should have at least one outside director and more than one–quarter of its board filled with outside directors. This increased to three outside directors and one-half of the board for firms with assets exceeding 2 trillion *won*. • Outside directors must not be related to the existing management in any way. • "Fiduciary duty" imposed on directors in addition to existing "duty of care."	KCC and regulations on securities listing
Management practice	• Legal responsibility imposed on "actual directors" who can exercise control on management without official positions. • Registration of dominant shareholders as director. • Abolition of secretary office recommended. • More restrictions on transactions between dominant shareholders and firms.	KCC and regulations on securities listing
Minority shareholder rights	• Lowered ownership requirements for exercising minority rights. • Cumulative voting rules for board election recommended. • Class action suits allowed for false reports on securities issues, tender offers and financial statements.	SEA and KCC
Institutional investors	• Voting rights restored on trusted shares except in the case of exercising them for controlling purposes. • Damages on trustee are imposed if fiduciary duty is not fulfilled.	Securities Investment Trust Act
Mergers and acquisitions	• Minimum purchase requirement abolished in a tender offer. • Less restriction on mergers and acquisitions by foreign investors. • Only "defense industry firms" are subject to government approval. • Board–approved purchase limit abolished. • Spin–offs and simplified mergers and acquisitions process introduced.	SEA and regulations on foreign investment
Accounting system	• Combined financial statements required for conglomerates. • Subcommittee established to select auditors of listed firms and affiliates of conglomerates. • Class action suit against outside auditors allowed and increased penalties.	Regulations on outside auditing

Source: Park (2000).

3   **The Remaining Agenda**

Significant progress has been made in improving corporate governance in Korea. Reforms are being undertaken in such areas as shareholders' rights, the role of boards, and accounting and disclosure practices. In addition, initiatives are being made to create an external corporate governance mechanism, for example, by creating a market for corporate control. Given these legal changes, the future of corporate governance rests on the implementation and enforcement of the reforms.

Companies governed by the *chaebol* have little incentive to implement these changes, however. Thus, it is important for the government to make these changes in corporate governance legally binding or mandatory for firms listed on the Korea Stock Exchange. At the same time, sufficient penalties should be imposed for the violation of relevant laws. This seems particularly important in the area of minority shareholders' rights, considering the fact that lawsuits and derivative suits against managers or dominant shareholders are rare in Korea. Table 12.7 shows that few penalties have in fact been imposed by the Financial Supervisory Service.

In addition to the implementation issue, more fundamental questions should be answered. Is Korea moving toward an Anglo-Saxon model of corporate governance, and is this move desirable? Some scholars argue that the Anglo-Saxon model is a more efficient governance mechanism than the Japanese or German model. The *chaebol*, on the other hand, argue that corporate governance should take history into consideration, advocating gradual changes in corporate governance mechanisms.

Table 12.7   Penalties imposed by the Financial Supervisory Service, 1995–98

Penalty	1995	1996	1997	1998
Prosecution			1	
Dismissal of officers			2	
Restrictions on issuance of stock			1	4
Designation of auditor	11	4	9	17
Warning	38	25	23	36
Request for correction	24	18	20	59
Total	73	47	56	116

Source: Financial Supervisory Service.

There seems to be no clear resolution to this issue yet, but over the last decade we have witnessed a global convergence in corporate governance. German and Japanese firms have adopted an American-style board of directors. American and British firms now listen more carefully to the voice of stakeholders other than shareholders. The most important force driving such convergence is the globalization of the world economy. To achieve competitive advantage, firms now benchmark against the best practices of other firms on a global basis. Corporate governance is certainly a key management practice that firms are benchmarking. Thus, although we witness convergence of governance from both sides, the Anglo-Saxon style seems dominant because foreign firms tend to benchmark American firms that enjoy competitive advantages in many global industries. This trend is visible in Korea as well.

Notes

1 The chairman of a *chaebol* has been considered the *de facto* CEO of all the affiliated firms.

2 Further, the desire to retain control has resulted in heavy reliance on external debt financing instead of equity financing. Debt financing has helped the chairman avoid the dilution of family shares and maintained his position as the largest individual shareholder. A by-product of the desire for control, therefore, is a high leverage ratio.

3 In 1999, thirty groups consisting of 616 firms were defined as "large business groups" under the Monopoly Regulation and Fair Trade Act. These industrial groups are both diversified and vertically integrated. A number of the industrial groups are reluctant to go public; only fourteen of the fifty-five companies in the Samsung industrial group, for example, are listed.

4 This rule can work as a defensive measure for target firms.

5 Shareholders can exercise appraisal rights within 20 days after the shareholders' meeting.

6 The rule did not prohibit a takeover of a firm by purchasing stocks in the over-the-counter market or from existing management.

7 Banks could call in, rather than roll over, the loans if they wanted.

8 The requirements for a derivative action suit must be met only when the suit commences, which would greatly facilitate the pursuit of the action.

9 With the new provision, many principal owners are now registering as directors.

10 Also, under "a small-scale merger," when the acquiring firm issues less than 5 percent of its shares to purchase a small company, shareholder approval is not required. In addition, spin-offs were recently allowed to be used in corporate restructuring.

11 The 10 percent limit on the investment in one company was relaxed to 30 percent and the tender offer prior-reporting rule was changed to a post-reporting rule.

References

Easterbrook, H. 1984. "Two Agency-cost Explanations of Dividends," *American Economic Review*, 78: 650–9.

Fama, Eugene. 1980. "Agency Problems and the Theory of the Firm," *Journal of Political Economy*, 88: 288–307.

Jang, Hasung. 2000. "An Analysis of Effect of Corporate Restructuring after Economic Crisis," Working Paper. Seoul: Korea University.

Jensen, Michael, and Meckling, William. 1976. "The Theory of the Firm: Managerial Behavior, Agency Costs and Ownership Structure," *Journal of Financial Economics*, 3: 305–60.

Korea Development Institute. 1999. "Corporate Governance in Asia." Seoul: Korea.

Korea Stock Exchange. 2000. "Survey Results on the Outside Director System."

McConnell, John, and Servaes, Henri 1990. "Additional Evidence on Equity Ownership and Corporate Value," *Journal of Financial Economics*, 26: 595–612.

Morck, Randall, Shleifer, Andrei, and Vishny, Robert. 1988. "Management Ownership and Market Valuations: An Empirical Analysis," *Journal of Financial Economics*, 20: 293–315.

Park, Kyung Suh. 2000. "Corporate Governance in Korea: Its Institutional Structure," Working Paper. Seoul: Korea University.

Rozeff, Michael. 1982. "Growth, Beta, and Agency Costs as Determinants of Dividends Pay-out Ratio," *Journal of Financial Research*, 5: 249–59.

Shleifer, Andrei, and Vishny, Robert. 1986. "Large Shareholders and Corporate Control," *Journal of Political Economy*, 94 (2): 293–309.

13   Conclusion: Whither the *Chaebol*?

Stephan Haggard, Wonhyuk Lim and Euysung Kim

This volume has shown that the *chaebol* as a corporate form cannot be divorced from a broader context that includes politics, policy and regulation, and a rapidly changing financial system. We summarize our findings by posing two questions of this complex of institutional relationships. The first is a balance sheet: how much change has occurred in Korea's system of corporate governance, broadly conceived, and what is the likely direction of change in the future? Is Korea moving toward a new model of business–government relations and corporate governance as a result of the crisis? Or are the *chaebol* form and the institutions that have supported it likely to persist?

The second question centers on the implications of such organizational changes for future economic performance. The *chaebol* were the main private agents of Korea's rapid growth in the three decades prior to the crisis of 1997–98. What does their transformation portend for the Korean economy? Is such change desirable, or neutral, or does it reflect a preoccupation with foreign models of corporate governance and an underestimation of indigenous organizational strengths?

To construct our balance sheet, we summarize the evidence presented in this volume in four broad areas: the political economy of business–government relations; reforms of the government–bank–*chaebol* relationship and the financial system; efforts to introduce competitive forces that would provide external discipline on the *chaebol*; and more direct efforts to change the corporate governance and internal organization of these firms. We argue that the changes that have occurred in the wake of the crisis have been extensive and that most are likely to have positive consequences not only for growth but probably for equity as well. Nonetheless, certain policy areas and institutions exhibit "stickiness." Some reforms of corporate governance have been circumscribed by political pressures on the government and resistance from managers, owners and other stakeholders. In other areas, however, institutional stickiness reflects the distinctive organizational strengths of the *chaebol*; throughout the conclusion we seek to disentangle these two.

1   The Political Context: Changing the Nature of Business–Government Relations

As we argued in Chapter 1, the *chaebol* form is in part a creature of politics. The Korean political system under both Park Chung Hee and Chun Doo Hwan was highly centralized and autocratic, but this fact did not preclude a complex set of exchange relationships with the private sector. In return for private sector support for shifting policy initiatives, the government provided direct financing through the state-owned banking system, guarantees to foreign lenders, and a wide variety of other subsidies and rents. These favors were directed overwhelmingly toward the largest business groups and contributed to a number of features of *chaebol* organization: their size, high degree of diversification and extraordinary leveraging. We have labeled this system a government–business risk partnership, underlining the potential benefits of these arrangements as well as the costs of moral hazard that they implied.

The long-standing debate about industrial policy in Korea and elsewhere has focused largely on the question of whether government intervention could be understood as an efficient response to market failures of various sorts (Rodrik 1995; Chang 2000). However, the analysis of government intervention must also address the politics of industrial policy. The Park government enjoyed a degree of independence from the private sector (Haggard 1990; Evans 1995), thus permitting it to effectively impose conditions on firms and monitor their behavior (Amsden 2001, ch. 6). But, as Kang (2002) shows, those relationships were not devoid of unproductive rent-seeking and corruption even if their extent was limited. Moreover, the corruption trials during the Kim Young Sam administration revealed that Chun, Roh and their allies amassed slush funds of staggering proportions in their effort to operate in a more competitive political environment (West 1997; Schopf 2001; Kang 2002).

Reforming the *chaebol* system is therefore not simply an issue of policy reform; it requires changing the *political* relationship between politicians, bureaucrats and the private sector. This involves two closely related tasks: to reduce outright rent-seeking and corruption; and to change the expectation that private actors can shift risk onto the public sector. An important means of mitigating moral hazard is establishing the precedents that firms can fail and that managers, owners and shareholders can experience losses.

The transition to democracy appeared to have some salutary effects in reducing rent-seeking and moral hazard (Schopf 2001). First, democracy implied greater freedom for groups in civil society, such as labor unions, public interest groups and independent media, to air their grievances against *chaebol* privileges. Second, competitive politics provided strong incentives for opposition politicians to expose the corruption of political incumbents, reduce the socialization of risk, and tighten the regulation of private malfeasance (Schopf 2001). Political competition increased the transparency of government and its responsiveness to the median voter. Such incentives were visible in the introduction of a real-name financial transaction system, in the corruption trials of the Kim Young Sam administration, and in the exposure of the political corruption surrounding Hanbo's demise in early 1997, and in corruption allegations brought against members of Kim Dae-jung's cabinet as well. Finally, democratization was accompanied by political pressure to bring greater accountability to other spheres of social and economic life, including the governance of the firm. An example of this phenomenon was the emergence of public interest groups such as People's Solidarity for Participatory Democracy, which focused public and media attention on the long-standing *chaebol* practice of expropriating minority shareholders.

All of these factors were visible in the Kim Dae-jung administration's management of the *chaebol* issue. Kim Dae-jung was more attentive to opposition voices than his predecessors and made the reform of business–government relations a centerpiece of his campaign. Because Kim Dae-jung was a political outsider, because he confronted an acute crisis and because he enjoyed an electoral honeymoon (albeit with fairly narrow electoral support), he was less beholden than his predecessors to the dictates of corporate support. Kim Dae-jung did use tripartism and government–business consultation to pursue these reforms but, as Mo and Moon show in Chapter 6, many of the early reforms of the Kim administration were clearly imposed on the private sector.

The policy tools for changing business–government relations under Kim Dae-jung combined the introduction of market forces with direct intervention and regulatory oversight. The creation of the Financial Supervisory Commission (FSC) and the strengthening of prudential regulation were explicitly designed to contain the socialization of risk. Among the most important examples of the exercise of such direct regulatory powers during the crisis were the FSC's restrictions on corporate paper and bond financing of the *chaebol* in 1998; the agency's active role in defining and later negotiating the Big Five's Capital Structure Improvement Plans; and the increasing use of prompt corrective action *vis-à-vis* the banking sector. The Korea Fair Trade Commission also became more active in enforcing antitrust law and regulating at least some inter-subsidiary transactions of the *chaebol*.

In any crisis of this magnitude, the government and taxpayers are likely to bear substantial fiscal costs, particularly for the rehabilitation of the financial system. But the management of important bank and corporate failures also showed the willingness of the government to limit the socialization of risk and commit to the market discipline of the firm. Even if the management of the Daewoo crisis was subject to important and costly delays (Chapter 7), the government did in the end allow the dissolution of the firm to take place. Both the Kim Young Sam and Kim Dae-jung administrations allowed a number of the other top thirty *chaebol* to fail as well. Through both court-supervised receiverships and out-of-court workouts, the management of many leading *chaebol* was displaced, and controlling shareholders saw their holdings either diluted or altogether wiped out. Of the thirty largest business groups in 1996, fourteen had gone bankrupt or entered workout programs by the end of 1999, and a number of others lost major subsidiaries. In sum, the Kim Dae-jung government provides important examples of how a democratic administration can build political support for limiting moral hazard, rent-seeking and corruption. We believe these changes constitute quite fundamental ones in the nature of business–government relations in Korea.

That said, it is important to also appreciate the political constraints that democratic rule places on governments as well. While democracy may provide political incentives to expose corruption and rent-seeking, it does not necessarily end it. Politicians still need financial backing, and democracy provides business the opportunity to advance its interests not only through public debate, but through other channels as well, including both legitimate and illicit campaign contributions. In Korea, *chaebol* control of the media is an ongoing issue of public debate. The ruling party and the opposition in Korea have colluded to water down provisions in anti-corruption and campaign financing laws, and even the Kim Dae-jung government – which ran on a clean-government platform – faced corruption within its own ranks in 2000 and 2001. Although these cases do not appear anywhere near as serious as those of the Chun and Roh periods, they are a reminder of the difficulty of fully eradicating corrupt practices.

However, the most powerful political weapon wielded by the private sector is the ability to mobilize support among creditors, workers, suppliers and other stakeholders who bear the costs of corporate restructuring. In Chapter 3, Byung-Kook Kim shows how both the Roh Tae Woo and Kim Young Sam administrations repeatedly backed away from reform of the labor market and the financial and corporate sector due to fears about the disruption such reform would bring. Although the economic crisis allowed Kim Dae-jung to break this pattern, his administration faced a variety of political constraints, some a direct result of the crisis such as rising unemployment and growing "reform fatigue." The government faced National Assembly elections in April 2000, and in September 2001 the president lost his majority in the National Assembly as a result of the defection of his coalition partners. These political changes virtually eliminated the likelihood of further legislative initiatives and weakened the administration's hand in purely regulatory issues as well.

These political pressures influenced the nature of the restructuring program from the outset. Most notably we see bias toward financial restructuring and forbearance, as opposed to more politically difficult operational restructuring measures such as shutting down unprofitable subsidiaries and divisions, laying off workers and selling assets. The Big Five (Hyundai, Samsung, Daewoo, LG and SK) were formally shielded from the corporate workout process and bankruptcy until Daewoo's problems became too egregious to ignore (see Chapters 6 and 7). The Big Deals, often wrongly interpreted as a populist measure emanating from the administration, in fact reflected corporate attempts to secure tax benefits and write-offs. Several of the largest business groups exploited control over non-bank financial institutions (NBFIs) to continue to take on debt in 1998, opening a second window for moral hazard in the bond market. Until Daewoo's collapse, creditors continued to prop up the largest business groups, expecting the government to shield them from bankruptcy.

The government was also slow to investigate any malfeasance or unlawful activities on the part of owner-managers, professional managers, and their monitors (such as accountants and auditors) whose firms or financial institutions had become insolvent. Where fraud and misconduct contributed to the demise of firms and financial institutions – and particularly where the government has used public funds to clean up nonperforming loans – aggressive prosecution is warranted. The government should also have closed loopholes that made it possible for the owner-managers of some firms to renege on loan guarantees and hide assets.[1] Clearly, moral hazard will continue if corporate managers draw the inference that they can shift the burden of firm failure onto the public. Yet it was only in 2001, three years after the outbreak of the crisis, that the government began to make coordinated efforts to address this problem (Board of Audit and Inspection 2001).

These important caveats aside, the change in business–government relations in Korea has been substantial, particularly since the onset of the crisis of 1997–98.

• Increased political competition, democratization and the emergence of public interest groups have increased the transparency of business–government relations and helped to reduce, although not eliminate, moral hazard and corruption.

• The development of new regulatory institutions, such as the FSC, and the strengthening of others, such as the Korea Fair Trade Commission (KFTC), have increased the independence of the government from the private sector.

• The government's willingness to impose losses on managers and shareholders in the wake of the crisis reduced the risk of moral hazard, even if some avenues remained for owner-managers to avoid losses at public expense.

• Nonetheless, political concerns about the social costs of restructuring provided the *chaebol* with an important political weapon and biased the restructuring program in favor of financial restructuring at the expense of more politically difficult operational restructuring and asset sales; it is to these financial issues that we now turn.

2   Government–Bank–*Chaebol* Relations, the Evolution of Financial Markets and Corporate Restructuring

The evolution of the *chaebol* as a corporate form was influenced not only by politics but also by rational corporate responses to highly imperfect markets, markets whose development was strongly affected by the terms of the government–business risk partnership. By far the most important component of this external environment is the financial system. As the economic crisis of 1997–98 made clear, the Korean financial system had been characterized by profound incentive problems in government–bank–*chaebol* relations for some time. Despite important reforms in the wake of the crisis, a number of these incentive problems persisted, affecting the corporate restructuring process in important ways.

Financial repression was a central feature of the Korean business–government risk partnership throughout much of the postwar period. In the aftermath of the drive to develop heavy and chemical industry, the government undertook important financial market reforms. It scrapped the industrial targeting approach and drastically reduced the preferential terms of bank lending.[2] Starting in the early 1980s, the government sold its shares in commercial banks and allowed several new entrants into the banking sector. Perhaps the most important financial development of the 1980s, however, was the growth of NBFIs. Restrictions on the licensing of NBFIs were relaxed in the early 1980s, and that segment ultimately overtook the banking sector in asset size. As the data in Table 13.1 shows, Korea appeared to be moving toward a system in which government ownership of banks was limited and financial intermediation

Table 13.1 Banking in selected middle-income countries, c. 1995 (%)

Country	Bank share in financial intermediation	State–owned bank share in total assets
Argentina	98	36
Brazil	97	48
Chile	62	14
Colombia	86	23
Mexico	87	28
Venezuela	92	30
Hong Kong	–	0
India	80	87
Indonesia	91	48
Korea	38	13
Malaysia	64	8
Singapore	71	0
Taiwan	80	57
Thailand	75	7
Japan	79	0
United States	23	0

Source: Guillen (2001: 185).

was moving from a bank-based financial system to one in which equity and direct financing played a greater role.

However this stylized picture ignores important aspects of the institutional context of Korean financial markets and is therefore highly misleading. First, as we have seen, Korea's bank-based system differed from the bank-dominated German system and from the Japanese main bank approach, in that the banks were almost completely agents of the government. Banks enjoyed little independent authority to monitor and discipline corporate management, and thus had few incentives to develop their capacity to evaluate risk. Even after their privatization, the government continued to exercise control over top managerial appointments.

But Korea's market-based system was also very different from the Anglo-Saxon model, in which capital markets play a more important role in corporate finance; these markets *also* exerted little independent influence on corporate management. As Joon-Ho Hahm shows in Chapter 4, this was due in large part to the fact that the *chaebol* themselves were major players in the development of the NBFIs. The emergence of financial entities directly linked to the *chaebol* thus limited the development of independent sources of market discipline. The shift to a nominally‑ market-based system did not necessarily solve problems of moral hazard either. The size of the corporate bond market and the dependence of important constituents on it made it extremely difficult for the government to stand aside when these markets exhibited instability or distress. In effect, the government–business risk partnership remained in place in important respects, but with the hand of the government weakened and the balance of power increasingly favoring the *chaebol* (Lim 2000).

The crisis had the effect of transferring nominally privatized commercial banks back to state ownership as the government injected public funds equal to about 30 percent of GDP to absorb nonperforming loans and recapitalize the banking sector. Prior to the crisis, the government held approximately 18 percent of total banking sector capital. By mid-2000, the Korean government owned 58 percent of commercial bank capital, including majority shares in three major commercial banks.

Despite its expanded role in the financial system, the government was reluctant to use its position as a controlling shareholder of the banks to aggressively push corporate restructuring. The government initially let the top five *chaebol* carry out their own restructuring efforts and ultimately to define the content of the Big Deals to a substantial degree. As Kyung Suh Park shows in Chapter 8, the restructuring process of the "6–64" *chaebol* was supposed to be led by the banks, not the government. Not until October 1998 did the government begin to realize that implicit government guarantees and *chaebol* control of NBFIs were creating serious distortions in the financial market, leading to the first efforts to cap financial institutions' exposure to corporate bonds issued by the *chaebol*.

What accounts for this initial stance? Market-oriented critics – as well as the *chaebol* themselves – argued that the bureaucrats should learn a lesson from the crisis and stop meddling with the market once and for all. The threat of litigation also limited the adoption of a more proactive stance, and as we have seen, the government was subject to a wide variety of political pressures. These pressures were compounded by the fact that the government was a significant creditor to the private sector and thus directly involved in politically sensitive decisions concerning the extension of credit, the disposition of assets and operational restructuring measures. It is impossible to tell whether government ownership *per se* compromised the restructuring process. In some ways, government ownership of banks facilitated restructuring, particularly if we consider that private banks faced perverse incentives with respect to the recognition of losses. But the delay in selling financial institutions, in addressing the Daewoo problem and in disposing of several of that company's subsidiaries all raised questions of whether political calculations slowed the momentum of corporate restructuring.

As Kyung Suh Park shows in Chapter 8, the concept of bank-led corporate restructuring was to some extent an oxymoron. In the immediate aftermath of the crisis, the commercial banks in Korea were in no position to lead the corporate restructuring effort; in fact, they faced perverse incentives with respect to it. Although these incentives are common to all bankruptcy settings, they are worth reiterating because the depth of the crisis after 1997 greatly compounded their effects (Claessens, Djankov and Mody 2001).

Immediately after the crisis, financial institutions were reluctant to take tough measures with respect to nonperforming loans because of the fear that their balance sheets would undergo yet further deterioration. The unprecedented closure of five banks in 1998 and massive layoffs in the financial sector itself only reinforced the banks' cautious stance *vis-à-vis* debtors. Pressures to improve balance sheets and to increase capital adequacy ratios were important in forcing banks to assess risk. Nonetheless, these measures had perverse effects in the short run, since they not only affected the propensity to lend but the incentive to make full provisioning against bad loans. In addition to the incentives facing each bank *individually* were the well-known collective action problems facing the creditors *as a group*, including how to coordinate the interests of different classes of creditors (secured versus unsecured) and those with different levels of exposure.

The incentives of the debtors are also well known, and once again potentially perverse. When faced with complete loss of control and the write-down of equity, managers and inside shareholders have little to lose; they may resort either to extraordinary risk-taking in the hope of salvation or to outright plunder of the firm. Even if the going-concern value of the firm exceeds its liquidation value – making it socially optimal to resort to court-led corporate restructuring – managers may not find it individually rational to do so. Moreover, managers confront their own political and organizational constraints in undertaking operational restructuring and much prefer forbearance to the difficult choices that such restructuring entails.

Last but not least, in the Korean case the legacy of implicit government protection against the bankruptcy of the largest business groups created perverse incentives for investors as well. Relying on market forces became problematic when "market expectations" themselves were distorted by moral hazard. As Dong Gull Lee shows in Chapter 7, Daewoo, in particular, took advantage of this situation and issued 17 trillion *won* (approximately $12 billion) of new corporate bonds and commercial paper in the first nine months of 1998. Investors, large and small, apparently believed that the government would not let one of the Big Five fail.

These incentive problems generated a corporate restructuring process in Korea that has been marked by a stop-and-go pattern. Starting in mid-1998, the government injected public funds to stabilize the financial system and improve the balance sheets of surviving financial institutions, moving more swiftly and aggressively than other countries in the region to accept the scope of losses. The creditors, in turn, began negotiating out-of-court workout deals with distressed firms. Yet as both Kyung Suh Park (Chapter 8) and Youngjae Lim (Chapter 9) show, many of the early entrants into the workout program were in fact not viable and should have been allowed to go bankrupt. This problem of forbearance received increased attention in the wake of the Daewoo collapse in 1999, which signaled new government resolve. The government introduced tighter forward-looking criteria for asset classification and loss provisioning to encourage financial institutions to take decisive action with respect to distressed firms.

Yet, in cases involving the largest firms, with potentially serious repercussions for the economy as a whole, the government tended to put off the day of reckoning. In these crucial cases, including both Daewoo and Hyundai subsidiaries, progress in restructuring stalled until market forces compelled the government or government-controlled banks to act. The resolution of problems at Hyundai Construction provides an example of the operation of these new market pressures, unleashed in part by reforms undertaken in the wake of the crisis. Hyundai Construction suffered more than $800 million of uncollected payments in Iraq and had carried a vulnerable financial structure for more than a decade. Nonetheless, investors expected that other Hyundai subsidiaries would ultimately come to the rescue if the firm had trouble meeting its obligations. By early 2000, however, familial infighting for corporate control, as well as changed rules governing inter-subsidiary transfers and guarantees, called this presupposition into question. The company's financial weakness became a cause of increasing public and market concern. Yet the government and government-controlled banks were slow to take tough measures, held back by the hope that asset sales and other self-rescue measures would suffice.

But, as in the Daewoo case, this business-as-usual approach was unsustainable. Hyundai Construction ran out of viable assets to sell.

Fearing litigation, creditors balked at providing fresh loans to the company and investors demanded higher and higher risk premiums on its corporate bonds. International financial institutions and credit-rating agencies also signaled that they viewed Hyundai Construction as a test for Korea's commitment to reform. After nearly a year of wavering, the creditors imposed a serious restructuring plan which included a massive debt-for-equity swap, an issue of convertible bonds, a major write-down of shareholder equity, and the installation of a new management team.

The government faced a number of other difficulties in breaking with the legacy of implicit government guarantees. Because prudential regulation had been weak in the past, regulators found it hard to apply principles of accountability to investors who had made their decisions under the old regime. The resolution of the Daewoo crisis in 1999 was delayed in part by this transition problem. Financial institutions had made easy money by "guaranteeing" corporate bonds, with an implicit understanding that the government would come to their rescue in time of crisis. When Daewoo's problems rippled through the bond market, the government used taxpayers' money to bail out small individual investors, allowing them to redeem up to 95 percent of the face value of Daewoo corporate bonds. Even the imposition of this small loss convinced investors that corporate bonds no longer had the implicit backing of the government, however, and they quickly converted corporate bonds at their guaranteed price and fled from investment trust companies into banks. As investors became aware of default risks, many firms also began to have trouble rolling over their corporate bonds.[3] In effect, Korea's bond market became deluged with junk bonds without an operational junk bond market in place to handle them. In 1999 and twice in 2000 the government felt compelled to address these problems in the investment trust companies, and in the corporate bond market more generally, by orchestrating stabilization measures that included partial government guarantees.

Developments in the bond market demonstrate clearly the constraints that governments face in making the transition from a financial system characterized by explicit and implicit guarantees. Imposing even a 5 percent loss on holders of Daewoo bonds represented a dramatic departure from the past, which had been characterized by moral hazard with respect to small investors as well as large business groups. Nonetheless, further progress in Korea's transition to a more market-oriented financial system depends on how quickly Korea can replace such stopgap measures with market solutions that induce the orderly exit of nonviable firms.

To summarize:

- Well before the crisis, the government had begun to liberalize and privatize the financial sector, but this process was not complete. The combination of incomplete liberalization, continuing government intervention, and weak prudential regulation generated moral hazard.
- These problems were compounded by perverse incentives associated with *chaebol* ownership of NBFIs, suggesting that in countries such as Korea the separation of banking and commerce (including NBFIs) may be necessary to strengthen the independence of the financial system and to ensure effective corporate restructuring.[4] Even if Korea manages to import state-of-the-art bankruptcy laws and institutions from abroad, the governance problem created by *chaebol* control of financial subsidiaries can distort the incentives for financial institutions.
- Swift injections of liquidity served to stabilize the financial sector and helped to initiate the corporate restructuring process. But the resulting government ownership of major banks complicated the government's role by placing it in the position of being regulator and shareholder of the banks at the same time.
- Government ownership of banks also created political complications for the government by involving it, albeit indirectly, in difficult corporate restructuring decisions.
- Korea's financial markets have changed a great deal since the crisis. Market pressures operate to a much greater extent than in the past, and banks have moved rapidly to develop their capacity to assess risk. Nonetheless, the dearth of autonomous financial institutions continues to limit the scope of market-led corporate restructuring.

3   Changing the Competitive Environment of the *Chaebol*

The rehabilitation and reform of the banking system and changes in financial markets constitute the central task in establishing external discipline over *chaebol* owners and managers. But, as Kwangshik Shin argues forcefully in Chapter 11, "the *chaebol* problem" is by no means limited to the moral hazard associated with the organization of Korean financial markets. In addition, the *chaebol* have long enjoyed, in Shin's words, an "entrenched market position in a non-competitive environment." Although the progressive removal of entry barriers increased competition in the 1990s, and the government continued to liberalize trade, it also exercised residual controls. Substantive restrictions on foreign direct investment remained, and the market for corporate control was weakly developed. Perhaps more importantly, implicit government guarantees against the bankruptcy of the largest business groups in effect served as exit barriers, distorting investment behavior and competition. In the wake of the crisis, therefore, in addition to addressing the moral hazard problem, the Kim Dae-jung government paid serious attention to other policy parameters that directly influence the competitive context of the *chaebol*, including the rules governing foreign direct investment, fair trade policy,[5] and bankruptcy laws.

The most important and extensive policy reforms occurred in the rules governing foreign investment (Chapter 10). The *chaebol* grew up under a foreign investment regime that was one of the most restrictive in Asia, providing firms with substantial protection in the domestic market. The liberalization of investment did not begin in earnest until the mid-1980s and accelerated after 1989. But the Kim Dae-jung administration brought a renewed urgency to the task. In the wake of the crisis, the government completely eliminated the ceiling on foreign equity ownership in the stock market. By lifting the requirement that foreigners obtain board approval for ownership of more than one-third of the outstanding shares of a firm, the government provided a powerful impetus to cross-border mergers and acquisitions. The real estate market was opened to foreigners and foreign exchange transactions were liberalized further. The central reform of the rules governing foreign direct investment came in a new Foreign Investment Promotion Act in November 1998. This law streamlined investment procedures, strengthened incentives, and created innovative new mechanisms for subnational governments to play a role in attracting foreign investment.

As Mikyung Yun demonstrates in Chapter 10, these new incentives – when coupled with sharp exchange rate depreciation and other changes in the business environment – had a marked effect on both direct and portfolio equity investment. The share of foreign investors in the market capitalization of companies listed on the Korea Stock Exchange more than doubled from 1997 to 2000, from 14.6 to 30.1 percent. Yun details a number of cases in which foreign firms played an important role in the corporate restructuring process, and the list can easily be lengthened. Troubled subsidiaries of both Samsung and Daewoo were sold to foreigners, including most significantly the signing of a memorandum of understanding to sell Daewoo Motors to General Motors in October 2001.

In addition to the infusion of funds and managerial expertise, increased foreign direct investment also had political economy effects. For example, the foreign management of the Korea First (Cheil) Bank, taken over by Newbridge Capital in 1999, not only changed the bank's operations but publicly questioned efforts by the government to orchestrate continued credit lines to firms deemed unworthy of further support.[6]

Although largely a success, the opening to foreign direct investment has not been altogether without difficulty. Public support for foreign investment has generally been high, but representatives of the private sector and particular firms repeatedly complained that they were being pressured – including by the IMF and the US government – to sell assets at "fire sale" prices. These arguments naturally resonated strongly with stakeholders in troubled enterprises who would be adversely affected by the operational restructuring that foreign buyers typically undertake. During the National Assembly election campaign in the spring of 2000, some opposition politicians actively exploited this issue.

Such protests might have had little effect were the government not involved directly and indirectly in asset sales to foreigners through its role as creditor and regulator of financial institutions. As we have already suggested, this involvement created somewhat contradictory policy problems. On the one hand, we have noted delays in some asset sales that appeared to be politically motivated. On the other hand, a desire to negotiate sales quickly without viable alternatives has had the effect of weakening the government's bargaining power. When Kia Motors was sold in 1998, the government used a competitive auction with fairly binding conditions. Beginning with Renault's takeover of Samsung Motors in early 2000, however, the government showed a preference for designating exclusive priority negotiating partners for some sales. The problems that the government faced in tying itself to General Motors in the Daewoo Motors case resurfaced in conflicts with AIG over the pricing of Hyundai Investment Trust and Hyundai Securities in 2001.

These caveats, however, should not diminish the accomplishments that Korea has made in the area of foreign direct investment. Renault's takeover of Samsung Motors and General Motors' bid for Daewoo Motors are but two examples that show how much has changed in Korea. Selling a major company in such a "strategic" industry as automobiles to a foreign buyer would have been almost unthinkable in pre-crisis Korea. In fact, when Kia Motors went bankrupt in 1997, the government's instinct was to nationalize the company if a takeover by another *chaebol* could not be arranged. Putting a distressed firm to international bidding is a post-crisis development.

The crisis also created an opportunity for reform in fair trade policy. From its inception under Chun Doo Hwan, the KFTC has enforced *chaebol* regulation as well as traditional competition policy. In the wake of financial and corporate crises, it is not uncommon for a country to take a relaxed approach to anti-competitive practices such as cartels; Korea has explicitly used such forbearance to manage downturns in the past. But the government actually *strengthened* its competition laws after the crisis. The KFTC tackled the problem of government-sanctioned cartels head-on and dismantled twenty of them in 1999. Compared with the pre-crisis period, it also began to impose much more severe fines on firms charged with anti-competitive practices.

The government's success with respect to regulation of the *chaebol* is more controversial. Since the mid-1980s, the KFTC has placed direct controls on *chaebol* investment decisions, bank borrowing, and entry into particular activities.[7] This interventionist approach stemmed from the belief that "the *chaebol* problem" was a result of the groups' sheer size, concentration of control rights, and high level of diversification. Concerns about excessive diversification and the benefits of greater specialization persisted into the Kim Dae-jung administration, but with a different rationale. The government wanted to reduce expropriation of shareholder value and encourage operational restructuring, but also sought to limit the further socialization of risk. The government believed that *chaebol* control of NBFIs and undue resource transfers from profitable to distressed subsidiaries threatened a whole new round of crisis.[8]

Further revision of the Monopoly Regulation and Fair Trade Act became a tool for achieving these objectives. These changes sought to loosen the management, financial and other business ties that knit the *chaebol* together, and thus to facilitate corporate restructuring, contain systemic risks, restore fair competition, and protect the property rights of shareholders. The principal means of accomplishing this was to impose controls on various in-group inter-subsidiary transactions, particularly loan guarantees.[9] After initially rescinding them, the Kim government also reimposed direct controls designed to contain in-group equity ownership among the top thirty *chaebol*.[10] "Undue" transactions in shares, real estate and particularly loans among *chaebol* affiliates, and "unreasonable" assistance among *chaebol* group members became priorities of the KFTC's enforcement efforts, although its success in securing compliance has been limited and it has even been the target of corporate lawsuits.

The transitional controls on in-group inter-subsidiary transactions were justified in the wake of the crisis by concerns about weak corporate governance. Over the long run, these direct controls should be replaced by court-based private remedies designed to protect shareholders' rights, such as class action suits. But in the absence of such measures, direct regulation of such inter-group transactions was a prudential measure to limit systemic risk.

Another area of policy reform that is crucial to disciplining the firm is assuring that mechanisms exist to preserve and rehabilitate viable companies in distress, while providing for orderly exit of those firms that are not viable. Prior to the crisis, few distressed firms used bankruptcy procedures overseen by the courts. Rather, one of three things would occur: banks would continue to support troubled firms through "anti-bankruptcy" or "bankruptcy suspension" loans and forbearance; the government would come directly to firms' rescue through various "rationalization" measures that constituted effective bailouts; or, since the debt of bankrupt firms was typically secured, firms would be liquidated on a non-judicial basis through civil procedure.

The process of reforming the bankruptcy system began in earnest in 1992, but met an unanticipated setback in 1996, just prior to the crisis. A toughening of the courts' stance *vis-à-vis* controlling shareholders produced a flight to more generous "composition" procedures that allowed management to maintain control. Korea's reliance on an out-of-court settlement process led by the government and the banks was thus not simply the result of the magnitude of the crisis and the corresponding strain placed on the courts. This choice was also influenced by the fact that the country had a bankruptcy system that permitted debtors to exploit important legal ambiguities and that was only newly, and incompletely, reformed.

Bankruptcy reforms in 1998–99 were a requirement of lending from the IMF and the World Bank, but as of September 2002 the system has still not been fully overhauled. The initial reforms of 1998 – legislated in haste – did not alter the fundamental framework but did expedite procedure. The changes tightened (but did not eliminate) the composition loophole, strengthened the commitment to wipe out the shares of controlling owners, and introduced a crucial change in principle. To qualify for judicial procedures required an assessment of whether the value of the firm as a going concern did in fact exceed its liquidation value. In further reforms introduced in 1999, this efficiency principle was strengthened by *requiring* the courts to rule in favor of liquidation when the returns from doing so exceeded value as a going concern; the principle was tested when Dong-Ah Construction was liquidated in 2001.

There can be little question that Korea's system for managing distressed firms has proven vastly superior to that in either Indonesia, where the courts have offered little protection to creditors, or Thailand, where the reform of bankruptcy laws was slow in coming and the weakness of court-supervised processes has undercut out-of-court negotiations. But these cases represent a low standard, and the use of the courts to force both reorganization and liquidation still has some way to go in Korea. As of late 2001, few large companies had passed through court-supervised reorganization or liquidation. As Youngjae Lim shows clearly in Chapter 9, even following the reforms of 1998–99, those firms which did go through the courts included a number that had little likelihood of becoming viable, suggesting that efficiency criteria were not strictly applied.

The main issue for the future is effecting a transition from a system dominated by out-of-court workouts – which was absolutely necessary to deal with a crisis of the magnitude of 1997–99 – to one in which court-supervised procedures play a more central role. There are several reasons why this transition is important. First, we have already seen how restructuring can be delayed by the negotiated nature of the workout process and by conflicts over the provision of new credit, over the treatment of secured versus unsecured debt, and over the distribution of losses among creditors, shareholders and the public. Court-supervised processes also involve negotiations, but statutes serve to resolve some of these disputes. Second, the integrity of the court-supervised process is critical in determining the bargaining power of the agents involved in the out-of-court workout process. In the absence of credible threats to force reorganization or dissolution, owners, managers and other stakeholders can defend their stakes at the expense of creditors and the public through pure delay. Third, the nature of this delay is also important to understand. As is well known in the bankruptcy literature, court-supervised procedures aim to overcome several collective action problems. One is the incentive for managers facing financial distress not only to avoid difficult operational restructuring measures, but also to engage in high-risk activities and even to strip the assets of the firm. It is beyond our scope to detail the outstanding areas of reform that are still required; Mako (2001) provides a useful list of changes that were pending at the end of 2001. But it is worthwhile to underline that the purpose of bankruptcy is not in the end punitive; it is to maximize the value of assets and to facilitate reorganization of the firm where possible.

In sum, the crisis generated pressures to change the overall competitive environment in which the *chaebol* operate.

• In addition to continued commitment to liberalizing trade, Korea has radically liberalized its regime governing foreign investment. Foreign firms now play an increasing role in the restructuring process. Nonetheless, continuing government involvement in asset sales has complicated the opening to foreign direct investment.

• Korea also has strengthened fair trade policy. The KFTC has begun to take a tougher stance on cartels and other restraints of trade. To facilitate corporate restructuring and to protect the property rights of shareholders, it has also placed a number of restrictions on in-group inter-subsidiary transactions, measures which are prudent given the weakness of corporate governance.

• Reform of bankruptcy laws and procedures was somewhat slower, but cases such as Dong-Ah Construction suggest that the courts are becoming less generous toward financially distressed firms.

4   The Changing Nature of the Korean Firm: The Corporate Governance of the *Chaebol*

The relatively weak performance of the *chaebol* was an important antecedent of the crisis (see Chapters 5 and 12). This weakness can be traced in part to deficiencies in corporate governance. The *chaebol* suffered from a variety of agency problems, including centrally the disparity between the ownership and control rights of founding families and the potential for expropriation of minority shareholder value that resulted. From very early, the Kim Dae-jung government focused its corporate restructuring efforts on improving the governance structure of the *chaebol*, beginning with the five principles of corporate restructuring announced in January 1998:

• enhancing the transparency of corporate management
• eliminating in-group inter-subsidiary debt guarantees
• improving firms' capital structure
• focusing on core competencies
• enhancing the accountability of controlling shareholders and managers.

Enhancing transparency and accountability was designed to address the problem of "arbitrary imperial rule" by the *chaebol* bosses, who exercised complete control over their firms with low ownership stakes and in some cases without even being registered as the chief executive. The other principles sought to break up the "convoy-style" management of the *chaebol*, under which resource transfers among legally separate subsidiaries often violated minority shareholders' interests.

These principles were given teeth during 1998 through a number of incentive-based measures that improved transparency and increased checks and balances on inside shareholders and managers (see Chapter 12). The government eliminated the system of "shadow voting," in which institutional investors had to cast their votes in proportion to other votes cast, and new internal governance standards required at least one outside director on the board.

Some of the most important reforms, however, centered on transparency. To improve financial disclosure and accounting standards, the new administration required that groups adopt global accounting standards and also produce consolidated and combined financial statements.[11] Korea had had laws prohibiting "window-dressing," but it was only in the wake of the crisis that the spirit and the letter of these laws were respected. One of the top accounting firms in Korea shut down due to its involvement in Daewoo's fabrication of accounting information, and the Supreme Court ruled that "window-dressing" could be regarded as fraud, not just a technical violation of the external auditing law. With the courts taking a principled stance and with a number of violators actually jailed, firms began to take accounting transparency seriously.

Along with these approaches to changing corporate governance based on markets, information and incentives, the reform effort also included measures that were decidedly more direct, control-oriented and bureaucratic. For example, the government sought to limit resource transfers among legally separate subsidiaries, not simply by making such transfers transparent but by completely prohibiting inter-subsidiary loan guarantees. In a particularly controversial measure in 1998, the government required the *chaebol* to reduce their debt–equity ratios to 200% by the end of 1999, overlooking the underlying incentives that led to high leverage in the first place.[12] As we have seen with the government's continuing involvement in the financial sector, it was not always clear whether the government had a well-designed plan to replace these discretionary stopgap measures with more rule-based and market-oriented solutions. But such a direct results-oriented approach can be justified as a transitional measure on the grounds that market- and incentive-based measures provided inadequate checks on corporate management and investment in the short run.

How much has the governance structure of the *chaebol* actually changed as a result of these reform measures? It is important to underline at the outset that the combined effects of the various policy changes we have outlined here might take years to affect the internal organization of the *chaebol*, and are difficult to measure. Nonetheless, we can assess these efforts by examining changes in the *chaebol's* ownership and capital structure, as well as by looking at the effects of institutional changes introduced after the crisis on corporate behavior. The message is a mixed one. While the ownership and capital structure of the *chaebol* have hardly improved from a corporate governance perspective, the increased threat of litigation is forcing corporate managers to think twice before they engage in malfeasance. Although much greater efforts need to be made to close loopholes and introduce effective private remedies, attempts to expropriate minority shareholders are no longer likely to go unnoticed. The threat of litigation is also forcing bankers, accountants and auditors to become more cautious in their dealing with their corporate customers.

As we showed in Chapter 1 (Table 1.1), there has been a nearly secular trend since the 1970s toward decreasing ownership share on the part of controlling *chaebol* families. Although there are composition effects arising from the fact that the list of the top thirty *chaebol* changes each year, this trend does not seem to have changed in the years immediately following the economic crisis; indeed, it may have even accelerated. Inter-subsidiary shareholdings increased in the post-crisis period as well.

These changes can be traced directly to the government's mandate to reduce debt–equity ratios to 200 percent and the simultaneous lifting of restrictions on inter-subsidiary shareholdings in 1998. The 200 percent debt–equity target was a radical measure designed to strike at the very heart of past *chaebol* practice: the high preference for debt, the implicit reliance on the government for guarantees, the propensity to "credit-led" diversification. On the surface, the measure appeared highly effective. A comparison of the twenty-three *chaebol* groups that were designated as among the top thirty *chaebol* by the KFTC in both 1999 and 2000 – thus controlling for composition effects – shows that the average debt–equity ratio of this group fell drastically from 363.2 to 164.1 percent (see Table 13.2).

When we look more closely at how this reduction of the debt–equity ratio was accomplished, however, we find that the underlying changes in *chaebol* organization and operations may be somewhat less than appears. Table 13.2 shows that these twenty-three *chaebol* increased equity, or the denominator, by an average of 79.2 percent while decreasing their debt – the numerator – by an average of only 18.9 percent New equity thus played a far greater role in changing debt–equity ratios than did a reduction of borrowing.

In corporate governance terms, the relative shift in the dependence on debt and equity represents a shift in principals: from debt-holders to equity-holders. Given the problems of moral hazard in the banking system, this might be interpreted as a positive development, particularly if the new equity came from foreign or institutional investors with a history of strong oversight. Yet when we consider this increase in equity in light of the data presented in Table 1.1 on in-group ownership, a much less optimistic portrait emerges. The *chaebol* clearly met the debt–equity target largely by having subsidiaries within the same business group purchase newly issued stock, and in massive amounts. These changes in ownership patterns could even reflect a further entrenchment of the control rights of the founder's family, the principal source of the agency problem in the *chaebol's* governance structure to begin with.

Table 13.2   Changes in debt–equity ratios of leading *chaebol*, 1998–99

Groups of *chaebol*	Total assets (A)	Total equity (B)	Total debt (C)	Debt–equity ratio (C/B)
23 *chaebol* (top 30 in both 1999 and 2000)				
1998	366.5	79.2	287.3	363.2
1999	374.8	141.9	232.9	164.1
Change	8.3	62.7	– 54.4	– 199.1p
Top 4 *chaebol* (Hyundai, Samsung, LG, SK)				
1998	227.7	53.1	174.6	328.8
1999	237.7	96.5	141.2	146.3
Change	10.0	43.4	– 33.4	– 182.5p
19 *chaebol* (Nos. 5–30 in both 1999 and 2000)				
1998	138.8	26.1	112.7	433.4
1999	137.1	45.4	91.7	201.9
Change	– 1.7	19.3	– 21.0	– 231.5p

Note: Excludes financial subsidiaries. 'p' = percentage points.
Source: Korea Fair Trade Commission.

Although the *chaebol's* ownership and capital structure suggest that their corporate governance may not have improved after the crisis, the behavior of corporate managers has been constrained in new ways (Chapter 12). Minimum shareholding requirements have been significantly reduced for exercising shareholders' rights, such as the right to take derivative action against company executives for misconduct, to request the dismissal of directors and auditors, to review accounting books, or to call for a general shareholders' meeting. Cumulative voting has been introduced, and a securities class action bill was submitted to the National Assembly for consideration in 2002.

These institutional changes are not without their shortcomings. For instance, a loophole in the legislation allows companies to preclude cumulative voting in the articles of association. As a result, only about 20 percent of publicly traded firms have adopted cumulative voting. Derivative actions face serious incentive problems. In derivative action, shareholders bring a suit against directors of a firm on behalf of the firm. Even if they win, shareholders are not directly rewarded because directors pay damages to the firm, in contrast to class action cases, reducing the incentives to file such suits. Moreover, the Korean legal system does not have discovery procedure. In order for shareholders to pursue a case against company directors for a breach of fiduciary duty,

they must somehow collect sufficient evidence on their own and overcome collective action problems in doing so. Last but not least, the
chaebol control of the substantial portion of the non-bank financial
sector weakens the possibility of imposing discipline on corporate
management by financial institutions. Even the banks and NBFIs not
directly controlled by the *chaebol* may need their business and take less
than a principled stance against them. These problems suggest that it
will take much more than a few rule changes to develop credible market
discipline by parties at interest.

Nonetheless, we should not underestimate the extent to which corporate governance reform since the crisis has affected the behavior of
corporate managers and their monitors. In contrast to the past,
attempts to expropriate minority shareholders are likely to be heavily
publicized.[13] Non-government organizations such as People's Solidarity
for Participatory Democracy have filed derivative action on behalf of
shareholders when major malfeasance is suspected. In a landmark case
at the end of 2001, a district court in Suwon ruled in favor of shareholder activists and ordered the chairman and nine past and present
executives of Samsung Electronics to pay compensation of nearly
100 billion *won* for misuse of company funds and undue resource transfers to other subsidiaries.[14] The increased threat of litigation is forcing
both corporate managers and their monitors to exercise greater caution
in making their decisions.

While these non-quantifiable changes in behavior are substantial,
more reforms are needed to make it easier for parties at interest to
monitor and discipline corporate management. Private remedies should
be made more effective by reflecting the incentives of shareholders. In
particular, the introduction of securities class action suits should make
it easier for ordinary shareholders to resort to private remedies even
without the help of public interest groups.

In sum:

• The government placed high priority on incentive-based reforms of
corporate governance that would insure that inside shareholder-
managers paid greater attention to shareholder value. These included
increasing the transparency of group accounting and reforming governance to limit the capacity of insiders to control the board, auditing
procedures and other checks.
• The government also employed a number of more direct, control-
oriented measures, such as limits on inter-subsidiary shareholding and
caps on debt–equity ratios in order to force firms to revise their corporate governance. These controls served to limit systemic risk, but
over time, they should be replaced with process-oriented measures
designed to put parties at interest in a position to monitor and disci-

pline corporate management. In particular, more attention needs to be given to external and legal changes, such as class action suits, that serve to monitor management and align the incentives of insider shareholders, management and minority shareholders.

* There is some evidence that the underlying financial structure of the *chaebol* has improved, including the reduction of debt–equity ratios, greater reliance on internal finance and improved coverage ratios. Moreover, these changes do appear to reflect the decline in government guarantees and closer monitoring of firms by banks and other creditors.
* Nonetheless, this evidence remains ambiguous on a number of points. Firms still vary widely in their performance, and at least some of the improvement in financial structure comes from measures such as inter-subsidiary purchase of equity that might reflect continuing efforts of owner-managers to retain control.

5 Conclusion: Globalization, Convergence and Divergence in the World Economy

Students of East and Southeast Asia have long sought a unifying model that would encompass the diverse experiences of these high-growth economies, whether through a focus on market-oriented policies (World Bank 1993), the existence of developmental states (Johnson 1983; Wade 1990), or even more fundamental processes of late development (Amsden 1989, 2001) or capital accumulation (Krugman 1994). Nonetheless, comparative research continually returns to the widely *divergent* paths that the countries in the region have pursued (Hamilton and Biggart 1988; Haggard 1990, 2000; MacIntyre 1994, 2002; Evans 1995; Guillen 2001; Noble 2000; Kang 2002). We have similarly straddled this divide between the general and the idiosyncratic, emphasizing some determinants of the *chaebol* form that are common to business groups in other countries, such as capital and product market imperfections and political connections, but also underlining features of the Korean experience that are distinctive. These include the central role of government-owned banks in Korean industrial policy, the unusually high levels of industrial concentration associated with the *chaebol's* rise, and a peculiar corporate governance structure that combines relatively low ownership stakes with high levels of control.

Yet as our summary in the foregoing sections suggests, Korea has undergone profound policy and institutional change in the wake of the Asian financial crisis. That change suggests a fundamental rupture with the past, *chaebol*-oriented system and convergence toward a new – albeit hybrid – model that more closely resembles patterns of corporate governance in the advanced industrial states. Previous opportunities for rents have been foreclosed and firms are being subjected not only to more intense market pressures, but a variety of new institutional checks and demands for accountability as well. The demise of major *chaebol*, particularly Daewoo, has reduced moral hazard by forcing small investors as well as large firms and financial institutions to reassess risk. Enhanced shareholder rights and regulatory enforcement have facilitated disaffiliation, blocking undue resource transfers between subsidiaries.

One source of these changes is political. Democratization altered fundamental features of business–government relations that were central to the growth of the *chaebol* and generated new pressures for transparency. The crisis of 1997–98 also produced an important domestic political realignment that supported a reassessment of policy in a number of areas germane to *chaebol* growth.

But it is equally clear that the pressure on the Korean model has come not only from the inside but also from globalization, by which we mean both the more gradual process of trade and financial integration that has been going on in Korea for several decades and the particular pressures to which the country was subject in the wake of the crisis of 1997–98. These external pressures for policy and institutional convergence take several forms, the first being the interests of foreign investors. Until the 1990s, neither foreign direct investment nor foreign participation in Korean capital markets was particularly great. This changed dramatically with the financial crisis. Many of the post-crisis reforms that we have catalogued were clearly aimed at easing the entry of foreign investment, including portfolio investment. International financial markets are not only a catalyst for policy change; they also act on corporations directly. Firms that seek foreign financing or that wish to sell assets to foreign buyers come under pressure to adjust to market norms and expectations.

A second way in which globalization operates as a force for convergence is through the international financial institutions. The concern with the intrusiveness of the IMF is as old as conditionality itself, but has grown with the expansion of the reform agenda. Beginning with the debt crisis of the 1980s, and extending to the "new" financial crises of the second half of the 1990s, the "Washington consensus" has steadily expanded to encompass a range of structural issues, including reform of the financial sector, regulatory institutions and corporate governance.

A third and related route through which globalization generates pressures on governments and firms is standard-setting processes, both public and private. These include standards with respect to capital adequacy in the financial sector, accounting and through the OECD, of corporate governance itself. Financial crises such as those that hit Korea in 1997–98 bring all of the forces outlined above into play: government sensitivity to the market and capital flight, intense engagement with the international financial institutions, and concerns about meeting market standards would all tend to push policy in the direction of international norms.

The analytic underpinnings of the convergence hypothesis are by no means clear. There are a number of theoretical reasons to believe that national policy and institutional differences might persist in the face of globalization.[15] With respect to patterns of corporate governance and organization, we can underline three. The first is that the link between both market-oriented and non-market-oriented reforms and actual patterns of corporate governance is indirect and subject to significant lags. For example, there is increasing agreement that neither banks nor capital markets adequately monitored the investment behavior of the *chaebol*. But the development of institutions with such capabilities is not simple, and requires changes in corporate and banking culture as well as the absorption of new skills.

A second source of inertia is political. The financial crisis of 1997–98 unleashed a quite fundamental struggle over the control of assets. *Chaebol* owners and managers did not easily relinquish prerogatives and in some areas, such as with respect to shareholder rights, have fought tough, rearguard actions to limit oversight.

The final reason why convergence might not occur is because existing patterns of organization were in fact efficient and it would therefore neither be socially optimal, nor individually rational from the perspective of the firm, to change *chaebol* structure and behavior. As Alice Amsden (1989, 2001) has argued most forcefully, the *chaebol* were efficient means of tackling a number of problems associated with late development, including the need to exploit potential economies of scale and scope in the course of technological catch-up.

We have sympathy with these arguments, and outlined in Chapter 1 the ways in which the *chaebol* form could be seen as an efficient adaptation to highly imperfect markets for capital, skilled labor and intermediate inputs. Yet with the benefit of hindsight, these objectives might have been met just as efficiently through other organizational forms, such as multi-divisional firms, rather than multi-subsidiary organizations, and with fewer adverse affects on minority shareholders. We have also suggested that the costs associated with rent-seeking and expropriation of shareholder value, as well as declining profitability, have weighed more heavily in the balance sheet over time. The dynastic squabbles associated with succession in a number of major *chaebol* are a reminder of the disadvantages of family control, disadvantages that are likely to become more pronounced as the third and fourth generations take over. The elements of the Kim Dae-jung reform agenda that remained incomplete at the end of his administration, such as the development of more autonomous financial institutions and private remedies to counter weaknesses in corporate governance, appear to stem from continuing political resistance from insiders. More and more, those insiders appear to be defending a corporate form which – despite its past glories – was becoming less and less able to meet the challenges facing the Korean economy.

Notes

1   According to the Board of Audit and Inspection Report released in November 2001, corporate managers of insolvent firms concealed a total of 7.1 trillion *won* of their personal wealth. Strictly speaking, it is not true (as alleged in some press reports) that these managers somehow found ways to siphon off public funds for their private gain. Public funds were injected into banks and other financial institutions, not directly into the firms. The net effect, however, is the same, because corporate managers in Korea typically make personal debt payment guarantees for loans extended to their firms. The Board of Audit and Inspection Report shows that a number of corporate managers bypassed these obligations by hiding their wealth or transferring their assets to their relatives or overseas. The government should have appointed a special team of public prosecutors, auditors and accountants to investigate any irregularities from the outset. Belatedly, the government is using Article 406 of the Civil Code and searching for the concealed wealth of corporate managers so that their loan guarantees can be honored.

2   The interest rate gap between general bank loans and export loans, for instance, was completely eliminated in 1982.

3   This change in expectations had a dramatic effect on the financing pattern of corporate investment. According to the Korea Development Bank, manufacturing firms in the pre-crisis period relied on external financing for more than 70 percent of their investment needs, primarily through bank lending and corporate bond issues. By 2000, retained earnings and depreciation charges accounted for more than 70 percent of investment funds, completely reversing the relative importance of internal and external sources of financing. We interpret this shift to reflect the decline of implicit government guarantees in the wake of the Daewoo crisis, and the exercise of greater caution on the part of both banks and bondholders in assessing corporate risk. The greater reliance on internal financing should also imply greater prudence on the part of management with respect to investment decisions as well. In fact, as banks increasingly focused on consumer and

housing loans, the share of the corporate sector in won-denominated bank loans (stock, not flow) declined from 77.2 percent at the end of 1996 to 58.8 percent at the end of 2000.

4 The government and the *chaebol* continue to control the lion's share of financial institutions. Although President Kim Dae-jung mentioned the need for a separation of banking and commerce in his speech of August 15, 1999, few concrete actions were taken.

5 We use the more expansive term – "fair trade policy" – because the mandate of the Korean Fair Trade Commission has not been limited to competition policy alone but has expanded to other issues that arise due to the unique nature of *chaebol* organization, including particularly inter-subsidiary transactions of various sorts; we address these in more detail below.

6 In addition to liberalizing foreign direct investment, Korea made major progress in trade liberalization by abolishing its import diversification policy in July 1999, which had been used since 1978 to contain the inflow of Japanese imports (justified on the grounds of Korea's large bilateral trade deficit with Japan).

7 At the same time, the government promoted small and medium-sized firms with various forms of targeted support designed to offset the presumed advantages of the *chaebol*.

8 Bong-kyun Kang (2001: 127–8), who served as Senior Economic Secretary and Minister of Finance and Economy in 1998 and 1999, acknowledges that implicit government guarantees against bankruptcy and inter-subsidiary resource transfers impeded the restructuring of the top five *chaebol*. In the absence of precedents for a Big Five failure and effective private remedies to stop undue resource transfers, "market-led" corporate restructuring was actually producing a perverse result. Moreover, the government feared it would take time to introduce institutional changes that would credibly signal a regime change. Faced with increasing systemic risks, the government decided to adopt two regulatory measures to facilitate corporate restructuring. First, it placed a cap on the exposure of financial institutions to corporate bonds and commercial papers issued by the *chaebol*. Second, it blocked undue inter-subsidiary resource transfers by strictly enforcing the Monopoly Regulation and Fair Trade Act.

9 A 1999 amendment to the law also allowed the formation of pure holding companies, albeit under restrictive conditions that limited second-tier subsidiaries and the holding of both financial and non-financial subsidiaries.

10 The administration's simultaneous preference for a more market-oriented approach to policy and the desire to facilitate restructuring led it to lift limits on inter-subsidiary shareholdings. The result of this liberalization measure was an *increase* in in-group ownership; we discuss this policy challenge posed by this unexpected development in more detail below.

11 When a business group produces combined financial statement for the entire group, it takes financial as well as non-financial subsidiaries as a unit and nets out inter-subsidiary shareholdings and transactions. The combined financial statement thus shows the overall financial health of the group. However, it is important to underline that combined financial statements do not necessarily address the issue of accounting fraud. In order for

combined financial statements to be reliable, *individual* financial statements have to be accurate.

12 In 1995, the average debt–equity ratio of the top thirty *chaebol* was 347.5 percent; by 1997 this had climbed to 519 percent.

13 Bae, Kang and Kim (2001: 2–3) document some of the most notorious expropriation cases involving Samsung and LG.

14 It is important to underline that the *chaebol* as a corporate form is based on a multi-subsidiary structure with different ownership patterns across the subsidiaries, rather than a multi-division structure with the same ownership pattern. If protection for investors' property rights is strengthened, it will become increasingly difficult for the *chaebol* founder's family to effect undue resource transfers between subsidiaries. The shareholders of a profitable subsidiary will balk at propping up distressed subsidiaries just to advance the interests of the founder's family. As a result, protecting shareholder rights is likely to accelerate the trend toward independent management, even in the absence of any draconian measures to "break up" the *chaebol*.

15 Guillen (2001) develops a wide-ranging institutional critique of the convergence logic that underscores path-dependent institutional advantages and the competitive gains from diversity. Extending the logic of fiscal federalism, Rogowski (2001) argues that different national jurisdictions are not likely to adopt similar policies because of the variations in preferences. Mobile capital may raise the costs of some policy options, but voters may well choose to pay that price, for example, through more stringent regulation. Kahler (2001) points out that "races to the bottom" – competition for more lax regulatory standards – are in fact rare and hinge on assumptions that are dubious, including mobile capital that is highly sensitive to small differences in policy and governments who compete for that capital and are highly sensitive to attracting it.

References

Amsden, Alice. 1989. *Asia's Next Giant: South Korea and Late Industrialization.* Oxford: Oxford University Press.
——. 2001. *The Rise of "The Rest": Challenges to the West from Late-Industrializing Economies.* New York: Oxford University Press.
Bae, Kee-Hong, Kang, Jun-Koo, and Kim, Jin-Mo. 2001. "Tunneling or Value Added? Evidence from Mergers by Korean Business Groups." Paper presented at the First Asian Corporate Governance Conference, Asian Institute of Corporate Governance at Korea University, Seoul, 14 December.
Board of Audit and Inspection. 2001. *Audit Report on the Management and Supervision of Public Funds* (in Korean). Seoul: Board of Audit and Inspection.
Chang, Ha-Joon. 2000. "The Hazard of Moral Hazard: Untangling the Asian Crisis," *World Development,* 28 (4): 775–88.
Claessens, Stijn, Djankov, Simeon, and Mody, Ashok, eds. 2001. *Resolution of Financial Distress: An International Perspective on the Design of Bankruptcy Laws.* Washington, DC: World Bank.

Evans, Peter. 1995. *Embedded Autonomy: States and Industrial Transformation.* Princeton: Princeton University Press.

Fields, Karl J. 1995. *Enterprise and the State in Korea and Taiwan.* Ithaca: Cornell University Press.

Guillen, Mauro. 2001. *The Limits of Convergence: Globalization and Organizational Change in Argentina, South Korea and Spain.* Princeton: Princeton University Press.

Haggard, Stephan. 1990. *Pathways from the Periphery: the Politics of Growth in the Newly Industrializing Countries.* Ithaca: Cornell University Press.

——. 2000. *The Political Economy of the Asian Financial Crisis.* Washington, DC: Institute for International Economics.

Hamilton. Gary G., and Biggart, Nicole Woolsey. 1988. "Market, Culture and Authority: A Comparative Analysis of Management and Organization in the Far East," *American Journal of Sociology,* 94: S52S94.

Johnson, Chalmers. 1983. *MITI and the Japanese Miracle: the Growth of Industrial Policy, 1925–1975.* Stanford: Stanford University Press.

Kahler, Miles. 2001. "Modeling Races to the Bottom." Unpublished MS, University of California, San Diego, at http://www-irps.ucsd.edu/faculty/mkahler/RaceBott.pdf

Kang, Bong-kyun. 2001. *Economic Development Strategy of Korea* (in Korean). Seoul: Pakyoungsa.

Kang, David. 2002. *Crony Capitalism: Corruption and Development in South Korea and the Philippines.* New York: Cambridge University Press.

Krugman, Paul. 1994. "The Myth of Asia's Miracle," *Foreign Affairs* 73 (6) (November–December): 62–78.

Lim, Wonhyuk. 2000. *The Origin and Evolution of the Korean Economic System.* Policy Study 2000-03. Seoul: Korea Development Institute.

MacIntyre, Andrew, ed. 1994. *Business and Government in Industrializing Asia.* Ithaca: Cornell University Press.

——. 2002. *The Power of Institutions: Political Architecture and Governance.* Ithaca: Cornell University Press.

Mako, William. 2001. "Corporate Restructuring and Reform: Lessons from Korea." Paper presented at the Conference on the Korean Crisis and Recovery, Seoul, May 18.

Noble, Gregory. 2000. *Collective Action in Asia: How Political Parties Shape Industrial Policy.* Ithaca: Cornell University Press.

Rodrik, Dani. 1995. "Getting Institutions Right: How South Korea and Taiwan Grew Rich," *Economic Policy,* 20: 55–107.

Rogowski, Ron. 2001. "Globalization, Policy Convergence, and Inequality." Paper prepared for the American Political Science Association convention, San Francisco, August 30–September 2.

Schopf, James. 2001. "An Explanation for the End of Political Bank Robbery in the Republic of Korea: the T + T Model," *Asian Survey* 41 (5) (September–October): 693–715.

Shin, Inseok. 2001. "Historical Perspective on Korea's Bond Market: 1980–2000." Korea Development Institute, Working Paper No. 2001–02. Seoul: KDI.

Stern, Joseph J., Kim, Ji-Hong, Perkins Dwight H., and Yoo, Jung-ho. *Industrialization and the State: the Korean Heavy and Chemical Industry Drive.*

336 S. Haggard, W. Lim and E. Kim

Cambridge: Harvard University Press for the Harvard Institute for International Development.

Wade, Robert. 1990. *Governing the Market: Economic Theory and the Role of Government in East Asian Industrialization*. Princeton: Princeton University Press.

West, James. 1997. "Martial Lawlessness: The Legal Aftermath of Kwangju," *Pacific Rim Law and Policy Journal*, 6 (1): 85–168.

World Bank. 1993. *The East Asian Miracle*. New York: Oxford University Press.

Index

Page references followed by *fig* indicate figures; those followed by *tab* indicate tables.